D1083243

DIALECTIC OF CIVIL SOCIETY

DIALECTIC AND SOCIETY

Lawrence Krader, Editor

Board of Editors

Agnes Heller, Budapest
Cyril Levit (Assistant Editor), Hamilton
Angel Palerm, Mexico D.F.
Peter Stadler, Zürich

Editorial Consultants:

Herman Bianchi, Amsterdam
Alessandro Casiccia, Turin
Stanley Diamond, New York
Margrit Eichler, Toronto
Ernest Gellner, London
Maurice Godelier, Paris
Manfred Hinz, Bremen
Marlis Krueger, Bremen
J. R. Llobera, London

Guido Martinotti, Milan
David McLellan, Kent
Claude Meillassoux, Paris
Ikenna Nzimiro, Nsukka
J. M. Ripalda, Madrid
Charles B. Timmer, Amsterdam
Bianca Valota-Lavalotti, Milan
Bärbel Wallisch-Prinz, New York

1. Lawrence Krader: THE ASIATIC MODE OF PRODUCTION: Sources. Development and Critique in the Writings of Karl Marx. 1975.

2. Lawrence Krader: DIALECTIC OF CIVIL SOCIETY. 1976.

DIALECTIC OF CIVIL SOCIETY

LAWRENCE KRADER

1976

VAN GORCUM, ASSEN/AMSTERDAM, The Netherlands

© 1976 LAWRENCE KRADER

No parts of this book may be reproduced in any form, by print, photoprint, microfilm or any other means without written permission.

ISBN 90 232 1428 5

Robert Manning Strozier Library

MAY 16 1979

Tallahassee, Florida

Printed in The Netherlands by Van Gorcum, Assen

To Meyer Fortes
and
To Angel Palerm
In friendship

TABLE OF CONTENTS

PREFACE

In this book the history and dialectic of civil society are explored in
outline. Civil society is the society of opposed social classes and the
state. Its history is the history of the transition from social bondage
to the formal freedom of labor in society. The history of modern
society, which is dominated by production of capital, requires such a
schema that arches over the histories of particular societies that make
it up, and is at once freed from the bondage to categories of European
history. For these reasons, negative and positive, the central place
is given to the history of civil society, both in reference to its basis,
the Asiatic, servile and modern modes of production, and to the origin
of the state. Bourgeois society is thus seen to be but a moment of the
history of civil society, whose theory Ibn Khaldun and Hegel fore-
shadowed. The book then has a unitary burden, whose several aspects
are examined in related essays. Most of these appear for the first time
in print. The last chapter, On the Dialectic of Anthropology, is reprinted with only a change in title, from the *International Review of
Social History*, v. 20, 1975, pt. 2, pp. 236-272, and pt. 3, pp. 424-449.
The chapter, On Value, with slight emendations, was given at the
Wenner-Gren symposium, Burg Wartenstein, organized in July 1976
by Ernest Gellner. The sense of the first chapter, and of the work
as a whole, has been expounded before interested persons at universi-
ties and academies in Amsterdam, Bremen, Budapest, Cambridge,
London, Mexico City, Milan, New York, Oldenburg, Paris, Turin,
Uppsala and forms the thematic principle of my seminar at the Free
University, Berlin. To those who have had the patience to hear me,
and for the courtesy of their invitation, my thanks.

INTRODUCTION

I

This book is complementary to the two earlier published, *The Ethnological Notebooks of Karl Marx*, and *The Asiatic Mode of Production*. Together, the three works form an interrelated whole, taking up the various sides of their common theme, the dialectic of human history. While the dialectic is here set forth as a system, it is not completed, no possibility of closure being contained therein; the negation of the closed system proceeds from the nature of the dialectic of human society, which is an unfolding.

Writing about the dialectic is now the fashion; the term appears in the title of articles and books by the score. It is often expounded as though there were a pure dialectic, with an empyrean existence, abstracted from human history, like the well-known method of Descartes. According to another tradition, the distinction is made between pure and applied dialectic, modelled on the distinction between pure and applied science, etc. This pure dialectic is the fantasy of a pure idealism which takes whole sciences for its province. For example, we read about dialectical anthropology. But what can anthropology be but dialectical? To be sure, some are less conscious of this fact than others. The fantasy of a pure dialectic has its mirror image: the dialectic is expelled from our earthly Eden with sword of flame.

Neither nor. On the one hand the dialectic is one with human history, connected to it alone, inseparable from it. On the other hand, there is no universal dialectic. The human kind is continuous with the order of nature, having no constituent part other than that which is found in the rest of nature. At the same time the history of the human kind is discontinuous with the history of nature. The dialectic is not an emanation of the spirit or mind; it is embodied in human history. It is the relation that the human kind bears to its history, or the relation in human society. That relation is twofold: 1. It is that which is related, recounted, accounted for in human history by the historical record. 2. It is at the same time that which is related, historically connected; it is the historical process. The history is twofold, the unwritten history and the written. The subject of history is fourfold: 1. The historical subject is the agent, the active factor in history, the social classes. 2. It is that which is written about, the struggles between the social classes. 3. It is the human kind as a whole. 4. It is the given society as a whole.

The dialectic is one with human history, which is the history that we make. As such it is opposed to natural history, the history we do not make. We human beings are not godlike, we have not made nature, nor shaped the natural universe. Nature is a given. Nor do we make natural history. There can be no dialectic of natural history, in the same sense that there is a dialectic of human history. Because there is no actual, real dialectic of natural and human history in any single sense, there can be no abstract dialectic, or pure dialectic common to both histories. There is no dialectic in itself, of and for itself. Human history contains its own active factor. It is at once the field or stage of activity of that factor. Human history is in this sense both agent and patient. As there is no dialectic of nature, so there is no active historical subject in nature, save that which has been introduced by the human kind. Thereby natural history is opposed to human social history.

The dialectic of human society is the relation of the historical subject to the object, which is its history. The subject is the human kind in its totality. (The dialectic, if it were the pure subject, divorced from history, would be that pure abstraction, the transcendental subject noted above, which is the fantasy of the Kantians, or the pure subject floated by the Cartesians.)

The historical subject is at once posited and negated in human history. Human history is both subject and object; as such it is both subjective and objective. It is both abstract and concrete. In its abstraction, human history is one; concretely it is many histories. The abstract history of humanity is plurality in unity, the concrete histories are unity in plurality. The abstract history of humanity is unitary; it is the course of the social evolution of the human kind. The concrete history of humanity is many, in which the histories of the particular societies are unfolded, as the Eskimo, Iroquois, Greek, etc. Human social evolution is an abstraction of the many social histories of the human kind: but the evolution of nature is wholly and solely concrete. The abstraction of evolution is the product of the human kind in relation to nature.

The dialectic of human history is not simple; it is opposed to the science of nature, or natural history, which comprises the evolution of the biological species. The biological evolution of the species, homo sapiens, is the history that we do not make. It is at once unitary and concrete. The alternative to this thesis is racism, in which a plural course of the biological evolution of the human kind is proposed. This is nonsense: the history of the twentieth century has shown how dangerous that nonsense can be. The biological unity of the evolution of humanity is one, its singularity follows from our not having made it. The social history that we make is other; it is many. The plurality of the social histories of the human kind is a factum; it is connected to the fact that that history is the work of the human kind. The unity that we make out of the many social histories is an abstraction. On the contrary, the biological evolution of the human species is unitary and concrete, it is not the product of our thought. By nature it is so, a natural given. But because the social history of the human kind is plural, it has been falsely assumed by some that the biological evolution is likewise plural. By attributing this false plurality to our biological unity we arrive at a racist inhumanity.

The dialectic of social history, economy and technology has been made complex by the manipulation of the sciences in the interests of particular social classes and parties, of the ruling class in Hitler's Germany, and elsewhere. Making the distinction between human and natural history we follow Giambattista Vico, who wrote that men make their own history; to this Karl Marx agreed, adding, "but they do not make it of their own free will." The history that we make is composed of circumstances that are handed down to us. The dialectic of human history and the science of nature are actually separate, potentially they are one. (This is the theme of the last essay, On the Dialectic of Anthropology.)

On the Definition of Terms

The problem of periodization of human history is comprised in the negation or overcoming of the history of primitive society, whereby the transition to its opposite is posited, which is the history of civil society. In the first essay in this book, the dialectic of civil society is set forth.

In all human societies, labor or work[1] is performed, whether it be labor in society, or any other sort of work or labor. Human beings go mediately to work, their work, or labor, being in all cases mediated by the instruments of work. All value proceeds from this mediate relation, but some work or labor produces no value. Thus it is not by virtue of the mediate relation of work or labor that value is produced.

[1] At this point, human society is referred to generally, and the terms work and labor are referred to without difference. The differentiation between work and labor will be made in the next paragraph and on: there too the differences between societies will be introduced. Primitive society and economy, however, are not differentiated.

Value is produced under those conditions of social production in which the differentiation between the relations of labor and work is made. The source of value is the twofold relation of labor,[2] the relation of labor to nature and the relation of labor in society:

(1) In its relation to nature the source of value is concrete labor, or work. The value produced thereby is concrete value. While in its relation to nature all work is mediate, yet the value produced thereby, being concrete, is direct or non-mediate value. By concrete labor, useful things are produced. (2) The relation of labor in society is likewise the source of value. This is abstract or mediate value; it is the product of abstract labor. Concrete labor, as it is human labor in relation to nature, is mediate labor. Abstract labor is non-mediate, or direct social labor, it is the labor of the direct producers in society.

The two sources of value are at once distinct from each other and combined. The distinction between the two is latent in the primitive economy; it is given expression only in the political economy.[3] Labor time, as it is reckoned up in the political economy, is the source of all value, abstract and concrete. Labor time implies the distinction between abstract value and labor on the one hand, concrete value and labor on the other. As abstract and concrete labor, so abstract and concrete value are the determinants of one another, each is the necessary condition of the other. Without concrete value there is no abstract value, without abstract value no concrete value. But without the reckoning up of labor time there is no value to begin with. Value is not reckoned up in primitive society. Concrete, mediate value is produced through the relations to nature, by working upon nature. This is the natural moment of value, or use value. Abstract value is the product of social labor, its source is the relation of production in society. This is the social moment of value, or exchange value. The natural moment of value is the product of concrete labor: the social moment of value is the product of abstract labor. The totality of value in social production is composed of the two parts, concrete and abstract value, which are separated from each other for the

[2] The concept of value has been called into question by Joan Robinson, *Economic Philosophy*, London 1962; *An Essay on Marxian Economics*, London 1966; and The Theory of Value Reconsidered, in: *Australian Economic Papers*, vol. 8, 1969. The question of value has been redirected by J. R. Hicks, *Value and Capital*, Oxford 1939; and *A Theory of Economic History*, Oxford 1969. Labor theory of value has been in part defended by Leif Johansen, Labour Theory of Value, and by Alfredo Medio, Profits and Surplus Value; both in: *A Critique of Economic Theory*, E. K. Hunt and J. G. Schwartz, ed. Penguin 1972. But value theory covers a wider range of historical economic matters than these twentieth century figures have taken up.
[3] Alfred Marshall, *Principles of Economics*, 8th ed., 1920, p. 43 held "political economy" to be the name of a science. However, there must be an object of this study. Economics studies a different object.

4

purpose of our analysis, but are inseparable in reality, in production and exchange in society. Value in its totality is produced in the political economy alone; there alone is labor time reckoned up. Only in the political economy is concrete value distinguished from abstract value. Abstract value is not produced in primitive society because labor time is not reckoned up; value, whether concrete or abstract, is not produced in primitive society, however, not because it is not reckoned up but because it is not exchanged. Labor is performed under the conditions of primitive life, as it is under all conditions of human life, mediately in relation to nature; concrete labor, not labor in general, is the human universal, but without the relation of exchange in society there is no abstract value; there is no abstract labor. There is no reckoning up of labor time without the abstract relation of labor in society. Since abstract and concrete values are the mutual determinants each of the other, there is no concrete value in primitive society, for there is no value to begin with there, in the absence of either. There is no exchange value in primitive society because there is no significant amount of social exchange there; for in primitive society, the units of production and consumption generally coincide. Distribution and the concrete moment of exchange are poorly developed under these conditions.

Value and labor are not developed as symmetrical relations, for, while concrete labor is performed in primitive society, as work in relation to nature, yet it adds nothing to say that under these conditions concrete value is produced. There, useful things are produced, but not use values, concrete value; these are the products of the relations of political economy, where they are opposed to abstract or exchange value. Concrete, mediate work is here performed in the relations to nature, as in the primitive case, but in the political economy it is transformed into value by the relations of exchange, or the social moment of value. It is abstract value, the product of social labor; its source is the relation of exchange in society, whereby the relation of social production is generated. As such it is distinct from the natural moment of value, and from concrete labor. The source of the abstract value is the distinction that has been generated historically between the unit of production and consumption, through the generation of exchange and the distinction between abstract and concrete labor; hence abstract value is distinguished from concrete value, or exchange from use value.

The production of a social surplus is generated under the same conditions which brought forth the opposition between abstract and concrete labor and between abstract and concrete value. The condition under which civil society is formed and determined is that in which a social surplus, hence surplus value, is produced. Production is thereby separated from reproduction; at the same time, production there comprises both the reproductive and the surplus production in society. The differentiation between value and surplus value is introduced by the differentiation in civil society between the direct producers and the social whole. The production of the social surplus is the condition whereby exchange is developed in society; the development of exchange between communities of tillers, producers, is the condition whereby the social surplus labor or product is developed. Each is the historical determinant of the other.

Primitive society is the society of primitive, undifferentiated economy; civil society is the society of political economy. Primitive society is undifferentiated society; civil society is class-divided, class-opposed society. Society as civil society is articulated into its substructure and superstructure; primitive society is without such opposition and articulation. Civil society is the organization of production of the society; as such it is part of the social substructure. Civil society is at the same time the bridge that arches over the difference between the social substructure and superstructure. The substructure comprises the social production and its organization, reproduction, distribution and exchange. The superstructure comprises, i.a. the political system, or political society, the state, law and right, civil right, property right, and the consciousness of all of these. Because it is the organizing factor of the substructure and at once the expression of the unity of substructure and superstructure of the society, civil society is contradictory in its internal relations, being at once the part and the expression of the whole. We are conscious of this contradiction. It cannot be resolved, being determined for us by the relations of society themselves.

The political economy comprises the relations of production in society. These relations are at once subjective and substantial, formal and informal, official and private, external and internal. As the economy of civil society, the political economy is the substructure of political society. Political society has its formal, substantial, official, external side, which is summed up in the state and the juridical system. It has no other side or aspect. The political economy is the set of relations of production, distribution, exchange and consumption in civil society, and is at the same time the relation of this set to the political system of state and law. Through civil society, the political economy is related to the social whole, that is mediately; civil society is the organization of the economy, whereby it is related to the social whole. The political economy is the relation of social production to the formal, official, external system of state, right, and law. Unlike

6

the relation between economy and society, which is an indirect relation, mediated by civil society, the relation between political economy and political society is direct. Economy takes in a vaster field of human activity than political economy, society takes in a vaster field of human relations than civil society.

The same contradictions governing the relations of civil society govern those of political society. They are not determined by our thought, but for it. These matters are taken up in the two essays of our book, On the Early History of the Labor Theory of Value, and its partner, On Value. The one treats the question of value through the course of its development, the other treats the same systematically. Both take up the dual relation of value, the relation to nature, and the relation in society.

Civil society is non-primitive society throughout its history, in ancient Egypt, China, Inca Peru, ancient Benin, Greece and Rome, and modern bourgeois society. One aspect of this development was traced in *The Asiatic Mode of Production*; there the unity and opposition between civil and bourgeois society was brought out. Here the opposition and unity of civil society and the modern society of production of capital is set forth, whereby the dialectical moments of the abstract and the concrete in history are explored. Civil society abstractly considered arches over many societies of traditional Asia, Africa, pre-Columbian America, Europe. It is at the same time the concrete society of modern capital production. The term for it comes from ancient Rome, its historical sources are far wider and more ancient, comprising the history of the Asiatic mode of production, as it is attested in ancient Asia, Africa, America and Europe (the last prior to the period of ancient slavery); the term likewise comprises the mode of servile production in ancient and medieval Europe, and the modern mode of production. Taken together, the history of civil society is the history of social labor both in its unfree and in its free conditions; it is the history of unfree social labor in the Ancient, Asiatic, ancient slave and medieval serf modes of production, and the history of social labor that is formally free in the modern mode of capital production. Abstract in its term of reference, civil society comprises many historical sources, and as such does not exist in any concrete form, but only as the sum of particular histories and economic formations, or their organization in society. It is concrete at the same time in its historical manifestation as the modern society of capital production. This historically concrete form has a bourgeois aspect, the civil society of the United States, West Germany, Japan, or France. It is at the same time generalized to include those modern socialist societies in which the production of capital predominates. Civil society is general and particular in its history, passing from the one to the other and from its abstraction to its concretion, through the revolutions of the twentieth century.

The dialectic of civil society has been mystified of late by learned writers, (see below, On the Dialectic of Civil Society, section VII). The result of this mystification is that the dialectic of the history of the social revolution in Europe, and in other parts of the modern world, has been obfuscated. One of the tasks of the first essay, and of the work as a whole, is to bring the use of the terms back into step with historical process.

In the last essay, On the Dialectic of Anthropology, the state and person are re-examined, whereby it is shown that they are the same historical composition, and of the same substance: the juridical person is the formal side of the human being, the state is the formal side of society. Each side is the determinant of the other, deep calleth unto deep. In the state, society of a given condition, class-divided society, has brought forth an institution which gathers together the formal, external, juridical relations. The human being, in order to relate to this formal social being, extrudes a formal, external side; that is, the juridical person is called forth by the relation to the state. The juridical person is not human, it is the personification of the human; the human being is fetishized as the person. This person, this formality exists so long as the state exists. When the social conditions that give rise to the state disappear, the juridical person will disappear. There will then be a new sociology, a new psychology, a new anthropology, with wholly different relations and categories.

The critique of the theory of reification in that same essay is conducted against Georg Lukács. It is a constructive critique, which continues and reverses his frame of reference. The critique is founded on the distinction between objectification and reification. Lukács had said that his real, perhaps his only – and important – error in his work, *History and Class Consciousness*, was just the identification of objectification and reification.[4] Two matters are to be added to this:

A. Objectification was not differentiated from reification first because abstraction was not differentiated from concretion. Abstraction and reification are both acts of all human beings. Objectification is an abstractive act; abstraction, on the contrary, is not objective alone: it is also subjective. Thus the relation between abstraction and

---

.[4] "Mit persönlicher Genugtuung las ich Ihre Kritik über Geschichte und Klassenbewusstsein... weil ich so oft aus Lukács s Mund *dasselbe* gehört habe. Er hat immer gesagt, dass sein wirklicher und vielleicht einziger – und wichtiger – Fehler in G. u. K. eben die Identifizierung von Objektivation and Verdinglichung gewesen war." Letter from Agnes Heller, 9. II. 76. Cf. Georg Lukács, *Geschichte und Klassenbewusstsein*. Berlin 1923.

objectification is not symmetrical; the opposite of abstraction, concretion, is the combination of object and subject in society as in thought. Ludwig Feuerbach had made objectification into the universal act whereby man becomes man. This is a hypostasis. To be sure, objectificaton of the world and of self is a panhuman act, but it is not the means whereby we become human. Feurbach in making the holy descent from Hegel took up one side of the Hegelian positing of abstraction, – and left it there. We do not abstract because we objectify; we do not become human because we have externalized ourselves. Abstraction is but a part of humanization; objectification and externalization are but a part of the same. Furthermore, to proceed from thought to reality, as from abstraction to objectification to externalization is a fantasy of the medieval realists, who conceived of universalia anterior to things. (Feuerbach later, in his vulgar materialist phase, turned this tenet around, and fancied that he had corrected the course of philosophy.)

Reification on the contrary is concrete historically. It is concretized in the class oppositions, whereas the different social classes, and all human societies, objectify, abstract, think, perform the acts of relating in thought, in non-different ways. Reification is determined by different relations of production in society of the opposed social classes; reification differs, varying according to the social class. The class of direct producers in society is reified, that is, literally transformed into a thing each day in the process of social labor. The direct producer is made into a passive something; his consciousness of the process is reified. At the same time he is active in the work process. He is at once agent and patient. He is both form and content of the relations of production in society. He is in the world of reality while at the same time he has a formal existence expressed in the legal contract governing the sale of his labor power. The capitalist, the other party to the same contract, is on the contrary the negation of the opposition of activity and passivity, just as he is the negation of the opposition of form and content. His only social being is the formality of the social relation of production. He is the personification of capital, capital endowed with a will and consciousness of its own. The capitalist is the juridical form of capital, the person in law. Actual and real are the relations of labor and capital in society. The reification of social labor is other than that of the capitalists. Both are concrete, each according to the relations of the corresponding social class. The society is the totality; objectification is the matter of the social whole. The process of objectification is the totality of human action and relation. Reification on the contrary is divided. The consciousness is reified according to the relations of the social classes. Objectification and the objectified consciousness is the total-izing process in thought as in society; the former in consequence of the latter. Lukács had posited the thesis. It is now a matter of negating it.

B. Objectification has not been differentiated from reification for a second reason, which is that theory has not been differentiated from practice. We begin with the practice, that is, with the opposition be-tween the social classes. Beginning therewith it is clear that the class of direct producers in the society has another relation to the reification of consciousness than all other classes of civil society. The theory of the difference between objectification and reification is determined thereby.

II

The central problem of human history and social evolution is usually given as that of periodization; in the nineteenth century there was general agreement that the history of the human kind was divided into three great periods or stages, savagery, barbarism and civiliza-tion. This was the finding of the social evolutionists of the time, E. B. Tylor and L. H. Morgan, and of Friedrich Engels, who composed his book, *The Origin of the Family, Private Property and the State*, in the light of the researches of Morgan. V. G. Childe sought to retain the general pattern of the three-stage theory, but in the light of more recent research, referred to the Paleolithic, Neolithic and Urban stages and the revolutions connected thereto. Still more recently, G. E. Markov, of Moscow, has distinguished between a producing economy in the Neolithic stage, and a hunting and gathering economy.[5] These various writers have set forth the thesis of the stages of evolution of human society. We are now concerned with the next step, which is the negation of the stages, the negation of their thesis, the antithesis of both. By this means the question of transition from one stage to the next is raised, or how the conditions of social life which constitute the primitive stage are overcome by those of its successor. According to this antithesis, the relations of society, the conditions of social life, are real, the stage itself is not. The stage theory was carried to an extreme by its nineteenth century adherents, in opposition to the thesis here presented. L. H. Morgan believed in the objective existence in reality of the stage (status, period); according to his tenet, the

---

[5] V. G. Childe. *Social Evolution.* London 1951. G. E. Markov, in lectures given at the Ethno-logical Institute, Free University of Berlin, Winter Semester 1976. The question may be a matter of terms. On the other hand it may be objected that production includes hunting, fishing and gathering activities, but that this is another sort of production from agricultural, metallurgical and electronic production.

stages alone are real, the individual peoples, Iroquois, Greek, in the respective stages of barbarism or civilization, are not.[6]

The theory of stages was dressed up at that time in the language of biological evolution. The laws of organic development were then attributed to human society; the relation between natural and human history was assumed to be not an analogy but a reality. Max Weber sought to attack the analogical theory of human evolution by his criticism of one part of it, the theory of agrarian communism. The attack that he made led him into a number of errors; he and his allies went too far. They attributed to the socialists the doctrine that the human being is by nature a communal animal; on the contrary, Weber and company declared themselves to be individualists, defending the thesis that the human being is by nature an individual animal, a simplification at once artless and artful of the issues.

In order to explore the question of the historical stages and their negation, a bygone polemic in the recent history of the social sciences is resurrected, concerning Max Weber and the theory of Agrarian Communism. It is shown that Weber's political interests led him into a hypostasis, the philosophy of individualism.

The negation of the stage theory of human evolution, but not in the sense that Max Weber has negated it, is exemplified in the transition from the primitive to the civil condition of society. This transition is falsely regarded in terms of historical stages, which are but a convenience, a construction, to be analyzed into the relations of economy and society. Take the problem of the origin of the state, which is a part of the problem of that transition. The state has been taken by some as a stage of evolution. It is not, any more than it is a god descending from the machine. It is a phenomenon of history, which comes into being when certain conditions in that history are brought out, the first being the formation and opposition of classes in the given society to one another. The determination of this opposition is effected by the separation and opposition of the units of production and consumption in the society, the development of exchange, thereby of commodities, the division of social labor, and the production of a social surplus by one of the social classes, together with the formation of another to which that surplus accrues. (See the two essays below, on value.) The state is not a prince, it is not a people, nor is it a society. The state is the abstract expression of the oppositions: (i) between the social classes, and (ii) within the social class to which the mentioned

[6] L. H. Morgan, *Ancient Society*. New York 1877. Part I, Ch. I. There the thesis was advanced that the culture pertains to the stage of evolution, whether savage, barbarous or civilized. The culture of the stage or period into which it is divided is distinct. The culture of the Old World, in the same period, accordingly, is distinct from that of the New.

surplus accrues. The state is the concrete organ for the regulation and control of these oppositions. The state as abstraction is a constant, invariant through all its forms. It is not eternal, but will pass away, it will be sublated when the conditions of its existence are abolished. The state as concretion is an agency for the control of the social class of direct producers. As such it is historically variable. The state is at the same time the organ for the control of the individuals in whose interest it has been organized, of the ruling class individuals. The control of these class individuals is all the more important because the historical phenomenon of the individuality and the social doctrine of individualism are generated and developed within that social class.[7] This is the error of individualism that Weber failed to grasp.

The aim of this book is to demonstrate that a series of problems currently faced can only be resolved by the dialectic of social evolution and history. The problems, whose resolution is here set forth, are the evolution and history of civil society, the historical periods and their negation, the controversy over the theory of value. These have been inadequately treated by even the most able of present writers because they have been treated in their abstraction. Stages of evolution, the state, value of social labor, are abstracted from history, treated synchronically, hypostasized.

This book is the conscious continuation of a radical tradition. Our history is made up of circumstances that are bequeathed to us. We cannot invent a tradition out of whole cloth. There are those who seek to invent a radical tradition ex nihilo; this cannot be done. The problems and theses that we have taken up here are the current statement of those taken up in the 1920s by Karl Korsch and Georg Lukács, which themselves carried forward the problem and themes set by Karl Marx.

[7] The origin of class oppositions in society lies in the Asiatic mode of production. It is held by some, e.g., Maurice Godelier and Ernest Mandel, that the Asiatic mode of production is a phenomenon of primitive, pre-class society, or else of the margin between pre-class and class society. This notion obscures the nature of class oppositions in society. The class oppositions in society make their first appearance in the Asiatic mode of production. But the relation is not symmetrical. The class of the direct producers, the tillers of the soil, retains its prior organization in communal institutions: here the village communities, clans, archaic gentes, continue their existence and activity long after the transition to the Asiatic mode of production and civil society in its Oriental form has been made. The ruling class is articulated as individualities, individual formal persons, class individuals.

On the contrary, the formal person in respect of the social class of direct producers is the community in the Asiatic mode of production. The community in the early history of civil society, whether the Roman familia, latifundia, clan, gens, is the unit of provision and collection of rent and tax. It is the unit of bondage of the tillers of the soil. Only under the conditions of the capitalist mode of production are the direct producers in society free. But their freedom is a freedom pro forma. These historical matters are discussed in *The Asiatic Mode of Production*, Pt. I, Ch. 7.

ON THE DIALECTIC OF CIVIL SOCIETY

ONE

ON THE DIALECTIC OF CIVIL SOCIETY

I. CIVIL SOCIETY AND POLITICAL ECONOMY

By civil society is meant a distinct kind of human society, one which is internally divided, being composed of mutually opposed classes of people. The abstract sum of many particular societies, civil society is counterposed to historically concrete societies which make it up, whether the society of ancient Rome or modern Italy, Japan both old and new, Egypt, Mexico, or Zaire. Civil society is society taken in its totality, being opposed, by virtue of its class division, to the concept, no less abstract, of primitive society; at the same time, civil society is the historical development out of the primitive society. Civil society has its history, in the course of which great forces of production have been unrolled. Yet, despite its undoubted antiquity, vast productive capacities, and geographic extent, which embraces virtually the entire globe, it is but an evanescent phase in the development of human society as a whole. Civil society is here taken as the whole of society, moreover, in still a second sense: Because it is taken as a whole, divided as it is, abstractly conceived and unitarily represented, it is opposed to that conception which holds civil society to be an aspect, attribute, or quality of society as a whole.[1]

Civil society, as it is taken up here, is society as the divided whole. It is in one sense coterminous with modern society, in another it points to the society in all its historical manifestations in which the state is the dominant political institution. In the first sense it is the society in which the modern mode of production of capital predominates, in the second it is the society of the political economy generally, given

---

[1] Those to whom the term is due, as Richard Hooker (see below), at one time held that civil society, in the second sense given here, is opposed to the ecclesiastical polity; civil society, according to another usage, is opposed to the state, as though government, civil right and law were brought down by a would-be Moses from the heights of sovereignty to the workaday men and women.

The theory of society as totality was expressed by Georg Lukács, *Geschichte und Klassenbewusstsein*, Berlin 1923. His statement is the initial thesis, which is historically determined and contradicted. See Lawrence Krader, *Ethnologie und Anthropologie bei Marx*, München 1973, ch. 3.

that the relations of political economy are not the concern of the society of modern capital production alone. On the contrary, the relations of political economy, being the production in society of surplus value and exchange value, are the concern of all the epochs of the economic formation of society that have been hitherto identified as such; these epochs are the Asiatic, ancient, feudal, and the modern modes of capital production. The relations of political economy arch over all the modes of production in society enumerated. Historically, civil society is identical with the society of political economy in general. It is modern bourgeois society in particular, but at the same time it is the expression of the Oriental society, the *societas civilis* of classical and feudal times, the *'umran* of medieval Islam, and the society of the production of capital in general.[2]

Between the particular and general meanings of civil society there is an opposition that has not been resolved. This irresolution is not the expression of confused usage, but the result of the working out of the oppositions within the subject matter designated by the terms. The relations of the Asiatic, classical, and feudal modes of production contained within themselves the potentiality for development that has been realized, being made actual by bourgeois and the generally modern modes of capital production in society Modern civil or bourgeois society is the organization of that production, in one of its modes, being the most highly developed and many-sided mode of its organization that has been as yet developed historically. Modern bourgeois society is the realization and actualization of the potentiality of development of civil society as a whole, just as the latter in turn bears the relation of realization and actualization of the potentiality of primitive society within itself.

[2] *Societas civilis* is a modern, not an ancient term. Nevertheless, the object designated by this expression existed in antiquity, being the form of society whose law was the civil law, *jus civile*. It was the practice in the sixteenth century, as we shall see, to denote such a society as the society 'constituted by civil law or right.' Ibn Khaldun (1332-1405) referred to civil society as *'umran*, literally, 'civilization, urban life.' See his work, *The Muqaddimah*. F. Rosenthal transl. New York 1958, v. 1, p. 89. Ibn Khaldun himself quotes Aristotle, *Politics* I, in part: "Man is by nature political." Ibn Khaldun adds, "By this is meant, he cannot do without life in *society*, which is made equivalent to *polis*" (i.e. *civitas*, city-state). (See also v. 2, p. 417.) On the relation between *'umran* and *polis* (Arabic *madina*) see E. I. J. Rosenthal, *Political Thought in Medieval Islam*. Cambridge 1962, pp. 86, 126. It will be shown in what follows that *civil society* comprises the *polis*; it is the *polis* and the *polis* in its relation to the economy, or the ground of the political economy.

On the epochs of the economic formation of society see Karl Marx, *Grundrisse der Kritik der politischen Ökonomie* (Rohentwurf, 1857-1858). Berlin 1953, pp. 375 et seq. Idem, *Zur Kritik der politischen Ökonomie* (1859) Foreword. (Marx Engels *Werke*, v. 13, pp. 7f). Further references in: Lawrence Krader, *The Asiatic Mode of Production*. Assen, Van Gorcum, 1975, Pt. I, Ch. III.

Civil society is at once the superstructure and the relation between the foundation and the superstructure of society. As the organization of production in society, civil society is the relation of the foundation, social production, to the superstructure, that is, the political, communicational, juridical, moral, educational systems, the systems of public health, etc., of society. But inasmuch as these systems are part of civil society, so the latter contains its own superstructure. It is at the same time the sum of means to the satisfaction of human wants.[3] Civil society is on the one side identical with modern society, being the overarching category which, with the political economy at its base, includes the systems of the superstructure. It is in this sense the interrelation of the political economy with the state, law, government. It is the field of their interrelation and itself the intermediating process. It presupposes the separation of the public and private spheres of social life and at the same time constitutes the means of their combination. On the other side, society and civil society are not coterminous. Modern society has many elements in the private sphere that are not directly interrelated with the public; likewise, there are in social life many elements of an informal nature which have no immediate relation to the formal systems of the state and law. Some of these private, informal relations are found in the play element in social life, in artistic creation, and the like. These may indeed have their own element of organization, and their own social character, but from the standpoint of civil society they constitute the unorganized and informal aspects of social life, and their relations to civil society and the state are wholly different from those that will be taken up in the following pages.

In the political economy generally there are two opposed relations of production in society: on the one side, the relation of work and labor of those who are directly engaged in social production, who gain their subsistence in this way, and thereby reproduce themselves; on the other, the relation of those who are not so directly engaged, but who profit from the work and labor of others. Throughout the history of civil society, two opposed classes have been constituted, conformable to these relations, the interests of either being opposed to each other. The great historical reach of these relations appears to lend them the semblance of lasting quality, but they are transient, as are those of the political economy and civil society generally. Their passing is

[3] G. W. F. Hegel, *Grundlinien der Philosophie des Rechts* (1821). *Werke* 7, Suhrkamp 1970, § 188, had conceived the satisfaction of wants to be the matter of the individual relation through labor. This is connected to society; the system of wants, as that of labor, is social, hence the matter of civil society. See below, sect. VI and IX D.

subject to mutually contradictory tendencies: on the one side, the mass of antagonistic relations is comprised within the social unity; yet that unity will not be burst asunder by quiet metamorphosis. On the other hand, if the given form of society does not comprise within itself the material conditions of production and exchange which are necessary for a classless society, any attempt to burst forth from it will be vain.[4]

Human societies have been classified according to their habitat, mythology, social structure. But our concern is not with the classification of societies by desert or mountain terrain, tropical or polar climate, of societies holding beliefs in ghosts or gods, or of their matrilineal or patrilineal organization; – it is with the relations of social production, according to which the economies are either primitive or political; and the respective societies are either primitive, that is undivided, or civil, that is, divided internally into opposed social classes. These relations of economy and society arch over the entire history of civil society from its most ancient origins to the modern bourgeois and socialist periods. Thus, landed property held the clue to the history of the ancient Roman Republic and to that of ancient China and India; it is not otherwise in the history of the ancient Incas of Peru, of ancient Mali and Ghana, Benin and Songhai; it is not otherwise in the history of the feudal period of Europe or Japan; and it is not otherwise in the history of the early centuries of capitalism, and of the Russian and Chinese revolutionary periods in the twentieth century. Aristotle faced, and partly solved, the problem of commensurability of the different forms of value in ancient Athens, such as are being faced throughout the world still, twenty-four centuries later.[5]

The discussion of the form of civil society and its internal relations was begun in classical times by Pericles, Aristotle, Cicero, and Augustine; it was carried forward by Thomas Aquinas, Albertus Magnus and Ibn Khaldun in medieval Europe and Islam.[6] A change in the quality of the discussion, which took place in the sixteenth century, has been noticed;[7] the explanation of that change is not far to seek: it took

---

[4] Marx, *Grundrisse*, op. cit., p. 77. Also p. 176.
[5] Marx, *Das Kapital* I. (*Marx Engels Werke*, vol. 23, pp. 73f.) Marx, *Kritik*, 1859, op. cit., incipit. Aristotle, Politics, I, 9.
[6] Karl Korsch, *Karl Marx*. London 1938, p. 138.
[7] Otto Gierke, *Die Genossenschaftstheorie und die deutsche Rechtsprechung*. Berlin 1887, pp. 442 sq. J. W. Allen, *Political Thought in the 16th Century*. London 1927, ch. V. J. W. Gough, *The Social Contract*. Oxford 1957, p. 49. A. P. d'Entrèves, *Natural Law*. London 1960, p. 56. Leo Strauss, *Natural Right and History*. Chicago 1965, p. 61n. F. A. Hayek, *Law, Legislation and History*, v. I. London 1973, p. 151. Ernst Bloch, *Naturrecht und menschliche Würde*. Suhrkamp 1972, p. 59.

place in the period of the emergence of capitalism.[8] It is not only the concept was now blessed with a name; it was now conceived as an essential being with the attributes of social contract, civil right and law, citizenship and natural rights, free and voluntary association, free and voluntary submission under sovereignty. The relations of contract and right, of freedom and its surrender by voluntary compacts were not conceived as historical events, but were given new meanings. Seyssel wrote of religion, justice, precedents and customs which reduced tyranny to civility; Melanchthon defined the state as society constituted by civil law.[9] Hooker appears to have been the first to apply the term *civil society* in the meaning which it had down to the present; he opposed life in civil society to any kind of private living on one side, to the society of all mankind on another, and to the ecclesiastical and theological communities in yet another.[10]

The new form which the discussion of the relation of society was given in the sixteenth century brought contract, natural right, freedom and free will together. Vico, to whom these questions were immediate (he was born in 1668), wrote against the doctrines of chance and fate, from which were conducted the political philosophies of natural right and social contract. "In this way Epicurus who wrote of chance is refuted together with his followers Hobbes and Machiavelli; Zeno is thus refuted and with him Spinoza, who wrote of fate."[11] This brilliancy is followed up by Bloch, who wrote, "Such strange brothers as

---

[8] Karl Marx, *Das Kapital*, v. I. 4th ed. Hamburg, 1914, pp. 682 sq.

[9] Claude de Seyssel. *Grant Monarchie de France*. I, 6-8. Precedent and custom constitute the *police*. Ibid. II, 17. Cf. A. J. Carlyle, *Mediaeval Theory in the West*, v. VI. Edinburgh 1962, pp. 220ff. Philip Melanchthon, *Commentarii in Politica Aristotelis*. 1530: The state is society constituted by civil law. "Civitas est societas civium iure constituta." Figgis interprets Melanchthon to mean, "The only *Civitas Dei* in any sense of the word commonwealth which is not purely metaphysical is the State." J. N. Figgis, *Political Thought*. Harper 1960, p. 85. M. Riedel, *Studien zu Hegels Rechtsphilosophie*. Suhrkamp 1969, p. 142.

[10] It is more practical and accordingly less utopian to speak of human society and not human community, as was the case from Immanuel Kant and on. Hooker wrote indifferently of civil or political society, meaning in either case particular societies and not human society as a whole. But civil society was not opposed to savage society by him, or to life in the state of nature. No less "modern" is Thomas More. in his *Utopia*. Richard Hooker. *Laws of Ecclesiastical Polity*, Bk I. 1593. § X, 12, and § XV, 2-3. Figgis, op. cit., treats Hooker as a "modern" writer; so does R. H. Tawney, *Religion and the Rise of Capitalism*. London 1926. A. P. d'Entrèves, *Riccardo Hooker*. Turin 1932 (idem, *The Medieval Contribution to Political Thought*. New York 1959 ch. V-VI) treats him as a medieval writer. The reader will judge who is right. On the other hand, the current judgment concerning the modernity of Thomas More is unambiguous. Cf. J. H. Hexter, *More's Utopia*. New York 1965. Russell Ames, *Citizen More and his Utopia*. Princeton 1949.

[11] Giambattista Vico. *Principi de Scienza Nuova* (1744). *Opere*. Nicolini ed. Milano-Napoli 1953. § 1109.

Huguenots (after the Bartholomew's Night) and Jesuits (in fighting the heretical state) prepared the theory of the bourgeois revolution through juridical legitimation of the death of tyrants; natural as opposed to written law achieved from that point a sharp form in politics as well as in method. Althusius (*Politics*, 1610) taught that resistance against unjust masters is not rebellion but preservation of one's own injured rights. For this he used the epicurean doctrine of contract which men *voluntarily* entered into for the foundation of a state."[12]

The polemic conducted by Vico against the political philosophers was intended as a defence of the acts of Providence, the political philosophers having posited life in society either through fortuitous agglomerations of atoms, or else by a predestination, predetermination, fatalism, preestablished harmony. The element of volition in Epicurus, however, is changed.[13] The bourgeois revolution had long ere this been instituted. The prince of Machiavelli is no different in his arts, (circa 1500) than the coeval merchant venturers of Genoa, Venice,

---

[12] Ernst Bloch, *Das Prinzip Hoffnung.* Suhrkamp 1959, p. 622. Bloch makes allusion on the one hand to the writings of Beza, Hotman, Languet, Duplessis-Mornay, i.e., to writings of the 1570s; on the other to the writings of Molina, Mariana, Suarez, who wrote in the 1590s and on. Franz Borkenau, *Der Übergang vom feudalen zum bürgerlichen Weltbild*, Paris 1934, had gone over this ground, but his chronology was even later. Here a distinction is to be made between the transition from feudalism to capitalism on the one hand and the preparation of the theory of the bourgeois revolution on the other. The transition from feudalism to capitalism had been prepared long before the preparation of the theory in the published accounts by the Huguenots, Jesuits, Jansenists. The theory of the bourgeois revolution was to account for the transition to capitalism. The preparation of the theory of the bourgeois revolution was closer in time to the transition from feudalism to capitalism than either Bloch or Borkenau believed, having been instituted at the beginning of the sixteenth century by the more astute actors and observers. Machiavelli and the peasants who composed the Twelve Articles prepared the theory and demonstrated their grasp of the transition. (see below, sect. III of this essay.)

Henryk Grossmann, Die gesellschaftlichen Grundlagen der mechanistischen Philosophie und die Manufaktur (*Zeitschrift für Sozialforschung*, Jahrgang 4, 1935, pp. 161-231, charged Borkenau with being inaccurate in his references to chronology and one-sided in his reference to Marx. Marx had located the transition to capitalism in the cities of northern Italy during the fifteenth and sixteenth centuries. Sporadic developments had taken place earlier. The mechanistic philosophy of Descartes is a matter of the seventeenth century. Borkenau concentrated his attention on the latter time period, Bloch on the late sixteenth century. The historical movement that Grossmann brought out on Marx's foundation is antecedent to both of them. The early formation of capitalism proceeded pari passu with the florescence of art and science than which no greater is recorded, released by the new forces of the economy and society.

[13] In reference to Althusius, Hobbes and Grotius, Bloch (*Naturrecht*, op. cit., p. 59) writes, "The new feeling of law came from the contradiction between new economic forces and the bound, overcome forms of commerce." This new feeling is found in Machiavelli, as Vico showed. Vico placed this new matter in society as had Shaftesbury before him; they were both in opposition to Hobbes.

Barcelona in theirs.[14] The terms of political philosophy, statecraft and law have therefore a new meaning. The term revolution itself has more than one meaning, on the one side, the transformation of production and exchange in society, such as is intended by "commercial' or "industrial" revolution, on the other the violence of civil war in "French Revolution." It is clear that the revolution of capitalism in trade, manufacture, finance went hand in hand with the forceful overthrow of thrones and landed estates. The new form of contract corresponded to the changed function of the commercial undertakings in which independent and free contracting parties associated with each other by voluntary acts, which were then expressed in the theories of political association and of the formation of states of the seventeenth century. It was convenient to this purpose that men were conceived to be free agents in the foundation of states as they were in the foundation of merchant enterprises. Volition and contract run together. The history of freedom, in modern times, follows more-over the historical process of the inception of capitalist institutions around the countries bordering the Mediterranean and the North Seas. The history of political theory and law follows the history of these processes, providing their justification and containing their ideological explanation.[15] The free will, whether in morality and politics or in moral and political philosophy, had sought, from the sixteenth century and on, to justify the charges of sin and guilt, just as that will had justified them in theory during the European middle ages; but free will now originated in the changed nature of capitalist society and associations.

The state is not identified with civil society; the two have been so identified in the past, but in error. Civil society is the organization of production in society; the state is not the organization of that production, it is the product of the relation between political economy and society. The organization of civil society is twofold. It is, to

---

[14] Fernand Braudel, *La Méditerranée et le monde méditerranéen à l'époque de Philippe II*. 2nd ed. Paris 1966. Braudel places his emphasis on the location, in the cities, in which the new kind of relations between capital and labor took place, instead of on the changed relations between them.

[15] Max Weber refers (*Wirtschaft und Gesellschaft*, 5th ed., J. Winckelmann, ed., Tübingen 1972, ch. VII) to the modern theory and practice of law (p. 387), modern law (p. 398), etc., in connection with freedom of contract, (p. 399), freedom of movement, freedom of conscience, freedom to dispose of property. It is new; it has not always existed. "The measure of contractual freedom, ... is naturally the function in the first place of the broadening of the market" (p. 398). Even Brentano, in his polemic against Weber, talks of the flowering of trade as the proximal cause, following which "the development of the mind as a whole was to a degree unitarily ordered by Machiavelli." L. Brentano, Puritanismus und Kapitalismus. *Der wirtschaftende Mensch in der Geschichte* (1923). Hildesheim 1967, p. 370.

begin with, not the inner organization of society such as the traditional community and society bring out, but an external organization imposed in history through the latifundia, plantations, irrigation systems, factory and trust systems, market and banking systems, etc. This external organization is linked in turn with the system of organization of the state, which is likewise wholly external and formal. The state is the organization of society for the control and regulation of the relations within and between the classes of society; the society in question being civil society.

The organization of social production, civil society as such, is the development of the relations of social labor. Labor in civil society is bound in all the economic formations of society anterior to the society of the production of capital; in the latter it is formally free. The bondage of social labor is effected and expressed by the force of tradition, or by the practices of slavery and serfdom, or by combinations thereof, as indenture, term slavery, clientage, and the like. The characteristic organization of bourgeois society is constituted by the relation of social labor in the condition of formal freedom, or the freedom to sell the labor capacity and power under terms stipulated by contract. The organization of the regulation and control of civil society by the state is the expression and perfection of these relations of bondage and freedom of social labor. The contractual relation of social labor in the society of capital production is a formal one, that is affirmed, enforced and hallowed by the state. The formalism of the contract relation perfects the relation of wage labor in society; the wage laborer becomes a legal person, which the slave and serf are not, which the peasant in the Asiatic mode of production is not. The formal side of the human individual calls forth formal expression of the society, which is the state. The organization of social production calls forth the formal organization for the control of civil society, to wit, the state. The relation of the state to the formal side of the human individual and to civil society is reciprocal.

II. PRIMITIVE AND CIVIL SOCIETY

In order to understand the nature of civil society, it is necessary to understand what it is not. Primitive society is the opposite of civil society, being society without the relations of political economy and the state. Primitive society, or the primitive condition of mankind generally, has been conceived as the condition of man in the state of nature. This is an error. Human beings, whether in the primitive or civil condition, are alienated from nature; their relations to nature are, without exception, intermediated by instruments of work. These economic relations are cultural, hence indirect, and not natural. The economic relations generally are in turn divided accordingly as they are primitive, or relations of the political economy. All the economic relations of the human kind, in society and to nature, are mediated by the instruments of work and of social labor, and by the technology and ecology that pertain thereto.[16] The alienation from nature that results from their intermediation likewise has its history. The primary, universal alienation of all human societies from nature is the condition common to primitive and political economy; primitive and civil society is the organization of this primary alienation. But whereas the relations to nature of labor and work are nothing other than indirect, the relations of labor in society are both direct and indirect. Here the distinction between work and labor is to be introduced. Work is concrete, it is human effort that is applied in the production of a socially useful object; labor is the same in abstract form, applied not in production but in exchange for social objects, things or services.

In primitive society, the economic relations to nature and within

---

[16] Technology is the lore and science of the instruments of work and labor; such activity is human, whether primitive or civilized, in its ensemble, whether accomplished in society or not. Ecology is the lore and science of the relations of the society to the natural surroundings. Economy, ecology and technology alike have their historical course and development, expanded as the lore and science of nature are expanded. The ecology of primitive societies is found in all places to be complex, in an intensive and localized form, as the body of traditional knowledge of the natural surroundings amassed by local groups. The technology of primitive societies, on the other hand, is by definition simple. Primitive societies are notably disappearing today, although all mankind once lived in this condition. Pygmies and Eskimoes when discovered were primitive in this sense, their ecology localized and complex, their technology adapted to their environment.

Technology has its history, so does the alienation of the human kind from nature, that alienation being from its very inception recorded in the history of technology. At the same time that the alienation of the human kind from nature is instituted by the human relation to nature, it is constituted by the relations in society. It is by the interaction of these two relations that human is differentiated from natural history. The human as part of the natural order is in history; it is the history that we do not make. The human as opposed to the natural history is the history that we make. The history of technology is increasingly the history of the alienation of the human kind from nature, just as the history of human society has been hitherto the history of the increasing alienation in society. The means whereby this twofold alienation is overcome lie in the relations of political economy and society. The history of technology, again, is the history of the material interchange with nature, on the one hand, that of the relations in society on the other. Cp. Vico, op. cit., § 331: "This civil world is certainly the work of men... The world of nations, or the civil world, which, because men have made it, they can come to know." His editor, F. Nicolini, relates this doctrine to the absolute historicism of Vico. See the footnote in Marx, *Kapital* I, op. cit., pp. 392 f., on Vico and the history of technology. Gramsci has developed the thesis of absolute historicism in regard to Marx, which is conceived by him as the philosophy of praxis, the terrestrialization, disenchantment of thought, the humanization of history (A. Gramsci, *Il materialismo storico a la filosofia di B. Croce. Opere*, Torino 1948).

the society are predominantly in the form of concrete labor, or work, the production, directly, of useful things. In civil society the relations in the economy to nature and in society are predominantly in the form of abstract labor, labor in short, labor for the purpose of its exchange against socially useful products in the form of commodities. In primitive economy and society all work who are able, whereby the conditions of life are produced and reproduced. In the political economy and society some are directly engaged in social labor, and form thereby a distinctive social class of immediate producers; they produce what is socially necessary for their own reproduction as a class, and a surplus; the surplus is applied on the one side to the expansion of production in the society, on the other for the maintenance and reproduction of those who are not immediately engaged in social production. The relations of production in primitive society are generally direct, in civil society they are both direct and indirect. The alienation in primitive society is primary, in relation to nature; in civil society the alienation is not only primary, in relation to nature, it is at once alienation in society, the social product being in part alienated from the immediate producer for allocation elsewhere in the society.

In the primitive economy, further, the distribution and exchange of the social product are not as highly developed as they are in the political economy;[17] commodity exchange and production is in this sense either low or nonexistent in the primitive economy. The category of the social is undivided in the primitive condition, being at once public and private, without distinction, whereas in the political economy, private labor is distinct from social labor, and private property from public property.[18] The distinction between public and private applies not only to labor and property but to the allocation of the surplus produced. In the primitive condition no distinction is made between the public and private use or abuse of the surplus, whereas in the political economic condition the social surplus is distinct from the private: In the primitive society generally and in the private sphere of civil society a surplus may be produced, but it differs in

---

[17] Joan Robinson, *Freedom and Necessity*. London 1970, ch. 2, refers to the isolated economies of primitive society.

[18] *Ager publicus* is mentioned by the ancient Romans both in regard to their own landholding practices and in regard to the ancient Germanic. See Tacitus, *Germania*. This implies a distinction between public and private and the transition to political economy, *societas civilis*. There is no distinction between public law and private law in the primitive economy. *Ager publicus*: see *The Ethnological Notebooks of Karl Marx*, Lawrence Krader, ed., Assen, 2nd ed., 1974, p. 414.

kind from the surplus produced in the public sphere of the political economy.[19]

[Teleology in the sense of the Aristotelian usage is a unilinear progression from one condition of being to another, as the progression from childhood to adulthood in the same species,[20] the progression being uniquely determined; the offspring of a cow does not have the adult horse as its telos. In social evolution, on the contrary, the primitive condition has more than one outcome; the political economy and civil society is the realization in actuality of but one of these. Further, the relations of political economy and civil society can reproduce a potentiality in the primitive society, and in human society generally, other than those of class division and opposition.]

In both the modern bourgeois and socialist economies there is a division and opposition between labor of head and hand, and between rural and urban production, as between countryside and city. These oppositions are found in the late feudal mode of production, and the mode of production of classical antiquity, but not in such a development in the Asiatic mode of production, which is a part of the history of political economy and civil society.[21] The production of a surplus in agriculture is a necessary condition for the development of modern urban industry, it was a condition for the development of industry in the ancient Asiatic mode of production as well, but that industry was not particularly urban, it was rural and urban without distinction. The production of a social surplus in agriculture is a necessary condition for the development of modern urban industry, for if the immediate agricultural producers consume all that they produce, then nothing will be left for the cities and industrial development therein. Poor and underdeveloped countries, lacking industrialized agriculture, must retain the greater part of the agricultural product for the reproduction of the agricultural producers. Therefore these countries cannot provide a surplus for the support of their urban industry.

---

[19] "Something extra – for a guest, for a feast" is produced and set aside in the primitive and in the private spheres. Cf. Joan Robinson, op. cit., p. 25; to this she added "tribute to whom tribute is due." In this case one would not speak of an isolated economy, for it would then be connected to a tribute system. The tribute is a relation of political economy. Ernest Mandel, *Traité d'économie marxiste*, Paris 1969, v. 1, ch. 2, distinguishes between simple and developed exchange, both in reference to primitive economies. There is not an absolute, rather only a relative division between primitive and political economies. Cf. Claude Meillassoux, *Anthropologie économique des Gouro*. 2nd ed. Paris 1970. Maurice Godelier, *Horizon, trajets marxistes en anthropologie*. Paris 1973.

[20] On teleology cf. sect. VI, below. Kurt v. Fritz, *Grundprobleme der Geschichte der antiken Wissenschaft*. Berlin 1971, pp. 278 sq. Etienne Gilson, *D'Aristote à Darwin et retour*. Paris 1971.

[21] On these relations of urban and rural production, cf. Krader, *Asiatic Mode of Production*, op. cit., Pt. I, ch. VII. See below section VIII.

In the industrially developed countries, on the contrary, the agricultural surplus supports the rich and ruling class on the one side and the urban industry on the other.[22] Here the movement of the surplus is twofold.

The urban center in antiquity was the city-state, *civitas*, the historical core of civil society. This point was grasped by Machiavelli, who is the father of urban sociology in modern times. He did not begin his history with a mythical state of nature, as did Hobbes, Locke and Rousseau, but with the movement from a dispersed social condition to a centralized one. The movement of centralization in modern capitalism is thus prefigured in the movement of centralization in the ancient society of Rome and Athens, and in the medieval society of Venice[23].

In the primitive economic relations, the activities of production and consumption are not separated; the unit of production and the unit of consumption are the same. The production is not separated, in this condition, as public and private, neither is the consumption. We have seen that the surplus that is produced and consumed is not a social surplus, being neither public nor private. The feasting of a guest is an act of surplus consumption, but it is not a public social act. Since the main part of what is produced is consumed at home, in the family, among the small group of kin or within the village, the product is to that extent an undifferentiated whole. The differentiation of the products into the component parts, such as are subsequently recognized as public and private, begins as the isolated communities of kin and neighbors enter into increasingly intensive intercourse with other like communities.[24] The exchange of products is then developed

[22] Extractive industry of the countryside must also be supported by an agricultural surplus. Unlike agriculture, the extraction of ores, etc., is not an interchange of materials with nature, but a one-way movement of the product. Only after many aeons are the interchanges "equaled out." Some refer to non-replenishable and replenishable resources in order to carry through this distinction. But civil society is a totality based on both types of movements. Limitation on development of the totality is discussed in Harrison Brown, *The Challenge of Man's Future*. New York 1954.
[23] Niccolo Machiavelli. *Discourses on the First Ten Books of Livy* (ca. 1513); on Rome and Athens, Book I, ch .1. On the beginnings of Venice see his *Florentine History* (1525), Bk. II,ch. 1.
[24] The process of relating the communities is one of successive further differentiations. The producer is only later differentiated from the trader. See Colin Renfrew, Trade and culture process in European prehistory. *Current Anthropology*, v. 10, 1969, pp. 151 sq. R. M. Adams (Anthropological Perspectives on Ancient Trade, ibid., v. 15, 1974, pp. 239 sq.) provides the following prehistory and history of exchange: the product is moved along a path, which thereby becomes a beaten track; so much is implied by the etymology of the word "trade." Adams continues: "Then, by the middle or later 16th century [in German, English, Dutch], the meaning broadens to include a habitual course of action or the practice of some occupation." The effect of customary practice on the relations between producing communities and the transformation of the traditional practices of exchange by the development of capitalism is shown by the history of the word. The research of Adams bears at once on the history of political economy generally,

on each side, whereby they are transformed into commodities. Adam Smith related the process of exchange to the sublation of the primitive economy and the related social condition: "In that rude state of society in which there is no division of labor, in which exchanges are seldom made, and in which every man provides every thing for himself, it is not necessary that any stock should be accumulated or stored up beforehand, in order to carry on the business of society."[25] The order of the thoughts is important: from division of labor to exchange, then to accumulation, whereby the primitive economy is overtaken and surpassed. The rude state of society is one in which wants are supplied by the immediate producers themselves, where everyone can make what others do.[26] The method of Durkheim in this connection was to trace the development of society from a stage of solidarity by similitudes, to a stage of solidarity which is due to the division of labor. In the first or more primitive stage, social solidarity is derived from resemblances between the individuals in the society, and is of a mechanical type.[27] The increasing division of labor has the function of effecting the transition from the primitive to the political economy according to Adam Smith; it effects the organic solidarity of society according to Durkheim.[28] The society of organic solidarity is civil society.

Malinowski described the economic relations of the Trobriand fishermen in these terms: "Let us see what happens with the division of the catch. In most cases only a small proportion of it remains with the villagers. As a rule we should find a number of people from some inland community waiting on the shore. They receive the bundles of fish from the fishermen and carry them home, often many miles away,

---

that is, over the entire course of existence of civil society, and on the transformation of both in the sixteenth century. The linguistic side of this analysis is due to Eric Hamp.

[25] Adam Smith, *The Wealth of Nations* (1776). New York, 1937. E. Cannan ed., p. 259. Joan Robinson, *Economic Philosophy*, New York 1964, p. 27, has identified the division of labor with specialization. The opposition of the perspectives of Herbert Spencer and of Emile Durkheim went further in this regard.

[26] G. W. F. Hegel, *Grundlinien der Philosophie des Rechts* (1821). *Werke*, v. 7, 1969, § 187, Zusatz, makes this the condition of the cultivated man; thereby everything is inverted from the primitive society. See Marx, *Kapital* I, op. cit., p. 329n. Here the heretical views of Hegel on the division of labor are remarked upon.

[27] Emile Durkheim. *De la division du travail social.* (1893). Paris 1973, pp. 35, 73f., 79ff.

[28] It is not the division of labor in society that was Durkheim's concern, but the solidarity of the society that was brought about thereby. His method was not to establish the economic relations whereby the effect on society was achieved, but to describe the progress of law from the imposition of repressive sanctions. Robert Nisbet, *The Sociology of Emile Durkheim*, London 1975, pp. 128f., has pointed out that Durkheim never returned to this idea again. The distinction between mechanical and organic solidarity is taken none too seriously by S. Lukes, *Emile Durkheim*, London 1973, p. 148. The problem of the division of labor remains.

running so as to arrive while it is still fresh. Here again we should find a system of mutual services and obligations based on a standing arrangement between two village communities. The inland village supplies the fishermen with vegetables: the coastal community repays with fish."[29]

The social surplus has been implicitly divided as private and public; offering food to a guest on the one side, tribute on the other, will exemplify this distinction. Pearson offers a distinction between relative and absolute surplus. His relative surplus is a quantity of goods or services set aside for some specific purpose; the absolute surplus is a quantity above an objectively ascertainable level of subsistence

---

[29] Bronislaw Malinowski. *Crime and Custom in Savage Society*. London 1926, p. 22. One must not be hypnotized by the word "savage." The point is, however, that these societies carry within themselves the means of their own dissolution and transformation. It is not western capitalism that serves as the midwife of history. The "standing arrangement" underlies the view outlined by Renfrew and Adams (see above); here are portrayed the means whereby the primitive economic relations are overcome within the primitive society. Richard Thurnwald, *Economics in Primitive Communities*, London 1932, p. 147, likewise traced the development of economic relations in primitive conditions from certain forms of exchange to their regularization as trade. See also K. Polanyi, *The Great Transformation*. Boston 1957, pp. 58f.

The postulation of a one-to-one transaction to account for exchange, trade, or commerce was an arbitrary assumption made for the purpose of abstraction as a convenience in the eighteenth century. See A.-R. J. Turgot, Valeurs et monnaies. Projet d'article. (1769). Repr. in his *Ecrits économiques*. B. Cazes, ed. Paris 1970. See p. 242. It is not only that the trader is isolated from his society; this was the criticism of Ricardo made by Marx. (See Marx, *Kapital*, I, op. cit., p. 43.) It is also that the trader in the fable of the Robinsonade is isolated from temporal continuity, repetition, regularization. This latter is brought out by Malinowski and Adams. Each mode of isolation implies the other.

Antonio Gramsci writes that "for a given human society there must be a given society of things, and that human society is possible only in so far as there exists a given society of things." (Antonio Gramsci, *The Modern Prince*. L. Marks, transl. New York 1967, p. 78.)

1. The categorical distinctions, *humanum societas* and *rerum societas* apply equally to primitive as to civil society, rubbing out the distinction between the latter two.
2. Gramsci's distinction points to the economy of man and nature as a unified one, i.e., of social man and socialized nature, which is the universal condition of alienation of humanity in relation to nature.
3. The movement is at the same time the material interchange or *Stoffwechsel* between man and nature.
4. The interchange between humanity and nature is counterposed to the movement of exchange, *Austausch*, in civil society.

(On interchange or *Stoffwechsel* see the last essay, on the Dialectic of Anthropology.)

needs.[30] Aristotle considered a surplus as the means to support the priests in Egypt, once the necessaries of life had been assured. This leisure class then developed mathematics; Hegel followed Aristotle in this judgment.[31] The surplus produced in primitive society is not applied to the support of a leisure class; the surplus produced in civil society, and this is the gist of Aristotle's insight into the problem, is so applied; the examples of the Egyptian priests and the philosophers of Athens will suffice for this. Aristotle defined the surplus in terms of the ratio between the amount necessary for reproduction of the immediate producers in society, and the excess over that amount, or in terms of the distribution of the social product. It is the present day writers who failed to define the surplus in relation to social production.

The material meaning of surplus was clearly set forth by Aristotle and Hegel in the formation of civil society as opposed to the primitive. Bodin opposed the Platonic doctrine of communism; the republic, he said, is ruined by ignorance of the difference between mine and thine. The relation between private property and civil power was clearly set forth by him, as a formal matter.[32] The formal relation of civil society and the state to private property, its demarcation and protection, was clear likewise to Hobbes, Locke, and Adam Smith.[33] The material and formal sides were further developed in their dialectical relations, in the theory of civil society. Property remained, as it

---

[30] M. J. Herskovits, *Economic Anthropology*. New York 1952, has defined the surplus as an excess of goods over the minimum demands of necessity. This is a subjective approach. Pearson's is not otherwise, although it claims objectivity. H. W. Pearson. The Economy has no Surplus. K. Polanyi, C. M. Arensberg and H. W. Pearson. *Trade and Market in the Early Empires*. Free Press, 1957, pp. 323-329. Cf. M. Harris. The Economy has no Surplus? *American Anthropologist*, v. 61, 1959. Pearson's example of the relative surplus is the Biblical story of grain storage in Egypt. Abstinence and saving are not the answer to a surplus, for then one might say that the farmer who stores his seed for the coming year's sowing has set aside a relative surplus. Joan Robinson deals only with a surplus of production over the necessities of subsistence, enumerates cases of a surplus, and eschews its social definition (1970, loc. cit.). See Karl Marx, *Kapital*, v. I, ch. 22, § 3 on Abstinence (op. cit., pp. 554 sq.).

[31] G. W. F. Hegel. *Wissenschaft der Logik*. 2nd ed., 1831. Vorrede. Aristotle, *Metaphysics* A1, 981b; A2, 982b. Neither Aristotle nor Hegel can be held responsible for overlooking the distinction between the surplus in relation to production and to reproduction, which was introduced after their time. Pearson's work appeared after this distinction was made, but he has not grasped it. He criticizes Marx, but does not know what he is criticizing.

[32] Jean Bodin. *Les six livres de la république*. Paris 1583, p. 949. By *republic* is meant the *state* (ibid., p. 124).

[33] Thomas Hobbes, *De Cive*. 1642 (*The Citizen*. 1651. I, 3. V, 8-10. VI, 1. X, 1.) *Leviathan·* 1651. I, 10. I, 14. II, 24. John Locke. *Two Treatises*, op. cit. II, ch. 5-8. Adam Smith *Wealth of Nations*, op. cit., pp. 669ff. P. Laslett, ed., Locke, *Two Treatises*. Cambridge, 1967. C. B. MacPherson, *The Political Theory of Possessive Individualism*. Oxford 1962.

is, a formal-legal consideration in the question of civil society in its relation to the state.

The binary opposition of primitive and civil or political society is other than the three-stage theory of the evolution of civil society from the stages of savagery and barbarism. The three-stage theory was first adumbrated by Ferguson,[34] it was further developed by L. H. Morgan side by side with the binary opposition between *societas* or primitive society, and *civitas*, or civil society. The three-stage theory, as formulated by Morgan has been modified in the light of subsequent data of archaeology and ethnology, by V. G. Childe[35]. Will it not be modified yet again?

The difference between the primitive and political economy, hence between primitive and civil society, is summed up in reference to the law of value. Adam Smith had discussed that law according to which the value of a commodity is determined by the amount of labor time applied in its production, but in so doing referred without distinction to primitive and political economy. Wrote Smith, "If among a nation of hunters, for example, it usually costs twice the labor to kill a beaver which it does to kill a deer, one beaver should naturally exchange for or be worth two deer."[36] In the subsequent discussion of the theory of value, the primitive was distinguished from the civil condition by Marx in the following way: "Moreover, the savage is guilty of weighty economic sin by his utter indifference to the expenditure of time, and applies, as Tylor accounts, an entire month to the preparation of an arrow."[37] The notion of a primitive nation of hunters making application of the labor theory of value leaves out of account the relation of exchange, hence of exchange value, in society, and the relation of abstract to concrete social labor. Social labor, in the relations of the political economy, is both abstract and concrete. As abstract labor it is a commodity and has an exchange value. As concrete labor in society, on the contrary, it is engaged in the production of useful

---

[34] Ferguson, *History of Civil Society*, op. cit.

[35] Lewis Henry Morgan, *Ancient Society*. New York 1877.
Friedrich Engels, *Ursprung der Familie, des Privateigentums und des Staats*. Stuttgart 1884.
V. Gordon Childe, *Social Evolution*. London 1951.
L. A. White, *Evolution of Culture*. New York 1959.

[36] Adam Smith, op. cit., p. 47. He distinguished in many places between rude or savage society (cf. pp. 63, 163, 653), barbarous (p. 753) and civilized society (pp. 14, 248), ibid. He likewise gives an account of the historical periods of this development (pp. 672ff.). But he failed to bring the periodization together with the problem of value.

[37] Marx, *Kapital*, II, 4th ed., Hamburg 1910, p. 414. Cf. E. B. Tylor, *Researches into the Early History of Mankind* (1865). Chicago 1964, p. 163. Paul Sweezy, *Socialism*, McGraw-Hill 1949, p. 138ff., discusses the relation between Adam Smith and Marx in regard to the theory of value. See below, sect. X, on the relations of primitive and political economy.

things, which have a use-value as such. The differentiation between the values of exchange and use of a thing, however, is applicable to the political, not to the primitive economy. It is the exchange value of a commodity that is reckoned by the time applied in its production, not its use value. The immediate producer in the primitive economy is engaged in production for use in the first place, and not for exchange, whereas, on the contrary, the immediate producer in the political economy is engaged in production for exchange in the first place, and not for use. We have seen that the unit of production is other than the unit of consumption in the political economy; but this distinction is not usually the case in the primitive economy. The units of production and consumption are related to each other by the process of exchange, and it is in this connection that socially useful things assume an exchange value, social relations which are either absent or else are not well developed in the primitive economy. The elements of these developments are referred to in the case of the Trobriand Islanders cited above

The consideration of the case of the nation of hunters by Adam Smith was taken up by Ricardo, but, while the view still prevailed in which the law of value in the political economy applied to the primitive as well, yet Ricardo reduced the nation of hunters to the isolated hunter.[38] But the law of value presupposes not only the distinction between primitive and political economy, it presupposes a social relation, and not an isolated individual, or primitive Robinson Crusoe. Marx has much fun with Ricardo and his Robinsonade.[39] Labor considered as a commodity, in its abstract relation, is labor in civil society; the distinction between the condition in which labor time is reckoned up and valued from the condition in which it is not implies the distinction between civil and primitive society.

The human being is everywhere a creature of society, both in the primitive and civil condition. The notion of a Robinson Crusoe isolated from society is a fantasy without relation to concrete social reality. The fable of the man-beast in isolation in the state of nature is a figment of the imagination of the same sort as Robinson. Both Hobbes, the author of the first fiction, and Defoe, the author of the second, anticipated the fable of the selfmade man, the captain of industry who starts with nothing to become the hero in history. Hobbes began without society; it was customary in the political philosophy of his time to make the presupposition that the individual exists prior to society; so did Descartes and Spinoza. Montesquieu began to question

---

[38] David Ricardo, *The Principles of Political Economy and Taxation* (1817). London 1911, p. 13.
[39] Marx, *Kapital*. I, op. cit., p. 43.

this presupposition. Defoe, however, cannot be made into the butt of the argument against the Robinsonade, for he conceived his hero as the product of his society. Robinson as represented by Defoe is the opposite of the man in the natural state, for his first task in establishing himself on his tropical isle was to rescue everything that time and his physical strength permitted from his wrecked ship. Defoe recounts the dangers that Crusoe braved, detailing in the most circumstantial way that which was brought to safety on the shore, before the ship disappeared beneath the waves, and the use to which he put the goods he was able to store up against the future. Defoe leaves us no room to doubt that *only* in this way was Robinson able to survive.

The fabulations of Hobbes and Defoe have been transformed into the theories of the hero and the great man in history by Thomas Carlyle. The literature of the nineteenth and twentieth centuries is full of such tales, whose tellers have spoliated the writings of the foregoing centuries, transforming them into theories of laissez-faire, of the rugged individualist, or the hero in history, which promulgate the vision of the free market, free enterprise, freedom tout court, the piratical spoliator of wealth from all possible sources, whom the agencies of the state seek to inhibit while cheering him on. Robinson becomes in this sense a mumpsimus of bigotry through adherence to a fallacy that has long since been exposed. He is the creature of society, and is so understood by Defoe; the reason for his having been miscast in the following centuries are related to those for which Ricardo recast the argument of Adam Smith: it is not only convenient, it is desirable to begin with the isolated individual. Adam Smith wrote scornfully of the "insidious or crafty animal, vulgarly called the statesman or politician" who inserted himself into the affairs of the economy.[40] Yet his effort to keep government out of business should not be confused with the attempt by others to separate economy and society. The allusions by classical political economists to the isolated primitive hunter are a frame story, the relations of the political economy are on the contrary relations in society.

III. CIVIL SOCIETY AND THE STATE

The discussion of the centralization of political rule over an entire society, city or empire was conducted in ancient and medieval times. Aristotle, Cicero, Augustine had held that the affairs of human society may be regulated by diffuse power and without specialized

---

[40] Adam Smith, op. cit., p. 435.
On the great man: Thomas Carlyle, *On Heroes, Hero-Worship, and the Heroic in History*, 1840.

organs of government, that is, by traditional means of conducting its affairs and composing its differences. Alternatively, as it was then held, these may be controlled and regulated by centralized power, by special organs of government, and by means, whether traditional or not, of conducting its activities. The traditional means in the latter case are matters of form alone, as we shall see. In the sixteenth century the discussion was given a new form, and the corresponding terms, civil society and the state, were introduced.[41] Civil society in particular comprises the negation of the diffuse and generalized means of government of society, such as may be found in primitive conditions, or in the societies of pure communism. Within civil society, the private sphere is separated from the public, the private interest is opposed to the public; the state is the particular organ of civil society whereby these private interests are regulated and controlled. The relation between the centralization of power and the control of the private interests is at the same time the matter of the control over the disposition of the surplus produced in the society.

The community of primitive society is negated in civil society. The immediate relation of production in society is still of a communal nature in the beginnings of the Asiatic, classical and feudal modes of production. This communal relation of production is negated by the relations of civil society which reach a peak in the development of production of capital. By this negation the individual is torn loose from the community on the one hand and from the immediate bonds to the means of production on the other.[42] The individual here pursues his private interest at the expense of the social whole, and at the expense of his own class as a whole. But the class interests are the indi-

---

[41] Machiavelli, *The Prince* (1513) refers to the state in the modern sense, perhaps the first to do so Thomas Starkey brought this usage to England in 1538. The terms appear in general use in the fifteenth century in a different sense. See O. Bloch, W. v. Wartburg, *Dictionnaire étymologique de la langue française*. Paris 1964, s.v. état. Also A. P. d'Entrèves, *The Notion of the State*. Oxford 1967, ch. 3. Prior to Machiavelli, Philippe de Commynes a.o. use the term to refer to personal or political status, etc.

[42] Friedrich Engels, *The Origin of the Family*, op. cit., has considered the state in relation to the ruling class.

The class interest of the individuality and the individual interest of the class are necessary to complete the theory of the state. This is shown in the notes of Marx on the work of H. S. Maine. Cf. *The Ethnological Notebooks*, op. cit., p. 329: "Erst Losreissung: First tearing loose of the individuality from the originally *non-despotic*... *bonds of the group*, of the primitive community, – therewith the one-sided elaboration of the *individuality*. But the true nature of the latter is shown only when we analyze the content – the *interests* of these "latter." We then find that these interests are themselves again common and characterizing of certain social groups, class interests, etc., thus this individuality is itself class, etc. individuality, and all these in the final instance have *economic conditions at their basis*. On these as bases the state is built up and presupposes them."

vidual interests. The class interests are at once the activation of the individual interests and their negation. The individual interests are summed up and realized in the social class, whereby they are made actual. They are at once negated in and by the social class, and its organ of regulation and control, the state. On the one hand the expression of the individual interests, and the negation of the communal interest, are the necessary conditions for the formation of civil society and the state. On the other hand, the individual interests are summed up in the collective interest of the social class of these individuals, the social class which is the expression of the sum of these mutually antagonistic individual interests. It is Hobbes' war of each against all. But contrary to Hobbes, it is not the condition of man in the state of nature; it is the condition of man in civil society. It is the condition of man in modern bourgeois society, which was projected by Charles Darwin into the natural kingdom by the process he described as the survival of the fittest.[43] It is civil society conceived by Hegel as the spiritual animal kingdom, or the jungle law carried into the streets of the city.[44] But these individualities are not those of the immediate producers in society; that society, such as is found in the beginnings of Mycenaean and Egyptian history, is comprised by communities of field laborers, and of a class of individuals who control that labor and consume the surplus in the society that is thereby produced. The social surplus is at the disposition of the ruling class through the individual interest. The state is at once the expression and the negation of the individual interest. That interest is concerned with the disposition of the social surplus, which is an interest of individuals as a social class, a class interest of individuals and the individual interest of and by the class. Those engaged in immediate production in civil society are at first bound to the means of production, in the first place, the soil; they are bound by ties of custom, tradition, by the

---

[43] He owed the phrase to Herbert Spencer. See Charles Darwin, *The Origin of Species by Means of Natural Selection, or the Preservation of Favored Races in the Struggle for Life.* (1859). New York Modern Library, n.d., p. 52. The phrase, Struggle for Life, was his own (ibid., pp. 52, 66). The outlook that is implied was shared both with Spencer and with Thomas Malthus (ibid., p. 53. See also Darwin, *Descent of Man*, ibid., p. 428.)

[44] Hegel, *Phänomenologie des Geistes* (1807). *Werke*, v. 3, Suhrkamp 1970, p. 294. Cf. Marx, Letter to Engels, June 18, 1862. Karl Marx and Friedrich Engels, *Selected Correspondence.* I. Lasker, transl. 2nd ed., Moscow, 1965, p. 128: "It is remarkable how Darwin recognizes among beasts and plants his English society with its division of labor, competition, opening up of new markets, "inventions", and the Malthusian "struggle for existence." It is Hobbes' *bellum omnium contra omnes*, and one is reminded of Hegel's *Phenomenology*, where civil society is described as a "spiritual animal kingdom", while in Darwin the animal kingdom figures as civil society ..."

bonds of debt, by clientage, slavery, and serfdom. The state is the organ for the extraction of surplus labor and product from them by means of the collectors, treasury agents, bailiffs, court officers, the military; the social surplus is extracted in the form of tax and rent, or a combination of both. In the transition to modern capitalism, the laborer is no longer bound to the soil, the workshop, etc., but is free to engage in contracts for labor time and wage. The result is the further extension of individuality and the further extension of control and regulation of individuality by the agencies of the state . The functions of these agencies, in the period of modern bourgeois society, multiply in type and quantity as a consequence of the extension of this new individuality. The centralization of state power is intensified by the proliferation of the individual interests.

The early history of that centralization is no less indicative of individual interests, but these are expressed only by a few, who are torn loose from the community. These few are of the type of Romulus and Theseus, who are not individuals, nor yet an era, but a class of individuals which gave an era its name.[45] In their hands the socially produced surplus was concentrated; it was thereby separated from the community of the immediate producers. In this way the common interest was dissolved and the private interest was expressed as opposed to the social and public interest. The public and social interest are, however, not one. The social interest is the interest of the whole; the private interest may coincide with the interest of the whole, whereas private and public interest are opposed to each other, by definition. The common interest in the continued existence of the community continues long after the transition from primitive to civil society, where it continues to be the form of organization of the immediate producers, coexisting with the private interests of the ruling class. The state is the organ of regulation and control of all these conflicting interests; it has no interest as such, being an abstraction. Those in control of the organs of the state apply them in their collective interest. The state is at the same time the organ of the ruling class of civil society for the control of other classes and the organ for the control of individual interests of all classes which are at variance with the interests of the ruling class as a collectivity. This conflict is exacerbated by the condition that the ruling class of civil society evolved the individuality in the expression of the interest of the class and the individual. The individual in the pursuit of his interest, for which the class was evolved, is in conflict

---

[45] L. H. Morgan, *Ancient Society*, Chicago 1907, p. 265, wrote, "It will be sufficient to regard Theseus as representing a period, or a series of events." Cf. *Ethnological Notebooks*, op. cit., p. 209.

with the interest of the class. This is the contradiction of the class interest of individuals; the state is evolved in part to resolve this contradiction, but cannot do so any more than it can resolve the conflict between the class of those engaged in direct production in society and those who are not so engaged. The former have no immediate interest in the state; it is the latter in whose interest the agencies of the state are engaged; the former are engaged in their own immediate production, and have lately evolved organs for the limitation on the conditions under which the social surplus is extracted from their production. These organs are combinations, associations, syndicates, unions and parties.

The centralized power in society was expressed symbolically in the art of the ancient Near and Far East. The slate of Narmer in Egypt (ca. 3000 B.C.) depicts a ruler commanding over subjects; inscriptions on oracle bones in the early history of China convey like scenes. This opposition was expressed in ancient Rome as *imperium* of the central power; the diffuse power was referred to as *potestas*.[46]

Machiavelli wrote that the Romans prior to the founding of their city, lived dispersed, referring in a like way to the founding of their respective cities by Athenians, Venetians and Florentines. Hobbes opposed the system of Machiavelli, together with its antecedents in the writings of Cicero and Augustine. Hobbes regarded power, authority and empire as all one, holding that man first lived in isolation, in a state of nature. In such a state there is no form of power of one over another, but violence; a peaceful if diffuse power, such as Machiavelli depicted among the Romans before their historical period, was excluded by Hobbes, just as the power of the people according to the views of Cicero and Machiavelli was excluded by him.[47] Power, according to Hobbes, is either concentrated or it does not exist at all; therefore there is no grounds for the distinction between power and authority, power and imperium, etc. Hobbes and Harrington after

---

[46] There is some confusion about the latter term. D'Entrèves, *The Notion of the State*, op. cit., p. 7, wrote against T. D. Weldon, *The Vocabulary of Politics*, London 1953, who had not distinguished between 'power' and 'authority', whereas the former, following Cicero, did do so. Cicero, *De legibus*, 3, 28, wrote "... potestas in popula, auctoritas in senatu sit." But Cicero also wrote of *potestas* in the hands of the praetoria (*Pro lege Manilla* 24, 69) and of the censors (*Oratio pro Cluentio* 27, 74), neither being of the people. Usually, centralized power or authority is referred to as *imperium*; *potestas* may be either diffuse or centralized. This is also the usage of Augustine (de civitate Dei 3, 24). The point at issue is not the meaning of *potestas*, *auctoritas* or *imperium*, however, it is the distinction between central and diffuse authority.

[47] Thomas Hobbes. *Leviathan*, 1651. I, 13. See also his *De Cive*, 1642. Machiavelli, loc. cit. On popular power, see his *Discourses*, op. cit., I, 58f. On Cicero see preceding note. Aristotle's *Politics* should also be counterposed to the view of Hobbes.

him were agreed that riches are power.[48] Hobbes opposed the public and private spheres to each other in civil society, and opposed civil society to the state (commonwealth or artificial man, the mortal god).[49] The system of Hobbes as it bore upon the relations of the state to society and to the relations within the civil society rested on two undertakings: Civil society was an association formed by free and voluntary contract between independent men as plenipotentiary parties; the state was formed by the submission of the associates under a sovereign power.[50] Spinoza, Locke, Shaftesbury, Mandeville, and Hume held this system in common.[51]

The earliest writers in modern times to have developed the theory of the state brought out its form, function and content. Machiavelli brought out not only the early usage of the word 'state' in its modern meaning, he also furnished an account of the historical circumstances under which the state is formed. For this he was endebted to Cicero and Augustine, but he carried his air far beyond them, into the modern era, and it is to his tune that we dance, not to Cicero's. The transition from the dispersed to the concentrated social life is the transition from primitive to civil society; Machiavelli well grasped the relation of this

---

[48] Hobbes, *Leviathan*, op. cit., I, 10. James Harrington, *Oceana*, 1656. See his *Works*. London 1771, pp. 37f.

[49] Hobbes, op. cit., Dedication and Introduction, also I, 14. Cf. his *De Cive*, op. cit., Preface; I, 2; V, 9; VI, 1; X, 1.

[50] Whether Hobbes envisaged two original contracts or two stipulations in one contract need not detain us. See Gough, *The Social Contract*, op. cit., pp. 108f.

[51] Spinoza, *Theologico-Political Treatise*, 1670, ch. 16 sq., (see also his *Political Treatise*, 1677, ch. 5 sq.) and Locke, *Two Treatises*, op. cit., stood close to Hobbes, although both denied the motivation of men to form an association through fear of violence. Lord Shaftesbury varied from Hobbes, being among the first to identify civil government and civil society. Shaftesbury ridiculed Hobbes' notion of the original state of nature, of human life in isolation, of mutual enmity, as he did the notion of a contract whereby civil society was founded: "How the wit of man should so puzzle this cause, as to make civil society and government appear a kind of invention and creature of art, I know not." Shaftesbury, *Sensus Communis* (1709). See his *Characteristicks*, 2nd ed. 1714, v. 1, pp. 110f. There is, accordingly, no such thing as an original asocial state of nature, as Hobbes would have it. Man is social throughout, herding, affection and fellowship being the true account of the constitution of society. Hobbes and Shaftesbury alike identified society and civil society; yet Hobbes' distinction between civil society and the state was without significance to the latter.
(Cf. Friedrich Meinecke, *Die Entstehung des Historismus*. 2nd ed. München 1946, p. 25.) Bernard Mandeville, *The Fable of the Bees*, ed. 1723, adopted and extended the system of Hobbes, making the distinction between public and private into the foundation of civil society. He derived public virtue from private vice. Hume, *A Treatise of Human Nature*, op. cit., pp. 475n., 537f., 543, distinguished between the civil and natural condition of man, closely following Hobbes, Spinoza, Locke and Mandeville. Hume affirmed the fictive nature of the social contract (*Essays, Moral and Political*, 1748). Cf. Gough, op. cit., p. 186ff. and Ernest Barker, *Social Contract*. Oxford 1960, Introd.

moment in ancient and medieval European history to the meeting of the human wants of sustenance and protection from the weather in society in general: this is the thought that Hegel developed in his theory of civil society. The transition from the diffused to the centralized power in society is the second moment; it is the historical moment of the formation of political society. It is in consideration of the opposition and combination of these historical moments that we have proposed to differentiate between civil and political society; if Cicero propounded the doctrine of the latter, Machiavelli and Hegel propounded the doctrine of both. The state has its origin in both these historical moments, behind which, and underlying them, lies the process of the division of society into classes, the historical relation of the state to civil society, and of civil to primitive society; Jean Bodin brought out the factor of private wealth in the formation of the republic, writing, "... in eliminating these two words *mine* and *thine* the foundations of all republics are ruined..."[52] Hobbes and Harrington brought out the relation between wealth and power, as we have seen; Locke held that civil society and the state are established for the defence of property.[53]

The men of law, Althusius and Grotius, formulated the new doctrine of the state in relation to natural and civil right, thereby bringing out the formal side of the state as opposed to the function. A false continuity between modern and ancient jurisprudence has been proposed in the Renaissance and Reformation, indeed down to the time of Fr. v. Savigny, as though the categories of Roman jurisprudence were valid throughout, without interruption. Following Hegel, in his controversy with Savigny, Beseler and Gierke opposed modern to ancient practice, and Germanic to Romanic. We have seen that Hegel's view has prevailed. Althusius and Grotius spoke another tongue, and their argument has not been answered in that tongue. Following the ancient Romans, they distinguished between natural and civil right, whereby all men have the former, some the latter. Roman civil right is the basis of modern civil right, Roman civil society the basis of modern civil society, accordingly. From this it would follow that the ancient Roman definition of the juridical person and of *civitas* is the modern, but this is absurd, because the ancient Roman person was a bundle of family, gentile, civil, etc., rights, which are not

---

[52] Jean Bodin. *De la république*. Paris 1583, p. 948. See ibid., p. 15.
[53] Locke, op. cit. Cf. C. B. MacPherson, *The Political Theory of Possessive Individualism*, op. cit.

found in the coeval Egyptian, Persian, Judaic, etc., polities.[54] Civil law and the law of nations (*jus civile* and *jus gentium*) were accordingly opposed to natural law (*jus naturale*), and civil society was regarded as the repository of civil law. The opposition of the civil and natural conditions of humanity was accepted accordingly without question by the theorists of civil society and civil right, from Hobbes to Rousseau. Practically this meant the formulation of the theory of the social contract as the fundament of civil society and its origin. Whence came this fateful theory whose banner is still borne aloft in the nineteenth and twentieth centuries?

The sixteenth century is not the beginning of the formation of capital which was produced in ancient times in Asia, Europe and elsewhere, nor yet of capitalism, whose beginnings are detected in Italy in the centuries prior to the sixteenth. But by the latter time, all the strands were tied together, the expansion of capital was developed, the companies for trading in the east and west were formed in Europe, labor was loosened from its bondage to the soil in parts in Europe, notably in Italy, England, the Low Countries. The relations of capital formation and of labor are contractual. The arguments of the theorists of natural right that society is a form of association had direct bearing on these contractual relations, even before the theory of social contract had been formulated.[55] In 1544, Salamonius asked, "If the state (*civitas*) is nothing but a kind of civil society (*civilis quaedam societas*), is any society ever formed without contracts?" His answer was, "No. There be contracts, tacit or express."[56] The lines of development from contract theory and from natural law led to the formulation of social contract as a pact of association. The theory of society implied was based on that of a commercial company or a trading society.

The debate during the nineteenth century over the history and

---

[54] Gaius remarked in his *Commentaries* that the *jus vitae necisque*, of life and death over the children, was a peculiarity of the *patria potestas* of Rome and was not common in this extreme degree with other peoples. Roman definitions of right, person, etc., have a general but in no way a specific bearing on modern definitions of the same.

[55] Discussion of contract as "the fundamental principle of feudal society" by A. J. Carlyle, *Medieval Political Theory*, op. cit., v. VI, p. 382, reinforces the conclusion that contract had changed meaning from the thirteenth to the sixteenth centuries. (See ibid., v. III, pt. I, ch. 2, 4; v. V, pt. I, ch. 7, 8.) Johannes Althusius, *Politics*. 1603. F. S. Carney, tr., London 1964. Otto Gierke, *Johannes Althusius*. 6th ed. Aalen 1968. Hugo Grotius, *On the Law of War and Peace*. 1625. The changed nature of the theory of society, in particular the concept of the corporation, had been brought out by F. W. Maitland, Introduction to Otto Gierke, *Political Theories of the Middle Age*. Cambridge 1900, p. xxviii.

[56] Marius Salamonius. *De Principatu*. 1544. Transl. J. W. Gough, *Social Contract*, op. cit., pp. 47f. Gough translates *societas* by 'partnership' .

function of the association is dimly to be perceived in theories of the twentieth which derive the state from forms of association. Lowie found the germ of the state to be the associations formed by Plains Indians for the purpose of policing the buffalo hunts.[57] The association in this case was not freely and willingly undertaken, but was a duty of the Indian hunters. In this matter, Lowie brought out the beginnings of differentiation and opposition between public and private interests.[58] The sib and gens are counterposed to the associations; Lowie opposed the theory of the formation of the state out of the dissolution of the ancient gentes, such as had been the idea of L. H. Morgan and Friedrich Engels.[59] The association is composed of associates who band together not by ties of kinship or of neighborhood, but for a common purpose independent of these. It is not the past that determines the form and function of the association but the expectation from common activity among the *socii*. A society (*societas*) was formed by contract, in classical Roman law, between two or more persons (*socii*), who, without forming a corporate body, obligated themselves mutually to a common end by means in common. This society was a matter of private law; the corporate body, corporation, had both a private and public character in the classical Roman law.[60] Etymologically, *socius* is derived from a root meaning 'follower, follow', i.e., *sequor*.[61] Later forms of the root term took on meanings of 'common', 'comrade', 'combination'; *socius* came to have a meaning of 'ally' in public law.[62] The societies formed by these *socii* have much in common with modern companies and firms. In the Germanic tradition the *Genosse*, 'companion, comrade', corresponded to the Latin *socius*, with this difference, that *Genosse* has little in common by its etymology, with 'follower'; *Genosse* has rather to do with *Nutz*, use.[63] The ancient Romans eschewed the idea that the entire Roman

[57] R. H. Lowie, *The Origin of the State*. New York 1927. (Summarized in *The Freeman*, July 19 and 26, 1922). R. M. MacIver. *The Modern State*, Oxford 1926.
[58] R. H. Lowie. Societies of the Crow, Hidatsa and Mandan Indians. *American Museum of Natural History. Memoirs*, v. 11, 1913, pp. 145-358. Cf. Heinrich Schurtz, *Altersklassen und Männerbünde*. Berlin 1902, pp. 1-82.
[59] L. H. Morgan, *Ancient Society*, op. cit. Friedrich Engels, *Origin of the Family*, op. cit.
[60] Max Kaser. *Das römische Privatrecht*. München 1971. I, pp. 302ff., 572ff. It is not clear that close kinship was different from other forms of private association, ibid., 73ff., 82ff. The private *socii* formed the model for naval units, *socii navales*. See Theodor Mommsen, *Römische Geschichte*, 6th ed. Berlin 1874. v. 1, pp. 515f.
[61] Julius Pokorny, *Indogermanisches etymologisches Wörterbuch*. Francke 1959, I, pp. 896f. Cf. A. Walde, J. B. Hofmann. *Lateinisches etymologisches Wörterbuch*. Heidelberg 1954. I, s.v.
[62] A. Ernout, A. Meillet. *Dictionnaire étymologique de la langue Latine*. 4th ed. Paris 1959, s.v. Cf. Mommsen, op. cit., III, p. 246.
[63] Pokorny, op. cit., p. 768. F. Kluge, *Etymologisches Wörterbuch der deutschen Sprache*. 20th ed. Berlin 1967, s.v.

society be modelled on the private association, *societas*. This idea was put forward by the European theorists of *civil society* in the sixteenth and seventeenth centuries. They were concerned with what has later come to have the meaning of 'society' in the treatment by social scientists of the nineteenth and twentieth centuries, a meaning which had to be purged of its ancient denotations in classical Roman private civil law, and likewise the connotations of public law in the early period of modern capitalism.

The *Genossenschaft* in early Germanic usage had a history parallel to the Roman *societas*, having been transferred from a usage in the private sphere to the public sphere, as the two became separated in history. The *Genossenschaft* was originally like the fellowship; later writers on the subject have sought to assimilate the idea of *Genossenschaft* in this meaning to that of *societas*. This consists in the identification of *societas* with 'fellowship', hence with *Genossenschaft*. Latterly, 'society' came to mean a group of masters and fellows, but that is a tiny segment of its entire meaning today.[64]

The theory of the *Genossenschaft* as it was developed by Gierke was not at first conceived in reference to any notion of 'society'. The two terms crossed paths in the discussion of an early form of the business firm, the trading company, *Handelsgesellschaft*, which was derived from a supposed, prior *Genossenschaft*, parallel to *societas*.[65] Gierke's task, however, was not to combine but to separate the Germanic from the Roman and later Romanic practice. Practically, Gierke intended to overthrow the attempt by B. Windscheid to adapt and thereby to continue Roman law into the modern time.[66] Theoretically, Gierke's task was to trace the historical root of the modern state and corporation to the ancient and medieval Germanic *Genossenschaft*, which, in this sense, ends as a voluntary organization. In its origin it therefore has the potentiality of becoming a body of freely willing members, on the one side, and of becoming the sovereign state on the other. (We will take these questions in order, returning to the state later.) The *Genossenschaft* in theory was parallel to the *societas* by the common feature of voluntary and free conjunction. This at once was contradicted by Gierke's dictum, "Hardly anywhere are

---

[64] Otto Gierke. *Das deutsche Genossenschaftsrecht*. 4 v. 1868-1913. (*Political Theories of the Middle Age*. F. Maitland, transl., op. cit. *Natural Law and the Theory of Society*, E. Barker, transl., op. cit.)

[65] Gierke, op. cit., II, pp. 938ff., 943ff., 949, 952-6. Cf. Gierke, *Die Genossenschaftstheorie die nud deutsche Rechtsprechung*. Berlin 1887, pp. 49, 45of.

[66] O. Gierke. *Das Wesen der menschlichen Verbände*. Berlin 1902. R. Hübner, *Grundzüge des deutschen Privatrechts*. 2nd ed. Leipzig 1913. P. Vinogradoff, *Outlines of Historical Jurisprudence*. I, Oxford 1920. Idem, *Custom and Right*. Oslo 1925.

the categories set forth by the Romanists of *universitas, societas, communio* maintained in connection with the Genossenschaft theory." He opposed the idea that the Genossenschaft is a legal fiction, arguing in favor of its reality (als reale Gesamtperson).[67] It is to this end that he traced the open trading society (die offene Handelsgesellschaft) back to the venture society (Vermögensgenossenschaft), thence to the ancient Germanic Genossenschaft.[68] His concept of Genossenschaft from the beginning and throughout is related to that of the association (*Verband*) as a part of the latter. The Genossenschaft is more than this, however. It is not only the form of association that gave rise to the trading company, it is at the same time, as it was in origin, connected by Gierke to the most ancient communal peasant practices, which in Dithmarsen and Fehmarn had virtually throughout a guild form and nature. It is in this connection above all that Gierke wrote of associations as resting on natural and historical foundations, and at the same time of the volitional character of Genossenschaft in the Germanic tradition.[69] The guild, the peasant community, the corporation and the state are elaborations of the Genossenschaft, in Gierke's theory.[70] The community and the state are the realization, accordingly, of the potentiality in the Genossenschaft. In these institutions of the history of the people, as in the corporation (Körperschaft) are realized the expression of the will of the members, as likewise of their freedom. The freedom and will of the state is deduced therefrom, whence is derived the freedom and will of the juridical persons which the state constitutes and recognizes. The realization and constitution is connected to the original potentiality of the Genossenschaft in Germanic history. In the technical sense, said Gierke, the Genossenschaft is a corporate body which rests on a free unity; it is an independent body as a legal person, the freedom being not that of each individual member, but that of the body that is so constituted. The will of the corporate body is therefore not derivative from the individual members, but from the state, as the overarching corporate body, to which the subordinate juridical persons are responsible.[71]

---

[67] Gierke, *Genossenschaftstheorie*, op. cit., pp. 3, 5, 339f. ("real collective person").

[68] Ibid., pp. 317 sqq., 864, 879. Cf. his *Genossenschaftsrecht*, I, § 69 passim and p. 983 n. 47, in ref. G. Beseler and J. Bluntschli.

[69] In this he opposed J. Möser and Kindlinger, and continued the work of G. L. v. Maurer, G. Beseler and G. Hanssen. See Gierke, *Genossenschaftsrecht*, I, pp. 411f., II, § 35 passim and p. 868. Cf. G. Hanssen, *Historische-statistische Darstellung der Insel Fehmarn*. Altona 1832, pp. 331f.

[70] Gierke, *Genossenschaftsrecht*, I, p. 5. II, p. 865, 992f., § 10 passim. Idem, *Genossenschaftstheorie*, pp. 307f.

[71] Gierke, *Genossenschaftstheorie*, pp. 607, 855 n. 1; ch. 1 and 5 passim.

Those who applied his theory, in particular, Tönnies and Barker, did not accept his idea of the will as emanating from the state.[72] The problem of Genossenschaft begins with the failure of Gierke to distinguish his usage from that of his forerunners, in particular, Maurer,[73] who wrote of the Markengenossenschaft as a traditional communal Germanic institution. Gierke assumed that his usage of Genossenschaft had not only current validity but that it corresponded to age-old Germanic usage, just as his theory of the practices corresponded to the ancient practices themselves. Gierke's usage is directly related to his ends, the independent derivation of German state and law (right) from the ancient Germanic institutions, to the exclusion of the Romanic. But Gierke was only partly aware of his ends and of his means. He made the state into a mystical superorganic body, founded on his theory of Genossenschaft, and for this he was criticized by Barker.[74] Gierke's translators, scholars no less eminent than he, had to struggle with an appropriate rendering into English of Genossenschaft; they failed. Maitland translated Genossenschaft as 'fellowship'; Barker followed him.[75] Genossenschaft was pursued by Gierke back to a time when all were free and equal. The *Genossen* were not only *socii* who freely compacted with each other to form a *societas* or Genossenschaft; the Genossen were the members of the original Germanic folk, endowed with the right to free association thereby.[76]

The theory of Genossenschaft is further complicated by its connection with the theory of the association or *Verband*, which has one meaning in jurisprudence, another in sociology.[77] In Gierke's usage, it is a purposeful, willed combination, distinct in one sense from the *Gemeinde*, commune, which is traditional and involuntary.[78] Hence

---

[72] F. Tönnies, *Gemeinschaft und Gesellschaft* (1887). 8th ed. Leipzig 1935. E. Barker, Introduction to Gierke, *Natural Law and the Theory of Society*, Cambridge 1950.

[73] G. L. v. Maurer. *Einleitung zur Geschichte der Mark-, Hof-, Dorf-, und Stadtverfassung.* München 1854. Idem, *Geschichte der Markenverfassung.* Erlangen 1856. Idem, *Geschichte der Dorfverfassung.* 2 v. Erlangen 1865-1866.

[74] Barker, op. cit., pp. xvii, lxix.

[75] Maitland, Introduction to Gierke, *Political Theories*, op. cit., p. xviii. Barker, Introduction to Gierke, *Natural Law*, op. cit., p. xc.

[76] Freedom in this sense has a different meaning from freedom in modern bourgeois society. On freedom in modern bourgeois society and its critique, see below, sect. IX. Marx had distinguished between the liberty, equality and fraternity of the ancient gentes and the same in regard to "the new system", "toward which modern society tends." Marx, Drafts of Correspondence to Vera Zasulich, D. Rjazanov, ed. *Marx Engels Archiv*, v. 1, 1926, p. 320. See also *Ethnological Notebooks*, op. cit., pp. 86f.

[77] H. J. Wolff, *Organschaft und juristische Person.* I. Berlin 1933, pp. 461 sqq. F. Jerusalem, *Kritik der Rechtswissenschaft.* 1948, pp. 392f.

[78] Gierke, *Genossenschaftsrecht*, I, pp. 657 sq. II, pp. 195, 214ff. III, pp. 36ff. Idem, *Genossenschaftstheorie*, pp. 210 sq., 226 sq.

the connection which he drew from the ancient Genossenschaft to the modern state, corporation, joint stock company pursued a different path.[79] Max Weber included in his theory of the association the categories of village Genossenschaft, the guild and the Markgenossenschaft. The activities of these associations, in Weber's theory, are based on the unity of the will of the members.[80] Moreover, as Gierke, Weber introduced the category of the will in the form of the arbitrary will (in the case of Weber, Willkür) into the state formation.[81] Neither the Genossenschaft nor the Association plays a central role in Weber's system, as the origin of the state therein. The society in the conceptions of Gierke is the realization of its full potentialities in the state, wherein he was at one with Aristotle. Aristotle, however, did not hold the state, in the form of the polis, to be a superior individual, endowed with a will and consciousness from which are derived the will and consciousness of its members, the juridical persons; such was incorporated in the system of Gierke. The latter began with the premise that human beings are what they are thanks to their unification with each other; he posited these unifications as associations which not only heighten the power of those who exist coevally with each other, but provide the possibility of their development.[82] That men are what they are by virtue of their combination in society, and that their power of development is thereby heightened is the foundation of all human science. Neither Gierke nor Weber went as far as the assertion of this truth. Gierke limited his assertion of its efficacy to the association; Weber made the individual into the source whence the social is derived.[83] Gierke's goal was the determination of the source of law and right and that of the right of the state. The state was taken by him as an original, undivided whole. Society did not exist in this schema, but was a derivative of it. The oppositions in society and the formation of the state for the regulation and control of these fell outside his conception. The formation of the state as the resolution of the divisions of civil society, as it was developed by G. W. F. Hegel, is not the same as the theory of the formation of the state as the means of control of the oppositions of civil society, yet Hegel's theory was

---

[79] Gierke, *Genossenschaftstheorie*, pp. 9off., 574ff., 603ff., 612ff., 642ff.

[80] Max Weber. *Wirtschaft und Gesellschaft*. 5th ed. Tübingen 1972, p. 423.

[81] Ibid., p. 508. Cf. Weber, *Rechtssoziologie*. Luchterhand 1967, pp. 298f.

[82] Gierke. *Genossenschaftsrecht*, I. Einleitung. Cf. his *Johannes Althusius*, 6th ed., Aalen 1968, pp. 264 sq.

[83] This is other than economic individualism, attributed to Weber by R. Bendix (*Max Weber*, New York 1962, pp. 44-48). On this individualism generally see Weber, *Gesammelte Aufsätze zur Wissenschaftslehre*. 3rd ed. Tübingen 1968, p. 439; cf. H. H. Gerth and C. W. Mills, Introduction to Weber, *Essays in Sociology*, Oxford 1946, pp. 55f.

developed indirectly by Gierke on one side, and by Marx as the mechanism of regulation and control on the other.

The two forms of association which have been set forth whereby the state has been formed, by Lowie and MacIver on the one side, by Gierke on the other, have the common features of voluntary combination as the expression of a common will. Further, they bring out in either case the formal process in state formation. Beside this they have little in common, for the data of Lowie, although derived from a wide study of the ethnographic literature of the South Sea Islanders, American Indians and the peoples of Africa and Australia, yet did not take in the Europeans of ancient, medieval and modern times. Lowie in particular did not deal with the process of state formation itself, but made reference only to the germ of the state in the association of the buffalo hunters, nomads of East Africa, etc.[84] Neither he nor Gierke went into the oppositions of civil society itself in the formation of the state.

L. H. Morgan regarded the state as the product of the dissolution of the ancient gentes, holding that all forms of government can be reduced to two. The first is the simpler and is earlier in time; it is founded on relations between individuals, its unit of organization is the gens, combinations of which form the ancient or primitive society, as a part of an organic series of wider groupings related by kinship and propinquity, or the phratry, tribe and confederacy of tribes. The second form "is founded on territory and property and may be distinguished as a state (*civitas*)." The opposition between primitive and civil society is made by Morgan into an evolutionary sequence, the state is identified by him as political society.[85]

The approach to the problem of the origin of civil society and the state of Morgan is not a formal one; it is rather by the history of the parts, the replacement of the tie of kinship by that of territory. The society based on property is not united thereby but divided into rich and poor. This civil form of society is the period of civilization, in which "... the outgrowth of property has been so immense, its forms so diversified, its uses so expanding, and its management so intelligent in the interests of its owners, that it has become, on the part of the

---

[84] R. H. Lowie, *Primitive Society*. New York 1947, ch. X, XI.

[85] L. H. Morgan, *Ancient Society*, op. cit., p. 6. On organic series, pp. 249, 266, 277f. The second form is also characterized as political society, pp. 249, 277, 284 and Part II, ch. X, XIII passim. On Morgan cf. Engels, *Origin of the Family*, op. cit.,; Marx, *Ethnological Notebooks*, pp. 95 sq. L. A. White, *Evolution of Culture*. Cp. Henry Maine, *Ancient Law*, London 1861, ch. 5. Heinrich Cunow, *Zur Urgeschichte der Ehe*. Stuttgart 1912. The views of Maine and Morgan are grouped together by Lowie and by White; they are counterposed to each other by Marx, *Ethnological Notebooks*, op. cit., pp. 390ff., 437.

people, an unmanageable power. The human mind stands bewildered in the presence of its own creation."[86] The reader will note the opposition between the property owners and the people, drawn by Morgan. The reification of the mind through property is unitary in his conception, as it was in the conception of Georg Lukács.[87]

The perspective introduced by Morgan, in which he was followed by Friedrich Engels, led from the state and civil society to property as their basis, property being, accordingly, the determination of the beginning of civil society by its introduction, and the termination of civil society by its dissolution. Property, held Morgan, contains the elements of its own self-destruction.

Property, however, is not itself the basis of civil society; it is the legal form as the expression of that basis. The expression of the legal form is summed up in the state, which is the gathering together of the legal forms. The state is at the same time the abstract expression of the content and function of the centralization of political power in society, or *imperium*; the concrete expression thereof is civil society.[88]

Yet the social relation of property is not a moment of the history of civil society alone, but the bridge to the substructure, the means of production. The freeing of the peasants from the bondage to the soil is the first of the moments of the negation of the relation of social labor in the history of the earliest period of modern capitalist society. The reverse of this same moment is the movement to the towns and the formation of an urban proletariat, a movement which took place not only in Italy at this time, but throughout northern Europe. These moments are related to at least one other in the movement of liberation that was embraced by the peasants of parts of Germany, Bohemia, Hungary in the first decades of the sixteenth century, and which are expressed in the third of the Twelve Articles of 1525.[89]   Here the peasants declare that they are no man's property; it is the moment of freedom from bondage to the soil. The second moment is the freedom

---

[86] Morgan, op. cit., p. 561. Cf. Engels, *Origin*, op. cit., in fine; Marx, *Ethnological Notebooks*, p. 139.

[87] Lukács, Verdinglichung und das Bewusstsein des Proletariats. In his *Geschichte und Klassenbewusstsein*. Berlin 1923. Reification is in the first place not the determination by the society as a whole; it is a social product, but it is differentiated as the relations between the classes in the society are differentiated, through the relations in production. See my work, *Ethnologie und Anthropologie bei Marx*, München 1973: Chapter III, Verdinglichung und Abstraktion in der Gesellschaftstheorie; both in relation to and in opposition to Lukács, reification is not unitary but divided, and its effect on the human consciousness likewise.

[88] On property see Krader, *Asiatic Mode of Production*, op. cit., Pt. I, Introduction and Ch. VII.

[89] The Twelve articles of the Peasants. *Translations and Reprints from the Original Sources of European History*. Vol. II. Dept. of History, University of Pennsylvania. Appended to: Friedrich Engels, *The Peasant War in Germany* (2nd ed. 1874).

of all from the sovereign authority. Luther's response was an evasion of both issues, advising them to bear their cross in suffering: Leiden, Leiden, Kreuz, Kreuz.

The peasants in the same article challenged the proprietors to show that the Gospel declares "that we are serfs." Calvin conceded the point, writing, "For some men, when they hear that the Gospel promises a liberty which acknowledges no king or magistrate among men, but submits to Christ alone, think they enjoy no advantage of their liberty while they see any power exalted above them."[90] The Gospel is therefore a weak reed for the constitution of serfdom to lean upon. Calvin clearly meant a liberty of a wholly different kind from that intended by these peasants who formed at that time the earthly-Christian utopian communities when he wrote, "Magistrates ought to apply their greatest diligence that they suffer not the liberty, of which they are constituted guardians, to be in any respect diminished, much less violated."[91] That liberty is the theocratic liberty, of the civil government which provides that the true religion which is contained in the law of God be not violated.[92] Civil society becomes bourgeois society, civil right becomes bourgeois right, civil freedom becomes bourgeois freedom; the citizen is the burgess of Geneva; his is the freedom of the city. [The freedom is not founded on but expressed by the fact of property through the rights accorded thereby.]

To hold that men are property is to reify them, in the most literal sense of the word. On the contrary, to hold that property is the active factor in history is to hypostasize it; in the same way, the tenet of freedom as the active factor is the hypostasis or etherealization of freedom and of history. The first moment is the grinding of men into the ground, the second is the puffing of property and of freedom into the air. The first alone is serious, having been held to be so both by the peasants and their antagonists.[93]

IV. CIVIL SOCIETY AND POLITICAL SOCIETY

Implicit in the usage of Melanchthon, Bodin, Althusius, Grotius and Hobbes is the conception that civil society is the society of civil right and law. If we take the Roman practice for our model, however, then

---

[90] John Calvin, *Institutes of the Christian Religion* (1559). J. Allen, transl. (London 1813). Philadelphia 1935. 2 vols. Vol. II, p. 633.

[91] Ibid., p. 640.

[92] Ibid., p. 635. The magistrates are the guardians and conservators of the laws (l.c.), the laws are "the strong nerves of civil polity" (ibid., p. 647). Which was to have been demonstrated.

[93] The second is taken seriously only by Benedetto Croce, the author of *History as the Story of Liberty*.

this identification is limited to the opposition between *civitas* and civil law; the idea of civil society was not expressed in ancient Rome, for *societas* was narrowly defined at that time, being contained as a category within the civil right; it was not then the overarching category, within which civil right and law were contained, that it has come to be. In order to gain this meaning, the concept of society in the modern sense, in which law, right, the state all take their places, had first to be developed. (The latter development was set forth by the critique of natural right, social contract and civil society by Hegel and Marx, as we shall see in the following chapter.) In order that the concept of modern society be developed, modern society itself had to be conceived.

In the nineteenth century a number of writers identified civil society with that society in which civil right, *jus civile*, was applied, among them Tocqueville and Fustel de Coulanges. Tocqueville opposed civil and political society, denoting the state by the latter term; civil society, accordingly, is the society of civil right. He described the conflict between civil and political society in Germany in the fifteenth century, which took the form of advocacy of Roman civil right and law by the university doctors of jurisprudence (légistes, who were trained in the law schools of Italy), and whose idea of society was civil society; opposed to them were the masters of "political society", who were charged with the conduct of the public affairs. This political society was opposed by Tocqueville, at the same time, to the ancient society of the Germanic peoples.[94] Fustel de Coulanges agreed with one of the propositions of Tocqueville, that civil society is the society of civil right, while the opposition between civil and political society was foreign to him. He wrote of civil society with Classical Rome as his model, opposing *civitas* to civil society in the nineteenth century sense; likewise, he opposed civil society to the more ancient society in which the family (gens) was the only form.[95] These usages notably influenced L. H. Morgan's terminology; Morgan's theory, on the contrary distinguished between the gens, which was composed of descendants in one line only, whether from father to son or from mother to daughter, and the family, which was composed of members of at least two differ-

---

[94] Alexis de Tocqeville, *L'ancien régime et la révolution* (1856). "Le droit romain," concluded Tocqueville, "qui a perfectionné partout la société civile, partout a tendu à dégrader la société politique, parce qu'il a été principalement l'oeuvre d'un peuple très civilisé et très asservi." Paris 1967, pp. 341-343. (Notes to the text by Tocqueville.) If his usage of civil society as advocated by the fifteenth century civilians appears anachronistic, so do we all labor under these limitations in terminology.
[95] N. D. Fustel de Coulanges. *La cité antique*. Paris 1864, Bk II, ch. X, § 4. This antiquarian sentiment was already outmoded in Tocqueville, as we have seen.

ent lines.[96] Morgan, as we have seen, identified *civitas*, political society and the state, in which he was consonant, with Tocqueville.[97]

The evolution of right and law in the scheme of the recent writings, for instance of Durkheim and Vinogradoff, who followed Maine and Morgan in this matter, proceeds pari passu with the evolution of civil society and the state. If Tocqueville falls outside the evolutionary camp in this sense, yet Fustel, Maine, Morgan, Durkheim and Vinogradoff participate in this school of thought. That they stand close to each other in this matter is made clear when their common doctrine is contrasted with the opposed one of natural right, natural law and the state of nature, expressed by John Austin.[98] Tocqueville continued the usage of political society made by the physiocrats of the preceding century; so did Austin.[99]

The terms 'civil society' (societas civilis, bürgerliche Gesellschaft, société civile) and 'political society' (société politique) were sometimes consonant, sometimes opposed in the usages from the sixteenth to the nineteenth centuries, which will be seen from the following table:

	Civil Society[1]	Political Society[1]
16th century	Hooker[2]	Hooker
17th century	Hobbes[3]	
	Locke[2]	Locke
18th century	Shaftesbury[3]	
	Vico[4]	
	Mandeville	
	Hume[2]	Hume
	Rousseau[2]	Rousseau

---

[96] L. H. Morgan, *Ancient Society*, op. cit. In this Morgan opposed Fustel de Coulanges. As an evolutionist, Fustel is more "up to date" than Tocqueville.

[97] This schema is implicit in Emile Durkheim, *Les formes élémentaires de la vie religieuse*. 3d ed. Paris 1937. See also Paul Vinogradoff, *Outlines of Historical Jurisprudence*. I. Oxford 1920, p. 158.

[98] The opposition between the content of the doctrine of evolution and that of the formalist school of Austin is reinforced by the conscious alignments of the writers: Morgan with Fustel, Durkheim with Fustel and Morgan, Vinogradoff with Maine, Morgan, Durkheim. H. S. Maine, *Lectures on the Early History of Institutions*, London 1875, ch. 12-13, contra John Austin, *The Province of Jurisprudence Determined*, 1832. Behind Austin stands Jeremy Bentham.

[99] Mercier de la Rivière. *L'ordre natural et essentiel des sociétés politiques*. 1767. Ed., E. Daire. *Physiocrates*. Paris 1847. Austin, op. cit., New York 1954, H. L. A. Hart ed., pp. 192f., 202f., 207f.

	Ferguson[2]	Ferguson
		La Rivière
	Burke[5]	
	Schlözer[7]	
19th century	Hegel[8]	
		Austin[5]
	Tocqueville[5]	Tocqueville
	Marx[8]	
		Fustel de Coulanges[6]
		Morgan[9]

Here we reaffirm what we have stated earlier: civil society is not the state; it is the organization of social production. The state as the political society is not the organization of that production, although the ideologists of the managerial theory of the state would have it so (James Burnham, Karl August Wittfogel). The state is the product of the relation between political economy and society. Its agencies usurp the organization of production.

[1] These usages have a bearing on selected writings in England, Germany, Scotland, Italy, France and the United States during the 16th-19th centuries. The term civil society is not in fashion, and is often replaced by 'political society'. However, the latter is at times confused with the state, or else it is identified as the repressive state, the tyrannical state, the bureaucratic state, and so forth. The etymological parallels between *civil* and *political* (respectively from Latin and Greek terms meaning, among other things, city-state, made it possible for Hooker, Locke, Hume, Rousseau, Ferguson to refer indifferently to civil and political society. (See the following note.)

[2] Richard Hooker, *Laws of Ecclesiastical Polity*, op. cit. John Locke, *Two Treatises of Civil Government*, II. An Essay Concerning the True Original, Extent and End of Government. 1690. David Hume, *A Treatise of Human Nature*, 1739. J. J. Rousseau, *Economie Politique*, 1755. Adam Ferguson, *An Essay on the History of Civil Society*, 1767.

On the confusion between political society and the state, see below, sect. VIII.

[3] Thomas Hobbes, *Leviathan*, op. cit., opposed civil society to the state. Rousseau and Schlözer (see below, note 7) did the same. on Shaftesbury see above, note 51.

[4] Giambattista Vico, *Scienza Nuova*, op. cit., referred to the *mondo* civile, the world of nations See above, sect. II.

[5] John Austin, *The Province of Jurisprudence Determined*, op. cit. Alexis de Tocqueville, *L'ancien régime*, op. cit. Both Austin and Tocqueville opposed political society to the state. Tocqueville opposed civil to political society. Edmund Burke, *Reflections on the Revolution in France*, 1790.

[6] Fustel de Coulanges, *La cité antique*, op. cit., opposed civil society to the state (civitas).

[7] A. L. Schlözer, *Allgemeines Stats Recht*, 1794, identified the bürgerliche Gesellschaft, societas civilis and civitas. He defined the state as societas civilis cum imperio (civil society plus sovereignty); see his work, Pt. I, §§ 17 and 44 note.

[8] On Hegel and Marx see the following chapters.

[9] L. H. Morgan, *Ancient Society*, identified civitas and the state with political society.

V. SOCIETY AND CIVIL SOCIETY

Vico used the term *society* to mean a trading company or merchant enterprise, writing, "… Spinoza speaks of the republic as of a society of merchants."[100] Vico grasped the narrow basis which was provided by the theory of natural right, in its particular form of the theory of social contract, for the theory of the state. He began the critical exploration of the nature of the state and of society in terms of the historical forces, popular traditions, national ways and arts; he proposed further that all nature and everything human is historical.[101] The work of Rousseau unknowingly, of J. G. Hamann and of J. G. Herder consciously, develop Vico's. They all alluded to irrational forces beyond the control of human will and consciousness in the working out of human history.[102] Vico is the further developer of Machiavelli's historical grasp.[103] The path that the human sciences took in the period from Machiavelli to Vico was not that of Machiavelli,

[100] G. B. Vico, *Principi di Scienza Nuova* (1744), § 335. His editor, F. Nicolini, adds the foot note, "That is, utilitaristically." (*Opere*, ed. Milan-Naples 1953, p. 481). That may be, but it is not because merchants are utilitarists that the charge was made by Vico. His charge against Spinoza was that the latter conceived the state to have been founded and run as merchant companies are founded and run. The Italian language still today preserves the turn of phrase from the time of the first trading companies of the capitalist period. Those established thereafter, in the Low Countries, Spain, France were referred to as anonymous societies, in England and Germany as societies of limited responsibility, beschränkte Haftpflicht. Vico attacked the theory of natural right and social contract in many different connections (ibid., §§ 550-553, 636-641, 971f.), which provided the basis for the conception of the state founded on the model of the trading society. But just as Bodin, Hobbes and Spinoza, Vico treated society as though it were adequately covered by the idea of the republic, commonwealth or state. The new science that was introduced by Vico negated this judgment at the same time, in proposing that the trading society is not an adequate model for the theory of the state. In the same way, the state is an inadequate model for the treatment of society, whether in the form of civil society or any other. Vico's usage was not different from that of Salamonius (v. supra), who conceived that a society was not founded otherwise than by contract.
[101] Vico, ibid., §§ 1101, 1108 and passim. See above, ch. II.
[102] Albert Soboul, *The French Revolution*. A. Forrest, transl. London 1974, p. 568, writes of "the obscure forces of feeling and intuition, exalted by Rousseau…," and the connection of these forces with the persistence of irrational currents which were utilized by the counterrevolution. This appreciation is quite different from the judgment of G. Lukács, *Die Zerstörung der Vernunft*, Luchterland 1962, p. 111, that "Rousseau as 'irrational romantic' is a product of the polemics against the French Revolution." The history of the symbol of reason in the hands of the aristocracy of the seventeenth, eighteenth- centuries (not reason itself) is other than the opposition to it of the symbol of sensibility in the hands of the bourgeois. This conflict was not fully cloaked by its representation as the quarrel between the ancients and the moderns by Brunetière and Rigault. The attempt by Georges Sorel, *Les Illusions du Progrès*, Paris 1908, to straighten out these lines has not been carefully followed through.
[103] Benedetto Croce, in his 1924 article, Machiavelli and Vico (*Philosophy, Poetry, History*, London 1966, C. Sprigge, transl.), writes that Vico was an "unwilling exponent of Machiavelli."

it was that of his enemies; Vico restored the study of human society as concrete history, so did Hamann, Rousseau and Herder. Tantae molis erat, so many pains were required then, but are no less a requirement today. The conflict of the bourgeois cult of sensibility with the aristocratic cult of reason engaged the political philosophers, historians and lawyers in the sixteenth, seventeenth and eighteenth centuries. On the one side the irrational forces, on the other, the control by human consciousness and will, were substituted by the symbols of the same as the would-be control of human history.

Civil society is the society in which the private and the public spheres are opposed, it is the society of the opposition in the public sphere of the private interests as class interests; the two oppositions are the determinants, one of the other. Machiavelli began with the oppositions between the prince and the people; the prince, however, is the conflict as such between the public and private interest, or the individual and class interest. The people were in this conception a historical concretion, negated in relations to nature and in society. It is not the bounty of nature but human effort that transformed Venice from a swamp to a flourishing city;[104] the people were accordingly an active historical factor, as an industrious, practical entity.[105] In opposition to Machiavelli, to Vico, Hamann and Herder, the attention was diverted from the popular life by Bodin, Descartes, Hobbes, Rousseau; the concern of the second group being with rules and orders by the reason and will over the public matter, res publica. The science of society is reduced to the science of politics in this sense; the end of the study was the constitution of the state. The activity of law-making and counselling was counterposed to the passivity of the study of traditions until the time of Bishops Hurd and Percy, and of Hamann and Herder who followed them.[106] The laws governing the traditions of the society were not at issue in the eighteenth century. It was only in the nineteenth and twentieth that the possibility of ascertaining their laws was recognized and pursued.[107] The social contract of Hobbes, Locke and Rousseau is in the literal sense the society established by contract; the utilitarian, sceptic and positivistic Hume, who had distinguished between moral and empirically verifiable judgments, had already shown the mythical character of this meaning of society

---

[104] Machiavelli. *Florentine History*. II, 1.
[105] Machiavelli, *Discourses*, I, 58.
[106] Cf. Meinecke, *Entstehung des Historismus*, op. cit., ch. 6.
[107] Maxime Leroy, *Histoire des idées sociales en France*. Paris 1947-1954, brings out the discontinuity from the eighteenth to the nineteenth centuries, F. Meinecke. *Die Idee der Staatsräson*, 1925, and Emile Durkheim, *Montesquieu et Rousseau*, Paris (1953) the continuity.

and of social contract. The affirmation of the general will by Rousseau does not introduce human history into the notion of society; in this regard he had not reached the point attained by Vico. Rousseau wrote of civil society as the invention of a single individual, after the fashion of the day: "The first man who, having enclosed a piece of land, bethought himself to say, This is mine, and found those who were simple enough to follow him, was the true founder of civil society."[108] The formation of civil society is represented as the opposition of the clever to the simple, the former being the propertied class, the latter the poor; beyond them, in the darkness of prehistory, are the natural men, without property and distinctions of the same. Rousseau asserts his "true" theory of history, which in a later century will be known as the vulgar materialist theory, whereby civil society is founded on self-interest. It is the theory of Hobbes and Bodin. To this "true" theory, which is one, false theory which is many, stands opposed: Among the many false theories of civil society is that of the Roman Patrician, Menenius Agrippa, who conceived civil society as an organism with belly, mouth and brain.[109] Plato, contrary to Bodin and Rousseau, thought civil society could be founded on the absence of the distinction between Mine and Thine. Rousseau was engaged in the composition of neither anthropology nor history; he submitted his draft of the constitution of civil society of Europe in the form of the various Discourses, and the pièce justificative of the constitution in the form of the above-mentioned fable.

By this thrust Rousseau set forth the relation between enclosure and civil society. Thomas More had written in 1516 that sheep were

---

[108] Rousseau, *Discours sur l'origine et les fondements de l'inégalité parmi les hommes*. 1755, Pt. II, beginning. (The *Political Writings of Jean Jacques Rousseau*, C. E. Vaughan, ed. Repr. Blackwell's 1962, v. I, p. 169.) The thought is already in Blaise Pascal, *Pensées*, I, ix, 53.

[109] In the dialectic of anthropology, everything is turned into its opposite; the appearance is revealed for what it is. The belly in Livy's account of Menenius Agrippa is the aristocracy, and is thus conceived by Shakespeare:

> There was a time when all the body's members
> Rebell'd against the belly...
> Your most grave belly... answer'd:
> "True is it, my incorporate friends," quoth he,
> "That I receive the general food as first,
> Which you do live upon, and fit it is,
> Because I am the storehouse and the shop
> Of the whole body."
>
> (Coriolanus)

The veritable organ of the nobility is the storehouse and the shop; the aristocracy is the class of tradesmen. Marx (*Kapital* I, op. cit., p. 381) refers to the 'ridiculous fable' of Menenius; its point at the hands of Shakespeare is the opposite.

eating men[110]; in the eighteenth century hedges ate men and sheep. That human beings in civil society are divided into rulers and ruled is the second insight of Rousseau; and that this division is made according to the criterion of property is the third. Rousseau in his fable begins with the relation of human beings to things; this is not the beginning of civil society, it is the beginning of its critique. It is, however, by virtue of the relation of human beings to each other in the political economy that men become things, to be treated as things. Civil society is a society like any other, being the expression of the relations in which human beings stand to one another and to nature. Antonio Gramsci conceived that two concepts were therewith combined: the society of men and the society of things. These two societies are not ordered in a chronological sequence, they exist side by side, each being the condition of the other. We can no more exist without relations to nature than we can exist without relations to other human beings; together these relations form the whole whose expression is the society. In the relations of the political economy, wherein the production of the social surplus, of surplus value, the alienation of the product from the immediate producer, and the exchange of commodities are comprised, human beings are transformed into things. Living labor is thereby transformed into congealed labor time, which is the process of reification, and concrete labor is transformed into abstract labor, which is the process of hypostasis. In the critique of political economy we begin with the thingly relations between human beings and the social relations between things. The order is important: Things in the form of congealed labor time and of commodities cannot enter into social relations until the human beings are transformed into things. Things have a life, will and consciousness of their own only in the fantastic world of the fetish-worshippers and the venerators of personified powers.

The history of the abstract social relations conceived in the form of commodities runs from Hobbes to the classical economists, Petty, Hume, Adam Smith and Ricardo, thence to Hegel and to Marx. Rousseau like Hobbes took up one side of this progression which is at once concrete and subjective in the account of the origin of civil society as a concourse of private interests. In the critique of civil

---

[110] Thomas More, Utopia. "Sheep," wrote More, "these placid creatures, which used to require so little food, have now apparently developed a raging appetite, and turned into man-eaters." "They're no longer content to lead lazy, comfortable lives, which do no good to society – they must actively do it harm by enclosing all the land for pasture that they can, leaving none for cultivation." The sheep convert churches into sheepfolds, farmland into wilderness. More's fable is no more ridiculous than Shakespeare's.

society, which was begun by Hegel, the subjective and objective factors are brought together; they are made historically concrete by Marx.

Kant followed natural law relating civil society to human history. Rousseau gave civil society the form of the general will; to this Kant added the content.[111] Fichte, like Rousseau and Kant, considered human history only abstractly.[112] The form is brought to the content. History is taken up concretely by Adam Smith, and by the physiocrats in matters of political economy. Political philosophy was not an abstract science, however, in the hands of Kant and Fichte; it was a matter of the science of morals and government. The doctrines of Rousseau, we have seen, were engaged in the cause of democracy, and at the

---

[111] Immanuel Kant, Idee einer allgemeinen Geschichte in weltbürgerlicher Absicht (1775): "The greatest problem for the human kind, to the resolution of which it is forced by nature, is the attainment of a civil society universally governed by right." *Werke*, 9. Darmstadt 1971, p. 39. Cp. ibid., p. 47.

[112] J. G. Fichte, *Von den Pflichten der Gelehrten.* (1794-1795). Hamburg 1971, pp. 78-81. Here philosophy is taken as the systematic history of the human mind. See also his *Beiträge zur Berichtigung der Urteile des Publikums uber die französische Revolution. Sämtliche Werke*, v. 6. Berlin 1845.

The philosophy of society of Kant was founded on the social contract, which served as the foundation of civil society, or the state. His model for the constitution of civil society is derived from the historical example of a joint-stock company. Kant, Uber den Gemeinspruch: Das mag in der Theorie richtig sein, taugt aber nicht für die Praxis (1793), ibid., pp. 143ff.,wrote: "Of the contracts whereby a multitude of men is combined into a society (pactum sociale)", "for the creation of a civil constitution." "The combination of many to any (common) and whatever is encountered in all social contracts." Society, accordingly, comprises a "common entity to the extent that it is found in the civil status." "The civil status thus taken only as legal status is founded on the following principles a priori: 1. Freedom of each member of the society as men. 2. Equality of these men with every other as subjects. 3. Independence of each member of a communal entity as citizen." (Ibid., p. 145). By society (civil society) Kant meant the state, as distinct from the people, writing, "The act whereby a people constitutes itself into a state, actually into the idea of a state, according to which its conformity to law alone can be conceived, is the original contract, whereby all (one and all) the people surrender their external freedom in order to take it up again at once as members of a common entity, i.e., of a people as a state." Kant, Die Metaphysischen Anfangsgründe der Rechtslehre. *Metaphysik der Sitten* (1797). *Werke*, 8. Suhrkamp 1968, p. 434.

The relation of external freedom to internal freedom is posited by Kant; the internal freedom is a relation of dependence which arises from the contractor's own legislative will (loc. cit.). Both relations to freedom are externalities; as externalities they are formal. The content of freedom is other than its inner relation, or the conquest of wants by the means available to a given society. The external relation of freedom is an abstract-historical relation; it does not take place in the history of any known people.

Justus Möser, *Patriotische Phantasien* III. Berlin 1778. LXIII: The Peasant Farm as Joint-Stock. (Der Bauerhof als Aktie Betrachtet.) This fantasy is inspired by the East and West India Companies. (*Sämtliche Werke*, Band 6, Oldenburg/Hamburg 1953, pp. 255sq.

Kant, by identifying civil society and the state progressed beyond Hobbes and Rousseau, making explicit the connection between the two sides.

same time in the cause of the counter-revolution at the end of the eighteenth century, for which they were not intended. These concerned not only the irrational sensibility, but also the notion of the will. Political philosophy was concerned, like Condillac's statue, with but some of the human traits and concerns at a time. The fancy that the human society was subject to the sovereign will preoccupied the philosophers who thought that they were dealing with the whole man. This is the error of the less vigorous thinkers of the eighteenth century. They had not come upon the thought of the whole society, or the whole of history, of universal history, which Vico and Herder sought to grasp, therefore the attempts to spread a net in which the whole man could be caught by politics alone was vain. The limitation of Vico, Hamann, Herder, in turn was that they had grasped only universal history, the anthropologizing perspective; they had not grasped the dialectic of the particular and universal historical judgment. Nevertheless they had already progressed past the point attained by Fichte. The particular concrete history of Voltaire, Gibbon, Schiller, and the concrete ethnography in the Jesuit reports, Hakluyt's voyages, Purchas' Pilgrims, Steller, Krasheninnikov, Strahlenberg, Müller, Georgi, Gmelin, Pallas, Deguignes, Duhalde, Abulgazi, were at war with the universal history of Iselin, Ferguson and Garve, Herder, Turgot, St. Lambert, Volney and Condorcet. The joint concepts of primitive and civil society in their opposition, and the oppositions of particular to universal history, emerged out of these conflicts.[113]

John Austin sought to do away with the category 'civil', through the claim that it is too confused; he does not know whether to pair it with law military, ecclesiastical, criminal, astronomical, canonical, barbarous, savage, alien, natural, international, political, or family.[114]

---

[113] Contrast the development of history in Hegel as the determinant of human destiny: the history of the world is the judgment of the world, with the judgment of Hume: "History's chief use is only to discover the constant and universal principles of human nature." The subordination of history to the science of the principles of human nature is the negation of history. The quotation from Hume is yoked by Becker to a quotation from Fontenelle: history is the retailer's treatment of man, morality the wholesaler's. Fontenelle, who makes the retail trade in the study of history the equal of morality as separate branches of the distribution of the commodities of knowledge, contradicts Hume. (C. L. Becker, *The Heavenly City of the Eighteenth Century Philosophers*. Yale 1932, headnotes, ch. III.) Hume and Fontenelle are an ill-matched pair.

[114] "The word civil has about twelve different meanings; it is applied to all manner of objects which are perfectly disparate. As opposed to criminal it means all law not criminal. As opposed to ecclesiastical it means all law not ecclesiastical; as opposed to military it means all law not military; and so on." John Austin. *Lectures on Jurisprudence* (1832). 1879. II, xliv, 780.

It is difficult to know what to make of this judgment. In one sense it is a mere debater's trick used by an otherwise serious thinker. If the word is used in context then it should be clear

The concern with society in general, as with civil society in particular, was given a new turn at the beginning of the nineteenth century. Laws of government of nations were no longer the sole object of thinking about society; yet this is what Locke, Montesquieu, Goguet, Linguet appear to imply. The classical political economists, Petty, Smith, Say, Ricardo, as well as the physiocrats Quesnay, Dupont de Nemours, had other concerns[115]; socialists and their immediate fore-runners, Saint-Simon, Comte, Owen, Pecqueur, Fourier, had a different perspective from the schools of natural right, social contract, political economy. At the same time, a holistic meaning of social movements was adumbrated by Turgot and Condorcet, and Franklin, Jefferson, as the framers of the American constitution, which was the commitment to the progress of humanity. Civil society was on the one side a stage in the advancement of society; on the other it was a means to the end of social advancement. As a stage it was opposed to primitive society; it is implied therewith that, just as the natural or primitive stage could be perfected and civil society established, so civil society could be perfected and surpassed. As a means, civil society was conceived as the active part of the whole, that which could be adjusted, perfected by constitutional means. The distinction between folk right and constitutional law lies in the consideration that constitutional law is written and rewritten. Paine criticized the English for having no written constitution.[116] Constitutions were drafted at that time throughout the world.[117] The nations, as they were conceived by Vico, the folk, as conceived by Herder, were not established by legislation, a conscious act of volition, but by nameless, partly unconscious tradition. This is not contradicted by Vico's dictum that history is made by human beings. Globally, human history is the sphere of human undertakings and relations in society

whether it is being opposed to military, criminal, etc., law. If it is not then the judge or editor should know how to clear the matter up if he is competent at his job. You cannot merely aver, as Austin appears to be doing, that the word ought not to exist. On Austin, cf. *Ethnological Notebooks*, op. cit., pp. 327-334. Further, H. S. Maine, *Lectures on the Early History of Institutions*. London 1875, ch. 12 and 13. Just as Austin in the nineteenth century sought to suppress the term 'civil', so in the twentieth, A. R. Radcliffe-Brown and David Easton have sought to suppress the term 'state', overtly at least on lexical grounds alone.

[115] See Krader, *Asiatic Mode of Production*, op. cit., Pt. I, ch. I.

[116] Thomas Paine, *Rights of Man*. 1791. See E. P. Thompson, *The Making of the English Working Class*. Pelican 1968, pp. 93 sq.

[117] They were not only drafted by official bodies but by private persons. See G. W. F. Hegel, *Die Verfassung Deutschlands*, 1802. It is not the German constitution that is at issue, but the Constitution of Germany; it is the constitution in political form of a body of people. "The German Constitution" referred to by T. Knox (*Hegel's Political Writings*, Oxford 1964), loses the point.

and to nature, and of no other than these. The acts of political constitution and of law-giving are but a part of the entirety of human history. The holistic perspective contradicts the legislative. The holistic perspective, however, was distinguished as progressive and conservative; Joseph de Maistre, his colleague de Bonald, as well as Ballanche, Saint-Martin and Lamennais, were no less holists than Turgot and Condorcet, but the former were theocrats, antiprogressist, enemies of the French Revolution and ideologists of the reaction and Restoration. Vico was a devout believer in Providence; politics, progress and holism have no intrinsic connection.[118] The holistic social perspective was further distinguished as static or dynamic. Maistre conceived of a larger whole than society; it was the city of God. But the interest therein was the perservation of a static, conservative and Catholic society. The dynamic holism was set forth by the utopian socialists of that time; their holism was not historical in particular. The historical table set out by Fourier is the opposite of historical, being hopeful and fantastic.[119] Maistre sought for the historical justification of his policy no less than Vico. Maistre's reaction was double: it was against the Revolution and against the present; it was for the past because it was against the Revolution and against the future. History is not only on the side of progress, neither is the concept of society. But progress without the concepts of history and society is utopian and fantastic. Fourier, Owen, Cabet and Pecqueur were aware of the ills of society, but lacked a concept of society. The phalanx in the case of Fourier was replaced by the small-scale unity of farming and industry in the plan of Robert Owen. Etienne Cabet established his commune of Icaria. Fourier was denoted as the architect of a new society[120]; the same can be said of Owen. Their unit of social planning however was the community and not the society. Thereby the opposition between communism and socialism is implied, an opposition which emerged only after the time of those utopian socialists. They were without exception inspired by the vision of communism and egalitarianism; the communities that they founded, in America and elsewhere, were in the form of a voluntary association. They had no plan to proceed from the establishment of the community to the reform of society, save by the multiplication of the communities.

[118] Marx in writing for the *New-York Daily Tribune* explained the entire Hegelian dialectic by the 'homely proverb, that extremes meet.' Far from being fantastic, it is proven not only in the revolution in China but in the doctrine of natural right, which was asserted both by Edmund Burke and by Tom Paine, as antagonistic a pair as ever were our present opponents, Condorcet and Maistre.

[119] Charles Fourier. *Théorie des quatre mouvements.* 3rd ed. Paris 1846, facing p. 32.

[120] This is the phrase of Parke Godwin, *Popular View of the Doctrines of Charles Fourier.* 1844.

The nature of society, of social classes, class interests and conflicts, individual interests, public and private divisions and oppositions, local interests and oppositions, were not their concern.[121] Their social theories were in part conscious; in part they expressed their social criticism,[122] with their feet.[123]

The characterization of the utopian socialists by Engels is still the determinant of our twentieth century views.[124] Noyes related the theories of utopian socialism as religious and non-religious; the religious communities being of traditional type. He distinguished the non-religious communities as associations, having the Fourierist phalanx in particular in view, and described others of these non-traditional communities as active joint-stock ventures.[125] The utopian socialism is the continuation of the capitalist mode of discourse by other means.[126]

VI. CIVIL AND BOURGEOIS SOCIETY. CITIZEN AND BOURGEOIS

Although the notion of civil society appears in German idealism, from Kant to Fichte, it was not taken up by Hegel expressis verbis until his last writings, the *Philosophy of Right* and the *Encyclopedia*. Prior to this he had taken up the family, the folk, the categories of the civil, citizenship, and the state, or state-society; in the *Phenomenology* the ethical world, the family and the folk are not separated. The relations male and female are natural; the family on the contrary is an

---

[121] Robert Owen, *A New View of Society*, 1813. Charles Fourier, *Le nouveau monde industriel et sociétaire*, 1829. Robert Owen, *The Book of the New Moral View of the World*, 1837-1844. Etienne Cabet, *Voyage en Icarie*, 1840.

[122] *Ethnological Notebooks of Karl Marx*, op. cit., p. 120. Cp. Engels, *Ursprung der Familie*, op.cit., near the end. Idem, *Socialism Utopian and Scientific*, ch. 1. (1880).

[123] The answer to the wants of the new man was the emigration to the new world – vide Fourier, Owen, Cabet, and others.

[124] See Friedrich Engels, *Socialism Utopian and Scientific* (1880). Originally, ch. 1 of Introduction, and ch. 1-2 of Pt. III in his work, *Herrn Eugen Dührings Umwälzung der Wissenschaft*, 1877. (*Anti-Dühring*). See further, Ernst Bloch, *Das Prinzip Hoffnung*, Suhrkamp 1959. V. P. Volgin, *Frantsuzskij utopičeskij kommunizm*. Moscow 1960. Martin Buber, *Paths in Utopia*. London 1948. Mark Holloway, *Heavens on Earth*. 2nd ed., New York 1966. F. E. Manuel. *The Prophets of Paris*. Harvard 1962. *Utopias and Utopian Thought*, F. Manuel, ed. Boston 1965. Jean Servier, *Histoire de l'Utopie*. Paris 1967.

[125] J. H. Noyes, *The History of American Socialism*. Philadelphia 1870, ch. V.

[126] See the critique of Saint-Simon by Karl Marx, *Das Kapital*, v. III, pt. 2. 3rd ed. Hamburg 1911, pp. 144-147. Lorenz v. Stein, *Der Socialismus und Communismus des heutigen Frankreichs*. 1842. Lorenz v. Stein, *Geschichte der sozialen Bewegung in Frankreich*. 1850. Cf. Karl Marx, Friedrich Engels, *Die heilige Familie*. 1845.
Saint Simon and Fourier alike had the joint stock company before them as the model of the new society which either of them envisaged.

ethical being in general.[127] In simplified form these categories were represented by Hegel in his Nürnberg period as an unresolved unity, save that the family is here considered as a natural society, in opposition to the state, which was defined as a juristic society.[128] Hegel, however, had earlier conceived of civil life as divided into the public and private spheres; the private sphere stands opposed to the political, and the citizen is implicitly separated from the bourgeois.[129]

Hegel conceived civil society explicitly in opposition to the state, implicitly in opposition to primitive society; civil society being the society which is divided into the private and public spheres, and into the opposed private interests, is the reverse of the undivided primitive society. In civil society the private interests are particular interests, and are opposed to the universal interest; here Hegel played a verbal trick: the public sphere is opposed to the private; the universal interest can reside in neither of these spheres; but the state is opposed to the civil society and the particular interest, it is the positing of the universal interest, just as the *categories* of particular and universal are posited in their opposition. Form and substance are opposed. The state as the universal is both form and substance. In civil society, the substance is made abstract; here the form is separated from the substance, and the externality from the internality.

[In order to resolve the opposition between the public and the private spheres, it must be shown that the universal in the state sublates both spheres, creating thereby a synthetic unity of the two. This would imply that the state is more than the public sphere, res publica, alone, that it is coextensive with society as a whole; further this would imply that Cicero, Jean Bodin and Thomas Hobbes had wrongly grasped the exclusively public nature of commonwealth, law of the state, state-right, this would imply, moreover, that as the state is both the private and public matter, it is both formal and informal social matter, both as subject matter and as materia. But this is absurd. – These matters were not demonstrated by Hegel, they were merely posited by him. His use of the term "universal" implies that it has the meaning of "all-sided" in respect of humanity and the human individual. This is the verbal trick. The Hegelian rightists and the various schools of Hegelian idealism abroad, e.g. in nineteenth century England, uncritically promulgated this doctrine; Marx on the contrary critically analyzed this, which is the hypostasis of the state and right.]

[127] G. W. F. Hegel. *Die Phänomenologie des Geistes*. 1807. *Werke* 3, Suhrkamp, 1974, pp. 328-336,
[128] Hegel, *Werke* 4, pp. 242f., 245ff. (Nürnberg, 1810 and on).
[129] Hegel, Über die Wissenschaftlichen Behandlungsarten des Naturrechts. *Kritisches Journal*, 1802-1803. *Werke* 2, pp. 493f.

Hegel himself overcame the hypostasis by the category of civil society. Civil society is the *external* state.[130] This external state is for itself, it is developed in itself, mediating between the isolated individualities. Its universality is the means whereby the external relation between the human individuals as persons is posited; the persons are the formal, abstract, subjectivities, the human individual taken as a particular, selfdependent asocial atom. The civil society is the sum of the formal, abstract interrelations of these individualities to each other; opposed to this externality is the ethical substance, or the state in its internal relation. The state in its external relation is in itself the civil society. Civil society is in itself and for itself, the form, the abstraction of ethical substance.

The state is the folk or people in history; a people, however, is not a state. The transition of a family, a horde, a tribe, a set of people into the condition of a state makes up the *formal* realization of the idea in it, in general. Without this form, the ethical substance would be lacking, being in itself the *objectivity* of the state in laws and purposive determinations. The independence of a people in the absence of these wants Sovereignty.[131] The state has had four concrete manifestations in historical empires, the Oriental, Greek, Roman and Germanic.[132] The state as a formal, public abstraction is counterposed to the concrete world empires; this is no more than a juxtaposition by Hegel. The state as the inner substance of civil society is the ideal state; it is the state as the source of life in human society, the theology of that society, the expression in modern terms of the relation drawn by Aristotle between family, community (*koinonia*), barbaric society and the polis, which latter is likewise the final end of man; it is the

---

130 Hegel, *Enzyklopädie der philosophischen Wissenschaften*. 3rd ed., 1830. *Werke* 9, § 523.: "Substance as spirit particularizing in many *persons* ... who are for themselves in independent freedom and as *particulars*, at first loses its ethical determination in that these persons as such have not the absolute unity but their own particularity, and their being for itself in their consciousness and for their purpose – this is the system of atomistics. Substance in this way becomes a universal, mediating interconnection of independent extremes, and of their particular interests. The totality of this interconnection, which is developed in itself, is the state as civil society or as *external state*." See also Hegel, *Grundlinien der Philosophie des Rechts* (1821). *Werke* 7, Suhrkamp 1970, §§ 183, 261.

131 Hegel, *Philosophie des Rechts*, op. cit., §§ 331, 344-349. The passage from the folk to the state is indicated by Hegel as a formal, abstract historical reversal. What he takes for the objectivity is its subjectivity; sovereignty is not the objective means of determining the independence of a people. The former colonial peoples have gained sovereignty but not independence, being still dependent on the great producers of capital in Europe and America.

132 *Enzyklopädie*, §§ 350 sq. Hegel does not complete the passage from the abstract state to the concrete historical manifestation thereof as empires. The state remains formal-abstract, the empires are idealizations – in both senses – of concrete history. See also Hegel, *Vorlesungen über die Philosophie der Weltgeschichte*. Meiner 1968.

ultimate condition whose realization is at once the realization of the potentiality of human nature. This relation of teleology is shared by Aristotle and Hegel.[133] The undoubted advance that Hegel made over Aristotle is the introduction of the history of civil society in relation to the political category of the state.

The history of the state is the conception of Machiavelli and Vico: the history of theocracy that of Spinoza. That the folk is a historical category is the conception of the British collectors of folkore in the eighteenth century, as it is of Hamann, Herder and Hegel. The categories of political economy are not made into historical phenomena by the classical economists; that transformation was the work of Marx. Civil society, political economy and the state are all social-historical, they are not abstract philosophical categories. Of these, Hegel had written the history of civil society, Marx the history of political economy and the state. The source of Hegel's system, however, is more immediate than the writings of Aristotle.

Bodin had written systematically of the state in relation to the family and civil society. All human beings live in a community, which is of two sorts, natural and civil. The family is a natural community. The civil communities are of two sorts, those having and those lacking sovereign power. The republic or state is the civil community governed by sovereign power, and may comprise either the natural communities directly, or non-sovereign civil communities. The latter include the corporations and colleges, hamlets, villages and towns. The state is not formed by voluntary association, but through slow cumulations of the combinations of civil and natural communities, whereby sovereignty, laws and punitive power over the communities are secured.[134] Bodin opposed the theories of natural right and social contract, and implicitly set out the nature of the state as a historical process. The transition from city to city-state (polis, res publica), and from non-sovereign to sovereign communities as history is not contradicted by Bodin, and is elaborated by him in an abstract way. The institutions of civil society, if not the integral concept, is counterposed by him to the family on the one side, the state on the other.

The admiration that Hobbes expressed for the theory of the commonwealth was high to the extent that the consciousness of civil society as the active principle in human history was low, in his estimation. The civil society was of interest to his theory of the state insofar as the state is the extrusion of the civil society; the state is a

[133] Aristotle, *Politics*, ch. I. Cf. sect. II, above.
[134] Jean Bodin, *De la république*, op. cit., pp. 474, 489. The republic may likewise be composed of civil and natural communities in combination. Within the civil community, some of these may form societies by their association and alliance (pp. 475, 477).

voluntary association of men who contract with one another to form a society; the contract will stipulate the formation of a sovereign power and the submission of the contracting parties to the sovereignty they have by their artifice created. The said parties are capable of contracting among themselves through their membership in the civil society. They are contracting agents by virtue of their being citizens; they are therefore capable of associating and of forming a sovereignty which they will then hold in awe.[135] It is citizens who make the state, whereupon they become its subjects. The chance agglomeration of a multitude does not make up a commonwealth; it is the purposive agency of the multitude or their common will which does. That will must be freely given, otherwise the contract is invalid. By the agency of the common will the multitude is transformed into a unity, whence are derived the commonwealth of Hobbes and the state and general will of Rousseau. The will is not natural according to Hobbes, but artificial and civil, the state being the product of these civil undertakings.[136] The civil society comprises the voluntary agencies, the associative agencies and the agency of sovereignty within itself; it is opposed to the natural agency of the family on the one side and the product of the will on the other, which is the state. The system of Hobbes recapitulates that of Bodin to this extent, making explicit in modern terms what was implicit in Bodin. Hobbes added to this the system of wants. The wants of man in the state of nature are opposed by wants of the citizen, or the member of civil society. The wants of the body politic are satisfied by the products of the civil society over which it rules, or by the exchange of those products against those of others. It is not the state that meets these wants; on the contrary it is the agency of the civil society that does so.[137]

This system of the relations of civil society, the state, the intermediation between the family and the state, and the system of wants are followed by Locke and Adam Smith. Hobbes had already expressed a theory of value, of surplus value and of commodity exchange and production in connection with that of the civil society. The entire system is formal in Bodin, Hobbes and Locke. It is the abstract representation of the concrete conditions of the war of the French against the Huguenots, or the Civil War in England, the Restoration

---

[135] Hobbes, *Leviathan*, op. cit., I, 13.
[136] Hobbes, *De Cive*, 1642, (*Of the Citizen*, 1651), VI, 1 note.
[137] Hobbes, *Leviathan*, I, 10 and II, 24; on the state I, 13-15.

that followed it, and so on. See the late work, *Behemoth*, by Hobbes.[138]

The historical composition by Hegel is likewise interested, the civil society that is set forth by him being itself composed as the union of contradictory moments; it is at once abstract and concrete. Abstractly, civil society is the form of society wherein atomism reigns supreme. Each is for himself, in his own private interest, as a person an abstract being. The state in its externality as civil society is an artificial composition of contradictory particles; in this abstract formality of social existence it then relates to the human individual in his abstract, formal existence as a juridical person. Each formality calls forth the other, the formal, external substance of the human being is dependent on the abstract formality of the being of the state, and conversely, the abstract, external state is dependent on the existence of the abstract, formal externality of his juridical personality by the human individual. The civil society is the sphere of private interests atomized in the law of the jungle – the spiritual animal kingdom; the family likewise belongs to the private sphere, but it is not atomized, it is the immediate or *natural* ethical spirit, the natural condition being opposed to the civil, as they were in this sense by Bodin and Hobbes. Civil society, however, is universal, as opposed to the family which is immediate determinate individuality; civil society is but the form of this universality.[139]. Hegel tries his hand at the abstract history of civil society in the same language as Bodin and Hobbes, but with a different result: "The expansion of the family as its passing into another principle is in existence partly the quiet expansion of the family into a folk, a *nation*, which thus has a communal natural origin, partly the gathering of dispersed family communities, either through lordly power or through voluntary union introduced by the binding wants and the reciprocity of their satisfaction." Civil society and the state are not the product of the quiet expansion of the family; on the contrary, each results from the introduction of a mutually distinct and opposed principle other than that of the expansion of the family: "Civil society is the difference which enters between the family and the state..." The difference is mediated through the principle of the form of the universality.[140]

The system of wants of man, according to Hegel, by its multiplica-

---

[138] *Theologico-Political Treatise* by Spinoza and Hume's *Essay on Human Nature* follow Hobbes' system. Hobbes, *Leviathan*, is the theoretical expression of the historical lessons of the Civil War. His *Behemoth or The Long Parliament* (1679-1682), F. Tönnies, M. Goldsmith, ed., London 1969, reveals the source in practice of his theory.

[139] Hegel, *Rechtsphilosophie*, op. cit., §§ 157ff. Unbridled market economy of capitalism, ethics of freedom as the form of the same.

[140] Ibid., § 181 (Anmerkung); § 182 and Zusatz.

tion differs from that of the beasts, whose wants are limited by instinct. Hegel fails to add what is now apparent, that the wants are both universal and particular among men. Being multiplied, and not limited by instinct, they are a matter of culture or nurture, and not of nature. Being nurtural and cultural, the wants are not uniform but variable. They have a common basis in the instincts of all men, as want arising from hunger or cold, but by being multiplied are different in the different social groups of humanity, being met in different ways. The common and the different are the joint condition of human wants; these, the universal and the particular are the dialectic of humanity. The beasts, species by species, are in contradiction to this, fixed and limited, there is no dialectic of wants in nature, aside from the dialectical opposition of the universal and variable wants in human nature. The variables in the system of human wants are the social wants, as opposed to the natural necessity; the mediation of the human wants and the means of their satisfaction is through labor.[141]

The civil society is a system of social relations of a formal character; the human individuals relate on the one side to each other, and relate to the civil society as a whole on the other. The relations of human individuals to each other, however, are both formal and informal, the relations of the individual and civil society are a matter of claims and rights and their reciprocal equalization: "Thus the individual has become *the son of civil society*, which has as many claims against him as he rights against it." This system of claims and rights is translated into the relations of the individual and the state as the establishment and reciprocal equalization of rights and duties.[142] The system of rights and claims is the language of private law, that of rights and duties the language of public law; the stipulation of their balancing and reciprocal equalization is valid in both kinds of law, and is a universal principle of the law of civil society and the state.

Civil society intermediates at once between the individual, the family, the state and the political state, which is in fact nothing other than the functioning state through its agencies. The theory of the separation of the formal functions of the state into the legislative, executive and judicial is adumbrated in the seventeenth and eighteenth centuries by Locke and Montesquieu; it is put into practice in the American

---

[141] Ibid., §§ 190f., 194, 196. On multiplication of wants, see James Steuart, *An Inquiry into the Principles of Political Oeconomy*, (1767), Book I, ch. VI, How the Wants of Mankind promote their Multiplication. Hegel wrote a commentary on a German translation of this work. (See Karl Rosenkranz, *G. W. F. Hegels Leben*, 1844. Repr. Darmstadt 1969, p. 86.) Hegel's *Rechtsphilosophie* is not concerned with Steuart, but with Smith, Ricardo and the other classical political economists.

[142] Ibid., §§ 238, 261 (cf. also § 155).

Constitution by Jefferson, Madison and Hamilton; the variation effected by Hegel bears upon his theory of civil society, whereby the state is divided into the legislative, executive and crown powers.[143] The judiciary function in Hegel's system of civil society is one of three authorities, together with the authority of the corporation and the public control or police.[144] The judiciary is, however, not directly related to the particular interest. Hegel writes: Civil society contains three moments: 1. The system of wants. 2. The actuality of the universality of liberty contained therein, the protection of property by the judicial system (Rechtspflege). 3. The concern for the contingent in the system of wants and the judicial system; the care for the particular interest as the common interest by the police or public authority and the corporation.[145] The judicial system is a universal concern, but its universality is that of the particular freedom or security of property. It is the universal in the private sphere. This is not consonant with the judgment in Hegel that the judiciary lies outside the spheres of the legislative universality and the executive particular; the contradiction is sublated only if the universal is shown to be both public and private, a formal matter. However, the concern of the state has the security of property for its substance; thus the private concern becomes the public; the freedom that is connected thereto is a universal concern, it is the actuality of the state. This contradiction arises from Hegel's concrete system which takes the form of the state for the content of the relations of human beings and institutions.

The new theme in Hegel's system of civil society is that it is treated historically. Further, the civil society is treated dialectically, being at once the society of the state, polis, res publica, commonwealth, and opposed to the state.[146] It is in a second, no less important dialectical opposition in history, being the general category of civil society and the particular civil society, whose creation belongs to the modern world.[147] The third opposition is that between civil society and the general category of society,[148] and the fourth is the opposition

---

[143] Hegel's critique of the three powers is that the executive corresponds to the particular, the legislative to the universal, but the judiciary is not the third element of the concept, for its singularity lies outside those spheres. Ibid., § 272 (Zusatz).

[144] The police is used in the sense given by writers from Seyssel to Adam Smith. The tripartition of the functions of the state in Hegel, op. cit., § 273. On Seyssel, see above. Adam Smith, *Lectures on Justice, Police, Revenue and Arms*, 1896. E. Cannan, ed.

[145] Ibid., § 188. The *richterliche Gewalt* and the *Rechtspflege* are here brought together.

[146] Ibid., § 258 (Anmerkung).

[147] Ibid. § 182 (Anmerkung).

[148] Primitive as opposed to civil society; society in general, without judges and laws, ibid., § 102 (Zusatz). Society in general, § 192. Society as civil society, "" 241, 242, 244. Cp. *Enzyklopädie*, §§ 502 (Anmerkung), 524, 526, 528.

of mutually antagonistic economic classes, the poor against the rich in society: "Poverty in itself makes none into a rabble: this is only determined by the sentiment connected with poverty, the inner incitement against the rich, against the society, against the government, etc."[149] This is the concept of divided society, in which the class antagonisms have combined the crude material expression of want and the ideological expression of hatred. Here 'society' can mean modern civil society, and no other. This society is the end toward which the foregoing forms of society have tended: "In law the object is the *person*, from the moral point of view the *subject*, in the family the *member of the family*, in the civil society the *citizen* (as bourgeois) – here from the point of view of needs it is the concretion of the conception which is called man..."[150]

Hegel adds to this discussion of the historical dialectic of society, from which all future critical science of society descends, the sham discussion of the political state,[151] as though there were any other. The hypostatization of the state also descends from Hegel in this way. The criticism of the state as the political state does not rest on the attribution of the patriotic disposition to the citizens in reference to their state[152]; that disposition is nothing but the sentiment that accompanies a well-integrated citizenry in a well-functioning state. The attribution of timeless qualities of spirit, idea to the state, and its removal thereby from history is the hypostatization of the state which Hegel introduced, and which destroys the validity of his historical and dialectical treatment of the state. The hypostatization is readily dispensed with; there remains the state in history, which is dialectically treated by Hegel.[153]

The movements in history of society and civil society[154] contain the

---

[149] *Rechtsphilosophie*, § 244 (Zusatz).
[150] Ibid § 190 (Anmerkung).
[151] Ibid. §§ 267, 273, 276.
[152] Ibid., § 268.
[153] Hegel had himself separated religion from the state (ibid., § 270). The state and religion are mediately connected through the ethical disposition (*Enzyklopädie*, op. cit., § 552).
[154] See above, sect. III.
Hegel anticipated the doctrine of the social nature of the human being through his study of civil society. Cf. A. A. Piontkowski, *Hegels Lehre über Staat und Recht und seine Strafrechtstheorie*. Berlin 1960 (J. Leschka, ed.), pp. 286f. Here it is brought out that the individual can only meet his wants if he is in a determinate relation to others. The satisfaction of the wants of that individual is mediated by the wants of others; the individual is satisfied only in that he at the same time satisfies the well-being of others. Piontkowski has reference to Hegel, *Rechtsphilosophie*, op. cit., § 182 Zus. (vide supra). (Hegel here has reference not to the individual but to the particular, not to the *Einzelne* but to the *Besondere*. The latter includes the corporate bodies. This is a social category, in the history of its development, in which Hegel participated.

moments of state and society in their opposition. The society as civil society is the realization of the potentiality of the society of the political economy. The state, on the contrary, does not stand to the civil society as the realization of its potentiality, as though in an arrangement of Chinese boxes. Civil society has as its attribute the state by virtue of the relations of the political economy, therefore of civil society. Civil society is not only the sum of past developments, as evolution over a period of time; it is the summation of the present or synchronic relations of the individual. Man is the overarching conception in its concrete form of the human being in the system of wants: man is the sum of the relations of person, subject, family member, citizen (as bourgeois) in a simultaneous interaction. What then is the overarching arrangement of the law, morality, family, civil society that corresponds to man? In one sense it is the state, and in the preparation for this sense Hegel introduces the law, the citizenry and the public order and private order. Moreover, man is the final end of these relations in the system of wants and their summation, just as the state in the final end and summation of the relations of law, right, morality, the family and civil society. This is the further hypostatization of the state by Hegel, hence of man. Each of the elements summed up in the state, law, right, civil society, has its history, and is in history; for example, in the exposition of the character of Antigone by Hegel, the history of the family is taken up.[155] We have seen that civil law, civil right, civil society are all treated historically by Hegel. Only the state, aside from its political manifestation, stands outside history. Hegel's conception of the state then is the transcendence of history, just as Dante's Paradise transcends the stages of the Inferno and Purgatory. It is in this sense that Hegel writes of the state as "the world that the spirit-mind-Geist has made for itself," as "a hieroglyph of reason," standing as high over physical life as Geist stands over nature. The state is therefore to be venerated as an earthly divinity.[156] As earthly, the state

---

Hegel thus stood in opposition to his own atomism, hence in opposition to the idealist conception of the human being of Leibniz and Kant, as well as of Hegel himself.) See the note at the end of this section.

[155] Hegel, *Phänomenologie des Geistes*, op. cit., pp. 348-354.

[156] Hegel, *Rechtsphilosophie*, § 272 (Zusatz), § 279 (Zusatz). It is the mortal god (Hobbes), the way of god in the world (Hegel) § 258 (Zusatz). The earthly divinity: Hobbes quotes the Book of Job: "There is no power on earth that can compare to it." This citation forms the superscript to the title page of the first edition of *Leviathan*. Beneath it is the figure of an armed man wearing crown and sceptre, rising over countryside and town, greater than all together. His shoulders, chest and arms are all that is visible, they being made up of a vast number of figures of little men who are regarding his face. "This being,", writes Hegel, "is

has its history, it is the political state; as supraterrestrial it stands apart from history, just as the laws of nature are divided by Plato into the sublunary and supralunary. The state stands to the summation of law, civil society, morality only as its hypostasized being, in the ideal world, or the world of fantasy.

The civil society has its history, corresponding to the history of the citizen as citizen and the citizen as bourgeois. The bourgeois is a dweller in towns, but the right of citizenship is not only the right of urban life, it is the right of civil life in general.[157] This was established as the form of social life in which civil law, *jus civile*, is in force. Historically this passes over into all other social forms that precede it, follow it, coexist with it. The right of urban life historically passes over into other forms of social life in the countryside, the world-city, etc. The bourgeois is a manifestation of modern man, the citizen of man ancient and modern.[158]

The service of Hegel is to have brought together the historical treatment of the civil society and the state, as it was developed by Machiavelli, Vico, Herder, and the abstract theory of the state as it was developed by Bodin, Hobbes, Spinoza and Locke. The paradox of

realized as independent power, in which the individuals are but moments..." (Loc. cit.) Hobbes and Hegel have here composed the figure or trope of metaphor.

But Hegel, loc. cit., in taking the further step, writes, "...es ist der Gang Gottes in der Welt, dass der Staat ist..." The positing of the way of god in the world, that the state is, constitutes the multiplication of terms without necessity.

[157] Compare Jean Jacques Rousseau, *Du Contrat Social*, I, 6: Of the name, city: "The true meaning of this word has been almost entirely obliterated by modern writers; most of them take town for a city, and a bourgeois for a citizen." The French, he writes, hold the term *citizen* to express a virtue, and not a right. (*The Political Writings of Rousseau*, C. E. Vaughan, ed. Oxford 1962. Vol. 2, pp. 33f.)

Urban life today is so lacking in virtue, is so misused and abused, that if Henri Lefèvre wishes to assert his right to the town, *ville*, to the bourgeois life, who will contest it?

[158] It is perhaps true, as it has been often stated, that the *Rechtsphilosophie* is a weaker book than his *Logic, Phenomenology* and some earlier writings. The *Encyclopaedia* does not go beyond the *Rechtsphilosophie* in this regard. But the weakness does not lie in its political program, which is said to be the ground for its weakness, it lies in the program of social science which is set forth in it. The science of society was developed only after Hegel did his work, and owes its strength in no small measure to his contributions. Two souls do not beat, ach, in Hegel's breast. This Manichaeistic view of science is an untenable one. There are many more Hegels than these, but one of them is relevant to our problems of science, and this one was brought forth by Marx. Among the others left behind are the Hegel-Spinoza, the Hegel-Kant, the Hegel-Feuerbach, and so forth.

the citizen and bourgeois which was set forth by Rousseau remains unresolved in Hegel.[159]

VII. CIVIL SOCIETY AND ITS CRITIQUE

The contradiction between the universal and the particular, and therewith the abstract and the concrete forms of civil society were brought out by Marx, who wrote:

"Through the emancipation of private property from the community the state has attained a separate existence alongside and outside civil society; the state however is nothing more than the form of the organization which the bourgeois, both for external and internal reasons, necessarily provide for themselves as the mutual guarantee of their property and their interests." "Since the state is the form in which the individuals of a ruling class assert their common interests, and in which the entire civil society of an epoch is comprised, it follows that all communal institutions are mediated by the state and attain a political form."[160]

Civil society has in this context a wider ambitus and a more comprehensive application than those of bourgeois society alone, while maintaining its strict reference to the latter at the same time. Civil society in general is opposed here to the communal institutions on the one side and to the state on the other. The emancipation of private property was effected in ancient Rome no less than in eighteenth century France and Germany; likewise, the communal institutions for which the state acts as intermediary, whereby they attain a political form, are the conditions of social life of the ancient world, as they are of medieval and modern Europe. Civil society is here taken both abstractly, arching over the historical epochs, and concretely; in the latter case it is the "entire civil society of an epoch." As such civil society bears its contradiction of the universal and particular form into

---

[159] Yet Hegel prepared the ground for his own surpassing. In his *Jenaer Realphilosophie* (notes to unpublished lectures, 1805-1806, J. Hoffmeister ed. Hamburg 1969, p. 249) he wrote: "In the extremes of the universal, which is itself individuality as government; it is not an abstraction of the state, but individuality which the universal as such has for its end, and the other extreme of the same, which the individual has for his end. Both individualities are the same. The same individuality takes care of his family, works, undertakes contracts, etc., and in the same works for the universal, has this for his end. In the first place he is called *bourgeois*, in the second he is called *citoyen*." To this Hegel added the marginal note: "Spiessbürger (petty-bourgeois, Philistine) and citizen of the realm, the one as much a formal Spiessbürger as the other." He is bourgeois because he is citizen, citizen because bourgeois. Moreover, each is equally the externality and formality of the human being, external because formal, formal because external.

[160] Karl Marx, Friedrich Engels. *Die deutsche Ideologie* (1845). *Marx Engels Werke* v. 3, p. 62.

the modern era. It came into expression in the eighteenth century, when the modern property relations had been worked out; civil society as such, in concrete form is first developed with the bourgeoisie. The form of civil society in the modern bourgeois period of history is abstract, being comprised in the state, itself an abstract and universal form of organization. At the same time, civil society is developed as a system of concrete relations arching over the particular stages of history:

> "*Civil Society* is the form of intercourse which has been conditioned by the forces of production existing at all the historical stages until the present time, and conditioning these in turn. Civil society as we have already seen has the simple family and the compound family, the so-called tribe, as its premiss and foundation, whose more exact determinants were already shown. This civil society as we see is the true hearth and theater of all history." "Civil society comprises the collective material intercourse of individuals within a given historical stage of the productive forces. It comprises the entire commercial and industrial life of a stage and to that extent goes beyond the state and nation, although on the other hand it must assert itself outwardly as nationality, and inwardly it must be composed as state."[161]

Civil society has as its end the civil-bourgeois society of modern European history, having been present among the ancient Greeks, albeit in a different, antecedent form, corresponding, again, to the different, antecedent, and as yet not fully released productive forces and relations of production in ancient Greece: "Civil society among the Greeks was the *slave* of the political."[162]

The critique that Marx directed against Hegel's conception of civil society followed the dialectic of both opposition and composition of the abstract and concrete, the universal and particular, the suprahistorical and the historical, which was introduced by the latter. The criticism made by Marx is that this dialectic is not dialectical enough. It is not consistently dialectical. The separation of the modern society into the civil, private sphere and the political, public, state sphere by Hegel is artificial, it is Hegel's contribution to history, and not the contribution of history itself; the Estates are introduced separately from civil society and are caused to mediate between civil society and the state: "The transaction between state and civil society appears as a *particular* sphere. The Estates are the *synthesis between state*

---

[161] Ibid., p. 36. Cp. Marx, *Zur Kritik der politischen Ökonomie* (1859). *Werke*, op. cit., v. 13, p. 8 (on eighteenth century meaning).
[162] Marx, *Zur Kritik der Hegelschen Rechtsphilosophie* (1843). *Werke*, v. 1, op. cit., p. 276.

and civil society." Civil society is placed as the *private Estate* in counter-position to the political state; civil Estates then become political Estates in the aspect of the legislative authority. This resolution, however, is a purely formal one, the reciprocal action of the two sides is overlooked, the dialectic is defective, forgotten. Civil society, on the contrary, is not separated from the political, it is a part of the latter, each in a reciprocal relation. Hegel's view of civil society reduces it to an abstract atomism of individual relations. "The atomistics into which civil society in its political act falls proceeds from the fact that the community, the communal being, in which the individual exists, is civil society separated from the state, or that the *political state* is *an abstraction* of civil society."[163] On the contrary, Marx held that civil society stands in a concrete relation to the state, which is derived from civil society at times through violence (*vide* the French Revolution).[164] Just as the modern state is the realization in actuality of the potentialities inherent in the ancient state, so civil society is the realization in actuality of the potentialities inherent in society. This separation of civil society and the state is the sin of the economists (Adam Smith), accomplished by implication. Their conception of society reduces everything to the individual.[165]

The separation of state and civil society is negated by Marx, in potentia in the society of classical antiquity, in actuality in modern: the ancient state had slavery, the modern state has civil society as their natural bases.[166] Through this transition, civil society achieves its concrete historical form. The civil society presupposes a determinate stage of production, commerce and consumption, comprising a corresponding social order, family and Estates or classes.[167] Civil society in its concrete form is the dissolution of the old feudal society.[168]

The history of the concept of modern civil society proceeds pari passu with its historical expression in concrete form. The society and its designation appear in the sixteenth century in a preparatory form

---

[163] Ibid., p. 270 (on synthesis); p. 277 (on legislative authority); p. 283 (on atoms, abstraction). Cp. also, on abstraction, pp. 328f., pp. 295ff. (on Estates). On non-separation of the political state from society, see Marx, Kritische Randglossen zu dem Artikel, "Der König von Preussen." (1844). *Werke*, v. 1, p. 401.

[164] Marx, Zur Judenfrage. *Werke*, v. 1, p. 357. See also his Einleitung zur Kritik der Hegelschen Rechtsphilosophie. Ibid., p. 389.

[165] Marx, Ökonomisch-Philosophische Manuscripte (1844). *Werke*, op. cit. *Ergänzungsband* 1, p. 557.

[166] Marx, *Die Heilige Familie*, op. cit., p. 120.

[167] Marx, letter to P. Annenkov, 28 Dec. 1846. *Werke*, v. 4, p. 548. Cp. Marx, Engels. *Manifest der Kommunistischen Partei* (1848). Ibid., p. 476.

[168] Marx, *Die Heilige Familie*, op. cit., p. 143. Marx, *Class Struggles in France* (1850), and *The Eighteenth Brumaire of Louis Napoleon* (1852), employed the same usage.

and came to maturity in the eighteenth. "Bourgeois society is the most highly developed and diverse organization of production in history."[169] The anatomy of civil society is to be sought in the political economy. The productive forces in the womb of civil society create at the same time the material conditions for the solution of the antagonisms of the process of production in society.[170] In the civil society of the eighteenth and nineteenth centuries, the opposition to bourgeois society is overcome; civil society is absorbed into bourgeois society; there is nothing left over but the empty shell of the old category.[171]

Hegel held the citizen to be the man of particular interests in opposition to the universal, hence the member of civil society is to be regarded as a "fixed individual"; the state, in the "fixed individuals" stands counterposed to the citizens. Marx criticizes Hegel who should have said that civil society is the determination of each state individual. But, writes Marx, it is not the same individual who develops a new determination of his social being. Hegel assumes that the different and separate empirical existences of the state are to be considered as direct incorporations of one of these determinations. The universal is directly confused with the empirical existence. That is the first point. Marx's second point is that the family man is not a fixed individual in the same sense as the citizen is, in relation to the state.[172] Hegel, we have seen, held the object to vary accordingly as the point of view in regard to it was morality, the family, civil society; these are all gathered together in the human being.[173] The state cannot serve as the summation of all the qualities of society in the same sense that the human individual can summate the different qualities of "person", "subject," "citizen", "bourgeois." Finally, it is utopian to imagine that an individual human being can summate the "person", "subject", "citizen", etc. Perhaps in a fleeting moment of insight, inspiration, etc., this can be done. But even in the lives of great men, Hegel or Marx, are recorded periods of unfruitful existence, alternating with great efforts of concentration and internal unity. The poet exists as disjecta membra side by side with the moments of unified being as poet. Alienation is the usual condition of social existence, unusual is the condition of inner coherence of the human individual.

The individual human being is only a fixture in an artificial sense;

---

[169] Marx, Einleitung. *Grundrisse der Kritik der Politischen Ökonomie* (1857-1858). Berlin 1953, pp. 5f. (on chronology); p. 25 (organization of production).

[170] Marx, *Zur Kritik*, op. cit., pp. 8f.

[171] Marx, *Theorien über den Mehrwert*, I. *Werke* v. 26.1, pp. 145f., 259, 383f. III, ibid., v. 26.3, pp. 57, 93, 257.

[172] Marx, Kritik. *Werke*, v. 1, pp. 243f. Hegel, *Rechtsphilosophie*, op. cit., § 289.

[173] Hegel, op. cit., § 190 Anmerkung.

in the sense of world history and human development the human being is subject to change. In this view, civil society is a historical category which bears within itself both the condition of its own change and that of the individuals who make it up and whose makeup in turn is determined by life in civil society. "A social formation never goes down before all productive powers are developed for which it is broad enough, and new, higher relations of production never take its place before the material conditions of existence of the new are incubated in the womb of the old society." This dialectical passage is completed by Marx: "A mass of opposed forms of social unity, whose antagonistic character is yet not to be exploded by quiet metamorphosis. On the other hand, if we do not find in society, as it is, the material conditions of production and the corresponding relations of intercourse, for a classless society hidden therein, all attempts at explosion would be quixotic." The condition under which the present civil (as bourgeois) society will be exploded is firstly the material one; secondly it is necessary to differentiate constantly between these conditions of material production and the forms in which men become conscious of the conflict in the material conditions and fight them out.[174] The form in the consciousness of the individual and the content in the material processes in society are parts of a whole, each is a necessary condition of the other, in the matter of social change. But more than that, the condition of individual change is dependent on the social change of material production; the latter is dependent on the change in form of the individual consciousness of the conflict. The form of consciousness, finally, is the field of battle in which the change of material production relations, civil society, and individual human life takes place.

Civil society has grown to a mighty organization of the production relations and productive forces because the individuals, far from being atoms, are connected to each other through relations of mutual dependence; correspondingly the various functions in civil society reciprocally presuppose each other.[175] Further, we have seen that the conception of civil (as bourgeois) society, hence of the citizen as bourgeois, develops as the means of production of society develop; the social determinacy of the latter grows in this way together, with

---

[174] Marx, *Kritik* (1859), op. cit., p. 9 (consciousness, womb of the old); *Grundrisse*, op. cit., p. 77 (metamorphosis). See also Marx, *Kritik des Gothaer Programms* (1875). *Werke*, vol. 19, p. 28.
[175] The businessman believes the opposite; the business enterprise is to him an individual, not a collective matter. It is in his business, financial interest to do so. Vide Thorstein Veblen, *The Theory of the Business Enterprise*, New York 1904, ch. 8, near the end.

and into the conceptual modus of civil society, forming an indivisible whole.[176] This is the social atom.

On the contrary, the members of civil society are no atoms. The real bond is the civil and not political relation and life; the state does not hold the atoms of civil society together; on the contrary, the state is sustained by civil society. The peasants in the French Revolution brought out the egoism of nationality as the spontaneous egoism of the universal state in opposition to the egoism of its feudal limitedness. Civil society thus reproduces everything in the form that it had fought against in its feudal and absolutist form.[177] Civil society is the social atom, determined as such through the development of commodity exchange and the division of labor in society, whereby the atomistic condition of its members is rendered impossible. In the Asiatic mode of production, on the contrary, the social atom is the self-sustaining village community. In this form the community is directly the state[178]; that is, it is without the intermediation by civil society, for in the beginnings of the Asiatic mode of production civil society is developed but in a rudimentary form. On the other hand, the community, the corporation, the association, as all social unities, whether traditional or voluntary, are mediated by civil society in relation to the state in modern bourgeois society, as they are in modern socialist society, with this difference: in the latter, the trade unions and other associations are absorbed directly into the Party which is the concrete agency of the abstract state in the Soviet Union. Civil society is not the invention of capitalism, nor yet of feudalism, socialism, etc. It is the product of the entire history of the political economy, from its earliest forms in the Asiatic mode of production to its fullest development hitherto, in the form of the production of capital in modern bourgeois society, and the modern socialist, all being comprised within the relations of political economy, civil society and the state. These relations are already present, partly in their potentiality, partly in their actuality, in the Asiatic mode of production.

The ownership of the means of production, the land above all,[179] in

---

[176] Marx, *Theorien über den Mehrwert* I. *Werke*, vol. 26.1, pp. 259, 383.

[177] Marx, *Die Heilige Familie*, op. cit., pp. 127f. *Theorien über den Mehrwert*, op. cit., p. 145. The atom is not only the liberum arbitrium as it was conceived by Thomas Aquinas, it is also the soul without a window, or monad, as it was conceived by Leibniz. (Cf. Nathan Rotenstreich, *From Substance to Subject*. The Hague 1974, ch. 4.)

[178] Marx, *Grundrisse*, op. cit., pp. 379, 392.

[179] Ibid., p. 375. The predominance of this means of production is the fact of life in all the modes of production that precede the capitalist, a predominance that does not end with the onset of bourgeois economy and society, but lasts until the industrial revolution. The predominance of industrial over agricultural production begins in England and the Low Countries, then in

the Asiatic mode of production rested in the community or in the state as the overarching community; the ownership of the means of production by private persons was then weakly developed. This relation does not proceed from the subjective, abstract and to the objective and concrete, however; on the contrary, being social it is at once objective and subjective, just as it is at once abstract and concrete. The society is the determinant of these relations, but it is at once society in general and the particular society in its given historical form that is the determinant. This relation in turn determines the social product as commodity, surplus value, capital. The internal relations and proportions of these components of the social product vary in the different historical social periods. Whether the social product is predominantly in the form of capital, such as is the case in the modern bourgeois economy, and in some modern socialist economies, depends on the given social relations in particular. The so-called perspective from the standpoint of society is an abstraction made concrete in a particular society as is the modern bourgeois; the abstract perspective taken alone overlooks the specific differences which express the social relations of Asiatic or modern bourgeois society, etc. Society in

---

other parts of neighboring Europe, and in America. The predominance of the capitalist over the feudal mode of production begins earlier, in the period of archaeo-capitalism, in Northern Italy, particularly Lombardy and Emilia, and in Flanders. The condition of this latter formation is the *freedom* of labor and the formation of *voluntary* associations of investment of capital both in the land (irrigation, channelization) and in commerce and manufacture. Cf. Marx, The British Rule in India. *New-York Daily Tribune.* 25 June 1853. Marx, *Kapital*, I, op. cit., pp. 478, 682, on beginnings of capitalism in Italy.

It is not the move of the proletariat to the cities that determines the formation of the capitalist mode of production, but the relation of labor, the immediate producers to nature, to the soil, the relation of the same in society, to the means of production, and the relation of the capitalist to capital. Under the capitalist mode of production these relations become free and voluntary.

The persistence of the closed town, the close corporation, and the enclosure of the town within bricked walls long after the formation of capitalism in Europe aroused the contempt of Adam Smith; because they inhibit competition, they ought to be destroyed, he argued (*Wealth of Nations*, op. cit., pp. 127, 128, 129, 437). The features of early (archaeo-) capitalist society recalled those of feudalism to J. S. Schumpeter (see his *Capitalism, Socialism and Democracy*, New York 1950, 3rd ed., Pt. II, ch. XI-XII). Lewis Mumford, *The Culture of Cities*, New York, 1961, ch. 14, and Fernand Braudel, *Capitalism and Material Life*, London 1973 (M. Kochan transl.), ch. 8, sect. 2, have emphasized the relation between capitalism and town life; they have overemphasized the minor point and missed the major one.

Just as labor was bound to the soil in the modes of production that preceded the capitalist, so it was bound, in the guilds and corporations, by rules and by-laws. (See J. P. Davis, *Corporations*. New ed., Introd. by Abram Chayes. New York 1961.)

The relation of labor under the new conditions frees it for the move to the towns, at the same time that capital is freed, so that its expansion, valorization, *Verwertung* is instituted and accelerated. The concentration of labor power in the towns and the concentration of capital go hand in hand, the freedom of labor and the freedom of capital do the same.

concreto consists of particular relations of workers, capitalists, citizens, etc. Society is the expression of the sum of the relations and connections in which the abstract human beings, individuals in general, stand to each other. Civil society is the expression of the relations of immediate producers in society, or their relations of social production and reproduction, surplus production, to the controllers of the surplus social products; these controllers are other than the immediate producers. The immediate producers are not human individuals in general; on the contrary, they are bound or free, slave, serf, or citizen, depending on the relations of society, which are historically variable. Society in general, man as man, the individual as such, are abstract categories. But just as there is a hierarchy of abstraction, so there is of concretion. Civil society is a category of the relatively concrete; bourgeois society yet more so; *this* society (America, Japan) yet more. *This* civil society has been replaced by the modern socialist societies; the abstract relation of civil society remains, and the relation of immediate producers, that of the reproductive, surplus production in society, capital, wage labor, commodity, exchange value and use value; here the state is connected to the production of capital, surplus value and exchange value through the intermediation of civil society. The civil society of the modern socialist type is abstractly other than the civil society of the modern bourgeois type.

More than half a hundred writers in the twentieth century have dealt with the problem of civil society in the light of the researches of Hegel and Marx. Karl Korsch has taken up the problem most critically. Marx, he writes, overturned Hegel's concept of civil society, having set forth its fundamental significance in the shaping of his materialism. Korsch phrased in his polemic against Kautsky the dialectical opposition of civil society and society already to be found in the young Marx, before his transition to materialism.[180] Kautsky had confused the historically concrete and the abstract civil society: "Within the community, smaller organizations of the most varied kinds can be formed. Over all of them stands 'the' society, as distinct from the smaller societies in it, also called 'civil', – société civile, not bourgeois."[181] In actuality, wrote Korsch, civil society in Marx's sense

---

[180] Karl Korsch, *Die materialistische Geschichtsauffassung* (1929). Frankfurt, 1971, pp. 47f.
[181] Karl Kautsky, *Die materialistische Geschichtsauffassung*. Berlin 1927, v. I, p. 712. The concept of society is much maligned, reduced to simple terms, skeletalized. The curiosity of the substitute society for the social whole need not detain us. But scarcely more than one or at the most two of those enumerated in these footnotes who dealt with Hegel, had given sign of an awareness that he intended much more than the abstract category, or the abstraction of the category, civil society. More to our purpose is the projection of the term on to the contemporary screen. Hegel sketched in the dialectic of civil society and society through the

is just the reverse – it is the société bourgeoise in opposition to the state as civil society (société civile): The community (Gemeinwesen) may contain smaller organizations; it is implied by Kautsky that community and society cover the same ground, 'the' society embracing the smaller societies within it, as smaller organizations can be found in community. This is a confusion of the history of community and society and the sociology of the two. In neither case do they stand in a dialectical relation to each other or to anything else, in the presentation of Kautsky. To this Korsch answers: Civil society, beyond the limits of the individual national states comprises the whole of capitalist society, and in fact coincides with 'civilized mankind'. But, continues Korsch, this is not a Marxist perspective, which instead opposes civil society to classless and stateless primitive communist society, and to the society of the future.[182] Thus 'civil society' comes to mean the society with classes and the state in all their forms; it is the society of political economy, which Marx subjected to his critique. In *Das Kapital*, beside the critique of the capitalist mode of production, which is the main burden of the work, and continuous with it, is found the critique of the political economy of the Asiatic mode of production,[183] the mode of production of Greek and Roman antiquity, including critical appraisals of Aristotle's theories of economics,[184] and the feudal. All of these are comprised by Marx in the overarching economic category, political economy, and the form of society corresponding to it, civil society. This point is made in part by Korsch, for it had been cast aside by Kautsky. The point needs repeating today no less than ever, for it is being distorted by some, and cast away by others, as we shall see in the following section.

Further, Korsch brought out that, without the clear grasp of civil society through the means of the political economy, the economic principle cannot be rationally comprehended. Hegel, writes Korsch, had already recognized and set forth the conditional nature of civil society through the political economy, and as such is in a continuum with Marx's critique of the same. The materialist knowledge of civil society, Korsch continued, does not spring from the highest spheres

moments of the private as opposed to the public spheres, civil society as the externality of society as opposed to its formality, civil society in relation to the system of wants in the classical political economy. He was followed by Marx who conducted the critique of political economy of capitalism, of civil society in its concretion as bourgeois society and the state.

[182] Korsch, op. cit., p. 48n. The state taken as *société civile* is a jeu d'artifice. The point is that the state is opposed to bourgeois society, bourgeois society being at once the same as civil society (in concrete form) and opposed to civil society (in abstract form). Cp. Idem, *Karl Marx*, op. cit., pt. 2, ch. 7.

[183] Karl Marx, *Das Kapital* I. *Werke*, v. 23, pp. 378f., 537. See also p. 102.

[184] Ibid., pp. 67f., 167n., 179.

downward; on the contrary, the state, in its entire historical becoming and being is rooted in the materialist life relations of civil society. Unless these steps are followed in the analysis of the state, it remains idealized, abstracted from history, timeless, hypostasized.[185]

It is in connection with Korsch's polemic against Kautsky that the theory of civil (capitalist, bourgeois) society in its relation to colonialism and imperialism in the capitalist period of history can be comprehended. Just as civil society stands to the political economy as the organization of the latter, so it stands to the political economy of the Asiatic, classical, feudal and modern capitalist modes of production in the corresponding forms of Oriental, antique, medieval and modern bourgeois societies as the overarching category of the latter; just as civil society stands in a dialectical opposition to society in general, as the becoming of primitive society and the potentiality of a future, liberated form of society by its own sublation, so it stands in a dialectical opposition to the state, the existence of which it mediates as its material underpinnings. The civil society has appropriated the surrounding noncapitalist world through the agency of its own capitalist entrepreneurs, the personifications of capital. The more highly developed in the production of capital then proceeds to subject the less developed to the relations of colonialism and imperialism. In classical antiquity the same historical processes, with the same opposed relations of homeland and colony, and the same between the public and private spheres were developed, with this difference, that the colonialization was at that time the enterprise of the res publica, polis or civitas, whereas it is given over to the tender mercies of private enterprise in the modern capitalist period.

The capitalist society has both internal and external relations, the internal being to the advantage of those segments, the ruling capitalist group of one society to the remaining classes of that society, and to capitalists and proletariat of the other societies. Externally, this capitalist society maintains relations to the non-capitalist world, both socialist and the third or the ex-colonial world. By virtue of the

---

[185] Korsch, op. cit., pp. 48-51, 68f. "Even when bourgeois social theorists appear to speak of other forms, their real subject matter is still the prevailing form of bourgeois society, whose main characteristics they find duplicated in other forms. When they speak of society in general, we can still recognize with only slight variations, in this figure of so-called general society the well-known features of present-day bourgeois society. This is most evident in the writings of the great founders of bourgeois social science in the seventeenth and eighteenth centuries and their followers, the German idealistic philosophers from Kant to Hegel, who naively used not only the term 'society', but even the term 'civil society', as a timeless concept." Karl Korsch, Leading Principles of Marxism: A Restatement. *Marxist Quarterly*, 1937. Repr.: *Three Essays on Marxism*. London 1971, p. 32.

more highly developed production of capital in the former, e.g., the United States, West Germany, a favorable, that is to say profitable, relation is maintained with the others in the production and exchange of commodities. These capitalist states are necessary for the economic life of all the countries of the world, whether socialist or capitalist, the countries of western Europe and North America being the chief source of the production of capital and its export, such as is useful and necessary to all. Capital rules the world,[186] its uninterrupted production and flow being the conditio sine qua non of all human life today, whether in Africa, Asia, South America, or in Europe and North America. It is so recognized by ideologists of both camps, the modern capitalist and modern socialist. The form of ownership of the means of production, of property, and the corresponding constitutions of the state are juridical and political accommodations to the relations of production and its organization in society.

The dialectic of civil society has far greater historical depth and present extent than the depth and extent of modern bourgeois society, arching over and determining the latter, both in its theoretical and practical moments. The transfer by revolutionary action of the ownership of the means of production in Russia in 1917 from private hands, and carried through by other means in the following decade, constituted the overturn of the relations of private property in its bourgeois form there and then. The negation of private ownership by the bourgeoisie of the means of production is not the same, however, as the negation of the relations of political economy and civil society in general. On the contrary, these relations continue in force. It is

---

[186] Tennyson thought it was property, and put this holy word into the mouth of his farmer; it is a vulgar materialism. There is a not inconsiderable literature in the twentieth century, which, after Tennyson, confuses the relation of property, a formal and legal relation, with the relation of capital. The latter, however, is not only a matter of form; it is a relation of production in society, and as such is at once form and content. On the question of production in society, in relation to property, see Krader, *The Asiatic Mode of Production*, op. cit., and references there cited.

It was capital endowed with a will and consciousness, and personified in its directors, that determined in the Spring of 1975 whether Britain should leave or remain in the European Common Market. The opinion of American, British capital, and Helmut Schmidt prevailed over the so-called left wing of British Labour, personified in Anthony Wedgewood-Benn, and over the USSR. How long will this relation of the opposed strength of the two systems of capital prevail? The posing of the question of capital and labor in this case is actually the question of personifications and symbols. Behind this question lies that of the increase of international influence of the USSR, and the relative decline in the same of the United States which yet, at this time, could marshal the greatest battalions. The question of far greater importance than all of these is how the social relation of labor can gain ascendance over the social relation of capital as the decisive factor in our history.

not the difference in standard of living between social classes, as the anti-Soviet ideologists were wont to say, that demonstrates the continuity of civil society in the Soviet Union after the Russian Revolution. It is the continued existence of the relations of production, whereby capital is produced and is subjected to the law of its expansion, that demonstrates this; social labor under these conditions continues to be wage labor. The critique of the political economy, as of civil society, in these relations is the condition of their abolition. It is the abstract condition, of which the theory of civil society is a part. The critique of the political economy in relation to civil and bourgeois society was begun by Marx. The continuation of this critique is here applied to the changed conditions of civil society a century later; thereby the critique of capital is continued. The capitalist is the personification of capital, capital endowed with a will and consciousness of its own. This personification has an ever more restricted and ever less useful (efficient) bearing on the relations of production of capital in the political economy in bourgeois society in general. A new form of ownership and control was substituted for it after the Russian Revolution, in competition with the old, still existing in America, West Germany, Japan, France, Britain, Sweden, etc.; the leadership of the USSR has been increasingly conscious and explicit in the matter of this competition.[187]

There exist several models of the management of capital production in societies of high output of capital per capita (e.g., U.S., Japan, West Germany, Sweden) and in the USSR. The theory of competition (e.g. by W. Hamilton in his article, Competition, *The Encyclopaedia of the Social Sciences*, New York 1930) no longer applies to any of

---

[187] One school of thought conceives the competition between the USSR and the United States to be comparable to competition between General Motors and Ford Motor Company. (E.g., Z. Brzezinski and S. P. Huntington. *Political Power*: USA/USSR. New York 1964). On the contrary, there are fundamental differences between the two systems, in particular regarding the social relation of capital production. The Soviet challenge rests on the proposal that capital production is more readily valorized in Soviet than American social conditions. It is not merely that capitalist (Adam Smithian, Marshallian, etc.) competition is being compromised by "state capitalism" or "state socialism." The pure model of capitalism is a utopia. The attack of Hayek against the German social market implies the changes in the capitalist economy there. (See F. A. Hayek, *Studies in Philosophy, Politics and Economics*. New York 1967, ch. 17 and passim). J. S. Schumpeter, whom Hayek admires, but not for this reason, asserted that capitalist evolution will destroy the foundations of capitalist society (*Capitalism, Socialism and Democracy*. New York 1962, pp. 42, 56, 61 and pt. II passim). By virtue of this process, free competition and free market economy of capitalism change their meanings; competition itself changes meaning in the Soviet system. State capitalism or social market capitalism is not the system of the Soviet economy; competition is likewise not limited to the bourgeois chapter of history of civil society. The Soviet system differs from the U.S. system in the formal relation of the means of production.

them. The rhetoric of ideology aside, it is clear that the modes of management of capital production in the United States and in the Soviet Union are different. The difference lies in the organization of production, and not in the process of production itself. That is, it lies in civil society and not in the political economy.

The relations of production in society which lie behind the change in character mask continue in existence; the personification itself has been changed. These relations and their various personifications are to be subjected to critique as any other. The critique of civil society is but the first step in the critique of the political economy, of which it is the organization, over the whole world. That organization continues, albeit in changing form.

Practically, the same relations are carried forward in the twentieth century, that were evident in the nineteenth. Aside from the nations of modern socialism, the earth is divided into colonizing and excolonized countries. The former, the so-called civilized lands of culture, form the capitalist society, divided into the different states, all together the various expressions of modern bourgeois society. The different lands of this society, being more or less capitalistically developed have the characteristics in common of the organization of production of capital in civil society, and the state in its present form. Marx, in his critique of the program of the German Worker's Party, wrote, "In this sense one can speak of the present-day state, as opposed to the future, in which the present root, bourgeois society, will have withered away."[188]

In the contemporary world, societies at different stages of development, low and high, exist cheek by jowl.[189]

---

[188] Marx. *Critique of the Gotha Program* (1875). Sect. IV. Marx Engels *Werke*, v. 19, p. 28: "Jedoch haben die verschiednen Staaten der verschiednen Kulturländer trotz ihrer bunten Formverschiedenheit, alle das gemein, dass sie auf dem Boden der modernen bürgerlichen Gesellschaft stehn, nur einer mehr oder minder kapitalistisch entwickelten. Sie haben auch gewisse wesentliche Charaktere gemein. In diesem Sinn kann man vom "heutigen Staatswesen" sprechen, im Gegensatz zur Zukunft, worin seine jetzige Wurzel, die bürgerliche Gesellschaft, abgestorben ist." – "Nevertheless, the various states of the various lands of culture, despite their colorful difference in form, all have this in common, that they all stand on the soil of the modern bourgeois society, but one that is more or less capitalistically developed. They therefore have certain essential characteristics in common. In this sense one can speak of the "present-day state", in opposition to the future, in which its present root, civil society, withers away."

[189] Some lands are more highly developed in their civilization than others at any given time; it is their relations of production that divides them. On this difference the more highly developed exploit the less, and on occasion transform the latter into colonies. Marx distinguished not only the different degrees of development, but also the difference that contact between peoples of different degrees of development has wrought on them. Thus he wrote that Arabs, Turks, Tatars, Moguls, who overran India, were quickly hinduized. The British conquerors, however, stood on a higher stage of development, and to them Hindu civilization was inaccessible; the

VIII. ON THE DIALECTIC OF EVERYDAY LIFE IN CIVIL SOCIETY

The dialectic is the empirical fact of civil society, whose negation is prepared in the class conflict which makes up its history. The consciousness of the dialectic in history is the work of the bourgeois society, not only in Hegel, Marx, but in its everyday life.[190] That consciousness is divided on the one side into the social consciousness of the bourgeoisie and its ideologists who act in defense of the status quo, and, on the other, the revolutionary consciousness which is aimed at the overthrow of the old order. Just as the consciousness of society and history is determined by the class struggle, and is accordingly divided, so is its reification determined by the relation in social production, and is accordingly so divided. The revolutionary consciousness is not the product of bourgeois society any more than commodity exchange and production is its product. On the contrary, bourgeois society is the product, the result of commodity exchange and production and the expression of these relations in the consciousness of its members, the bourgeois and the proletarian; that consciousness is no more a whole than is the society. It is a whole, and at once is not, just as the society is at once whole and divided.[191] In ancient Greece and Rome, in the developed periods of feudalism and of the Asiatic mode of production, commodity exchange, the production of capital, expansion or valorization of the same, the production of a social surplus, were all developed. They were not as highly developed, nor was their organization as complex or as systematically carried through as it is in the bourgeois mode of production; but the presence of these relations as the defining conditions of these foregoing modes of production is well attested historically. Moreover, the beginnings of the revolutionary consciousness can be discerned in the foregoing social epochs, witness the Spartacus movement in ancient Rome; and, just as these movements have had their fantastic expression in the utopias of the bourgeois period (not only in Fourier, Owen, Pecqueur, Cabet, but also in Campanella, More) so the idea of utopia

British destroyed it. (Marx, *New-York Daily Tribune*, 8 August 1853. *Werke*, op. cit., v. 9, p. 221.) These statements are objective, and can be shown to be either true or false. (Cf. Krader, *Asiatic Mode of Production*, Pt. I, ch. II, III.)

[190] Karl Korsch, Dialektik des Alltags. Vortrag, Berlin 1932. The dialectic runs its course throughout human history, attaining a more intensive and extensive expression in civil society, an expression that is yet more intensive and extensive at once in the moment of modern civil society. This expression attains a more heightened form still in the moment of revolution. The consciousness of these moments go far back in history. In the modern period that consciousness was given exemplary expression by Hegel, but a further development by Marx. The dialectic of everyday life is the material of this consciousness.

[191] Krader, *Ethnologie und Anthropologie bei Marx*. Hanser 1973, ch. 3.

was promulgated in the societies of the Orient, classical antiquity, feudalism. The civil society in its bourgeois expression has summed up the foregoing developments; the latter can be grasped, its key is found in the later development.[192]

Continuity is paired with discontinuity. On the one side the Asiatic, ancient or feudal economic formations are regarded in their totality, as progressive stages, each leading to the next. On the other side, they are to be understood in terms of their own categories.[193] That totality, we have seen, is the unity of political economy and civil society, a unity which is at the same time a disunity, or opposition. Civil society, as the category that arches over the whole of the society of political economy and the state is subjected to an inner dynamism, or development, of which three moments are here singled out: A) the moment of the political economy, B) the moment of civil society, C) and the moment of the conscious expression of both. All these moments are to be taken up in their relations of scission and of totality.

A) The political economic moment, which has in its inner organization the relations of labor, commodity exchange and production. The movement of labor in the political economy is that from the bound to the free condition. In the Asiatic mode of production labor is bound to the means of production by tradition and habit; in the ancient mode of production in classical antiquity labor is bound by the ties of slavery and clientage; in the feudal mode of production labor is bound to the means of production, which is the soil in the first place, by the ties of servility. The transition to the bourgeois mode of production is at the same time the transition of labor to the condition of freedom to contract for the sale of labor power as an agent that is family the equal to its purchaser who is the capitalist. Each is a party to the contract whereby the labor power is freely alienated as a commodity. The labor power is reckoned in abstract form as its exchange value, the component units of which are the labor time. The free market for the contract of labor is a formal freedom whose content is bound by the system of wants.[194]

Thc system of wants is the content of the bondage of labor in the condition of formal freedom.[195] The worker is free to contract with this capitalist or that; the nature of the contract for the sale of his labor power is the same in the one case as in the other. The worker

---

[192] Marx: The anatomy of man is the key to the anatomy of the ape. – *Zur Kritik der politischen Ökonomie*, 1859, op. cit. Foreword.

[193] Korsch, Principles of Marxism, op. cit., pp. 35f.

[194] See above, sect. VI. On the leap from the realm of necessity to the realm of liberty, cf. Marx, *Das Kapital*, vol. III, 3rd ed., Hamburg 1911, Pt. II, p. 355.

is not thereby freed from the necessity to meet and renew his wants, and to reproduce his labor power thereby. The wants are not the biological needs, but their expression, in political economic terms, as commodities whose value is the abstract expression of the labor power applied in its exchange in equal measures and amounts. The relation of the system of wants is thus the dialectical moment of the content in its passage into its opposite, which is in the form of the contract as the expression in the society of the content. It is at the same time the passage of the concrete biological needs into their opposite, the abstract expression of the exchange value as a com-

[195] F. A. Hayek, *The Constitution of Liberty*, Chicago 1972, p. 162, writes, "Individual liberty in modern times can hardly be traced back farther than the England of the seventeenth century." This statement is made in the chapter entitled, The Origins of the Rule of Law. He rests his case in part on Acton, but the latter could not, any more than Hayek, separate the issue of freedom of conscience from that of the constitution (Lord Acton, *Lectures on Modern History*, 1906. Repr. London 1970, pp. 198f.)

Liberty or freedom is connected to the rule of law, but it is not the content, it is the form of freedom that is connected to it. The achievement of the law in the seventeenth century in England, Germany, Holland (Coke, Althusius, Grotius) was to express and summarize freedom and equality which were developed in the preceding century. That freedom and equality were expressed as natural right on the one side, and as freedom and equality of contract on the other. The two sides are connected to each other. The models of society and of freedom brought out in the seventeenth century had been adumbrated earlier by Machiavelli, Guicciardini, Salamonius. The importance of freedom and equality in contracting for sale and purchase of labor power in exchange for a wage, and in contracting to associate in the formation of a commercial society, or trading company, is well attested. The formal freedom of contract embraces and assures these relations in the law. These are not only formal, they are external relations. The content of freedom has as its first measure the mastery of the system of wants in general in the society, whereby the individual is freed from wants in particular. For neither the society nor the individual is free in any but a formal and external sense as long as they are bound by the system of wants.

Hayek has a concrete plan of freedom, which is the defence of the institutions of capitalism (free market, free contract, freedom from governmental interference), in which he is joined to L. v. Mises, *Theory and History*, London 1958, pp. 347ff.

The discussion of liberty by Hayek is one-sided, taking the form for form in relation to content, and externality for internality in its relation to outer form. He appears not to be aware of the history of the subject, freedom in relation to contract, freedom in relation to society, equality in relation to both. Although in this work and in his subsequent *Law, Legislation and Liberty*, London 1973, he refers to Descartes and Spinoza, he does not take into account the change in the discussion of freedom from the earlier time to the present. Freedom was discussed by these men in reference to bondage by the passions, whereby the liberation from human bondage is effected by reason. But bondage is effected not only by subjection to the passions, it is also effected through custom, enslavement, the relations of which lie concretely in society and not in human nature abstractly. The social moment of freedom was made clear by Hegel and Marx; this is its historicity. (See Krader, *Asiatic Mode of Production*, op. cit., Pt. I, ch. V, incipit). We are not freed by liberation from social slavery alone; nor are we freed by liberation from an abstract servitude imposed by our human nature. On the contrary, liberation is effected by both moments, each in relation to the other.

modity. For this, labor is expressed as labor power; the unity of living labor is broken down into the units of labor time, labor is given expression thereby as an abstraction, in the form of exchange value of that labor power, and is freed from its erstwhile condition of bondage in order to do so. For no contract made under duress, or bondage, is valid. The passage from the land as the means of production to the factory and workshop proceeds pari passu with the formal change of the labor relation.

B) The moment of civil society. The division of labor in the political economy into a relation of production in society and into a relation of reproduction brings with it a division of the society into a relation of the part and of the whole. The part of the society that is engaged in the reproduction of the relations of production and the forces of productivity is alone capable of meeting the wants of the social whole, that is, reproducing these in reference to the social whole. Contrariwise, the proletariat in sublating itself sublates its opposite at the same time, which is the social whole. The sublation of the part is thus the revolutionary transformation of the social whole. The entirety of civil society is the summing up of these antagonistic relations. The antagonism becomes ever more critical, approaching the moment of crisis in the course of the historical movement of civil society.

At the present time the antagonisms are expressed in the modern bourgeois and modern socialist systems. In both the contradictions between the process of reproduction and that of surplus production, between labor of hand and head, between urban and rural production are carried forward. On this basis, civil society and the state are established; their joint historical being is the expression of these contradictions; their joint task is the mastery of the manifestations of these contradictions (acts of terror, general work stoppages, deterioration of civil morale). The difference between the modern socialist and modern bourgeois forms of civil society lies in the theoretical form of the two: in the one the ownership of the means of production by private hands has been abolished. In practice the revolutionary overturn of the production of surplus and its unequal distribution, of the state and its agencies of repression and suppression of the class struggle in all its forms, of the conversion of the relations of political economy and civil society, to the conditions of the content of freedom and equality, hence of the abolition of these relations, is still to be accomplished everywhere.[196]

[196] Cf. Karl Korsch, Why I am a Marxist. *Modern Quarterly*, 1935. Repr.: *Three Essays*, op. cit., pp. 68-70. Also his Lenin's Philosophy, Some Additional Remarks. *Living Marxism*, v. IV, 1938, no. 5, pp. 138f.

C) The moment of consciousness. The history of civil society is the history of the formation of social classes, of mutual struggle and antagonism between them and of the development of the consciousness of this struggle; these doctrines were first expressed by Marx and Engels, they were carried into the twentieth century in the aftermath of war and revolution by Korsch and Lukács.[197] The struggle between the social classes, becoming ever more clearly expressed in the consciousness, makes its way divided thereby. This thesis has been posited by Lukács: "Although the social form of the bourgeoisie first allowed the struggle to appear in a pure form, and although it at first had fixed it historically as a fact, yet theoretically as well as practically it must do everything it can to cause the fact of class struggle to disappear from the social consciousness."[198] Marx had brought out the antithesis to this: It is the task of the proletariat to act in the opposite direction and to heighten the consciousness of the fact of class struggle.[199] The consciousness of mankind in the civil state is not unitary but divided. But it is not only the bourgeoisie that wills the fact of class struggle to disappear from the consciousness, it is the agency of the state everywhere to do so. The state, in the condition by which it prolongs its own existence, by which it assures itself that it will neither be abolished nor abolish itself, is the means to the continuation of the relations of political economy and civil society, or the antagonisms of the social classes expressed therein. (The state does not prolong its existence directly but mediately, acting through its agencies and instrumentalities; nor does it guarantee its own abolition directly, but only through its agencies. The state is an abstraction, its agencies are the concretion of the same.)

Lukács in positing this thesis has conceived the social consciousness to be a whole. The next dialectical step is to conceive this consciousness in its inner division. To conceive it as a whole and no more is to reify it, and to hypostasize the form of society in its totality of which it is the conscious expression. The doctrine of the social whole and of the whole social consciousness in its indivision is the affirmation of the unity of civil society. The doctrine of Lukács is not therefore a comfortable one to those in whose interest it is to affirm the social whole and the units of consciousness relative thereto. The common

---

[197] Karl Korsch, *Marxismus und Philosophie* (1923. 2nd ed. 1930) Repr. Frankfurt/Main 1966. Also vide supra. Georg Lukács, *Geschichte und Klassenbewusstsein*. Berlin 1923. See M. Merleau-Ponty, *Les aventures de la dialectique*. Paris 1955, ch. II, III.

[198] Lukács, op. cit., p. 74.

[199] *Die Heilige Familie. Werke*, op. cit., v. 2, pp. 35 sq.

interest of the state in capitalism as in the modern socialist civil societies lies in this, that the fact of class struggle in either is separated from the social consciousness, relative to those totalities.

The social consciousness is the consciousness of the whole of civil society, having in any period in civil society at once a unitary and a divided form. It has its prehistory and its current history. General de Gaulle, on being informed that Jean Paul Sartre was advocating social revolution, proclaimed, "On n'arrête pas Voltaire." The dialectic of everyday life in modern bourgeois society is the recognition that the revolutionary phrases are normal to it. The state in its French as in any other of its manifestations acts to restrain the more egregious forms of this contradiction, between the revolutionary norm and the normal-revolutionary.

IX. DIALECTIC OF ECONOMY AND SOCIETY. A.

1. The amount of time expended in producing useful things, or in production generally, is reckoned up in the primitive economy, or may be; but if it is reckoned up, it is not so as it is in the political economy. The unit of production in the primitive economy, be it a village community, clan, gens or sib, tends to coincide with the unit of consumption; hence exchange of products and circulation do not play an important part under these conditions. Labor time in the political economy is reckoned up in connection with exchange; here the unit of production and the unit of consumption diverge from each other, for which reason, labor time is reckoned up in connection with the accounts of exchange value and market price. As value per se labor, abstractly reckoned up in the political economy as labor time, is at once a concrete and abstract relation in production; it is social labor, and the production social production. Labor and labor power are reckoned up in units of labor time which has an exchangeable value measured in abstract units thereof. By this reckoning labor in the mode of social labor is transformed into a commodity, as any other. The abstract units of value are the exchange value of social labor and as such are separate from the concrete production of useful things, or use values, just as abstract labor is separate in the political economy from concrete labor or work. The producer in the primitive economy, since he is not primarily engaged in production for exchange purposes, does not have these grounds to reckon up or account for the amount of time expended in production.

2. The division of labor takes place within the unit of production in both the primitive and the political economies. In the primitive economy, however, the unit of production is generally self-sustaining;

the division of labor under this condition is that within the family, the village community, etc., it is not the divided and combined labor in society. The division of labor in the primitive condition is developed through differences in age, sex, strength, or health, whereas in the political economy, being developed through the organization of production in society, it becomes the social division of labor.

3. The transition from the primitive to the political economy is brought about through the development of exchange between communities, the relation introduced by the increasing degree of mutual dependence of the communities, or the units of production generally; these communities thereby become no longer self-sustaining. The exchanges become customary, traditional, whereby the things exchanged acquire, by the establishment of the usage, an exchangeable value; things exchanged are thereby transformed into commodities.

4. In consequence of the exchange practiced between the communities, the production of the things exchanged becomes transformed into the production of commodities, or the abstract representation of the exchange.

5. Labor gains an abstract expression by means of this transformation, measured in the exchange value of the product, which is in turn measured by the amount of time expended in its production. The abstract expression of labor value is abstract labor; it is now distinct from concrete labor, and the political economy distinct from the primitive.

6. By virtue of the distinction between abstract labor, or the commodity of labor, and concrete labor, or work, the difference between social and private labor is introduced. Social labor is the system of abstract and concrete labor; in private labor this distinction is not introduced. The distinction between social and private labor, as between abstract and concrete labor, is specific to political economy, as opposed to primitive economy. Social labor is the production by a social unity other than that which consumes its product. Social labor, again, is distinct from private labor in the political economy.

Social labor is labor for another; it is distinct from communal labor and from private labor. By communal labor is meant labor in which each works for all, or the whole, of which the immediate producer is a part. The whole is in this condition not broken down into the relations of labor by one for another. Labor for the whole is therefore communal, as opposed to labor for another, or social labor. Communal labor is neither abstract nor concrete, neither social nor private; these differences are not posited in the primitive economy as they are in the political economy.

7. Labor in the primitive economy is neither free nor unfree; in

the political economy it is either free or unfree. In the beginnings of political economy and civil society, it is unfree; that unfreedom is in the form of bondage by custom. These customary bonds, bonds of usage and tradition, are the communal bonds in the Asiatic mode of production, whereby the relation of immediate production in society is in the form of communal labor; the immediate producer is not torn free from the community. On the contrary, those for whom the labor, work or toil is performed are individuals torn loose from the communities. The communities as wholes together make up the class of immediate producers in society, the class of those for whom the labor is the class of individual interests.

8. Social labor in the beginnings of the history of civil society, or the Asiatic mode of production, is bound to the means of production, which is above all the soil. Social labor has evolved from its relations of bondage by custom to the relations of bondage by slavery, clientage and serfdom in the later stages of the economic formation of society.

9. The communal bonds of social labor in the beginning stages of the political economy are the positive connections of the human individuals within the communities in the Asiatic mode of production. These are positive relations, present in the periods of classical antiquity as well, likewise in the early periods of feudalism in Europe. In the later periods of the Asiatic, classical and feudal modes of production these positive communal bonds are negated. In the Asiatic mode of production they are converted into the bonds of colonial labor of the capitalist mode of production in its early period (i.e., the sixteenth to eighteenth centuries). In the economic relations of Europe in the period of classical antiquity in its middle and later stages, the positive communal bonds are converted into the negative, or the restraints of slavery; in the later stages of the feudal mode of production the positive communal bonds are converted into the negative, or the restraints of serfdom.

10. In all these modes of production, which precede the modern bourgeois, or capitalist, labor is unfree, hence it is not distinct from labor power. It is indeed a commodity, having and producing social value, having and producing abstract value of commodities. But since social labor is in these conditions bound as communal and customary, colonial, slave labor and serf labor, it is unfree. The one or the class for whom the social labor is performed disposes of the entire, undivided time of the immediate producers, measured in their living day and life time.

11. The limitation of the amount of labor time expended in production in society is introduced with the freeing of the immediate producers from the direct bondage to the means of production.

This is the specific difference, within the political economy, of the modern bourgeois or capitalist mode of production. The bondage of labor in the feudal manor, in the guild and corporation workshop is gradually loosened. The immediate producer in the capitalist mode of production is free to contract for the sale of his labor time with whomsoever will purchase it.

12. Labor power as labor capacity in this condition is subject to contract for its sale and purchase. The units are the working day, and segments thereof, and the working period, and segments thereof. Labor in the conditions of colonial labor and guild labor, is indented, whereby it is contracted for in segments of multiples of years. This practice is replaced by contract for sale of labor power in small units of time in the subsequent periods of the capitalist mode of production, whether hours, days, weeks.

13. Contract as a legal form is valid only if freely engaged in, and forced contract, as coercion in purchase and sale, is invalid. The bondage of labor to the means of production is overcome in modern civil society, wherein the immediate producer has the formal freedom to contract for the sale of his labor power in temporal units. The formal freedom is the conversion to the condition of political economy in the modern civil society of the form and content of bondage in the Asiatic, classical, feudal and early colonial conditions.

14. The form of social labor in the economic periods in which the production of capital predominates is wage labor. These periods are the modern bourgeois and socialist. In both these periods and in both conditions of production which predominate in them and determine them, labor power is distinct from labor, it is free social labor, subject to contract for sale of time and payment of wage. In the modern bourgeois and socialist modes of production abstract labor is distinct from concrete labor, social labor from private, as it is throughout the history of the political economy. The public sphere is distinct from the private sphere in these forms of civil society as it is through the history of civil society.

15. Whereas the form of social labor is generally communal in the beginnings of the political economy, whether Asiatic, feudal, etc. modes of production, it is individual in the condition of the modern political economy, whether bourgeois or socialist modes of production. In the modern cases, it is free wage labor, subject to labor contract.

16. The political economy is distinguished from the primitive by the social production of a surplus that is over and above the quantity expended in the maintenance of the immediate producers as a class, or the reproduction of that class. The primitive economy is characterized by its nondivision into such classes; for all here work who are

able and produce for each other, as for the communal whole. The political economy and civil society are throughout divided into a class that produces in society for its own maintenance and its reproduction as a social class; it produces at once in an amount expended for the maintenance and reproduction of another social class, consisting of an excess amount, or surplus social product.

17. In the primitive economy the relations of production are not separate from the relations of reproduction. In the political economy, in all its forms, whether Asiatic, classical, feudal, bourgeois and modern socialist, the relations of social production are differentiated from the relations of social reproduction.

18. This distinction between social production and social reproduction, whereby a surplus in society is produced, is the basis for the distinction between two classes in society in all epochs of the political economy, the class of immediate producers in the society, and the class of those who enjoy the social surplus produced. The social surplus produced is measured in surplus value. The primitive economy and society generally have produced no social surplus.

19. Through the relations of political economy, civil society is divided into two social classes, the one of the immediate producers in society, who produce for themselves and for others; the second is the class which disposes of the social surplus produced. That surplus is twofold, both for the reproduction of those who are not its immediate producers in society, and for the reproduction of the means of production. In the organization of production in bourgeois economy the social surplus is converted into the means of expansion of capital.

20. Social labor, being labor in which one works for another, is a reciprocal relation; society is the expression of the sum of the reciprocal relations in which given individuals stand to one another. Civil society, however, being the society in which surplus value is produced, is the negation of this social law, for surplus value is produced by the non-reciprocated labor of one for another. The relations of civil society are the contradiction of the relations of society; labor in civil society is at once social labor and the contradiction of social labor.

DIALECTIC OF ECONOMY AND SOCIETY. B.

1. Civil society is the organization of the political economy: it is the means for the intermediation between the private and the public spheres of social life, presupposing as it does the separation of the private and social labor. This separation is not extant in primitive

society; it is an alienation which is specific to civil society as distinct from the primitive society.

2. The system of wants in civil society is expanded over that of the primitive society, being at once more extensive and more variable than the latter. The alienation of the private from the public spheres is at the same time cause and effect of this extension and variation. The nonseparation of the units of the production and consumption, or the coterminacy of these two unities in primitive society, is overcome and surpassed in civil society. On the one side, we feel ourselves to be less subject to the reign of custom by this sublation; this is a subjective judgment. On the other we are more alienated from nature, and set in a secondary alienation thereby. We are by the same process reified, subject to the things whereby the mediated wants are met; we become thereby more of a thing, the reified subject in civilized society.

3. Civil society is the means whereby the process of socialization is carried forward, which had been first begun in primitive society. The organization of production in society and exchange therein, or the separation of social production from consumption, have the separation of the public from the private spheres as their result. The private sphere becomes the sphere of consumption, in the interference with which the wants are directly and subjectively felt. The public is that sphere in which production in society is organized, the sphere of social labor and production. It is the sphere of objectification of the wants.

4. The public sphere is at the same time the sphere of the state and law. The law in the public sphere includes the legislative act, or the conscious will personified in the law; it includes both public and private law. The private law is the intrusion into the private sphere of this sector of the public law.

5. The right of civil society is either private or public; it is both private and public. The public right, *jus civilis* in the strict sense, is separate from the private, which is not an intrusion as is the private law. The private right is the stronghold of the human being from the attack, repression and alienation of right by the agencies of the public sphere, of the state and law, both public and private.

6. The public sphere, on the contrary, is the stronghold of the formal relations of civil society; the constitutional right (Bill of Rights, etc.) is the intrusion into the public sphere of the private right from its stronghold.

7. The formal relations of civil society, the state and law call forth the formal relations, the public face or persona, of the human individual. The civil person, the juridical person, or persona ficta is

the form in which the human individual appears before the law, state and civil society. The human being has a standing in the law only insofar as he is a formal person, capable of right, in consequence of being legally recognized as capable of bearing such right. The formal person is the human being in relation to the public right and to public and private law. The state and law extrude the person; the person extrudes the state and law.

8. The system of wants of the human individual, however, is covered only in part by the public and formal relations of the person. The private relations of the human being are no less a proper part of his system of wants than are the objectifications of the public sphere.

9. The relations of reproduction of the political economy are the means of bringing together the public and private segments of the system of wants. The production in society necessary for the continuation of the immediate producers as a class is thereby secured. To this end both the public and the private elements of the system of wants are called forth in civil society.

10. The concrete wants of the particular human being, eating, drinking, sexual reproduction, then the pleasures of eating, drinking or the act of sex, are allusions to the private elements of the system of wants. Public are the elements, such as architecture in relation to the concrete wants and needs of housing; technology and science in relation to the material arts of life; medicine and the institutions of public health in relation to the wants in respect of illness, epidemics, their prevention and cure; publication of books, discs, tapes, the galleries, museums, theaters and concert halls in respect of the dissemination of knowledge and of forms of art; the university in respect of the dissemination of the same; the elementary schools in respect of the same to the young.

11. The subjective and objective moments of the system of wants are present in both the public and private sectors of the system of wants. The private moment is both subjective and objective: the procreation of the family, group, class, nation, the human species, is both objective and subjective; the reproduction of the social class of the political economy and civil society is both objective and subjective. The relation of biological procreation and that of reproduction in the social relation of the political economy are private, particular and concrete; they are at once public, and universal and abstract. These are related both as contradictions and as polar opposites. They cancel each other out and they each complete the other.

12. The system of wants in civil society is completed by the communal relations of production, such as the quilting bee, housing bee,

husking bee of the early history of the American frontier. These are the voluntary associations on the one side, the communal and customary collectivities on the other. The communal bonds are not voluntary; the communal relations are the bonds of custom. The communal relations of the village community, kin village community, house community, clan, gens, etc., are here opposed to the voluntary relations of associations, societies (Roman *societas*, Germanic *Genossenschaft*, etc.).

13. The relation of citizen completes that of the person; the person is the formal and legal, or public fact of the human being, the citizen is the complement of the person, relative to other elements of civil society than the law. The human being in respect of civil society is the citizen, in respect of civil law the person, in respect of the state he is the subject, and in respect of the political economy the free contracting party to the sale and purchase of his labor power. The human being stands in an outward relation to the political economy, civil society, the state and law of the same. Other than the relation of citizen, person, associate, subject, the contracting party and the family member, etc., is the inward relation of the human being.

14. In civil society the inward relation is alienated from the outward relation. The product of artistic, scientific, etc., creation is made into a commodity in the political economy, the art gallery, concert, laboratory, university lecture hall, sells the product of art and science, as any other commodity. Here the work of the hand and head is outwardly displayed and marketed. The internal relation of painting, thinking, composing is externalized. It has an exchange value.

15. The civil society generally is particularized as bourgeois society and the citizen as bourgeois; the political economy of capital generally is particularized as the production and expansion of capital. The modern socialist society no less than the bourgeois is the society of exchange value, wage labor, the society of the production of surplus value, of class division and the state. It is opposed to the modern capitalist society in its ideology, a difference in the superstructure of the societies. The modern bourgeois and socialist societies are alike those in which the production and expansion (valorization) of capital predominates.

16. In civil society the public and private spheres are separated, the formal and informal relations in society no less so. The individual is a formal, juridical person, standing in a formal, juridical relation to the state in civil society. In the modern bourgeois, as in the modern socialist economies and societies, the formal, juridical relation of the state calls forth the formal, juridical relation of the individual as person, citizen, wage laborer. The individual is rendered increasing-

ly abstract, the private sphere increasingly alienated from the public. The private sphere in consequence can only be related to the public by the intermediation of civil society, that is, by the formal person in relation to the state as the sum of juridical forms.

17. The communal being, or community of immediate producers, is opposed to the individualities at the beginning of the history of civil society. These communal human beings are transformed into individualities, with their class of individual interests, at the end of the history of civil society; these interests are opposed to the interests of the class of individuals torn loose from the community at the beginning of the history of civil society. The inner development of civil society follows the transformation of the communal to the individual form of right and interest of the immediate producers in society, or their passage from communal social being to individual social being. But whereas the individual interest of the ruling class is internally opposed and contradictory to the interest of other individuals of that class, the individual interests of the class of immediate producers in society are internally consonant with each other, and stand only in contradiction to the interests of the ruling class. The consonant interests of the immediate social producers are on the one hand the continuation and transformation of the interest of the community at the beginning of the history of civil society. On the other, the interest of the proletariat contains within itself the interest of the social whole. But that whole has been transformed from the expression of the social relations at the beginning of the history of political economy and civil society.

18. The person is the abstraction of the human individual, and abstract no less is the form of wage labor in civil society. The relations to nature and in society are increasingly abstractions in the history of political economy and civil society.

19. Civil society comprises both the public and private spheres of social life, arching over the form and content of the former. The public and private spheres of civil society are related *pro forma*. The content of the private sphere cannot be directly connected to the public, formal, official side of life in society; the connection and control thereby would constitute a monstrous act, even beyond the reach of most tyrants.

THE DIALECTIC OF ECONOMY AND SOCIETY. C.

1. The relation of labor in the political economy is reckoned up in quantitative terms, the reckoning being made in amounts of labor time that have been expended in production. Labor in the primitive

economy is also reckoned up, albeit differently from labor in the political economy. Labor in the political economy is social labor.

2. Labor time is differently reckoned up in the various modes of production of the political economy. It is not only the subject of the contract of wage labor in the capitalist mode of production in bourgeois society, it is also the subject of the relation of the immediate producers in the community to the state in the Asiatic mode of production, of the relation of slave and master in the antique, and of serf and lord in the feudal modes of production. All labor, be it communal or individual, private or social, involves the expenditure of labor time.

3. Labor in all the relations of the political economy, whether Asiatic antique, feudal, capitalist or modern socialist, is a commodity, inasmuch as all these economic formations are engaged in the exchange and production of commodities. It is a commodity because it has value, which is the abstract expression of the amount of labor time expended in production. That value is its exchangeable value, or abstract value, value in short, which is separated in the relations of the political economy from its useful value; this, its use value, is its concrete value and is distinct from its abstract or exchange value just as concrete labor is distinct from abstract labor. Throughout the relations of the political economy, concrete labor is the production of useful things, abstract labor being the production of exchange values. Abstract labor is the commodity of labor, as concrete labor it is work, or useful toil. The distinction between abstract and concrete labor in the political economy bears upon the labor in society, or the sum of the private labors, in which each individual works for another.

4. Labor in the political economy is either bound or free. As bound labor it is labor in short, as free labor it is laboring power. The relations of labor in all forms of the political economy other than the modern bourgeois and socialist are bound; on the contrary, labor as wage labor, labor power, contract labor, in the modern political economies of capitalism and socialism is free, for here the immediate producer, or working man disposes of limited amounts of his labor time.

5. Wage labor in the modern economies is labor subject to sale by the immediate producer through a contract, the quantity bought and sold being fixed thereby. This is a relation between private parties to the contract for the laboring power of the immediate producer. It is also fixed and delimited by public law which determines the maximum amount of time that can be so expended.

6. Where the amount of labor time is not fixed by private contract,

it is not fixed by public law. Where it is not fixed and delimited, no distinction between labor and labor power is made. In ancient Rome or India, and in modern colonial conditions, labor was and is sold that comprises the entire lifetime of the workingman, who becomes the bound laborer, slave or client of him who has thus become, by virtue of the sale, his master.

7. The right to dispose for a limited time over the labor is the right or power over the labor time of the individual workingman, or his labor power, in the modern political economies, as distinct from the unlimited disposal over the labor of the immediate producer in the Asiatic, antique and feudal modes of production.

8. The form of bondage in the Asiatic mode of production is imposed through custom and tradition, in the antique mode of production through slavery, in the feudal through serfdom. The form of bondage through custom is a communal form of labor, the form of bondage through slavery and serfdom is either communal or individual. Entire village communities are bound in their labor relations in these cases.

9. In all these modes of production, it is a limited amount of labor time that is disposed of by tradition, by capture in war, or by contract of purchase and sale. If the labor is placed at the disposition of the employer, master, or lord through bondage by tradition or by capture, the limitation in time ends with the death of the worker, the individual reproducing not himself but his labor or labor power.

10. In the primitive as well as in the political economic relations, labor time is reckoned up. E. B. Tylor and Karl Marx conceived that the amount of time expended in production by the primitive producer is a matter of complete indifference to him. This cannot be taken to mean that labor expenditure or outlay is not measured in terms of time. On the contrary, two communities or kin groups, etc., may produce and consume a quantity of products, the amount of which may move from one to the other and back, being evened out to the satisfaction of both over the course of several generations . Such arrangements of mutuality are exemplified in marriages between primitive groups. A spouse may move from one community, band, or kin group to another. This movement is accompanied by mutual gifts, feasting, services performed by the one for the other. A movement in the opposite direction may take place in the following generation. There are cases in which three communities are involved in such movements, whereby a spouse moves from group A to group B, group A receiving a spouse from group C; group B providing in its turn a spouse to group C, thus:

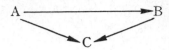

Such a movement, accompanied likewise by gifts, mutual prestations, incorporeal respect, honor, and the like, may take two or even three generations to be evened out. The amount of labor expended in such movements, in the acquisition of fruits, meats, peltries, etc., suitable for mutual feasting and gifts is known to all, and it is reckoned up.

11. In these conditions of primitive economy and society it is not the individual alone who is involved in the movement, it is the entire group, and indeed the group in its existence over several generations. The labor time is thus reckoned differently from the way it is reckoned in the political economy.

DIALECTIC OF ECONOMY AND SOCIETY. D.

1. Freedom in civil society in general is an external and formal relation, freedom in the modern civil society of the production of capital is no different. Civil society in general, modern bourgeois and modern socialist societies in particular are constituted of the externalization of human relations, which is summed up in the state as the formalization thereof.

2. Bondage is an external relation which is not only that of unfreedom but also that of inequality. Not all are bound in civil society; outwardly and formally, some are bound and some free. Hegel thought that in the civil society of the Asiatic mode of production, or Oriental society, one is free; in the society of classical antiquity some are free. Those who are free in these relations are not the equals of the unfree, any more than the serf is the equal of the lord, in the feudal society. Unfreedom and inequality are mutual determinants of each other in these social formations.

3. In modern bourgeois society lawyers have written of contract as the greediest of relations, swallowing up all the others. Contract is not only a greedy relation, it is a relation between free and equal parties to it.

4. Labor in both the modern capitalist and socialist modes of production, as social labor, is wage labor or labor subject to contract for the right of disposition over labor time of the immediate producers, who sell their laboring power in quantities limited by private and public law; the limitation imposed in the sale by private law is through contract, by public law through the regulatory agencies of the state. The sale of labor power is a form of contract, as that for the purchase

and sale of any other commodity; every seller must have a buyer, every buyer a seller. Whereas contract was of limited scope, importance and content in the civil society of the ancient, Asiatic and feudal modes of production, it has flourished in the modern, in which the production of capital predominates.

5. The development of capital production, contract and wage labor go hand in hand. They are transformed together, and together express the transformation of civil society into the modern bourgeois society. The freedom of labor and the freedom of capital are each the condition of the other, each the determinant of the other; the expression of the two freedoms takes place coevally. The freedom of labor is at the same time the equality of the workingman and the representative of capital. The freedom of capital is the freedom of the expansion of capital through its valorization. The process of expansion of capital takes place in relation to its surplus component, whereby it is reproduced and expanded; it also takes place in reference to the reproduction of the working class.

6. Contract is no less important for relations of capital than it is for the relations of capital and labor. The freedom of formation of voluntary associations of capital is of importance in the history of capitalism early and late.

7. Contract is a social relation that is necessarily free, it must be freely entered into and maintained. Proof in law that force was exerted either in its undertaking or fulfillment is ipso facto ground for its invalidation. An unfree contract is an invalid contract. Free parties to the contract are equal parties; freedom and equality go together, just as unfreedom and inequality. The American and French Declarations that accompanied their respective revolutions refer in many instances to freedom and equality and the right of all to the same. They followed by several centuries the inception of freedom and equality of labor to contract for the selling and buying of labor power at the beginning of the period of modern capitalism.

8. Freedom of contract of labor proceeds in history *pari passu* with freedom of association by contract of capital through its representatives, the capitalists. These forms of voluntary association in companies, societies, multiply in the period of the production of capital together with labor and wage contracts.

9. Partnerships, voluntary associations, companies and societies founded on contract are the model for the conception of civil society and the state in the sixteenth century. The theory of social contract in the conceptions of Hobbes, Spinoza, Rousseau and Kant is the further extension of this model. Marx was conscious of the importance of voluntary association not only in commerce but also in water

control in the early period of capitalism in Lombardy and Flanders.

10. The forms of civil society and the state that were created by the Russian Revolution of 1917 are based on voluntary association. Lenin wrote in 1914 on the right of nations to self-determination, hence to secession, in the case of states founded through revolution. National unities then are forms of voluntary association. Further, he wrote that this unity and amalgamation in international association is created by the working class. The nature of the working class and its social revolution is determined by its relation in social production, while the particular form of its association in nations and states is voluntary.

11. The freedom of labor, as of the men and women in the working class, in the contractual relation of civil society is an external, hence formal freedom. The voluntary associations of capital and of labor are externally and formally free amalgamations and associations. The forms of political combination and association are externally free during the historical period in which the production of capital predominates in society.

12. The political party is a form of voluntary association within civil society. The party is a part of the social whole, willing that it stand for the whole; yet it is not identical with the whole of society. The party wills, by delegation of power, to represent the social whole in its own interest, identifying that interest with the interest of the social whole. But that interest is not a reciprocal relation. The identification is a substitution of the part for the whole. It is a twofold substitution: on the one hand the party is a part of political society, on the other, the political society is a part of the social whole.

13. The party is a voluntary association in respect of the election of its members. Candidacy for membership in the party is a subject of will and decision by the individual; admission to membership is a matter of election by the members. The party is the expression of the general will of its members; the particular will of the individual is no longer free.[200] The theory of the party is founded on the doctrines of individualism, the will, the general will, and election.

14. The political party is a close corporation, having a determinate membership and interests. As a corporation, the party is a self-perpetuating body. It is in a particular, not a general relation to the social whole. That is, it does not necessarily act to perpetuate the political society of which it is a part; the party may seek the overthrow of the political society.

[200] Rousseau did not have a theory of society in mind when he asserted his doctrine of the general will. The modern day political parties are the expression of Rousseau's *volonté générale*. The whole of society is manipulated by the Rousseau model.

15. The vote is the means whereby the general will of the party is ascertained and expressed. The vote is a formal device that is far older than the political party; the vote was taken in ancient Rome long before the introduction of the party organization into civil society.[201]

16. The fiction of the free individual and free will is maintained in voting procedure. The manipulation of the vote, however, is attested in ancient and modern times.[202]

17. The system of formal party organization, formal voting, delegation of power and representation of the political-social whole has been carried forward from the modern bourgeois to the modern socialist civil society.

18. The political parties of modern bourgeois society hold themselves superior to the political parties of modern socialist society because they are many, and that of the modern socialist society is one. This difference is a formality, compounded of the difference in external organization of the civil society. It is a difference at once in the ideological sphere.

19. The ideological history of Europe in the twentieth century is the inverse of that history in the nineteenth. Capital and capitalism were exported then by the fulfillment of two conditions: A. Labor, already liberated in England, the Low Countries, North Italy, was made formally free in western and central Europe, then in parts of eastern Europe, by the effect of the French Revolution. B. The self-expansion of capital proceeded pari passu with the liberation of European labor.

The Concert of Europe, the Holy Alliance, and the Restoration did nothing to impede the extension of capital and capitalism; on the contrary, these reactionary forces, together with the bourgeois revolutions of 1830 and 1848, jointly gave an ideological stamp, the Russian reforms of the 1860s a legislative seal to historical acts whose impetus lay elsewhere. The movements set under way in 1789 were practical and concrete; their ideological comprehension by right and left hastened to embrace the fact of expansion of capitalism. The history of capital in Europe during the nineteenth century is unambiguous.

20. Civil society is at once a process and a stage of history. As a

---

[201] Voters in ancient Rome affirmed proposals of legislation with the letters, U. R. (*uti rogas*); they rejected proposals with the letters A. P. (*antiqua probo*).

[202] The manipulation is a reification. The means are tacit, unconscious, whether by imitation, playing on sentiment and disposition, or else explicit and conscious, by bribery, coercion, threat of the same, by appeals to cupidity, fear, anxiety, by flattery, or by insistent repetition.

stage it is in one sense an element of the social evolution of the human kind, in another it is an invention to illustrate the processes of history and evolution. In the first sense the stage is an ontological substance of evolution and historical being, in the second it is an epistemological construction. The ontological substance and the epistemological construction are juxtaposed to each other; their resolution is not a dialectical but a metaphysical problem. A stage, civil or political society, succeeds another, that of primitive society. The process whereby the succession takes place is the destruction of both. Either element in the succession is necessary for the other, the civil stage as the terminus into which the primitive emerges, the primitive as the terminus out of which civil society proceeds. Neither stage is eternal, neither is necessary for the human kind as a whole. Yet at the same time they are types in the theater of history, which give way to others when the new history is made.[203]

21. Bourgeois society in the nineteenth century and socialist in the twentieth in each case has conceived of the whole of human history in terms of historico-evolutionary stages. It is a triumphalist progression which the bourgeois society of today, in the hour of its recession, abandons. Stage theory is conditioned by historical events. The modern socialist mode of the civil society, as the bourgeois mode before it, considers itself as having attained to that which no other before it has reached. Alike they have made the stage theory into an ideological weapon, intended to prove that either has progressed out of a preceding stage.

22. Aristotle in regard to the theory of the polis held that some men, the Greeks, had already attained a stage that all men will one day reach; his was a consciously teleological conception of history. The theory of social evolution expressed by bourgeois ethnologists and historians in the nineteenth century (Herbert Spencer, Henry Maine, i.a.) likewise held that some men had attained a stage of social evolution that others would reach, a concealed teleological conception. Bourgeois society was without rival in the nineteenth century; the advocates of the stage-career of the human kind did not defend positions, nor abandon them. The ideology of modern bourgeois society is now seriously threatened by that of the modern socialist society, in particular, the Soviet Union.

23. The stage theory is an incomplete dialectic; its antithesis

---

[203] This is contradicted by the action of the machine-breakers, Luddites in the Midlands and north of England at the beginning of the nineteenth century. The contradiction is resolved in the course of time.

remains to be introduced. The historical process is the negation of the stage. The stage is consumed in the process of history.[204]

CIVIL SOCIETY AND THE EXTENSION OF ITS CRITIQUE

As a Marxist, L. Althusser has begun a critique of civil society in an attack against the dialectic of Hegel and Marx, the Marxism of Althusser being a dialectic, wherein the good is praised, the bad, Hegelian-oriented dialectical Marx abhorred. The aim of Althusser has that of B. Croce before it, with this difference, instead of separating what is living from what is dead in Hegel, it is to separate the living from the dead in Marx. Althusser proposes to demonstrate that what is living in Marx's doctrine is the structuralist thinking expressed therein, the dialectical being at most a mere trope.[205] Indirectly he conducts a critique of the categories of civil society in their relation to modern capitalism and socialism. The categories that he has taken up are those of social classes and class struggle, the state, ideology, the historical subject, historicism and the dialectic itself. But in doing so, he dispenses with the relations of change from one society to another, which the dialectic of the categories reveals, and his problem is resolved into the static representation of the categories themselves. That they stand in a dialectical relation to each other, to the society, to the political economy, hence of necessity to the observer, Althusser, is alien to him. He is of the structuralist wing among the intelligentsia of the French Communist Party, and the opponent of the dialectic. He is neither materialist nor idealist, but both at once, being unable to compose the passage from one to the other; each exists side by side in his work, separate from each other. On the one hand he is a skilled dialectician, in the sense of Abelard and Schleiermacher, who held the dialectic to be a rhetorical figure. On the other, his analysis of the esthetic of Michelangelo, who, in creating his artistic product by the negation of the unformed marble posited in that which envelops the material the form to be disclosed, proves itself to be indeed materialist.[206] Althusser's dialectic is in this case the materialist expression of a virtuoso who displays a composition which is not his own. He proposes a structuralism, in opposition to the philosophico-idealist structuralism of Cl.

---

[204] A. R. Radcliffe-Brown, *A Natural Science of Society*. The Free Press 1957, recommended against the concept of process. As an antagonist of the stage theory he ought to have recommended in its favor.

[205] Louis Althusser. *Pour Marx*. Paris 1966. Idem, *Lire le Capital*, 2 vol. Paris 1966. Idem, Avertissement. In: Karl Marx, *Le Capital* I. Paris 1969. Idem, *Lénine et la philosophie*. Paris 1972. Idem, *Reponse à John Lewis*. Paris 1973. Further references infra.

[206] Althusser, *Lire le Capital*, op. cit., v. 1, p. 44n.

Lévi-Strauss,[207] but his own structuralism differs little from that of Lévi-Strauss. The object of Marx's *Capital* is that of theory in relation to practice, but that relation is, according to Althusser, a philosophical one, in the sense of being an epistemology. The object of Marx's opposition to classical political economy is given thus by Althusser: "by means of what concept or ensemble of concepts can one think the determination of the elements of a structure, and the structural relations existing between these elements, and of all the effects of these relations by the effect of this structure? And a fortiori by means of what concept or ensemble of concepts can one think the determination subordinated by a dominant structure? In other words, how can the concept of a structural causality be defined?"[208] The object is not to negate the relations of production in society that have the classical political economy as their expression, it is the thinking of the determination of the elements of a structure; it is not the negation of the social relations of the classical theory of political economy, the ruling class in relation to the working class, it is the thinking of the determination of dominant to subordinate structure. History is not the history of class struggle, according to Althusser; on the contrary, there is an object in history, which is the construction of the historical concept.[209] The repetition of the concept of concept in relation to political economy as to history is nothing more than the practice of Hegelian idealism without the dialectic. This is made clear by the formulation given above: historical causality does not lie with the proletariat nor is it defined thereby in the struggle with capital and against the capitalist class; historical causality is a structure, according to Althusser, that is defined by relations between concepts. Nor is the possible relation between them brought out by him. The cinema is reduced to a series of still photographs, the concepts have no dynamism, they are immobile structures. They are, however, the reflections in thought of the categories of civil society, as we shall see. These relations are not consciously brought out by Althusser, but his relation to them is a complex one. The dialectic as expressed by Althusser is a hit or miss affair, the materialism likewise; now the latter appears, in the reference to the aesthetic of Michelangelo, now it disappears, in the references to the classical political economy and to the historical object. This is a vaudeville, the turn of the prestidigitator.

---

[207] Althusser, *Lénine et la Philosophie*, op. cit., pp. 37f.

[208] Althusser, *Lire le Capital*. op. cit., v. 2, pp. 166f.

[209] Ibid., p. 59, "... the object of history is, beyond historical investigation itself, *the production, the construction of the concept of history*." Italics Althusser's.

History was conceived by Montesquieu, according to Ernst Cassirer, as simply a moving totality. Not so, according to Althusser; Cassirer, he says, misses the point, and "does not express Montesquieu's most profound thought. For [Montesquieu] intends there to be in the last instance *a determinant term: the principle*". What is set aside by Althusser is the totality of history and its movement, which, said Cassirer, Montesquieu had expressed. This is of no interest to Althusser. He is attracted only by the discovery of an abstraction in the work of Montesquieu, which is the latter's "most profound thought", and the reason why we should read him. That abstraction is in the form of a principle or principles: "The force of the principles draws everything to it": "The corruption of the government generally begins with that of the principles"; "There are very few laws that are not good while the state retains its principles".[210] Montesquieu's construction of history is not at issue, nor yet Cassirer's grasp of that construction. The issue is what Althusser singles out for praise, which is Montesquieu's abstraction of history, and its static principle: laws, the judgment whether good or bad, corruption of the government, etc. This is of a piece with the reduction of history by Althusser to the construction of a concept, a structuralism of a philosophico-idealist nature, for the judgment of law and government as bad or corrupt ensures a static historical grasp, in that the elimination of the bad or corrupt will return the law and government to their prior state of goodness.[211] The dialectic would have helped Althusser in this case, had he but grasped it, to overcome his static historical conception. The want of a materialist, i. e., scientific grasp of history in this case is the root of the issue.

Althusser pursues novelty for its own sake, he overthrows determination, and inserts overdetermination, which he borrows from the language of psychoanalysis.[212] The overdetermination posited by Althusser is designed to overcome the law of contradiction of Hegel

---

[210] L. Althusser, Montesquieu. In: *Politics and History*. London 1972, B. Brewster transl., pp. 51f. Montesquieu, *Spirit of the Laws*. Ernst Cassirer, *The Philosophy of the Enlightenment*. Princeton 1951.

[211] This is the philosophy of prison reform brought out by Jeremy Bentham: Remove the evildoer from his environment, isolate him in a prison cell, and his innate goodness will assert itself; reformed he will return to society. It is this renovation of the human character that Tocqueville and Beaumont wished to inspect in practice in America. It implies a static human nature, an ideal which Althusser likewise implies, imputing it to Montesquieu and adopting it for his own spiritual ancestor.

[212] Overdetermination is used by him "as an index and as a problem." In the work of Lacan it is a psychoanalytic category located in the symbolic determination. Althusser, *Pour Marx*, op. cit. p. 100. Cf. Jacques Lacan, *Ecrits*, Paris 1966, pp. 52, 678f., 802 and passim; Althusser, *Lire le Capital*, op. cit., v. 1, p. 15n.

and to substitute the concrete model of the conception of history for the abstract model of contradiction reflected in it.[213] Althusser had written, "The object of history, as a theoretical discipline, is the production of the concept of specific determination of variations of historical existence, which is nothing but the existence of the structure and process of a determinate social formation, coming from a definite mode of production." To this Althusser couples the concrete history, but not as a dialectic.[214] If they were coupled as a dialectic then the theory of overdetermination would have been unnecessary, and the entire task of Althusser with it. The theory of overdetermination, as index and as problem adds nothing to the theory of determination save the multiplication of terms without necessity, for the determination of the abstract conception and concrete history is a mutual relation, they each are the measure and index of the other, as they are each the problematics of the other. Each arises out of the other as index and problem, as measure and as motive force.

Because he has suppressed consciously the dialectical relation of the abstract and concrete in history in general, Althusser cannot grasp it in particular. He takes it as given that Marx took over the term civil society from Hegel. "No doubt," he writes, "Marx still speaks of *'civil society'* (particularly in the *German Ideology:* a term which is imprecisely translated as 'bourgeois society'), but it is in allusion to the past, to indicate *the place* of his discoveries, and not to take up its *concept.*"[215] On the contrary, it is precisely in *The German Ideology* that the dialectic of the abstract civil society and the concrete bourgeois society is raised; the term is not imprecisely rendered as "bourgeois society'; that is one of its meanings, the concrete meaning, the opposite of its abstract meaning. Marx does not pluck it forth from the past, but sets forth the dialectical passage of the past into the present, the abstract into the concrete, the potential into the actual, civil society into bourgeois society. On one level this dialectic is a continuum from its expression in Hegel to its expression in Marx. In the expression, the signal is higher, the noise lower in Marx than in Hegel. On another level, the potentiality inherent in the opposition is systematically expressed by Marx. Hegel did not develop the system of wants as a concrete social category, as we have seen; on the contrary, the system of wants that he expressed was conceived as an invariant,

---

[213] Althusser, *Pour Marx*, op. cit., p. 106. Althusser seeks in this place to cut the link between the dialectic of Hegel and the work of Marx. The analysis of civil society that follows is found ibid., pp. 107-111.
[214] Althusser, *Lire le Capital*, op. cit., v. 2, p. 59.
[215] Althusser, *Pour Marx*, op. cit., pp. 107f.

throughout human society. Being invariant, the wants have their history only in their juxtaposition to the instinctive wants of beasts, according to Hegel, who composed their natural, but not their social history. Marx in his polemic against the classical political economists caused the system of wants to enter into social history, and from their abstract form converted them into a concrete moment. Althusser[216] rejects the thesis advanced by Marx that his dialectical method is the "direct opposite" of Hegel's, that he turned Hegel's dialectic "right side up".[217] His point is that Marx and Hegel speak different languages, therefore the one cannot be the reverse or opposite of the other.

Althusser reports the theory of civil society in Hegel with the following terms: it is the system of wants; it is the economy; and it is the world of economic comportment of individuals and its ideological origin. It is in modern times one of two societies, the other being political society or State.[218] This is an inaccurate reporting of Hegel who did not identify civil society with society in modern times alone, nor did he identify civil society with the system of wants, nor yet with the economy. Hegel did not identify the State with political society, but wrote of the political State, as opposed to the ethical State, the constitutional State, etc.; Marx understood Hegel to make these distinctions in his Critique of the Hegelian Philosophy of Right, as we have seen, and himself applied them in the 1840s. Althusser has caricatured Hegel in order to prove that Marx's critique is not the opposite of Hegel's dialectic; it is Althusser's intent to make Marx into a structuralist of his own devising, as the God of the ancient Jews stood to them. But Marx has made merry in reference to these reflex categories: "Such expressions of relations in general, called by Hegel reflex-categories, form a very curious class. For instance, one man is king because other men stand in the relation of subjects to him. They, on the contrary, imagine that they are subjects because he is king".[219] Althusser holds that Marx is a structuralist because Marx stands to him as such, whereas on the contrary Marx is a structuralist only because Althusser stands in relation to him (Marx) as such.

The system of wants[220] that was expressed by Marx has a concrete

---

[216] Althusser, Avertissement, op. cit., pp. 21 sq. *Pour Marx*, pp. 69f. Sur le Rapport de Marx à Hegel. In: *Lénine et la Philosophie*, op. cit.

[217] Marx, Postface to 2nd ed. of *Capital*. (London 1873). F. Engels, ed. English transl., New York 1937, p. 25.

[218] Althusser, *Pour Marx*, op. cit., pp. 107, 109.

[219] Marx, *Capital*, op. cit., p. 66 (in English transl. only).

[220] If we insist on this way of translating of *Bedürfnisse* it is not merely because Marx has already done so. (See his note on N. Barbon, on the first page of *Capital* (v. 1, ch. 1 of all editions). To be sure, this translation is not popular, and T. M. Knox and Nathan Rotenstreich

historical basis; it is his way of referring to historical man. More than a poetical trope, it was the means whereby he expressed early and late his reference to concrete man, eating, drinking, etc. The system of wants are brought out in this way in the *Economic-Philosophical Manuscripts* of 1844, in the chapter on Feuerbach in *The German Ideology*, in the *Notes to Adolph Wagner's "Textbook on Political Economy."* [221] The difference between the early expression of the system of wants is that it was brought out as a program which was later filled out; in both the first and last mentioned works the history is concretely expressed, wants are a historical variable. In the reference to wants in the *Economic-Philosophical Manuscripts,* it is not "man as man", but a concrete, historical man, an Irish peasant who in 1844 suffered want in the potato famine. This is the inversion of Hegel by the passage from the historically abstract to the historically concrete. It is of antiquarian interest that Ludwig Feuerbach wrote of wants both abstractly and concretely, but our issue is not the descent of that holy ghost; at issue is whether Marx invented a new language of wants or inverted the system of Hegel; whether he stood in a continuum which at once controverted the Hegelian dialectic, or whether he broke with the Hegelian dialectic to become the first of the structuralists.

The idealism of Althusser hides the fact that Marx in his history of human wants, just as much as in his history of the theories of surplus value, in his polemic against the classical economists as against Thomas Malthus, struck a blow against the society that profited from their conceptions. The classical economists had held the laws of profit, the market, labor value to be eternal laws; if so, then the political economy

have vetoed it. The words themselves, as Humpty Dumpty knew, are easily adaptable to anything. Wants and needs are opposed, and the distinction is important. They are the same matter, the one in political economy and social science, the other in psychology and biology. J. M. Ripalda, *The Divided Nation*, Assen (in press 1976) has another view of the issue. See the last chapter, in which the dialectic of wants and needs is pursued.

[221] Marx, *Werke.* Ergänzungsband 1, pp. 514f., 546 et seq. Ibid., v. 3, p. 28. Ibid., v. 19, pp. 362f.: "They [men] begin, as any animal, *to eat, drink*, etc., hence not to "stand" in a relation, but to *comport themselves actively*, to control particular things of the external world by the deed, and thus to meet their want. (They begin therefore with production.)"

Cf. *Werke* v. 3, p. 21: men begin to differentiate themselves from the beasts as soon as they begin to produce their means of subsistence.

Both the concrete wants of eating and the means of meeting them are active relations to nature. Insofar as they are human wants and means they are indirect relations, i.e., hunting with bow and arrow, and not with claw and fang. The system of wants and means to meet them are variable in human history. They are variable in natural history, but that variation has another meaning, just as does the history. In nature the variable unit is, as a rule, the species; in the case of the human kind, the variable unit is, as a rule, the social group, and not the species as a whole. Agnes Heller, *La teoria dei bisogni in Marx*, 2nd ed., Feltrinelli 1975, contains an excellent analytical conspectus, with bibliographic notices, of the theory of wants.

of profit, the market, labor value was likewise eternal, standing outside history. The interests of groups and classes were at stake, the disclosure of these interests was a weapon in the struggle against them. This is the historical kernel within the abstract shell of political economy; the critique of the history thereof is the dialectical passage into the socially opposed interest. The insertion of the idea of history and its concept by Althusser is the abstraction and idealization of that which Marx had made concrete.

Althusser has written of the object in history; we have seen that this object is wholly abstract, in his system it is idealized. The object stands in a dialectical relation to the subject, however; if that relation is severed by the fantasy of human thought, then the subject likewise is rendered into an abstraction, an idealized, fantastic representation of historical reality. It is severed from its concretion. The subject is removed from history: "the category of the subject is constitutive of all ideology," writes Althusser; ideology, he continues, has the function of "constituting concrete individuals as subjects." [222] This transition from the abstract to the concrete is a marvel of the dialectic; but it is only a pseudo-marvel, a prestidigitator's marvel. Nowhere does the subject in ideology, or the concrete individual, manifest itself as a human being, still less as a social class, as a human being in society, in human history, in a conflict between social classes. Nowhere does this ideological concretion descend from the empyrean in order to join the historical object. The ideological subject remains a hypostasis of the concretion. The pious horror that Althusser evinces at the expression by Marx, that ideology has no history, is an act of hypocrisy. It is hard to believe that Althusser is unaware of what he is doing and of its effects. His direction of the charge of positivism against Marx [223] is made in order to free himself of the relation of substructure to the superstructure, to enable him to adopt and to promulgate his abstract, philosophico-idealist tenets. (The charge of positivism against Marx fails because it rests on the prior charge that Marx assumed metaphysics to have no history; on the contrary, Marx made ideology into a category of civil society, hence of history.)

We have seen that Althusser brings political society together with the State, and has severed it from civil society, a seemingly theoretical point which has consequences in practice. Putting civil society on the one side, political society on the other is not a mere etymological solecism; it bears fruit in his distinction between the state power and

---

[222] Althusser, Ideology and the State. *Lenin and Philosophy.* B. Brewster, transl. London 1971, p. 160. (Cp. Le Rapport de Marx à Hegel, op. cit.)
[223] Althusser, Ideology and the State, op. cit., p. 150.

the state apparatus; state power is a matter separate from the state apparatus as it is from the objective of the political class struggle.[224] The state apparatus contains: the government, the administration, army, police, lawcourts, prisons (p. 136). He notes (loc. cit., n. 7) that A. Gramsci added to these the institutions of civil society: church, schools, trade unions. He then distinguishes between the repressive and the ideological state apparatus, assigning government, army, police to the former; included in the latter are in addition to the above: family, political parties, press, television, radio, literature, arts, sports (p. 137). His historical world is that of bourgeois, capitalist society, in which bourgeois law is operative, in which most newspapers, churches, parties, trade unions, families are private (loc. cit.). In addition, the period of Russian history down to the death of Lenin is allowed. Stalin, the Second World War, do not exist. This means (p. 139) that the ruling class in Russia other than the proletariat has succeeded in gaining control of the educational ideological state apparatus, despite the opposition of Lenin, and has succeeded in prolonging its existence, for the Soviet proletariat had seized the state power in 1917, but not the state apparatus; failing to secure the educational ideological state apparatus, it could not have seized control of the state apparatus (repressive); failing to seize the latter it could not secure the future of the dictatorship of the proletariat; failing to secure the latter, it could not ensure the transition to socialism. He cites (p. 139, n. 10) a text of Krupskaya in 1937 who related the history of Lenin's efforts.

A note on Althusser's style. The style, we know, is the man himself. Althusser reports Lenin's "anguished concern" over the separation of the Soviet proletariat from the ideological (educational) state apparatus, the "pathetic text" of Krupskaya, the history of Lenin's "desperate efforts." Anguish, pathos, desperation, all in a half-dozen lines on p. 139. Here is a critique of the fate of the social revolution of 1917. But it is not: the judgment is not made, something is held back; Krupskaya relates only "what she regards as his [Lenin's] failure." (p. 139n.). The subjective judgment, "what she regards" is not the aweful sentence of history, it is but one person's opinion. Who else shares it? Althusser? This is a hesitation before the court of world history. Better to flee to the safe philology of texts.

A second note on the style of Althusser. The class struggle (p. 134) is political, the October Revolution is social. The social relation is the determinant of the political. Althusser writes (p. 139): "no class can hold state power for a long time without at the same time exercising its hegemony over and in the state ideological apparatuses." Then the

---

[224] Ibid., p. 134. The ensuing points bear upon Althusser's exposition there, pp. 131-141.

hegemony of the ruling class over all other classes, and not merely of town over countryside, or of head over hand labor, extends in the Soviet Union down to the present day. The nationalization of the privately owned means of production is but a shift in the superstructure and in the juridical form of the same, not in the economic foundation. The "political" of Althusser which characterizes the events of October is nowhere associated to the economic foundation of the society. The events of October shook the ruling class of England, France, America, Germany, abolishing the former ruling class of Russia. But the relations of the proletariat to the means of production remain unchanged, for the latter continues to reproduce its relation to production in society;[225] it produces the surplus value by its relations of social production in the modern socialist and capitalist worlds.

A third note on style. Althusser refers to the category of 'civil society', by means of a reference to Antonio Gramsci (p. 136, n. 7). Civil society, class-divided and opposed society, includes the categories of church, schools attributed to it by Gramsci, and to this attribution Althusser associated himself. Civil society has different forms in the different modes of production (Althusser, p. 137 n.), one of which is the civil society of the USSR. Althusser implies but does not assert this judgment, and hesitates to write of civil society in this connection.

From this it follows that Althusser engages in a limited critique of civil society; he is loathe to break with the party of October. His attack on the dialectic of Hegel and Marx is a substitute for a critique of the Soviet society of today, and its ruling class. He abolishes the dialectical relation between the society and the categories of society, but he has not abolished the dialectical object and its critique thereby.

L. Kolakowski has broken his connection irrevocably to socialist Poland, and found a haven in unsocialist England. He considers that the Marxist doctrine of alienated man is founded on its canon of the separation of civil society from political society, and avers that Marx

---

[225] The reproduction is associated to the family (p. 137, n. 8) by Althusser. This is a simplification. Reproduction takes place in the apprentice hall, as well as in the factory; the place of the family is not the central one in reproduction in modern capitalist society. Marx, *Kapital*, v. I. Moore-Aveling, transl., p. 629: "The reproduction of the working class carries with it the accumulation of skill that is handed down from one generation to another." (Engels ed. New York 1937). ("Die Reproduktion der Arbeiterklasse schliesst zugleich die Ueberlieferung und Häufung des Geschicks von einer Generation zur andren ein." – *Kapital* I, op. cit., p. 573). By separating the process of reproduction of labor from the process of production in society, and by relocating it in the family, where it does not belong in modern bourgeois and socialist conditions of production, Althusser has obscured the question of the nature of the proletariat in the period following the proletarian revolution of 1917 in Russia, and the nature of the proletariat in modern society generally. Althusser is not prepared to confront the problems of the proletarian revolution, of the Party in the revolution, and the relation of society in both.

anticipated the identity of civil and political society, on which the future socialism will be based. This is a myth, according to Kolakowski; political society is the state, as opposed to civil society. Real communism, accordingly, appears in totalitarian form, i.e., as political society, replacing all crystallizations of civil society by the coercive organs of the state. The destruction of civil society therefore leads to the unbridling of political society and the unleashing of the coercive force of the state. He ends up as the defender of pluralism: the protection of the private sphere is the promulgation of civil society; the minimum of administration of things is opposed to ownership by one body of everything.[226]

Kolakowski's past is present: The condition of socialist Poland is socialist in the matter of juridical form. That juridical form rests on the interested tenet that ownership of property is the determinant of the mode of production, a tenet which is fundamental in the Soviet ideology. It is in the interest of the ruling class to advance that tenet, and to substitute the form of socialism for its content; on this Jacek Kuron and Karol Modzelewski are clear.[227] Kolakowski begins with the same elements of doctrine as Althusser, but goes in a different direction. His critique is not directed to socialism but to the abstraction, man. Both Althusser and Kolakowski begin with the separation of political and civil society, the form of repression in its relation to the content of economic reproduction and exploitation. Neither has brought the two sides together; in neither case is the determination of the form of repression by the content of production, reproduction and exploitation expressed. Althusser rediscovers in theory what Emile Durkheim had introduced in practice, namely, the replacement of the church by the school as the vindicator of the public social morality.[228] What Althusser fails to do is to trace the changes in production and reproduction in society which underlie the changes in these superstructural relations. Plainly, big capital in France, which established itself in power not at the beginning but at the end of the nineteenth century, found the church an impliable instrument for the training of the increasingly skilled army of labor in the industrial development of the country, whereas the civil schools were more suitable to its purpose. Durkheim was a willing framer of the educational policy of the separation of church and state. The difference in the French

---

[226] L. Kolakowski, in: L. Kolakowski and S. Hampshire, *The Socialist Idea*. London 1974, p. 21. Back to Adam Smith.

[227] J. Kuron and K. Modzelewski, An Open Letter to the Party. *New Politics*, v. V. 1966, no. 2, pp. 6-46; no. 3, pp. 72-[99]. French transl., 3rd ed. Paris, 1969: *Lettre au parti ouvrier polonais.*

[228] Althusser, op. cit., p. 149.

bourgeoisie is traced in the contrast between the representation of the bourgeoisie by Fourier, Cabet, and Pecqueur on the one hand, by Marx in *Capital* on the other. The structural method of Althusser has opposed and suppressed the historical factor in the relations of civil society.

Kolakowski and Althusser both regard civil society as the private sphere; more than that, it is the countervailing influence against the excesses of political society. In both political society is personified in the organs of coercion, being the public sphere endowed with a will and consciousness of its own. Lacking a materialist interpretation of socialism, they have each a view of history that hypostasizes the state. Their common aim and method is the criticism not of capitalism and socialism but of the state. On the one side, Althusser begins with the axiom that the era of capitalism is ended and that the critique of the party of Lenin must be begun. He has not gone so far as to express the axiom clearly, still less to spell it out in practical measures. But he has taken the first effort in formulation, and that is no small matter, costing great mental pain and toil. Kolakowski on the other side, begins with the axiom that the materialist explanation of Stalin, as of socialism, is nonsense, that the political explanation of the deformation by tyranny of socialism is sufficient, that the absence of the safeguards of the private sphere, of civil society are all that is required to account for Stalin. What is lacking, he says, is the control of the public sphere. This is a devil's theory; wicked men, avid for power, have taken control of the state for their own ends, manipulating the whole of society from above down. Althusser applies the materialist explanation, but he does not bring it into close connection with the economic relations in Russian or French society. His problem is not that of the categories in their relations in society, it is that of their abstract expression. He has detected the nature of the problem he is to deal with, but permits himself to be seduced by his own brilliancy. The party is in power in the Soviet Union; as the representative of the ruling class, it controls the production and expansion of capital in society, the separation of surplus value from the immediate producers. The proletariat is exploited in all the societies in which capital is produced. Objectively it is exploited through the production of a social surplus; the manifestations of its struggle against this exploitation are both objective and subjective.

What Althusser has begun in a hesitant, contradictory way is the critique of the Communist Party of France, next, of the Communist Party system. The step now to be taken is the critique of the political economy and civil society in which the Communist Party of the Soviet is comprehended.

If Althusser faces unwillingly forward, Kolakowski faces uncompromisingly back; his socialist passion properly bears the name of economism. He writes, "I believe that socialist thinking which is centered on its traditional topics (how to ensure for the working society more equality, more security, more welfare, more justice, more freedom, more participation in economic decision) cannot at the same time be infatuated with prospects of the perfect unity of social life." [229] These traditional topics are nothing other than those of the revisionists, The Worker's Cause, around the years 1900-1902. Morally these aims are unexceptionable. Who is not for more justice, equality? They are the topics, by now tradition, of Tories, Christian Democrats, Republicans of the Nelson Rockefeller variety. The Volkswagen management is not contesting the theoretical issue of sharing control of economic decisions with the trade union, the question is rather the practical one, how much? Kolakowski agrees that Bernstein's idea of revision is all that is left of socialism that is acceptable, for human nature is imperfect. The imperfection of socialism follows. By separating the issues of civil and political society Kolakowski makes the despotism of bureaucracy, the tyranny of power, political control by the state one with the utopian kernel of Marxism which has led to these horrors.

Let us rip out the twentieth century, the Russian Revolution, Stalinism; they are abolished by the abolition of utopianizing Marxism. The fault lies with those who commit crimes in the name of impossible moral tenets, says Kolakowski. This is an unnatural world, governed by sin and crime, which being punished by having the appropriate label attached to it will be purged of its culpability. The repristination of the world is assured by the naming of names.

The *real* to Kolakowski is the working society, all other societies are imaginary; the dream of utopianism is counterposed by him to the real conflicts of civil society. This is again morally unexceptionable, but it is an incomplete dialectical passage. The juxtaposition of utopia and reality is dialectically to be completed by the composition of the two. What follows from the juxtaposition is not the reduction of Marxism to utopianism, for that is mere economism; what follows dialectically is the transcendance of utopianism practically. Kolakowski has identified the social content of his perspectives of culture, polity and economy, but he has failed to identify the relation of Marxism and utopianism; he believes that economism is the healthy residuum of the equation, Marxism minus utopianism. His trope of indignation is carried too far. If the operational term in his conception is the *working society* then he cannot set himself forward as the vanguard of that

---

[229] Kolakowski, op. cit., p. 34.

society. The theoreticians of the vanguard of the proletarian revolution made the assumption that the working class could not go farther than economism, if left to itself; it followed therefore that the strategy of revolution by the party of the vanguard was a complement (born of necessity) to the limited aims of the working class. Now the working class is potentially but it is not actually the entire society. "If the proletariat wins," wrote Marx, "it thereby becomes by no means the absolute side of society, for it wins only by abolishing itself and its opposite. The prolerariat as well as its conditioning antithesis, private property, thereupon disappear." "[The proletariat] cannot free itself without abolishing all inhuman living conditions of modern society, which are comprised in its situation." [230]

The working class in Marx's perspective is not the working society, for it is not a society save under the condition of socialism. The transition to that condition, according to Kolakowski, is the achievement of economism, Bersteinian revisionism. But Marx had made, unknown to Bernstein, but available to Kolakowski, if not known to him, two conditions for the transition to socialism, each dependent on the other: one, the fulfillment of the necessary material conditions; two, the breaking of the mold of the old society. [231] A new whole as social totality proceeds from the old part. The constant throughout, from old to new, from potentiality to actuality, from part to totality, is the transformation by labor and work. The new whole is the working society, whereby the totality of inhuman working conditions of modern society are abolished. Grains of these concepts in barely recognizable form are to be found in Kolakowski. The sense of the whole is lost to him, for it is at this point that he balks. He accepts not the combat with the whole but with each part: security, equality, justice, for, he says, the struggle for the whole leads to utopianism, the struggle for utopianism leads to despotism.

The working class becomes the whole by abolishing its opposite, the means of production in the hands of those who do not work with them. This is the abolition of alienation in its principal form throughout the history of the political economy. The condition of socialism is that of the working society, in which there are no idle or leisured hands, in which social labor is defined as labor of each for all others, as opposed to labor in society by some for some others. The part does not become the whole thereby; on the contrary, one whole becomes another. The

---

[230] Marx, *Heilige Familie*. Karl Marx, Friedrich Engels, *Historisch-Kritische Gesamtausgabe* (MEGA), I, 3, pp. 206f.
[231] Marx, *Grundrisse*, op. cit., p. 77.

whole in theory becomes the whole in practice.[232] But the practice
is not conceived as such; it is consciously falsified by an interest that is
contrary to the whole.[233] Kolakowski is a holist and utopianist. Whatever may be the motives he has for turning his back on the argument
that he represents as utopian, the end result is the same: the socialist
tradition remains what it was before his attack. Before and after,
socialism seeks what he admits that it seeks. Some of the terms of the
quest that he has agreed to are holistic: equality, justice, freedom.
They are impartible, as any American trade union with Jim Crow locals
can prove. Security and welfare on the other hand are quantities,
material, and therefore partible. The qualitative and the quantitative
goals are mutually dependent and mutually supportive; without the
indivisible goals, no divisible ones, and conversely, without the divisible
goals, the immaterial ones are beyond reach.

The point is not to try conclusions with L. Kolakowski. The point
is that the socialist tradition is critically opposed to the social whole
which it seeks to overcome and to the social whole which it constitutes
thereby. Stubbing one's toe does not disprove Bishop Berkeley; we must
first agree that the frame of reference of the act and its interpretation
are the same to both sides. Kolakowski's criticism then becomes a
cavil. Despotism has arisen in the name of socialism. Socialists are
jailed in the Soviet Union for advocating socialism. But this unjust
incarceration is not the result of the inefficacy of the socialist dream.
The injustice arises from a material ground, the past condition of
inhuman exploitation and poverty in Russia, a condition not yet
overcome. It likewise results from the failure of the world revolution
in the 1920s, and the concomitant and resultant capitalist encirclement.
The history of material conditions are the grounds in which are to be
sought the ensuing formality of socialism, the unsocialist socialism of
the USSR. The contradiction of utopianism which Kolakowski has
extravasated is nothing other than the fallacy of misplaced concrete-
ness.

[232] Society is at once a whole and it is not a whole. In its form as civil society it is a mutually
divided and antagonistic whole. Georg Lukács, *Geschichte und Klassenbewusstseein*, Berlin 1923,
took up the question of society as concrete totality (see the chapter, Klassenbewusstsein, pp.
61f.). In the well-known chapter of the same work, Reification and Proletarian Consciousness,
he examined reification as a whole. This is the thesis, to which the antithesis is: If reification
is a whole, it is an internally antagonistic one, just as is civil society. (Krader, *Ethnologie und
Anthropologie bei Marx*, op. cit., ch. 3).
[233] The interest is that of property in its various forms, whether private or public. Where there
is either there is opposition between the two; there is civil society. The forms of property, however, do not constitute the driving force of history, they are the container in which the driving
force is enfolded. The driving force itself is the relation of the social classes to each other:
history is the history of class struggles.

Jürgen Habermas has juxtaposed primitive social forms, with tribal organization and kinship status, on the one side, to societies with social-economic classes, centralized organization and state power on the other. The latter are civilizations, with technological development and social division of labor as their basis. The category of civilization in the philosophy and sociology of Habermas is coterminous with that of civil society to that extent.[234] The classification of societies is not his ultimate concern, it is a means to something else. "Capitalism," writes Habermas, "is the first mode of production in world history to institutionalize self-sustaining economic growth.[235] It has generated an industrial system that could be freed from the institutional framework of capitalism and connected to mechanisms other than that of the utilization of capital in private form."[236]

This is an otherworldly universe inhabited by Habermas, in which the Soviet Union does not exist. There the "could be" of Habermas is, however, made into actuality. The social production of the USSR is connected to mechanisms "other than that of the utilization of capital in private form," nor do the ideologists of the USSR speak otherwise. Habermas appears to argue that the abolition of the private form of capital in the USSR is not the abolition of the industrial system of capitalism. But the industrial system of capitalism has been abolished in the USSR precisely through the abolition of capital in private form. What has not been abolished is the industrial system of capital; one form of that system has been abolished and another substituted. The argument put in this way yields the judgment that, without the abolition of the content of the industrial system of capital, the abolition of the form of its ownership is without significance; form and content are related. The historical frame of reference in this case is the abolition of the particular form of political economy and civil society, which is the category arching over modern capitalism and modern socialism.[237]

It is possible to restate Habermas' problem as the relation between the production of capital on the one side, and capitalism on the other. On the one hand it is the relation of the political economy, civil society

---

[234] Jürgen Habermas, *Technologie und Wissenschaft als 'Ideologie'*. Suhrkamp 1968. "Civil society" is to Habermas an old-fashioned term, of historic interest only, which appears in his account of Hegel and the French Revolution. See his book, *Theorie und Praxis*. Luchterhand 1967. Our concern is not with the terms but with what they indicate, and the critique that may be produced by their application. Habermas, however, uses "critique", "critical", in a different sense. See his *Erkenntnis und Interesse*. Suhrkamp 1968.

[235] That is summed up in the term *Verwertung*, which has the operation of the extraction of a social surplus attached to it in the system of Marx.

[236] Habermas, *Technik und Wissenschaft*, op. cit. (*Toward a Rational Society*. J. Shapiro, transl. Boston 1971, p. 96.)

and the state, the relation which arches over the USSR, the United States, West Germany and Japan, since all have the production of capital in common; on the other hand it is the relation of civil society as bourgeois society in the United States, West Germany and Japan, as countries of capitalism. The approach to the same problem by Kolakowski has made this restatement unmanageable. His is a political solution, and he sees no relation between economy and society in the USSR. Civil society there is reduced by him to the political form of society, political society. On the contrary, the form of civil society is determined, just as it is under capitalism, by the organization of production in the USSR; here a relatively high degree of the organization of production has been achieved, when compared with other countries' organization. But unlike the United States or West Germany, in which the high degree of the social organization of production is connected to a high degree of diversification, the organization of production in the USSR, high though it is, is connected to a diversification which is relatively low, when compared to that of the United States. The two sides of this contradiction are not unrelated. In the United States and West Germany, production in society is highly diversified because it is highly organized, whereas in the USSR, on the contrary, social production is comparatively little diversified because it is highly organized. The form of civil society is given public political expression as the state in modern capitalism as in modern socialism. The form of the state may differ on either side. The prepotency of the political form of civil society in the USSR is a surface phenomenon; there, as in the capitalist lands, civil society has the political form of the state. Civil society everywhere comprises both the public and the private spheres of social life, arching over the form and content of the former. Sleight of hand cannot reduce the entirety of civil society in the USSR or anywhere else to the political side alone.

The relation of the substructure to the superstructure in the society of capitalist production and of the production of capital generally has been falsely put by Habermas. The reason for his mishandling of the

---

[237] The matter is central to our discussion: the system of capitalism has been abolished in the USSR, the ownership of the means of production in private hands having all but disappeared. The political economy has not disappeared in the USSR; on the contrary, there is no system of political economy, with the possible exception of the United States, which exerts a greater influence internally and externally at present. The Soviet Union is one of the main systems of the production of capital in the world today. The civil society, which is the organization of the political economy of capital production is highly developed in the Soviet Union. In relative terms it is no less highly developed than the civil society of any other country in the world at present, although it is not as diversified as the organization of production of the United States or West Germany.

relation of social production to the juridical form of ownership of the same, or the matter of ownership of the means of social production, need not detain us. The end result is that he has not thought or fought this problem through to the point that others have. Althusser has to this extent gone beyond him, for, wherever his tenuous, exiguous, tentative critique may lead, nevertheless we can detect that here, however much less forthright it is than that of Gramsci, his great forerunner, the critique from within has begun. The passage from theory to praxis of this critique takes its infant step, already its echoes are heard in Spain. To the sounds of this passage the ears of Kolakowski and Habermas are closed, as Pushkin sadly wrote of his anti-hero, Eugene. They live in a world of hypostatic structure where lie the unmoved movers, the world of Platonic ideas, in the translunar, extrahistorical sphere. This Althusser has mistaken for his own. But the error of Althusser does not lie in the direction of his praxis, it lies in the direction of his thought, more exactly, in its expression. The unmoving structures of Kolakowski and Habermas are the social categories whose dialectical moments they fail to grasp. Hence they are bound in theory as they are worlds removed from practice. With Althusser it is other. The social categories of the critique of the PCF or the PCI are not seen by him as dialectical moments, which is what they are really are. He has fetishized these historical moments by translating them into the hypostatic structures of overdetermination and the rest. But his error is at once more interesting and actual, hence more profound, than that of the others mentioned: he foreshadows in practice that for which he has failed to find the theoretical expression. Because the social-historical movements in Italy and France have not yet come to the point of inner practical critique, the expression in theory thereof is yet to be found, hence it is jejune.[238]

---

[238] The leadership in this direction is taken by the south European parties, both of communism and socialism, roughly, Italy, Spain, France. Here the development of capital, as of capitalism is less advanced, less strong, than it is in West Germany, which, in the system of the European Market has profited from the relation of strength and weakness. The capitalist class in West Germany has played on the loyalty of the working class in that country to internationalism, to the greater goals beyond the nation-state, as it has on the false consciousness of the enmity of the East. But it has overreached itself. The Christian Democrats and the right-wing of the Free Democrats have waved the banner nationalism, hatred of Poland, fear of the Russians. Trivial tactical victories in Lower Saxony and the Saar by the CDU and FDP disclose no more than that the consciousness among German working class of the European slogan is false. (Berlin, February 1976.)

AGRARIAN COMMUNISM

I. The History of a Controversy
II. Mark, Mir and Zadruga
III. Community and the State in Civil Society

TWO

AGRARIAN COMMUNISM

I. HISTORY OF THE CONTROVERSY

The theory of agrarian communism is widely held and widely disputed. At the basis of the theory is the premiss that the tillers of the soil in primitive societies and in the early periods of civil society held their land in common; the social unit that held the land in common was bound together by ties of kinship or proximal residence, or both. The form of this social unit was a village, or kin-village, gens, sib, clan, phratry, tribe. The landholding here took the form of ownership by the social unit as a whole; individual and family relations to the soil were in the form of possession, which is distinct from property, whether common or individual.[1] This body of practices, according to the theory of agrarian communism, is found both in ancient and modern times; it did not withstand the extension of the systems of slavery and latifundia in ancient Greece and Rome, and of dominion over the land by feudal lords in medieval Europe. Opposed to this theory is that of early landholding in severalty, or the projection of modern landholding practices on to the earliest historical records. The controversy that has thereby arisen, in academic circles, has been discussed as a rule in isolation, excluding any question other than that of the form of property itself; but such an approach is fallacious, for the question of early landholding is connected to the theories of society, social history and evolution; further, it is related to theories

---

[1] Property is distinct from possession and simple occupancy. Landholding and land tenure are used indifferently, likewise ownership and property. Tenure of land by individuals and by families in any form is counterposed to tenure by other holders. Collective and common holding are related but are not the same, the unit of the collectivity being more general and more variable than the unit of the community; communal holding, commonalty stand in the same relation to collective holding. The collectivity includes the community, the kin village community, gens, etc., but not the family. Our discussion will deal chiefly with the European peoples, in particular, the Germanic and Slavic. On ownership as opposed to possession in the ancient agrarian communes, cf. Lawrence Krader, *The Asiatic Mode of Production*. Assen, 1975. Introduction, Part I (ch. IV), and Part II (passim, containing notes by Karl Marx to M. M. Kovalevsky, *Obščinnoe Zemlevladenie*. Moscow, 1879).

of human nature. Theory and practice of agrarian communism are a part of the social and political struggles of the past century as well as of their scientific and philosophical reflection. It has frequently happened that those involved in the struggle, in particular, those who called the theory of agrarian communism in question, have purported to argue on scientific grounds alone; but this has made their argument no less politically intentioned, even if secretly so.

The idea that agrarian communal life was at the foundation of European history was given a distinctive historical form in Napoleonic and Restoration Europe[2]; this form, born of revolution and counter-revolution, was reworked a generation later.[3] The literature on agrarian communism was studied closely by Karl Marx and Friedrich Engels, and became part of the socialist doctrine.[4] It was attacked by Fustel

---

[2] The practice of collective landholding was discovered or propounded in reference to different parts of the world by European writers in the sixteenth century, that is, soon after the beginning of the Age of Discovery. It was given new impetus, however, when it was expounded simultaneously and independently in different parts of Europe early in the nineteenth century. See C. A. van Enschut, *Over de Bevoegdheid der Markgenootschappen*. Groningen, 1818. Vuk S. Karadžić, *Srpski Rječnik*. Wien, 1818. J. Csaplowics, *Slavonien und zum Theil Croatien*. Pesth, 1819. Karadžić in the first edition of his dictionary limited himself to translation of the term *zadruga* as "Hausgenossenschaft", "plures familiae (more Serbico)". Zadruga and Hausgenossenschaft are not, however, plures familiae. The problem of the zadruga raised thereby was resolved by Karadžić in his subsequent work on his dictionary through the detail given in ethnographic examples added to the original entry: – vide his subsequent edition of 1852 and the posthumous ed. 1898, (date of Introduction to 3rd ed.) and subsequent reprintings. The Latin term is ignored; the equation of the Serbian and German usages remains as his lasting contribution. Cf. also the collection, Vuk Stefanović Karadžić, *Etnografski Spisi*. Beograd, 1964, p. 480. No significance is attached to the variations, Hauskommunion, Hausgemeinschaft, Hausgenossenschaft, house or family community, etc. in this context.

[3] Georg Hanssen, *Agrarhistorische Abhandlungen* (1835, 1837), I, 1880. August v. Haxthausen, *Studien über die inneren Zustände, das Volksleben und insbesonderen die ländlichen Einrichtungen Russlands*, 3. v. Hanover,1847-1852. Georg Ludwig v. Maurer, *Einleitung zur Geschichte der Mark-Hof-, Dorf- und Stadtverfassung*. Munich, 1854. The work of van Enschut, Hanssen and Maurer took up the Germanic past, that of Karadžić, Csaplowics and Haxthausen the Slavic.

[4] See *The Ethnological Notebooks of Karl Marx*. 2nd ed. Assen, 1974. Lawrence Krader, ed,, Introd., pp. 58-76 and 377-386. The agrarian commune in European history held landed property in common; Marx recalled that his father had talked about the ancient Germanic survival in the vicinity of his native Trier, on the Hunsrück, until shortly before the young Marx's time. (Marx, letter of March 25, 1868. Karl Marx and Friedrich Engels, *Selected Correspondence*, Moscow, 1965, p. 201.) Marx's father died in 1838; this communal system did not survive the French invasion of the Rhine and the Napoleonic wars. The Russian peasant commune, wrote Marx in a draft of a letter to Vera Zasulič, finds the system of capital in a crisis that will only end by the elimination of the latter, by the return of modern societies to the "archaic type of landed property"; "the new system" toward which the modern society tends," said Marx, "will be a revival in a superior form of an archaic social type." *Marx-Engels Archiv*, Bd. I, 1926, pp. 339f. Cf. *Ethnological Notebooks*, p. 139.

de Coulanges, Max Weber, G. v. Below, and A. Dopsch.[5] But behind their attack on this theory lay something more.

The conflict over agrarian communism concerned an original communism by cultivators of the soil in Europe, calling into question the practice of holding in common what was not the individual's or the family's. At issue was the land, the form of holding of the homestead and garden plots, arable, pasture, paths and ways, forest, waste and livestock. Two questions were excluded: 1. Water resources as they had been introduced in the study of Asia, and the Asiatic mode of production did not enter this debate. In European history, generally, water, particularly flowing water, was regarded as an enemy to be fended off at will.[6] The traditional European riparian right was less concerned in this case with water for agricultural purposes than with water for purposes of transportation and boundary demarcation. 2. The theory of agrarian communism leads to questions of the holding of hunting grounds, fishing banks, land for collecting of wild plants, by primitive hunting and gathering peoples; these questions and the related one of the longhouse or the bohio, land of the entire clan, are relevant to the issues raised, but they were not discussed. Fustel de

---

[5] N. D. Fustel de Coulanges, *La Cité Antique*. Paris, 1864. Id. Le problème des origines de la propriété foncière. *Revue des Questions historiques*, v. 45, 1889 (Repr. Id. *Questions historiques*. Paris, 1893). Id. *Recherches sur quelques problèmes d'histoire*. Paris, 1885. Max Weber, Der Streit um den Charakter der Altgermanischen Sozialverfassung. *Jahrbücher für Nationalökonomie und Statistik*. III. Folge. 28. Band, 1904. (Repr. *Gesammelte Aufsätze zur Sozial- und Wirtschaftsgeschichte*, Tübingen, 1924).
Id. *Wirtschaftsgeschichte*. 3rd ed. Berlin, 1958. Ch. 1. Id. *Wirtschaft und Gesellschaft*, 5th ed. Tübingen, 1972.
Georg v. Below, Territorium und Stadt. *Historische Bibliothek*, v. 11, 1900. Id. Das kurze Leben einer vielgenannten Theorie. *Probleme der Wirtschaftsgeschichte* (1920) 2nd ed. Tübingen, 1926. (*Allgemeine Zeitung*, Munich, 1903, no. 11, 12. Beilage).
Alfons Dopsch, *Die wirtschaftlichen und sozialen Grundlagen der europäischen Kulturentwicklung*. 2 v. Wien, 1923-1924, v. 1, ch. 1 and 2.
Carl Stephenson, The Common Man in Early Medieval Europe. *American Historical Review*, v. 51, 1946, followed Dopsch, et al. Cf. R. Koebner in *Cambridge Economic History*, Cambridge, 1966, M. Postan, ed.

[6] The form of this legal fixed phrase is usually "Flowing water is a common enemy, to be fended off at will." It is discussed in my article, The Environmental Threat and Social Organization, *The Annals of the American Academy of Political and Social Science*, v. 389, 1970. The dialectic of private ownership of land in European history, which is at issue here, makes the word "common" into the opposite of itself: A drives off the water as he would a stray cow from his land; it becomes B's enemy. They do not share the water driven off, nor do they share the problem that it raises, save by a voluntary and limited undertaking, for they do not customarily meet such problems by common action in modern European history. Water is controlled by government agencies, or by some like authority, as the Bishop of Ely, who caused fenland to be drained. Water is a common enemy in the eye of the legal philosopher, who can regard its problems with equanimity, externally; abstractly it is a common problem, concretely an individual one, in Europe.

Coulanges limited himself to the questions of ancient land tenure in Graeco-Roman, Germanic and French history. The others mentioned constrained themselves in a similar way. The restriction on the field of inquiry is not called into question, but Fustel de Coulanges supported his viewpoint through appeal to religious and family factors in history, Weber by appeal to political and religious factors. It is the theory of socialism that is called into question, and on two grounds as then propounded: First, the economic interpretation of history; second, individualism versus communism. As to the economic interpretation, it was simplified; Marx made precise that the economic relation is not that of tenure of land, a formal-legal aspect of the economic factor in history. In the conflict over the theory of agrarian communism, the further question raised was that of individualism and individuality versus community of landholding; this will be our main concern. It was then maintained that no good case has been made out for the holding of land in common by early European cultivators of the soil. From this it would follow that a future communism of an archaic type, such as certain of the utopian socialists had advocated, or of a higher type, such as Marx and Engels proposed, was against human nature, alternatively against the grain of European history, against the nature of homo Europaeicus. Weber went further than the others in expounding his position, but neither he nor the others mentioned stated the case fully, in its implications for social politics, social philosophy and social evolution. Evolution and evolutionism are called into question by Weber; his alternative for the analysis of social history was anti-evolutionary and anti-communist. The discussion which has followed Weber's indications in regard to scientific objectivity and anti-communism has not improved on his positions.

Emile Durkheim advanced an alternative sociological explanation of agrarian communism in connection with the evolutionary doctrine. His explanation of agrarian communism was directed at the same time to a generalized collectivism, which was conceived as a holism. Durkheim sought a generalized relation to social ends which he shared with the socialists. For this reason his underlying theory, which is only in part made explicit by him, is here characterized as collectivist, whereby his own doctrine is related to the general stock of ideas of the socialists, utopian and Marxist. This linkage remains on the level of theory, not of practice.

The examination of agrarian communism had a negative result: The existence of agrarian communist institutions in Europe in the nineteenth century had to be accounted for. The opponents of an Urkommunismus attributed the historical phenomenon of agrarian communism to fiscal and feudal practices, removing social evolutionary significance from it. For this reason, the Russian agrarian communal institutions were separated from the South Slavic and Indic definitively within Weber's system, but partially and unclearly by Durkheim. The three traditional institutions had been integrated into a single evolutionary system by Sir Henry Maine. There are two further movements relative to their separation: the South Slavic and Indic practices were related to family holdings in common; thus, the position of Marx, which had distinguished family from other types of holdings in common, is to be separated from the position which combines them. Further, the East Slavic and South Slavic practices of landholding in common, as they were maintained in the nineteenth century, are to be distinguished from each other.

As an alternative to a communist explanation of the phenomena is an individualist. The doctrine of individualism leads to the conception of the individual human being as the end and goal of history. The counterposition of the agrarian commune in history to the individual in history is connected to the individualist theory of history, the ideology of capitalism, and to the 'great man' theory of history, which is the caricature of both. This last was brought out by participants in the debate over agrarian communism, Henry Maine on the one side, and opposed by L. H. Morgan, on the other; it has a bearing therefore on the more general questions of individualism and communism. It takes its place in the conflict of socialist and capitalist ideologies, and the theories of both. That we are faced with a conflict over the interpretation of social evolution, history, theory and politics which goes beyond the academic limits of these is clear. The ideology of the collectivity is opposed to the ideology of the individuality; the latter has been developed by Thomas Hobbes, Thomas Carlyle, Herbert Spencer, and most recently, by Sidney Hook.

The theory of the individuality has a spurious unity. It is a mixture of different tenets and standpoints that bring together Hobbes, Carlyle, Max Stirner, Fustel de Coulanges, Maine, Weber, Vilfredo Pareto, Hook into one internally oppositive camp. We will see how the different lines of this theory come together and part. They have no unity save that which is lent to them by their various services in the support, historically, of capitalism. They form a theory of mankind, but it is one-sided, as that of Kant, bringing out only the individual aspect of humanity, leaving out the collective. The theory of the individuality which is here brought out is as various as capitalism itself; the latter is at once a body of practices of political economy, a theory of the same, a social formation, and an ideology relative to all the foregoing. The ideology of capitalism has, in one of its components, the ideology of individuality; these were given expression in the sixteenth century, in the earliest period of the capitalist formation. These various components of theory and ideology serve as background for the understanding of the debate over agrarian communism.

Max Weber's philosophy of history is nowhere made so clear as it is in his writings on an original or early historical group versus individual landholding. For here he made his determination of the weight of the different historical factors, economic, political and religious. "To place landlordship at the spearhead of the history of social development is as dubious for the Germanic peoples as for the peoples of antiquity. Also, for the latter, the theory of landlordship is overplayed." Weber continued to a second point: "The oldest social differentiation in Germanic as in Mediterranean prehistory is, as far as we can see, primarily political and in part religious, but not primarily economically determined. The economic differentiation must in any case be understood as the consequence and epiphenomenon, or, if one wishes to be ultramodern, as the 'function' of the first two rather than the opposite."[7] Weber raised a third point, his antipathy to the theory of stages of development of culture, a theory which he found in writings by W. Wittich and R. Hildebrand: This theory, said Weber, is one of the numerous attempts to apprehend cultural development according to a kind of biological process, as a regular sequence of different 'culture stages' which are universally repeated."[8] Weber naively believed that landlordship, Grundherrschaft, is the economic factor. On the contrary: Landlordship is a form, an abstraction of an economic relation itself. To place the political, and therewith the religious factors, as the preeminent ones therefore, is

---

[7] Weber, Der Streit, op. cit., p. 469. H. H. Gerth and C. W. Mills, Introduction to Weber, *Essays in Sociology*. New York, 1946. H. Albert, in: *Werturteilstreit*. H. Albert and E. Topitsch, ed. Darmstadt, 1971, pp. 200-236. It is held by his supporters, Gerth and Mills, that in Weber's position, neither religion nor economics alone is the motor of history; thus, Weber is made out to be more balanced than Marx. This is fallacious. Albert defends Weber against the attack by Leo Strauss, *Natural Right and History*, Chicago, 1953, who asserted that Weber's theory is individualist. Strauss is accused by Albert of an "unanalyzed essentialism and value objectivity." But Albert does not meet Strauss's objections to Weber. The positions of Weber and of Fustel de Coulanges overlap in two regards: the religious factor and the individualist thesis of landholding. Weber, Below, Fustel de Coulanges have all adopted a doctrine of individualism with reference to the constitution of human society and human being; they have likewise adopted, in their methodology, an individualist approach to social history, in which only the individual fact is real. The two individualisms, the constitutive and the methodological, are connected.

[8] Weber, op. cit., p. 437.

all the easier if the economic is thus reduced to a mere form or abstraction.

Weber later drew a schematic picture of an old German village,[9] composed of five concentric rings. The innermost ring contains the peasant homesteads; the second, the fenced-in garden plots; the third, the arable; the fourth, the pasture (Almende). "Each household has the right to drive the same amount of livestock to the pasture; it is not, moreover, communistic, but is appropriated according to fixed shares." The same is the case in ring five, forest; here the right to cut wood, litter, bed straw, mast is shared equally among the village inhabitants. "House, dwelling plot, individual shares in garden land, arable land, common pasture and forest are together called *hide* (Germ. *Hufe*, etymologically related to have, having)." "The hide was appropriated by the individual, and was indeed inheritable." The arable was divided into shares, these into strips. Although the size of the hide was variable, frequently the normal amount was as much land as a normal family could sustain itself with. The unit of measurement was the size of a strip of land that a plough ox could turn in a day without tiring; this is the "Morgen", "Tagwerk", or day's work. The normal family hide was 40 Tagwerk in size; the house sheltered a small family of parents, children, sometimes also grown sons. The village is a kind of association; an association of several villages is a Markgenossenschaft.[10] This latter appropriated the common mark, which included forest and wasteland, and is distinct from the common pasture. "The origin and earliest form of this 'Markgenossenschaft' are dark, but they are older than the political

---

[9] Weber, *Wirtschaftsgeschichte*, pp. 19 sq.

[10] Ibid., p. 24. Weber applied a theory of the village association in his ideal picture of the early Germanic agrarian organization in historical times. The hidemen formed a community, who appropriated jointly the land to be brought under the plough, over and above the shares of the arable which was individually appropriated. The community in question was formed only by the village members with full rights. Only those who had some possession in each of the three divisions of the land were such full members, or hidemen. The common mark, which comprised forest and waste, was appropriated not by the village association but by a still larger association, composed of several villages. Cf. Weber, *Wirtschaft und Gesellschaft*, op. cit., pp. 220, 431 sq. The thesis of a prehistoric clan organization, together with landholding in ancient Italy had been advanced by Weber, however, in keeping with the views of Theodor Mommsen (*Römische Geschichte*, vol. 1, 6th ed. Berlin, 1874). But while Mommsen did not distinguish clearly between Gemeinschaft and Genossenschaft, Weber did in *Die Römische Agrargeschichte*, Stuttgart, 1891, pp. 81 sq., p. 125: The Italic was an associational (genossenschaftlich), rather than a clan settlement; the essentially economically organized association succeeded the clan organization "as among most nations of whose most ancient organization we are informed". This comes close to a Stufentheorie, which he later denounced. On Mommsen's relation to Weber see Marianne Weber, *Max Weber, Ein Lebensbild*. Tübingen, 1926; J. P. Mayer, *Max Weber and German Politics*, 2nd. ed., London, 1956.

division of the Carolingians, and are likewise different from the hundred." In principle and in origin the agrarian system was here dominated by strict equality among its members. Other village inhabitants were without hides: younger sons, craftsmen, and other hands "who stood outside the Verband of the hide members." A distinction arose between the peasants (hidemen) and another class of village inhabitants. "The latter belong to the village only through their ownership of a house, but have no share in the arable; yet they could acquire a share if a peasant, with the agreement of the village head or its landlord (Grundherr, which was originally the kin group, Sippe) sold them a part of his share in the arable, or if a part of the common pasture was let to them. Such parcels were no longer submitted to the special obligations of hide possession and of the jurisdiction of the lower court and were freely alienable; on the other hand, their occupants had no share in the rights of the full hidemen." The peasant population was divided into two, according to the mode of land possession, hidemen on one side, those outside the hide association on the other. "But above the full hidemen there was formed a special grade of possession which, with its pieces of land, also stood outside the hide association. This grade was the *Bifang*, which acquired the land at the origins of the Germanic system so long as there was a surplus, which they cleared and fenced. Otherwise it belonged to the common mark." This *Bifang* (from *fangen*, 'grasp', 'seize') presupposed cattle and slaves, and was possible as a rule only for princes and landlords.[11] Weber's ultimate formulation does not reveal the

---

[11] Here ends Weber's general description. The different forms of land in the five categories are held as possession (Besitz) by the members of the village or the village association. The house, but not its site, is property (Eigentum) of non-hidemen *Wirtschaftsgeschichte*, (p. 25). On the other hand, the king or landlord took over (angeeignet) the office of Mark overseer, also the wood-court of law (p. 24). The hide, the homestead and gardenland and the share in the arable were appropriated (appropriirt) by the individual. The community of hidemen appropriated the rest of the arable. The Markgenossenschaft appropriated the common Mark. But cf. common landholding by the Markgenossen in: G. L. v. Maurer, *Einleitung zur Geschichte der Markverfassung*, op. cit., p. 184ff. Id. *Geschichte der Markenverfassung in Deutschland*, Erlangen, 1856, p. 163-166. Karl Müllenhof, *Die Germania des Tacitus*. Berlin, 1900, p. 365. Cf. p. 371f: Müllenhof wrote, "We find community of possession of field and arable in the primitive condition of all peoples", in Germany (Trier, Ditmarschen) down to recent times. (Repr. Amsterdam, 1970). See Rudolf Much, *Die Germania des Tacitus*. Herbert Jahnkuhn, Wolfgang Lange, ed. Heidelberg, 1967, p. 338: "Das die Aufteilung der Äcker, von der die Rede war (i.e. Tacitus on the ancient Germans), nicht sogleich zu vollständigem Sondereigentum führte, liegt an der unentwickelten Art des Ackerbaus." If the division of the fields did not lead "sogleich" to complete ownership in severalty, then this last conception lies closer to that of Maurer and Müllenhof than that of Weber, Below, etc. Heinrich Cunow, in issuing the 2nd ed. of Maurer, *Einleitung zur Geschichte der Markverfassung* in 1896, lists G. L. v. Maurer, F. C. Dahlmann, Wilhelm Roscher, F. W. K. v. Thudichum, H. v. Sybel, Georg Hansen und Karl Lamprecht on

premisses of his thinking on agrarian commonalty or individuality of landholding. His thinking here is opaque; his system was carried over, in outline, into his other writings without revealing their further intentions. Therefore the polemical article mentioned above is all the more important, both for what it reveals, and, as we shall see, what it does not.[12]

Max Weber set forth his opposition to an original agrarian communism, and hence to an original agrarian commune. The conflict over the character of the ancient Germanic social system had been made, in the last decades of the nineteenth century, a matter of landlordship. The period between Tacitus and the Carolingians had comprised the establishment of distinctions of classes of landlords and peasants.[13] Weber offered in evidence his reading of Caesar and Tacitus, in opposition to the interpretation of ancient Germanic life by those who saw in it the communistic practices of freedom and equality.[14] Caesar wrote, "neque quisquam agri modum certum aut fines habet proprios, sed magistratus ac principes in annos singulos gentibus cognationibus que hominum, qui una coierunt, quantum et quo loro visum est agri attribuunt atque anno post alio transire cogunt." ("None of them" – i.e., the Germans – "has a particular piece of land as his own; the magistrates and chiefs allot to the gentes and kin groups who join together determining how much land will be allotted to them and where it will be located, and the year after cause them to relocate elsewhere.") Weber objects to those who find that this passage "should point to 'strict field-community' with communistic tillage." "In any case it may be remarked", continued Weber, "that the indication of agrarian communism is not

---

the side of the agrarian communism of the ancient Germans, Justus Möser, Georg Waitz, Jakob Grimm, E. M. Arndt, K. F. Eichhorn and Landau on the opposed side. (Einleitendes Vorwort. 3rd ed., K. Dickopf, ed., Aalen 1966, p. 358) Dickopf, ibid., p. 396, adds to the list of Maurer's heirs and advocates R. Schröder, H. Brunner, K. v. Amira, Cl. v. Schwerin, H. Conrad, K. v. Inama-Sternegg, R. Kötschke, G. Philippovic, A. H. Post and J. Kohler. The list can be extended. An early contributor was the Danish expert Olufsen, *Bidrag til Oplysning om Danmarks indvortes Fortfatning i de aeldre Tider, isaer i det trettende Aarhundrede.* Kopenhagen 1821. (*Neues staatsbürgerliches Magazin*, III, pp. 77 - 126. ed. Falck).

[12] Weber, *Wirtschaft und Gesellschaft*, op. cit., p. 83, wrote of the agrarian commune (Feldgemeinschaft) as the result of burdens imposed by the landlord or political lord on the peasant community (Gemeinde): the landlord or fiscal agrarian commune (grundherrliche oder fiskalische Feldgemeinschaft). On the other hand the house-commune (Hausgemeinschaft) and house-communism are connected with each other; Weber excluded the employment of the term 'communism' in connection with the agrarian commune (p. 214; generally, pp. 212-222). See also his *Rechtssoziologie*, J. Winckelmann, ed. Luchterhand, 1967.

[13] Weber, Der Streit, op. cit., pp. 433-435 and passim.

[14] Ibid., pp. 436f., 441-463.

absolutely enjoined."[15] This is not the language of a fair-minded man; it is the language of one who is caught in a trap of debate and struggles to free himself. Weber adopted a position of anti-communism and could not make the facts adjust to the interpretation that he wished to propound.

The death of the theory of collective ownership as the original ownership of land was celebrated by Below: The true systematizer of history, he wrote, will be suspicious of the view that a broad, universal system unites the peoples, as has been suggested after jumbled comparisons. He continued: "Above all, the belief in a primitive condition of all peoples that more or less dispenses with individualities will be the object of his suspicion."[16] He attacked the comparative method in the social sciences and the evolutionary basis of national histories; these are bound to analogical arguments, such as those which Hanssen used to propound the theory of communal property in land; the error of analogical argument for the same or related purposes was committed by H. v. Sybel and G. L. v. Maurer.[17]

Rachfahl found that the eighteenth century cameralists had already proposed the idea of occupancy of the soil by individuals (Einzelhöfe) in history, and he attributed to Finanzrat Albert the discovery that the agrarian commune was an arrangement made by the landlordship of the Middle Ages.[18] Rachfahl concluded that in Germanic antiquity, as shown by the sole written source, there was no private property in land; land was the common property of the

---

[15] Caesar, *Gallic War*, Book 6, ch. 22. Weber, op. cit., p. 450. "Immerhin mag doch bemerkt werden, dass die Deutung auf Agrarkommunismus keine absolut gebotene sei." See *Ethnological Notebooks*, op. cit., pp. 240, 412f.

[16] Below, Das kurze Leben einer viel genannten Theorie, op. cit., pp. 23f.

[17] Ibid., pp. 4-6; on analogy, pp. 7f. K. Lamprecht was guilty of evolutionism. Below directed his suspicions, further, at W. Roscher, H. S. Maine, E. de Laveleye, K. Bücher, L. H. Morgan, H. Brunner, R. Schröder, R. Hildebrand, W. Wittich, F. Knapp. This is the caricature of a polemical article, but it is mentioned in passing because it had at one time a repeated circulation, and was referred to by others as being authoritative. The author scorned others for unproved assumptions concerning communal landholding. He did not stop to think that he had not proved or justified his own assumptions in any way. Making individualities alone the object of historical investigation is no less an assumption as any other. The practice of taking up each case in history by itself, as though isolated and unconnected with any other, is called systematic thought by Below. But Below's task was not to write a scientific paper; it was to compose a necrology in the form of such a paper.

[18] F. Rachfahl, Zur Geschichte des Grundeigentums. *Jahrbücher für Nationalökonomie und Statistik*. III. F. 19. Bd. 1900, pp. 1-33, 161-216. On Albert, pp. 12f.; on ownership and possession, p. 18. His article is a critique of R. Hildebrand, *Recht und Sitte auf den verschiedenen wirtschaftlichen Kulturstufen*. Jena, 1896. Teil I.

people.[19] Rachfahl shared with Hildebrand certain fundamental premisses, in particular, the stage or level theory of social-cultural evolution; according to Rachfahl, the ancient Germanic peoples were found by Caesar at the stage of lower agriculture; by the time of Tacitus they had made the transition to higher agriculture. Further, there was among them the division of labor according to sex; the men hunted and fought in war, women tilled the field.[20]

Fustel de Coulanges proposed that there were peoples who knew of no private property in land. Such were the Tartars (i.e., Turkic and Mongol nomadic pastoralists), who had private property of herds, but not of land; likewise the ancient Germans, who owned the harvest of the land, but not the land; he mentioned also a portion of the Semitic and Slavic peoples, who originally had no private property in land. On the other hand, he wrote, the peoples of ancient Greece, Italy and Israel, from the earliest times, had private property in land.[21] Fustel de Coulanges held that the ancient Germans had *both* private and communal property in land: it was not held by individuals, if we follow Caesar; it was so held, according to Tacitus; but the contradiction is resolved if we recognize the diversity of the Germanic peoples of that time, and of their customs. This was his later view, in which he concluded, "A certain co-parcenary (indivision, joint possession, Gemeinschaft des Besitzes) and several modes of ownership *pouvaient* (could have: my italics. LK) been practiced, according to whether one looked at this or that people, this or that class."[22] Still later he reviewed the various theories of agrarian communism put forth by P. Viollet, d'Arbois de Jubainville, Maurer and K. Lamprecht (concerning ancient Greeks, Gauls and Germans). Fustel de Coulanges found that none of them had proved their case, holding that the Germanic Mark and the Russian mir are relatively modern, hence

---

[19] Rachfahl, op. cit., pp. 24 and 188f. He also concluded, through Tacitus, that the ancient Germanic peoples lived in kin groups, large and small, the latter forming spatial unities. (Ibid., pp. 171f.) This depends on the translation of *propinquitas* (Tacitus, *Germania*, VII) as 'neighbor'. But it also means kin. Rachfahl is probably right, but not for this reason. See *Ethnological Notebooks*, note 111, pp. 377f.

[20] On stages, cf. Hildebrand, op. cit.; Rachfahl, p. 193; the transition was completed in Frankish times (p. 196). On division of labor by sex, Hildebrand, p. 6 (hunters); Rachfahl, p. 188. Rachfahl attributes the "discovery" of this division of labor to E. Grosse and K. v. d. Steinen; he knows nothing of Engels or of other earlier writers.

[21] Fustel de Coulanges, *La cité antique*, op. cit. livre II, ch. 6. The ancient Hebrews, like the Greeks and Romans, had private property in land; Fustel de Coulanges attributed these particularities to the religions of these peoples, and to their family life.

[22] Fustel de Coulanges, *Recherches sur quelques problèmes*, op. cit., pp. 258-294. See also his article, Les Germains connaissaient-ils la propriété des terres? *Séances et Travaux de l'Académie des Sciences Morales et Politiques*. N.s., 45, 1885. T. 123, pp. 705-776. T. 124, pp. 1-162.

that modern observations of family communal property and co-ownership of land by a village do not prove an original communal property; further, he said, co-parcenary is not communal ownership of the land if it is a domain belonging to a landlord.[23]

Dopsch argued that the life of the Germanic Suevi, as it had been observed by Caesar, was not their normal life. Their practice of communal ownership was an innovation. "Am ehesten *könnte man*, meine ich (my italics, LK): Far rather *could one*, in my opinion, speak of a 'state socialism' naturally brought about by wartime, which was adapted to its special needs." Dopsch assumed that private property in land was already in existence among the Germans in the time of Tacitus.[24] The language of Fustel de Coulanges and of Dopsch is speculative. The state socialism is put between quotation marks by Dopsch, but the appeal to wartime conditions is not.

Dopsch makes a point which he claims is derived from Wietersheim and from Weber; Weber had written that "the indication of agrarian communism is not absolutely enjoined." Wietersheim is reported to have preceded Weber and Dopsch in this matter.[25] But Wietersheim said nothing like this. He held that the Germans had migrated, the Suevi had maintained half-nomadic practices longer than others. During the time of migration they had no landed property in severalty, Sondereigentum; this was rather a matter of livestock. Whole communities, smaller or larger, had common camping grounds and pasture. Caesar's report bears upon the Suevian migration period. This does not deny possession in severalty (Sonderbesitz, possessio). Each small kin group or family (cognatio) had its pieces of land designated by the leaders. Wietersheim considered that Suevi had common ownership (dominium) and individual possession.[26] This is not at all the construction that Dopsch has made out of Wietersheim; it cuts exactly opposite to that of Dopsch, who argued *against* communal property in land among these ancient Germans, save as "state

---

[23] Idem. *Questions historiques*, op.cit., pp. 115ff. (Le problème des origines de la propriété foncière. *Revue des questions historiques*, 1889.) The implied method is a parody of thinking *more geometrico*: There is either private or communal landholding. But communal landholding has not been proved. We know that private landholding exists today. Therefore that is the original system of landholding. QED. Corollary: Communal landholding is introduced historically by taxation and landlord practices. Therefore it is not the original system. QED. This method underlies the thinking of Below and Weber.

[24] Alfons Dopsch, *Europäische Kulturentwicklung*, op. cit., vol. I, p. 63 (state socialism); p. 75 (private property).

[25] Dopsch, op. cit., p. 63; Weber, vide supra.

[26] Eduard v. Wietersheim. *Geschichte der Völkerwanderung.* 2nd ed. F. Dahn, ed. Leipzig, 1880, vol. I, pp. 45f.

socialism" (an abnormal case). But to Wietersheim the Suevian case was normal, not to wartime but to the time of migration, separating the question of land from stock.

Weber in his chapter on the Agrarian Systems and the Problem of Agriarian Communism, mentions beside his own works, those of Rachfahl and Below, "zur Orientierung über Entstehung und Verlauf der Kontroverse."[27] Previously he had mentioned Maurer, whom he intended to refute, as opposed to Dopsch, who denied agrarian communism. Below, in this matter, was one with Weber, but Rachfahl advocated the selfsame theory of evolution by stages which Weber had castigated as a biological organicism in reference to Hildebrand. IIe should have added that Rachfahl had interpreted Caesar as having reported communal property among the Germans, which Weber denied. Rachfahl, Below and Weber were not of one mind; if Rachfahl's views prevail then Weber's will not.[28]

Weber was ambivalent in the matter of the agrarian commune and its place in early history. Thus, on the one hand he found only permanent appropriation of share by hidemen in early Germanic history, and excluded the agrarian commune in the strict sense. But on the other hand, he held that dominium of the landlord replaced the original dominium over the land by the group of kin, the Sippe.[29] Note: The Sippe is a kin group that is greater than the family, or other than the family.[30] The historical development then is from the kin group, whether sib, clan, or gens, to the dominium of the landlord in political society. The Sippe competes with the political association. There is further (implied) argument by Weber in favor of an original agrarian communism. Weber wrote that the origins of the Markgenossenschaft are dark; yet it antedates the division

---

[27] Weber, *Wirtschaftsgeschichte*, op. cit., note on p. 20.

[28] Rachfahl, op. cit., was a collectivist or communist, writing of Gesamteigentum of the land by the ancient Germans (p. 24), and Gemeindebesitz (p. 32). The individual member of the Germanic tribe had territorial rights only in his capacity as member of the group or collectivity (pp. 26f.).

[29] On Sippe, cf. Weber, *Wirtschaft und Gesellschaft*, pp. 219ff., 404f., 622. See also his *Rechtssoziologie*, op. cit., pp. 138f.

[30] The peasants sell land "with the agreement of the village warden or of the landlord (originally of the sib)" ("mit Zustimmung des Dorfschulzen oder des Grundherrn ursprünglich der Sippe"). The group of kin is replaced by the landlord. (Weber, *Wirtschaftsgeschichte*, p. 25). Ibid. p. 24: The Carolingian Gaue appear after the Markgenossenschaft, whose origins are dark. – The historical movement leads from the primitive condition (life in a sib, mark) to life in the civil condition, indicated by the activities of bailiff or warden, landlord, the institution of the Gau. These categories are at once evolutionary and historical. Weber did not free himself of the charge of stage thinking that he had made against Hildebrand.

of the realm into Gaue by the Carolingians. The Markgenossenschaft, or union of several villages, appropriated the common Mark, including forest and waste, prior to the dormation of the political institution. The movement in history, or its development, is from a collective institution, originally a Genossenschaft, to a political institution, the administrative districts, Gaue, as part of the Carolingian empire. Sippe and Genossenschaft in connection with agrarian economy and society are agrarian communal/collective organizations. This is not friendly to his thesis of anti-agrarian-communism, or to Below and Dopsch, for the practices stated or implied, represent an original, prehistoric holding and disposition of the land as a collectivity by those who tilled it, gathered wood from it, etc.

Weber's system was not equal to the task that he set for himself; yet Weber was a stronger thinker in this matter than most of his contemporaries; the frame of reference of Weber's case goes beyond the limitations of Fustel de Coulanges, Below, Hildebrand, Rachfahl, Dopsch.[31] His basic contradiction is all the more profound and interesting by comparison. Above, mention was made of Weber's position on objectivity. He asserted that the social science interest is the "real, hence the individual form of the social cultural life given to us in its universal and therefore naturally no less individually formed connection." This exposition of an "objective" interest is preceded by the following declaration:

> A cosmic "original condition" which might have had a non-individual character, or less of one than the cosmic reality of the present would naturally be a meaningless thought: – but does a remnant of similar conceptions not haunt in this field the assumptions of economic-social "original conditions" without historical "accidents", now verified by the inferences of natural right, now by observations of "primitives" ("Naturvölker"), – thus of "primitive agrarian communism", of sexual "Promiscuity", etc. – from which the individual historical development arises as a kind of fall of man into the concrescence?"[32]

This intention to advocate a social science separated from value judgment[33] is here coupled with debater's tricks: here the allusions to "primitive agrarian communism" and sexual "promiscuity" are not

---

[31] See also R. Koebner (*Cambridge Economic History of Europe*, op. cit., ch. 1); *Ethnological Notebooks*, pp. 383f.

[32] Weber, Die "Objektivität" sozialwissenschaftlicher und sozialpolitischer Erkenntnis. *Archiv für Sozialwissenschaft.* Bd. 19, 1904, pp. 47f. (*Gesammelte Aufsätze zur Wissenschaftslehre.* 3rd ed., Tübingen, 1968, p. 172.)

[33] Ibid., 1904, p. 22. See also his article, Der Sinn der "Wertfreiheit". *Logos*, vol. 7, 1918. (*Wissenschaftslehre*, pp. 489-540.)

chosen by chance alone, but are designed to play on the prejudices of the conservative academic world of imperial Germany. The use of quotation marks and the trope of irony all serve to heighten the impression of senselessness of Weber's opponents.[34]

There is nevertheless a matter of substance that is posited. The argument of Weber proceeds from a universal or cosmic human nature that was neither more nor less individualistic in the deepest past than it is at present. This is a conflation of assumptions: 1. that there is a universal human nature; 2. that it then was individualistic as it is today. It is however just as specious to argue one side of this as the other. They are what were to have been proved. They cannot be handled on either side by mere assertion and sarcasm, irony and the like.

II. MARK, MIR AND ZADRUGA

Weber distinguished between the landholding by a commune and a house community or house-communism; the *zadruga* of the South Slavs (Serbs, also neighboring Slavonians, Croats, and to some extent Bulgarians in the modern times) corresponds to this latter. This house community or family community is thus distinct from the village community (*mir*) of the Great Russians. Weber identified the mir and the Russian commune in general, or *obščina*, while he had nothing to say on the rise of the mir; he simply reports that the Russians are divided on the issue. Weber thought that the most widely held opinion among Russian scholars was that the mir was not a primordial institution, but a product of the tax system and of serfdom.[35]

---

[34] Lucio Coletti, *From Rousseau to Lenin*, London, 1972 (J. Merrington and J. White, transl.), p. 38, for a related view of the same subject.

[35] *Wirtschaftsgeschichte*, p. 34; *Wirtschaft und Gesellschaft*, p. 742. This is a one-sided position by Weber. The development of the tax system is certainly as old as the Russkaja Pravda; (see below). The system of serfdom, however, is several centuries later than either the law code or the tax system of the earliest formation of the state on Russian soil; according to another widespread interpretation, serfdom was introduced only after the Time of Troubles, i.e., in the seventeenth century.

N.B. Weber made out the case for Leibeigenschaft, serfdom, not for feudalism in general. Thus we may conclude that he attributed the relation of serfdom to the earliest period of Russian history, to the Kievan period (c. ninth century). But he did not disprove the theory that serfdom in the strict sense, in the meaning of a permanent *adscriptio glebae*, was introduced only in the seventeenth century, by the joint action of the landlords, the Romanov dynasty at its inception, and the Church. The three dominant forms of land tenure from that time to the 1860s in Russia were: pomest'e (private landlordship), state ownership (including church-lands) and crown ownership. The emancipation of the serfs followed these three forms in the 1860s. See Johannes Engelmann, *Die Leibeigenschaft in Russland*, Leipzig, 1884. A. A. Korni-lov, A. S. Lappo-Danilevskij, V. I. Semevskij and I. M. Strakhovskij. *Krest'janskij Stroj*,

The distinction that Weber made between the mir and the zadruga is just. Yet it is equally important to distinguish those collective institutions of the Russian peasants that arose in history out of the administration and manipulation by levies in kind and labor from those which antedate the rise of the state and its agencies in Russia.

The explanation of the formation of the mir exhibits the fundamental defects of Weber's theory of history. The explanation is not his own, but it is favored by him; the weight of scientific opinion is reported by him to lie behind it. This is intended as a blow againt the theory of primitive communism. It is the opposite of an economic determinism; it is a political determinism of the history of such institutions. Weber did not consider that the thesis of determination of peasant communism by means of the agencies of the state, which are said to have imposed taxation and servile conditions on the peasants, assigns great power to the state and its agencies. Thus he assumed what he set out to prove.

B. D. Grekov has defended the distinction between the obščina and the great family; it is further to be distinguished from the zadruga, or house community, family community, etc.[36] Grekov further identified the mir with the obščina and the Germanic mark.[37] In the ancient Russian law code, Russkaja Pravda, the mir was both a rural settlement and an administrative unity of the monarchy. Grekov held that beside the administrative, fiscal functions of the mir it functioned also as a peasant kind community; in his view, the latter survives into the period of the formation of the state from an earlier period. The early law codes and related records bear upon the period of the eleventh to twelfth centuries, but the kin community organization is of the eighth to ninth centuries A.D.[38] His thesis is that the public authorities brought out one aspect of the mir, which they applied in tax collection and punishment of crimes, for which the wergeld was imposed. But these authorities did not create the mir ex nihilo, nor its communal

v. 1, St.-Petersburg, 1905. N. M. Družinin, *Gosudarstvennye Krest'jane*, 2 v., Moscow 1946-1958. Družinin describes the order in which the different categories of serfs were emancipated, relative to the mode of their bondage in Russia, as private, state, crown serfs.

[36] B. D. Grekov, *Krest'jane na Rusi*. Moscow-Leningrad, 1946, pp. 72f. See also Grekov, *Kievskaja Rus'*, Moscow-Leningrad, 1955, ch. 4, pt. 1. The point is directed against S. V. Juškov, who held that the rural community and the zadruga were the same.

[37] Grekov, in: *Pravda Russkaja* II. M.-L., 1947, p. 101. Also see Grekov, *Krest'jane na Rusi*, p. 81, *Kievskaja Rus'*, loc. cit., and M. N. Tikhomirov, *Rossija v XVI stoletii*. Moscow, 1962, pp. 62 sq.

[38] Grekov, *Krest'jane na Rusi*, p. 81. See also his *Kievskaja Rus'*, loc. cit. Parts of the Russkaja Pravda are of the ninth century (*Krest'jane*, p. 69). M. N. Tikhomirov, *Posobie dlja izučenija Russkoj Pravdy*, Moscow, 1953, is of the opinion that the body of the text is of the tenth-twelfth centuries.

bonds, of kinship or territory, out of nothing. They did not create the relation to the soil of the collectivity out of nothing. This is Grekov's position.

We have the position of Weber on the one side, of Grekov on the other. In order to grasp them more fully we must see whence they came; and for this we must dip into the conflict of opinions of the nineteenth century. The question of the family in whatever form, house-community, zadruga, extended or great family, etc., is set aside at this point, to be discussed below.[39]

J. Ph. G. Ewers, in his edition of the Russkaja Pravda held that it dealt with the formation of the state, more precisely, with the transition from the tribe to the state of ancient Rus'. His edition with commentary on the ancient law code expressed this interpretation. The unit of the social organization in the formation of the state, accordingly, was the tribe; the combination of the tribes formed the state, which succeeded the tribes and replaced them in the organization of society.[40] The Russian historians S. M. Solov'ev and K. Kavelin followed the interpretation of Russian history by Ewers. But a new feature was introduced by Haxthausen, the mir in the discussion of Russian antiquity.[41] Haxthausen did not take up the problem of the historical source, but only the characterization of the Russian rural communal life, its antiquity, and its role in shaping Russian national life. The Slavophile K. S. Aksakov took up the thesis of the obščina, in opposition to Solov'ev and Kavelin. Aksakov denied the existence of the tribe; families together formed the obščina.[42] Aksakov argued in favor of the unbroken continuation of the obščina from antiquity, whose democratic and communal spirit would be the health of the nation.

B. Čičerin and V. I. Sergeevič attacked the views of the Slavophiles, albeit from different standpoints. Čičerin started from the assumption of the prehistoric existence of the community, obščina, which dis-

---

[39] (F. I. Leontovič.) See below. The work of the late M. O. Kosven, *Semejnaja Obščina i Patronimija*, Moscow, 1963, is learned, with a survey of wide literature in a brief compass; but it obscures the distinction between family and community.

[40] J. Ph. G. Ewers, *Das älteste Recht der Russen in seiner geschichtlichen Entwicklung*. Dorpat-Hamburg, 1826. He espoused the view that all the goods of the ancient Slavs were the property of the tribe, which is the family expanded. The concept of the tribe was unclear. The same general interpretation as in Ewers is found in A. v. Reutz. *Versuch über die geschichtliche Ausbildung der russischen Staats- u. Rechtsverfassung*. Mitau, 1829.

[41] A. v. Haxthausen, *Studien über die inneren Zustände*, op. cit., vol. I, pp. VI sq., vol. III, pp. 115-161.

[42] K. S. Aksakov, *O drevnem byte u slavjan. Moskovskij Sbornik*, 1852. See his *Polnoe Sobranie Sočinenij*, Moscow, 1889, vol. I.

appears with the formation of the state in Kievan Russia. Thus the mir, he said, or obščina, of historical times is discontinuous with the ancient community; the modern community is the creation of the state.[43] Sergeevič denied any existence of the obščina in ancient times; he opposed the idea of an original communal ownership of the land, asserting that it had been privately held from the beginning.[44] Čičerin's views were widely known and quoted in Germany and in France. They were attacked by I. D. Beljaev, who affirmed the existence of the ancient obščina as a landholding system, but one that was not based on consanguinity.[45]

M. M. Kovalevsky traced the evolution of the house-community into the obščina in ancient times; the earliest mode of land tenure in Russia was the house-community, these undivided households having the village communities as their immediate successors. Kovalevsky attached himself to the thesis of H. S. Maine; Kovalevsky himself is quoted with approval by B. D. Grekov.[46] However, Kovalevsky and Grekov are not of one mind. Grekov did not trace the village community directly out of the undivided family, as did Maine and Kovalevsky; Grekov traced the village community, obščina, from the *rod*, gens or clan. This is closer to the viewpoint of L. H. Morgan, whom Grekov also quotes with approval. It is not exactly Morgan's viewpoint, for he did not write of the community; but Morgan distinguished the family in any form from the gens.[47]

We have seen that Grekov identified the mark and the mir; but Kovalevsky identified the mark as the territory owned by the community, as opposed to the mir, or the community itself. The second difference between them concerns the relation between the un-

[43] B. Čičerin, *Oblastnye učreždenija Rossii v XVII v.* Moscow, 1856. Also his *Obzor istoričeskogo razvitija sel'skoj obščiny v Rossii. Russkij Vestnik*, 1856. The activity of the government tax-collection and of the landed aristocracy jointly brought about the suppression of the original obščina, according to Čičerin.

[44] V. I. Sergeevič, *Veče i knjaz'*. Moscow, 1867. Sergeevič. *Russkie juridičeskie drevnosti.* 2nd ed. 3 v. St. Petersburg, 1902-1911. The parallel to the views of Fustel de Coulanges is known.

[45] I. D. Beljaev, *Krest'jane na Rusi. Russkaja Beseda*, 1859, I. See his *Lektsii po istorii russkogo zakonodatel'stva.* 2nd ed. Moscow, 1888. Surveys of the literature and conflicting views are found in: J. v. Keussler, *Bäuerlicher Gemeindebesitz in Russland.* 3 v. Riga, 1876, v. 1, pp. 1-112 (Repr. Aalen, 1970). B. D. Grekov, *Krest'jane na Rusi*, pp. 59-82. Id., *Kievskaja Rus'*, 1955.

[46] M. M. Kovalevsky, *Modern Customs and Ancient Laws of Russia*. London, 1891, pp. 75-78. The work is dedicated to Henry Sumner Maine. See also Kovalevsky, *Obščinnoe Zemlevladenie*. Pt. I (all publ.) Moscow, 1879. See *Ethnological Notebooks*, pp. 360f. Grekov, *Krest'jane na Rusi*, p. 64; also *Kievskaja Rus'*. Karl Marx attacked this thesis of Maine and Kovalevsky. See my *Asiatic Mode of Production*, op. cit., pt. I, ch. IV and V.

[47] Grekov, *Krest'jane na Rusi*, p. 59. L. H. Morgan, *Ancient Society*, New York, 1877. See Krader, *Ethnological Notebooks*, p. 43. Morgan had no theory of the agrarian community at all.

divided family and the mir. Grekov was writing, in relation to the mark and mir, and to Kovalevsky, only in generalities.

Weber's judgment that the most widely held conception relative to the origin of the mir was that of Čičerin is wide of the target; it can be explained only if we assume that Weber made a cursory survey, in which the antagonists of the collective theory of its origin were sought out, but not the views of its defenders. Weber was selective in his citations.[48] We have here been guided by the researches of Grekov and Tikhomirov; Grekov's organization of the Russian materials is the best that we have. Grekov held an evolutionist premiss foreign to Weber, and had both a formal and a material opposition to the views of the Russian legal historian, F. I. Leontovič, who expounded the doctrine that the family community, semejnaja obščina, had evolved into the village community, sel'skaja obščina.[49] This is the view Kovalevsky had espoused. Grekov criticized Leontovič.[50] However, the sequence from the zadruga to the mir-obščina is not a proper part of Grekov's theory. The relations in political society are other than those in primitive society; the institutions of primitive society do not simply emerge in a direct way as the corresponding institutions of political society, which would be implied by the sequence, family obščina – village obščina. The role of the classes in society, the opposition between the classes, in the village as in the society generally, the role of the agencies of the state in tax collection, the role of the landlords must be taken into account in the study of

---

[48] Weber, *Wirtschaftsgeschichte*, p. 32, mentions in regard to the origin of the mir only the advocates of a theory of original ownership in severalty: Keussler, op. cit.; A. A. Čuprov, *Die Feldgemeinschaft, eine morphologische Untersuchung*, Strassburg, 1902; and V. G. Simkhovič, *Die Feldgemeinschaft in Russland*, Jena, 1898, in addition to his own work. Collectivist theory was not given a hearing in Weber, Roscher's partisanship was opposed by him. Russian historians of that time, Ključevskij, a.o. held a view opposed to Weber. S. F. Platonov, *Lektsii po russkoj istorii*, 9th ed. St. Petersburg, 1915, held that the ancient Russians lived in a patriarchal tribal organization, divided into clans. Cp. *Entsiklopedičeskij Slovar'*, Brokgauz-Efron, St. Petersburg and Leipzig, 1890-1907, v. 47 (XXIV), Pozemel'naja obščina, s.v. Drevnjaja Rus', Velikorossija, (N. Vasilenko). K. R. Kačorovskij, *Russkaja Obščina*, St. Petersburg, 1900, pp. 125 sq. wrote that in the primeval occupation of the soil, the mir figured as the owner (*khozjain*) of it. V. O. Ključevskij, *Kurs Russkoj Istorii* (1904-1910), Moscow, 1956, v. I, p. 118: The ancient Russians had *rod* (clan) holdings still undivided when their historical record began.

[49] F. I. Leontovič, Zadružno-obščinnyj kharakter političeskogo byta drevnej Rossii. *Žurnal Ministerstva Narodnogo Prosveščenija*, July 1874. See also his O značenii vervi po Russkoj Pravdy i Politsiskomu Statutu. Ibid., April, 1867.

[50] Grekov, *Krest'jane na Rusi*, p. 63.

the earliest formation of the village communities in civil society.[51]

Jan Peisker had criticized the theory of the agrarian commune and of an original collective landownership. The view of Fustel de Cou-langes was here the accepted one; according to Peisker, neither the zadruga nor the mir-obščina was a primordial institution: They both came into existence late, as the result of taxation practices; the zadruga as the result of the Byzantine hearth-tax, the mir as the result of the head-tax introduced by Peter the Great.[52] Weber, without taking up the question of origins, true to his theory of the political interpretation of history of landholding, repeatedly stressed the administrative functions of the mir within the political system of historical Russia.[53]

The political position of Weber was conservative. His activities in the Verein für Sozialpolitik were those of an enlightened bourgeois who fought against social injustice; the Verein included, i.a., the Kathedersozialisten, G. Schmoller and L. Brentano. Weber had nothing but coolness and reserve toward the working class movement, socialism and Marxism.

Emile Durkheim took up the question of the mir and the zadruga as a collectivist rather than an individualist. Durkheim sought to estab-lish an ideal type of the various forms of social solidarity; in this regard, his method was one with that of Max Weber, whose name is more closely associated with the method and theory of the ideal type. Unlike Weber, Durkheim's approach to the question of these groups, which include the mir and zadruga, was developmental and evolution-ary. His sequence was taken from Morgan, *Ancient Society*, proceeding from the horde, which is a social aggregate without definite form or organization, as the true social protoplasm from which all the social types have emerged. Out of this germ emerged the clan, which is a primitive social organization of a family type; the communism in regard to property which is practiced by this family-clan is the result of their cohesion, whereby the individual is absorbed in the group, the part into the whole. The development of mutual interdependence of the groups, whereby the division of labor in society assures an increase in organic solidarity, transforms the social unities from the

---

[51] Weber introduced the factor of the village bourgeoisie, the kulaks, into his analysis of the mir; (to be sure at the end of the history of the mir, but the origins of these antagonisms are not found at the end of the history of the mir. The kulaks are rich peasantry of the capitalist period). Weber, *Wirtschaftsgeschichte*, p. 33.

[52] Jan Peisker, Die serbische Zadruga. *Zeitschrift für Sozial- und Wirtschaftsgeschichte*, v. 7, 1900. Cf. Peisker, *Slovo o zadruze*. Prag, 1899. (This is the same with greater literature.) Reprinted from Národopisný Sborník českoslovanský, Svazek IV and V. Prague, 1899. Also T. Peisker, in: *Cambridge Medieval History*, Cambridge, 1913, ch. 14.

[53] Weber, *Wirtschaft und Gesellschaft*, pp. 202, 546, 737, 742.

type of the family clan to the political clan.[54]   The question of the
relation between mir and zadruga is not a straightforward one.   Durkheim, as we shall see, considered some of its complexities, but his
discussion obscured rather than clarified the problem.   Further parts
of this discussion must now be introduced.   Durkheim was a lifelong
friend of the socialist leader, Jean Jaurès; he wrote a book sympathetic
to the socialist idea.   But the book dealt with socialism from the
standpoint of the forerunner of the utopian socialists, Saint-Simon.
Marcel Mauss considered that Durkheim sympathized with socialism;[55]
but Durkheim's sympathy was only with an ideal, without consequences in practice.

Durkheim was critical of the thesis of Jan Peisker regarding the
formation of the zadruga and mir by tax collection practice and
policy; he rejected the thesis of Fustel de Coulanges in this regard,
giving substance to the theory expressed in his work on division of
labor in society; here he accepted the primacy of private property
in the family as the unit of social, hence of economic organization
at the point where history begins.   He differed from Fustel de Coulanges insofar as the latter made religion the basis of history, whereas
for Durkheim, religion is the effect, not the cause.[56]   In his review of a
work that criticized Peisker's thesis, Durkheim wrote that the zadruga
existed before the taxation system of the Byzantine empire; therefore
it was not created by these historical events.   The critic of Peisker,
A. Stanischitsch, had, however, in Durkheim's opinion, too readily
conceded the recent origin of the village.   "If the Russian mir, in its
present form, is not ancient, it does not follow that, from the beginning,
there had not been, beyond the domestic community, another community, more extensive, which was also of a family nature.   Here as
elsewhere we tend to think that the whole precedes the part, or, more
or less, is contemporary with it."[57]   Durkheim's theory gives signs of
having been hastily formulated.   The doctrine of the whole and the
part is well-known to be his doctrine; but what are we to make of a
family community that is other than the domestic community of the
zadruga, but which underlies the village community?   Evidently,
Durkheim intended to distinguish the prehistory of the mir from that
of the zadruga, leading both, by different ways, from his conjectural
prehistory of the horde and the family clan.   But his suppositions

[54] Emile Durkheim, *De la division du travail social* (1893). Paris, 1973, p. 149-152.
[55] Durkheim, *Le Socialisme*. Paris, 1928. Introd. by M. Mauss.
[56] Durkheim, *Division du travail social*, p. 154.
[57] Review of A. Stanischitsch, Ueber den Ursprung der Zadruga, 1907. *Année Sociologique*, v.
11, 1906-1909, pp. 343-7.   Repr. E. Durkheim, *Journal Sociologique*, Paris, 1969, pp. 639-642.

are no less conjectural; he brought the kinship system of the family into the formation of the institutions of political society, as did Kovalevsky. Weber and Grekov were clear about the differentiation of the two.

Henry Sumner Maine proceeded from Savigny's distinction between property and possession, to Maurer.[58] However, Maine began his story of landholding with the joint family, which he found in India during his period of service there in the 1860s.[59] Maine considered that the house community (zadruga) of the South Slavs is the continuation of the joint family of the Hindus[60]; he thought to trace the prehistory and history of landholding thereby, believing that as both the Slavs and Hindus are Indo-European peoples, they had preserved forms of landholding which had later evolved into the Roman, German and Anglo-Saxon forms.[61] The house community then developed into the village community.[62] This confection is but one of many such schemes of evolution of the nineteenth and twentieth centuries. It assumed that because Indo-European philology had established a series of linguistic relations between speakers of Indic, Latin, Slavic, Germanic languages, therefore, the economic practices and legal customs of the present-day speakers of these languages have a common historical root. The subsquent history proceeded through developmental stages, accordingly, represented by the joint family, the house community and the village community. The most archaic stage was the joint family, still found in India; the next stage was the zadruga, still found in Serbia; the next was the mir, still found in Great Russia. Therefore, Maine argued, the ancient Anglo-Saxons and other Germanic-speaking peoples can examine their living past before their eyes. Yet he had to face the difficulty of descent in the female line that L. H. Morgan had put to him. Morgan had argued that the lowest group after the horde (mentioned above in connection with Durkheim's survey of Morgan's ideas) was the group built around

---

[58] H. S. Maine, *Ancient Law*, 1861. Cf. F. C. v. Savigny, *Das Recht des Besitzes*. 1802. Krader, *Asiatic Mode of Production*, op.cit., ch. V.

[59] Maine, *Village Communities in the East and West* (1871). London, 1890. *Dissertations on Early Law and Custom*. London, 1886. See *Ethnological Notebooks*, pp. 34 sq., and notes. Maine. *Lectures on the Early History of Institutions*, London, 1875. Cyril Levitt is studying this question.

[60] Maine, *Early Law and Custom*, pp. 240f. See also his *Village Communities*, Lect. III, pp. 65 sq., and Lect. IV, pp. 103 sq.

[61] For the South Slavs Maine relied on V. Bogišić; cf. his *Na "Ocjenu" Zbornika Sadašnjih Pravnih Običaja u Južnih Slovena*. Spljet, 1877. Maine had a report by F. Demelić, *Le droit coutumier des Slaves méridionaux d'après les recherches de M. Bogišić*. Paris, 1877. In addition to these, see O. M. Utiešenović-Ostrožinski, *Die Hauskommunionen der Südslaven*, Wien, 1859.

[62] Maine, *Early Law and Custom*, p. 261.

the matriliny and matriarchy.[63] The next stage after the matriliny-matriarchy was the patriliny-patriarchy.[64] Maine, after earlier holding the principle of a universal primacy of father-right, ultimately reached a compromise with Morgan in regard to matriarchy versus patriarchy. Maine wrote: "One of these two groups did not really succeed the other, but the two co-existed from all time, and were always distinct from one another."[65]

Maine was communist only in regard to the beginnings of human history, and regarded the reign of individualism in his own civilization as the end toward which human evolution tends.[66] He borrowed the thought of the Hero in history from Alfred Lyall and ultimately from Thomas Carlyle. Maine's explanation 'of the origin and growth of society among the higher races of mankind' follows that of his illustrious colleagues: "A mighty man of valour, with his kinsmen and retainers, founds a clan." "The communities which were destined to civilisation seem to have experienced an attraction which drew them towards one exemplar, the pure clan, generally exogamous among the Semites, but always believing in purity of paternal descent, and always looking back to some god or hero as the first of the race."[67]

Maine's theory of the original practice of communal landholding is the complement to that of Morgan; Morgan made no mention of a community other than that bound together by bonds of kinship; a territorial community was not known to him, neither in his description of the Iroquois nor of the Aztecs.[68] The territorial community is

---

[63] The reader will note changes in the terminology of Morgan and Maine. Morgan did not distinguish between matriliny and matriarchy, nor between these and matrilocality. Maine did not distinguish between Indo-European peoples (so-called) and peoples speaking Indo-European languages.

[64] Morgan, *Ancient Society*, op. cit.; *Ethnological Notebooks*, pp. 97-241. Morgan, too, thought that Indo-European speakers and peoples were the same. An earlier form of the theory of the matriarchy was given by J. J. Bachofen, *Das Mutterrecht*. Stuttgart, 1861.

[65] Maine, op. cit., p. 287.

[66] *Ethnological Notebooks*, pp. 34 sq., pp. 44 sq., pp. 58 sq. *Asiatic Mode of Production*, ch. V.

[67] Maine, *Early Law and Custom*, pp. 280, 281f. Sir Alfred Lyall. *Asiatic Studies*. London, 1882, Ch. 6, esp. pp. 182f., 185ff.

[68] Morgan, *Ancient Society*, Pt. II, ch. 2 through 7. A. Alföldi, *Early Rome and the Romans*, Ann Arbor, Michigan, 1963, found that there is historical evidence of landholding in ancient Rome by a collectivity (tribe, clan, gens). E. Benveniste, *Le vocabulaire des institutions indo-européennes*, Paris, 1969, v. 1, p. 308, finds that the form of the nominal theme *weik-, *woiko- points in two directions among the Indo-European languages: 1. In one group of languages it indicates a kin unity of several families, e.g. vis-, "clan" (Indo-Iranian); 2. in others it has slipped into meaning "village, burg" (Latin, Ancient Slavic, Gothic). Eduard Meyer, *Geschichte des Altertums*, 3ter Bd., Stuttgart 1954. H. E. Stier ed., pp. 372f. mentions only land tenure by individuals in Greek antiquity. On the contrary, J. B. Bury, *A History of Greece*, 3rd ed., R. Meiggs ed. London 1951, pp. 106f., considers in reference to the same passages of Hesiod a past

accounted for by Morgan only in connection with the formation of civil or political society. Morgan had a critical attitude to the hold that property maintains over the human mind; in our era, it is in the form of private property. Maine held no such criticism; the reign of private property is the end toward which human evolution tends. In Maine's doctrine the different strands of the ideology of his civilization come together: private property, individualism and its special province, the cult of the hero. His evolutionary doctrine is a simple succession of stages, save that the English in India have had the beneficial effect of intervening in the Indian evolution in order to bring them further on the way to private property in land. The mark and the mir are halfway to the final form of landownership, in Maine's position.

III. COMMUNITY AND THE STATE IN CIVIL SOCIETY

Marx traced more than one kind of an "original" landholding system. He wrote that the form of the natural community of the Incas is the state. Here there is an entirely closed natural economy of the state; their community does not engage in exchange of commodities. This has two moments: 1. *The state as community*, being closed, has no exchange with other communities, hence no commodity exchange or production, Circulation as the moment of exchange takes place only within the community, in this case. The product is consumed where it is produced, within the community. 2. *The community as the state* yet encompasses a further distribution within its limits. A surplus is produced and consumed within the community, but with

---

of undivided land tenure among the Greeks. Michael Ventris and John Chadwick, *Documents in Mycenaean Greek*, 2nd ed., Cambridge 1973, pp. 273ff. propose that in Pre-Homeric Greece land tenure was both in the hands of private overlords and shared by the people of a village. The village had two sorts of holdings: 1. holdings by full-time cultivators (men of the village); 2. holdings by artisans (men of the tool), part-time cultivators. The holdings of the artisans reverted to the village, where the land right resided. Parallels to Hittite practices are drawn by L. R. Palmer, *Achaeaens and Indo-Europeans*. Oxford 1955. Cf. A. Goetze in: *Ancient Near Eastern Texts*. J. B. Pritchard ed., Princeton 1950. According to these indications Pre-Homeric Greece and the Hittites had land tenure practices that fall within the category of the Asiatic mode of production; here the presence of private and communal land holding is found; likewise the land rights of cultivators in the village are 'superior' to those of artisans resident in the villages. Throughout the Asiatic mode of production division of labor in the village takes place between handicraftsmen and cultivators. Here the distinction is made between land-ownership by the village and by the overlord, as opposed to land possession by the cultivators themselves. The rights of the cultivators were superior to those of craftsmen resident in the villages and working the village land in Mogul India. See Lawrence Krader, *The Asiatic Mode of Production*, op. cit. Eva Cantarella is studying the history of land rights in antiquity along these lines. Guido Martinotti has been helpful in the matter.

an exchange taking place. As the community is the form of the state, the product is not the community product but the social product. But this presupposes the relation of social labor. The separation and relation between private labors by division of labor in society has taken place; there is production by surplus labor of a surplus product, but in the absence of commodity production. Formally the old Peruvian system of labor is communal labor; in its content as in its effect it is social labor.[69]

In the Inca system an early form of political economy, civil society and the state is found, in which the community does not exist apart from the state; at the same time, community and society in form are one. Civil society is not as yet fully formed. On the contrary, under the conditions of formation of civil society, the differentiation between community and society takes place; at the same time, the public and private sectors of social life are distinguished, and pari passu the distinction between the public and private forms of landholding. In the Inca system, as in the early form of the Asiatic mode of production, community and the state are not distinguished, and the land is held by the community as the state. In the later period of the Asiatic mode of production, however, state and community are differentiated, likewise, the state and civil society are separated. This differentiation and separation are measured by the introduction of the distinction between public property in land, communal property, and private property. It would be untenable to consider this distinction as the motor of history; it is but a formal consummation of a separation whose incentive lies elsewhere. The form of property in land is the civil announcement of the separation. The agency of the state in the later period of the Asiatic mode of production is now opposed to that of the community and of the individual. The ager publicus which was at first the property in land of the community, the state, civil society, the public, without distinction, is now the subject of contention between different sectors which are ever more clearly marked and opposed: community and the state, public versus communal on the one hand, private on the other. The opposition between the communal and the private sectors is at no stage fully expressed in the history of the Asiatic mode of production, for the community retains its right as landowner down to the nineteenth century, while individual private property in land is but poorly

---

[69] Marx, *Das Kapital*, II. 4th ed. Hamburg, 1910, pp. 88, 120. See also *Kapital*, I, op. cit., p. 54. Marx. *Grundrisse der Kritik der politischen Ökonomie* (1857-1858), Berlin, 1953, pp. 377 sqq. See below, ch. 3 and 4.

developed[70]; the immediate cultivator of the soil is in possession of his share, he does not own it. This mode of production has the production of value, exchange between community-producers of value, hence exchange value; the social producer is no longer the same as the social consumer of the product. Social labor is distinct from public and from communal labor. The surplus product and commodity as product are now differentiated. The community as the state is the proprietor of the land, which is the property of the state. The community as the state is the proprietor of the land as public property as distinct from the natural community of immediate producers as collective proprietors. In the degree that private property in land or its product is poorly developed, even the monarch in the old realms of Asia is not an owner of the land or of its surplus product in his private capacity. The entire surplus product of the realm is made over to him, he has it at his disposal, but he is its possessor, not its owner. The individual cultivator of the soil bears the same relation to it as the prince to the surplus product. On the other hand, the community of the cultivators bears the same relation to the soil as does the state: the soil is the property of the community and of the state as the overarching community. Labor is communal labor (labor for collective purposes within the community), public labor (labor in the collective undertakings of the state as the overarching community, as water control); private labor and social labor are now differentiated. Community and society are now fully separate; civil society has been developed; the state has been extruded by the society.[71]

We here posit the opposition between community and society; but it is only in civil society that the two are mutually opposed. They do not, however, stand to each other in the order of succession, from community to society, as though this were a sequence over time. They stand to each other as a synchronic opposition within the given condition of civil society, in the Asiatic, classical-antique, feudal and capitalist modes of production. Therefore the opposition between community and society, as it was proposed by F. Tönnies, is not a developmental one in the sense of an evolutionary sequence, from

---

[70] It is a late development as well. In the Mogul Empire there was a struggle between governors and military leaders in border provinces, on one side, the central state power on the other over endowments of land to the former; the civil and military leaders sought to make them into hereditary grants.

[71] Marx, *Grundrisse*, pp. 371, 278f., 391. *Kapital* I, op. cit., pp. 54, 322f. *Ethnological Notebooks*, pp. 255, 329. See *Asiatic Mode of Production*, op.cit., ch. VII, sect. E.

community to society.[72] We have to solve the developmental-evolutionary sequence in another way.

The Slavic community in historic times was not based on a kinship relation, it was based on the contribution of labor by the members. Those who labored on the soil had the right to a share in it and its product, those who did not had no such right. The zadruga had a different foundation, even in the nineteenth and twentieth centuries; the right to a share in the soil and its product was founded on kinship and not on labor.[73] This differentiation between mir and zadruga is the product of a millennium-long process of taxation by the state, of regulation by the landlords. But the mir was not the same in its form encountered in the nineteenth century, as it had been in the millennium before then. It was nevertheless a community distinct from the state; the mir was at that early time an element of civil society. The state was not introduced among the Slavs of Kiev by the Varangians in the ninth century; civil society, and an early form of the state is reported among the eastern Slavs, out of which the Kievan kingdom arose, in the centuries before the arrival of these Varangians.

The formation of the ancient Slavic community, the community in the Asiatic mode of production, and the ancient Peruvian form were all secondary. To the internal relations to the soil, the external relation of conquest is added. But the combination of the gentile principle and the act of conquest leads to formation of castes, no more. So long as the kinship principle remains in the tribe, no completed aristocracy or higher order is formed in society.[74]

The ancient Germanic community, as an institution of civil society, was separate from the state; it has developed from the Genossenschaft. The form of property in land was different, among these ancient Germans, from the form among the Slavs and in the Orient, as it was from the Roman form.[75] To conceive the German form of property in land as a separate mode of production, just as the Asiatic, the feudal, the capitalist, etc., is an error. A mode of production is defined by the relation of labor, the relation of the society to nature, the relation of the immediate producers to each other, to the means of production,

---

[72] F. Tönnies, *Gemeinschaft und Gesellschaft* (1887). See opposed to this: Otto Gierke, *Das deutsche Genossenschaftsrecht.* (1868) Graz, 1954, v. 1, ch. 1. Id. *Die Genossenschaftstheorie und die deutsche Rechtsprechung.* Berlin 1887, pp. 5, 307f.

[73] Lawrence Krader, Recent Studies of the Russian Peasant. *American Anthropologist*, v. 58, 1956. The Transition from Serf to Peasant in Eastern Europe. *Anthropological Quarterly*, v. 33, 1960.

[74] *Ethnological Notebooks*, Krader, Introduction, pp. 14-16, 183; *Grundrisse*, pp. 390f.

[75] Marx, *Grundrisse*, p. 382. *Ethnological Notebooks*, pp. 238-241.

to the surplus product, to distribution, to exchange and production in society. The fact of property determines nothing; it is the formal side of but one of the relations; where landownership is in question, it is the formal side of the relation to the soil. The form of property in land is an expression of something else. The presence of the Germanic form of property in land beside the Asiatic, antique, and Slavic[76] is but as a member of a list of categories of property; it is not the basis for construction of a separate mode of production.

L. H. Morgan held that the original unit of landholding in the transition from ancient society to civil society was the kin group. This is an important part of the issue that we are concerned with; it is not the whole of that issue. The collective holding or tenure by a community that is or is not bound by kinship is at issue; that community may be composed of kin or neighbors.[77] Maine sought to combine the two issues by tracing the evolution of the original landholding by a kin group, the joint family, in a stage of society before the formation of civil society, to the form of landholding by the mark or the mir, in civil society. In this he was followed by M. M. Kovalevsky. Maine also brought the kin relation, both in the form of the family and the cognatic group, into the formation of civil society; accordingly, it is not by the dissolution of the kinship relation in the clan or gens that civil society is formed, such as was the thesis of Morgan, Marx and Engels. Maine's thesis concerning the joint family obscures the issue concerning the mode of landholding, which is other than the issue concerning the internal relations of the landholding group, whether kin or neighbors; Kovalevsky's does likewise.

Maine was unclear about the process of formation of civil society and the state; Marx directed his critique against Maine in this regard, on four counts: 1. Maine had held that the actual direction of the forces of society by its sovereign is shaped, limited, and forbidden by the "vast mass of influences which we may call for shortness moral." Marx wrote that Maine ignores the economic factor, the much deeper one. 2. Maine assumed with John Austin that the state really exists, concretely. Marx on the contrary held that the state is but an appearance, it is not independent, but an excrescence of society; this

---

[76] *Grundrisse*, p. 395.

[77] Morgan, *Ancient Society*. See also *Ethnological Notebooks*, p. 139. F. Engels, *Origin of the Family, Private Property and the State* (1884). The problem of the evolution of the clan, gens, etc., is different from that of the evolution of landholding; the two overlap, but are not the same. But Engels, *Anti-Dühring*, 1878, also held that it is the dissolution of the agricultural community, and not of the kin community alone, that provides the origination of the state. The account of the origin of the state in the polemic against Dühring is broader and at once more to the point than the later account.

appearance will itself disappear when the society in which it is found attains a stage which it has not yet reached. 3. Maine had thought that the state is the prior organization in history. Marx responded that where the state exists, in politically organized society, it is by no means the prius; it only appears to be so. 4. Maine had proposed that the individual in the primitive community had lived in the despotic chains of the group. Marx held that the primitive community indeed had such bonds over the individual, but they were satisfying and comfortable.[78]

Marx criticized Kovalevsky for bringing the Asiatic mode of production within European feudalism, for explaining primitive land settlement by means of conquest, and for making the factor of consciousness a causa efficiens of history, rather than the factual events of history themselves.[79] Maine and Kovalevsky brought out the family as the direct constituent of society, hence the family landholding as the fundamental unit of the archaic agricultural economy. This was sharply criticized by Marx with respect to another of Maine's allies, Phear; the criticism obtains the more strongly against its leading partisan, Maine.[80]

Marx separated the question of the house community from that of the village community, in opposition to Maine, to Kovalevsky and Phear. On the one side, he derived support from Morgan, who had distinguished the family from the gens. On the other, Marx understood Tacitus to have supported the idea of landholding in common by the ancient Germans.[81]

T. G. Masaryk held Marx and Engels to have been unclear about whether they should or should not see in Russian agrarian communism the germ of the communist development of Western Europe.[82] The polemic by Masaryk has the advantage of being clearly an attack against the socialist doctrine, in contrast to the concealed attack by Weber, Below, a.o. Since Masaryk wrote, however, the drafts of the correspondence prepared by Marx with V. Zasulič have come to light, as well as the materials on the subject in his notes on Morgan,

---

[78] Maine, *Lectures on the Early History of Institutions* (1875). 4th ed., 1885, pp. 327, 356, 359. Marx, *Ethnological Notebooks*, p. 329.

[79] M. M. Kovalevsky, *Obščinnoe Zemlevladenie*, op. cit. *Ethnological Notebooks*, pp. 36of. Krader, *Asiatic Mode of Production*, op. cit., Pt. I, ch. IV.

[80] Sir John Budd Phear, *The Aryan Village in India and Ceylon*. London, 1880. *Ethnological Notebooks*, p. 281.

[81] *Ethnological Notebooks*, pp. 3of.

[82] T. G. Masaryk, *Die philosophischen und soziologischen Grundlagen des Marxismus* (1899) Osnabrück, 1964, p. 356.

Phear, Maine and Kovalevsky.[83] The place of the Russian peasant commune is not that of the germ of the future communist society; the latter will have a form superior to that of the peasant commune of the past. The peasant commune, at the same time, will not necessarily proceed through the historical period of capitalism in order to achieve the higher form of the communal life.

Masaryk raised a point regarding the class relations in the past agrarian communes that requires clarification. Gomme, says Masaryk, "... extends and corrects the views of Engels, as far as they touch England; especial consideration is due to his proof that, in the original gentile marks, special classes of serfs arose. Gomme makes it probable that one could assume the same state of affairs in India and indeed in other lands, and among the most various races."[84] In his eagerness to disprove Engels (and by implication Marx) Masaryk undertook too much upon himself. Gomme writes of unfree classes in the early population of England, "... one of the results of which has been the creation of the now famous formula of the village community in serfdom under a lord."[85] This reference in no way takes up the "original gentile marks" (ursprüngliche Gentilmarken) which Masaryk mentions. The unfree servants of the community in old England are not the same as the unfree village servants in India. The question is confused by Masaryk. The case of the Indian village servants, the so-called 12 employments, is different because the form of unfreedom is different. The Indian village watchman, blacksmith, barber, carpenter, dancing-girl, cowman, etc. are people who have no land rights themselves in the villages, receiving instead the income from the village crops in return for their services. The village cultivators are bound to the soil in India not by the laws of serfdom, nor yet of slavery, but by "habit and feeling." This difference was the determination made by Phear.[86] The question of the 12 employments was discussed by T. Munro, M. Wilks, G. W. F. Hegel, Marx and others.[87] The form of serfdom in England is not a proof that the village communities themselves were exploiters, but that they were embedded in the feudal system which was exploitative. The feudal system, in turn was removed, toto coelo, from an original gentile constitution, which

---

[83] The drafts of the correspondence with V. Zasulič were published by D. Rjasanov in *Marx Engels Archiv*, 1926, v. 1. The notes by Marx on Morgan, Maine, Phear, Kovalevsky have been referred to above. Cf. *Ethnological Notebooks*, op. cit.

[84] Masaryk, loc. cit. (note).

[85] G. L. Gomme, *The Village Community*. London 1896, p. 271.

[86] Phear, op. cit., p. 59. Cf. *Ethnological Notebooks*, p. 255.

[87] See my *Asiatic Mode of Production*, op. cit., Pt. I, ch. II.

was the point at issue. The "original gentile marks" antedate the period in which the English village was held in serfdom under a lord. The original gentile marks were not constituted of the lord-serf relation. The question of ownership of village lands by the village cultivators, as distinct from holdings in the hands of the Ayangadees, men of the tool, or handicrafts has been raised in regard to Mycenaean Greece and Hittite Anatolia.[88]

It has been said, by E. B. Leach a.o., that evolutionists have merely asserted, but have explained nothing. In fact, a motor of history is implicit in Tylor, Morgan, Durkheim,[89] but it is not developed by them. The social division of labor, the interrelations between communities, the resultant formation of the political unities are accounted for by the evolutionists, but only in part; the part that they do not take up is the account of the relations of production in society, and therewith of the individuality (the order is important). The greater the development of these relations, the higher that of the individuality at present. The mechanical repetition and local particularism are overcome by the increase in the mutual dependence by exchange between communities (hence commodity production), and the increase in the division of labor, whereby it is transformed into social labor.

The individuality begins at that point where the formation of social classes, hence of class individuality, begins. The individual great man is he who is torn loose from the bonds of the commune, and becomes the spokesman of the wider interest of a class of the overarching community, which would be a spokesman for the whole, the communitas communitatem (Althusius). The group of individuals around the prince, his retinue, the aristocrats, the nobility, the rich, are the first individualities. Opposed to them, the communities and the bondage to the communities remain within the society already divided into opposed classes. In the Asiatic mode of production this bondage is that of tradition and custom, habit and feeling; in the ancient Roman latifundia it is the bondage of slavery; in feudalism it is the bondage of serdom. Labor in society is bound in all these modes of production, both formally and materially until, in the capitalist mode of production, it is formally free. The evolution of the individuality is a movement of the social classes in their re-

---

[88] See Ventris and Chadwick, Palmer and Goetz in Pritchard, all cited above.

[89] The discussion in the twentieth century cannot be held to have gone beyond the points raised in the nineteenth, save in the accumulation of more reliable data. The original perspectives are unchanged. What is needed is the relation of unilinear, and multilinear evolution as a dialectic, and, in this connection, the relation of the abstract and concrete evolutionary movements.

lations to each other. The formal freedom of the individual alone is in question; the relation of mastery and bondage in society is the material bondage of both sides.[90] There are four movements in this evolution: 1. the class interest of the individuals, hence the class individuals, is opposed to the social whole; 2. the social whole is increasingly integrated by the mutual interdependence (commodity exchange, division of social labor); 3. the ruling individualities gain dominance in the overarching community of the civil society; 4. these individualities are in opposition to the communities of the peasants, over whom they stand as rulers, tax collectors, slave drivers, landlords. The concrete historical movements have in no way overcome, or even appeased, ameliorated the contradictions between the individualities and the social whole, and between rulers and governed; on the contrary, to these age-old oppositions, two new factors in the capitalist mode of production are added: the contradiction between formal freedom and material bondage of the working class, on the one side; the ideology of individualism and its complement, the ideological opposition to socialism and communism, on the other.[91]

If Rousseau was ambivalent concerning the individualistic versus the communistic nature of the human subject, Max Weber was not. He was an individualist. He made mention, in the guise of an objectivity, of the weaknesses both of natural right individualism and agrarian communism, but it was only the latter that he sought to demolish in its material base. On the contrary, he limited his attack on individualism to its ideological expression. His sardonic reference to natural right in this connection merely indicates how weak that reed is for the defence of individualism. His attack on the communist doctrine, however, is directed not only against its ideological expression, but against its material, the historical base. The only "natural" communism that Weber allowed was that within the family[92]; but the identification of family and communal interest, or the family as imperium in imperio is an individualist tenet, and was understood as such by Bodin, Hobbes, Hegel and Marx.

The movement of individuality and the ideology of individualism takes place in civil society from the center of political power outward.

---

[90] Marx, *Ethnological Notebooks*, p. 329 (on the first individuality of classes); p. 255 (on bondage in Asiatic mode of production). *Grundrisse*, p. 375 (on bondage to the soil generally). Hegel, *Phänomenologie des Geistes*. 1807 (Herr und Knecht). Cf. *The Asiatic Mode of Production*, op. cit., pt. I, ch. III and ch. VII.

[91] Cf. Roman Rosdolsky, *Zur Entstehungsgeschichte des Marxschen 'Kapital'*. Frankfurt-Wien, 1969, pp. 486-499, on the projection of the problem of individuality under socialism.

[92] Weber, *Wirtschaft und Gesellschaft*, pp. 582f. The communistic socialism is referred by him to the Marxist ideology (ibid., p. 61).

But the polar opposite is the movement of collectivity and the collectivist doctrine that is associated with it. The doctrine of individualism achieved its most forthright expression in the sixteenth and seventeenth centuries; thereafter, Rousseau, Kant and Bentham and the classical economists are its epigones. It appears again, in caricatured form, in the works of Carlyle and the Social Darwinists; and in Herbert Spencer. Having seen no good in defending the doctrine of individualism, Weber took the other course open to him, the destruction, within the limits of his methods, of the doctrine of agrarian communism. We have seen some of the ill-founded tactics, the weakness of the arguments and of the data which he marshalled in his attempt to defend the cause that was already lost.

Nevertheless, the question of agrarian communism is not a simple one; nor does the controversy over agrarian communism stand alone. It is related to a concrete political matter of Marx's lifetime; the Russian socialists had put to him the question of the future of the rural commune, which he related to the future of capitalism and the paths, direct and indirect, in any case plural, to socialism. In the academic world, the question of agrarian communism is a question of history, relative to the reading of texts in Caesar and Tacitus, and the interpretation of tax legislation and land tenure in Byzantine and Russian historical sources. Further, the question of the commune is related to the ideology of socialism in opposition to the ideology of capitalism. The question has a bearing on the conception of man in the Theses on Feuerbach by Marx. There he wrote: "The human essence is no abstraction indwelling in each individual. It is in its reality the ensemble of the social relations." Finally, the question has a bearing on the evolution of humanity, as it was developed in the nineteenth century in general. The ethnologists, historians and sociologists sought to reduce the question to an interpretation of the texts, just as the philosophers sought to reduce the world to the various interpretations of it. The question of individuality and society cannot be so reduced or simplified.

Agrarian communism was reduced to an empirical question by Fustel de Coulanges, Max Weber and others.[93] Yet this reduction of

---

[93] Cf. Emile de Lavelaye, *De la propriété et ses formes primitives*. Paris, 1874; Karl Bücher, tr., with new material added (*Das Ureigentum*, Leipzig, 1879, from 2nd Fr. ed.). Lavelaye had been attacked by Fustel de Coulanges and Denman Ross, and made answer in the 4th Fr. ed., Paris, 1891. V. Pareto, *Les systèmes socialistes*, 3rd ed. Geneva, vol. 1, 1965, p. 141, also thought that Fustel de Coulanges had made an adequate answer to Lavelaye. Pareto cited R. v. Pöhlmann, as though here lay the ultimate authority. Lavelaye was a socialist in the same sense as John Stuart Mill, on intellectual and moral grounds, but without practical consequences. Bücher, *Die Entstehung der Volkswirtschaft* (1893), 9th ed., 1913, adopted a collectivist thesis; Below,

the question is a spurious simplification; the question of agrarian communism stands in direct relation to the opposition of socialism and capitalism, as part of the respective ideologies of collectivism and individualism; further, the theories of social history and social evolution of humanity are connected thereto. Karl Marx took up the various aspects of the questions of landholding in ancient times, and of their implications in the political struggle, in social history and evolution. Here we have been concerned with drawing the different strands together.[94] The object of the attack by Weber was now Urkommunismus, now Agrarkommunismus. That is, a distinction was implied between primitive peoples in a communist condition (Urkommunismus) and agricultural peoples in the protohistoric and early periods (Agrarkommunismus) of European history. Engels did not make this distinction. His position, which was adopted "in the light of the researches of L. H. Morgan", excluded the consideration of the territorial unit as distinct from the kin unit in landholding in the periods of full development of barbarism, before the transition to civilization. Further, Engels brought primitive communism and agrarian communism together under one heading; more precisely, he applied the materials of agrarian communist social life (vide

Das kurze Leben, criticized him as an analogist. B. H. Baden-Powell, *The Indian Village Community*, London, 1896, pp. 4 sq., 398 sq., criticized Maine; socialism was now mentioned, but if this dart was aimed at Maine it was wide of its mark. Maine and his successor, Paul Vinogradoff (*The Growth of the Manor*, 2nd ed., London, 1911; cf. pp. 29, 92ff.) were collectivists, but in no way socialists. Maitland expressed his doubt about a 'communalism as old as individualism,' in F. Pollock and F. W. Maitland, *The History of English Law*, 2nd ed., 1898 (S. Milsom, ed., Cambridge, 1968, vol. 1, p. 688). Maitland was answered by Vinogradoff, *Outlines of Historical Jurisprudence*, Oxford, 1920, vol. 1, pp. 306ff.

[94] Friedrich Engels, *Ursprung der Familie*, op. cit., took up a position that was close to L. H. Morgan's. Engels and Morgan were followed uncritically by Karl Kautsky, who, together with W. Eichhoff, translated Morgan (*Die Urgesellschaft*, 1891). Engels was followed critically by H. Cunow, Soziologie, Ethnologie und materialistische Geschichtsauffassung. *Die Neue Zeit*. vol. 12, pt. 2, 1893-1894; and Die ökonomischen Grundlagen der Mutterherrschaft. Ibid., (l.c.) vol. 16, pt. 1, 1897-1898. Eduard Bernstein, Bemerkungen über Engels' Ursprung der Familie. Vorrede zur italienischen Ausgabe. *Sozialistische Monatshefte*, vol. 4, 1900, undertook a critical attitude toward Morgan, and by implication, of Engels. But this criticism of Morgan is without foundation. See *Ethnological Notebooks*, op. cit., pp. 391f. A more precise criticism of Morgan in the matter of an original landholding in severalty is made by Marx. Morgan had thought that reference to fencing proved the existence of private landownership in Homeric Greece. Marx (*Ethnological Notebooks*, pp. 134f.) wrote that Morgan errs if he believes this.

Plekhanov who responded to the "great man" theory of history from a socialist standpoint, did not reply as strongly as Marx, nor did he raise the points that Marx had raised against that theory. The ideology of individualism attains an extreme expression in the "great man" theory, which is, more exactly, not the theory but the cult of the great men. P. Kropotkin, *Mutual Aid*, London, 1902, attacked the capitalist ideology in its form as individualism, expressed in the guise of Social Darwinism.

Haxthausen, Maurer) to the problems of primitive communism.[95] In this regard his position is diametrically opposed to that of Max Weber.

We cannot separate the historical question of an agrarian communism from the evolutionary question of primitive communism, whether in the form of Urkommunismus or urwüchsiger Kommunismus. Both are part of a series of related questions: The development of the thesis of an Urkommunismus into agrarian communism is by way of communal property. The communal property is posited as original property, Ureigentum, by its proponents, it is opposed by Below and Weber, who raise the questions of systematics and global or cosmic conditions, in order to ward off the dangers of speculation and analogy. The dangers of speculation are not evaded by either tactic. The speculation, on the contrary, resides in the attempt to resolve the question of a particular historical origin beginning in isolation, as though it could be separated from the implied "cosmic" "primitive condition." It is plain that hard facts cannot resolve a single historical problem of origin by themselves. It is only by taking the general evidence of social evolution together that particular problems of origins can be solved in regard to a given historical line. In this case, the reports of Caesar and Tacitus remain important, but are not decisive save as they are taken in combination with the evidence of the mir, the ancient histories of the Greeks, Romans, and the like. Further, the evolutionary sequence is coupled with a philosophy of human nature, and an orientation to a political outcome of present-day struggles. Beside Marx, few have been clear about the battlegrounds on which these issues were and are being fought out. There is an inherent lack of clarity about what Weber and company were about, in part because they themselves were unclear. They expressed themselves aggressively and their expressions were explicit ideological engagements; but they kept within the academic battlefield, hence it is not immediately evident that they were attacking collectivists in general, socialists in particular. Durkheim sought to draw the discussion beyond the empirical limits, and to relate it to the general issue of collectivism, but was ineffectual.

The question of agrarian communism, is to be sure, a matter of

---

[95] In the note to the Eng. tr., London 1888, and the 2nd German ed., Stuttgart, 1890, of Karl Marx and Friedrich Engels, *The Communist Manifesto*, incipit, Engels refers to "primitive communistic society", "urwüchsige kommunistische Gesellschaft." His references are to Haxthausen and Maurer. The object of their research is placed by Engels in line with that of Morgan, whose objects were the more primitive societies, and with his own summation of the same in *The Origin of the Family*.

empirical evidence, in part. But it is not only an empirical question. Contemporary research supports the tenet of landholding by a collectivity in ancient Pylos and Rome, and among the early Slavic and Germanic peoples. There is some question whether these collectivities were kin groups, as sibs, clans, gentes, tribes, or whether territorial groups, as villages. Whether collective tenure was the exclusive mode of landholding; whether there was both property and possession, is still unclear in the early history of a number of European peoples. Yet Fustel de Coulanges, Weber et al. were wrong in their contentions; agrarian communism was practiced in ancient Europe. The implications which they drew from their positions are no less wrong.

If we examine the social life of the ancient Germans or Slavs we are by no means close to an "original" human nature. The concealed premiss in this quest is that of Rousseau, Freud, the ancient primitivists, the modern Romantics: civilized man is damaged, the primitive state is pure, the examination of the primitive state will tell us what human nature is really like. The further premiss of Below and Weber is that the human being is individualist by nature, a premiss which goes back to the early centuries of capitalism, to the school of natural right. The notion of an original human nature, and of an individualism, as the original, are equally untenable, being onesided. The human being is at once product and producer of the social conditions, forming them, being formed by them. The premiss of the doctrines of natural right and of social contract is that the human individual exists prior to the formation of society and enters it by a voluntary compact. The early capitalist ideology sought to make this individualism into an eternal law, just as the early capitalist economists sought to make the laws of the market place into eternal laws. Mercantilists, physiocrats, utilitarians, classical political economists, the cultists of the "great man", of freedom, have allied themselves with these doctrines. Their spokesmen are Carlyle, Spencer, Weber, Maine.

The socialist doctrine is not proved by proving of agrarian communism, the capitalist doctrine is not proved by disproving it. That man is a social animal, a collective animal, who works in combination and not in separation, will not depend on proving that the ancient Suevi held land in severalty. The doctrine of freedom of and for the individual, according to the ideologists of the French Revolution and the American War of Independence, no more than the doctrines of natural right and law, are disproved by the evidence of the mark and mir. Social scientists, we have seen, naively sought to eliminate the ideological side of these problems, and to resolve them into empirical formulations alone, whereby they would be solved by bringing historical, ethnological, sociological facts to bear upon them. They evade the debate over the political, ideological issues, retreating into empiricism, separating what is not to be separated. The academic discussion of the ancient agrarian communes has been bound by rules of a positivist provenience, maintaining a pose of being above the battle. As a result, even the best of the participants have been constrained to know nothing of the issues outside their immediate scholarly competence, whereby they have reduced and simplified the matters without warrant, being either less than candid, or unable to probe deeply or extensively into the issues raised. The initiative in the debate has been left in the hands of conservatives of a bygone era, the socialists having been trapped by the same separation of the political from the scientific issues, ceding points they ought not to have ceded; that separation is untenable for political and scientific reasons.

The debate over the ancient mark and mir has had an indecisive outcome; yet the question of an ancient or original land ownership in common is not an outmoded one. For the central issue in this connection is not the conception of this given feature of human history or evolution. On the contrary, the central issue is the struggle over the future of the human kind. It is in the light of this struggle that the attempt at a coherent interpretation of the world is then made; the debate over the reports of Caesar and Tacitus then takes its place in the latter, which is the lesser issue.

EARLY HISTORY OF THE LABOR THEORY OF VALUE

THREE

EARLY HISTORY OF THE LABOR THEORY OF VALUE

The labor theory of value as it is here traced is the product of the modern capitalist period, having its roots in ancient and medieval thought both in the east and west. But whereas prior to the modern period the theoretical expressions were obscure, they received increasingly clear formulation from the sixteenth century and on. The history of the theory was set forth by Karl Marx in relation to his research on surplus value[1]; since then it has had not so much the history of its development as the history of its attack and defence.[2] Our concern is not, as it was with Marx, to trace the historical development of the theory of value in terms of its system, but on the contrary, to trace its systematic development in terms of its history, particularly in Europe during the sixteenth to eighteenth centuries. To this end, the two components of the theory have been separated: the relation of labor in society, and the relation of labor to nature. These two components were not treated conjointly by the forerunners of Karl Marx; indeed their synthesis was not effected through explicit statement until the two relations were brought together in the treatment of value in use and value in exchange, on the one side, and in the treatment of labor abstract and concrete on the other, such as will be found in the chapter on the commodity in Marx, *Das Kapital*, I, 1. The two sides of the theory are separated abstractly, hypothetically, concretely they are inseparable. The labor theory of value

---

[1] Karl Marx, *Theorien über den Mehrwert*. K. Kautsky ed. Stuttgart 1905-1910. Marx Engels *Werke*, Bd. 26. Berlin 1965-1968. Marx, Randglossen zu A. Wagners "Lehrbuch der Politischen Ökonomie." *Werke*, Bd. 19, 1962, pp. 355-383. Marx, *Zur Kritik der politischen Ökonomie*. Berlin 1859. Erstes Kapital, A. (*Werke*, Bd. 13, pp. 37sq.).

[2] Rosa Luxemburg, *Die Akkumulation des Kapitals*. Berlin 1913. N. I. Bukharin and E. Preobraženskij, *Azbuka Kommunizma*, Peterburg 1920. Rudolf Hilferding, *Das Finanzkapital*, Wien 1927. I. I. Rubin, *Očerki po istorii stoimosti*. Moscow-Leningrad. 3rd ed. 1928. Roman Rosdolsky, *Zur Entstehungsgeschichte des Marxschen 'Kapital'*. Frankfurt/Main, 2nd ed. 1969. Eugen Böhm-Bawerk, *Karl Marx and the Close of his System*. Answer to foregoing by R. Hilferding. P. Sweezy ed. New York 1966. F. Oppenheimer, *Ricardos Grundrententheorie*, Berlin 1909. Ludwig v. Mises, *Die Gemeinwirtschaft*, Wien 1932. Joan Robinson, *An Essay on Marxian Economics*, London 1966. See also her Introduction to Eng. tr. of R. Luxemburg, *Accumulation of Capital*, New York 1951. R. L. Meek, *Studies in the Labour Theory of Value*. 2nd ed. London 1973. Eric Roll, *A History of Economic Thought*. 4th ed. London 1973.

has been erroneously attributed to Marx, perhaps by the process of what is called by the philologists retrogressive assimilation, but he himself made no claim to its invention. The working class makes use concretely, daily, of the theory according to which the value of commodities is determined by the labor time needed for their production. An economic law of the classical political economists, William Petty, Adam Smith, David Ricardo, it has since become an embattled ideological slogan. Yet it is bound in the capitalist historical period to the science of nature and of natural relations on the one hand, and to the science of society and of social relations on the other; the two sides were developed in their separation pari passu. Thus we shall see that the twin categories of John Locke, of the labor of the body and the work of the hands, played their part in the development of the theory; however, although the two categories were merely juxtaposed to each other by him, yet they stand as the inverse categories, each of the other.

In north Italy, England and the Low Countries, in the sixteenth century and on, labor was formally free to contract as a party equal with capital for the sale of labor power, being no longer bound to the means of production, the soil above all. There and then, capital was introduced into the period of its self-expansion (Selbstverwertung, self-valorization).[3] The process of self-valorization is not only one of the two differentia specifica of the capitalist form of the social production process, it is the central one in the relation of capital to surplus value, just as the release of labor from its bondage is the central one in the relation of labor to the mode of value formation in capitalism generally.[4] These two conditions sine qua non of capitalism did not come forth for the first time in history, nor had commodity exchange and production made its first historical appearance then; but these conditions, and the formal institutions of contract, market, joint-stock companies, instruments of credit and banking, which are related to them as form to content, were given new functions at this time. The national form of the state and the clear separation of the public from private spheres of social life were now fully developed.

[3] Karl Marx, *Grundrisse der Kritik der politischen Ökonomie* (1857-1858). Berlin 1953, p. 375. Cf. Lawrence Krader, *The Asiatic Mode of Production*. Assen 1975, pp. 214-230.
[4] Marx, *Das Kapital* I, 4th ed. Hamburg 1914, p. 330, refers to the Selbstverwertung of capital as a particular means of producing relative surplus value. In a philological note (*Le Capital*, J. Roy, transl. Paris 1873, p. 257n.) it is stated: "Il nous semble que le mot *valorisation* exprimerait le plus exactement le mouvement qui fait d'une valeur le moyen de sa propre multiplication." This movement is proper to the production of capital; it is not so to the exchange and production of commodities, such as is developed in the Asiatic mode of production or in the economy of Aristotle's day.

Corporations underwent structural changes, from being close in their encasement of labor or capital, they were now open and voluntary. Value was not discovered for the first time, but the formulations of its laws were restated, and its two aspects, of value in exchange and in use were indeed brought out for the first time.

The distinction between chrematistics, or acquisition of wealth, and political economy, was put forward by Aristotle; value equivalence between commodities was then brought out by him. The distinction between the household economy and political economy proper, or production, exchange, distribution and consumption in society, were likewise well-known to him and his successors.[5] The new elements that were brought out in the sixteenth century were these: freedom and equality in economy, law, politics, society generally were fixed in the people's minds at this time, if not fully realized, then as the beginning of the process. The freedom and equality, however, are formal matters only; they are to this extent an illusion. But that illusion was accepted as real. From the sixteenth to the twentieth centuries we have seen the extension of this illusion, as a popular prejudice which existed at first in posse and now exists in esse everywhere. Aristotle had no such illusion; he had another, according to which the organization of human beings in society conformed to a biological distinction between the labor of the hand and the head. This distinction is a popular prejudice among the university elite today, widespread, as though nothing had happened between Aristotle's time and our own.

At the beginning of the sixteenth century, Machiavelli and Luther undertook to rethink these relations. Machiavelli conceived that wealth comes from the labor of the hands; it does not come from the head, nor from nature; nature is the indirect source of wealth, which is to be shaped by human industry.[6] Now the relation of labor is twofold: it is labor in relation to nature, or the labor upon the natural resources in the production of useful things. This is concrete labor. Labor is at the same time a relation in society; on the one hand it is the relation of social labor in general; on the other it is the relation between human beings in particular economic formations of society; it is the relation of labor in the family, in the community, village, clan or tribe; it is the relation of labor in the factory. The value of labor in production and exchange was grasped by the human mind during the sixteenth and seventeenth centuries in either of two ways:

---

[5] Aristotle, Politics, Book I. On Slavery, 1253b-1255b; (household and property, 1253b-1254a). On value and chrematistics, 1256a-1260ob.

[6] Niccolo Machiavelli, The History of Florence (1535). Book II, ch. I.

either it was labor in society in general, or it was labor in relation to nature. At this time, labor was considered both concretely, in relation to the production of useful things, and abstractly, in relation to exchange of things produced. In order to effect such exchanges, a value had to be put upon the labor. The act of exchange and its expression in terms of abstract measures of value were not introduced for the first time; but the theoretical expression of the exchange was now promulgated, at first slowly, and only much later became widespread, in the later seventeenth and eighteenth centuries, with the full development of the capitalist mode of production in western Europe.

The path to the expression of the value of labor, we have seen, was pointed out by Machiavelli. But he did not give the value an expression, and he related labor only to nature and not to society; human industry was directly coupled to the winning of natural resources for social wellbeing, it was not abstracted from nature by him. Luther at the same time grasped the other side of the relation, but not the first. Labor time is abstract measure of gain or wages; he did not regard it as the producer of useful things. The merchant's time is subject to computation of the amount of labor which it contains, according to Luther. It is clear that he only partly grasped what he had before him, because the labor was separated by him from capital: His concern was with usury. But usury points in two directions, backward to the middle ages and antiquity, as an instrument of evil, and forward, still as an instrument of evil, but inseparably connected to the self-expansion of capital. Luther sermonized against usury at various times: Von Kaufshandlung und Wucher, 1524; An die Pfarrherrn wider den Wucher zu predigen, 1540. This concern is toto coelo removed from production; it is solely concerned with economic relations within society. The trade of merchants is distinct from usury, that is, circulation of commodities is distinguished by Luther from financial arts and great bankers' dealings (Fuggerei). Money is not like other goods; he distinguished between money as means of purchase and money as a means of payment; usury falls on the side of the latter usage.[7] But trade, that is, buying and selling – strictly, he said, "buyer and seller" – is a worthy thing: cattle, wool, grain, butter, milk come from the earth and are distributed among mankind. He did not conceive that these goods are the products of human labor, they are gifts of God. "Es sind Gottes Gaben, die er aus der Erden gibt, und unter die Menschen teilet." The merchant is advised to

---

[7] Martin Luther, An die Pfarrherrn wider den Wucher zu predigen. Vermanung. 1540. Cf. Karl Marx, Das Kapital I, op. cit., pp. 99, 155, 556.

compute the time and amount of his labor, and find out what a common day laborer earns. "After this, reckon up how many days you have taken to get and acquire the commodity, and how much labor and danger you have withstood therein. For great labor and much time should also have that much more wages."[8] This is a method of computation of labor according to the delimited time and effort, hence of the labor power. The unit is the earnings of the common day laborer. But the merchant withstands danger(!) – Will his unit of earnings then not be the multiple several times over that which the common day laborer earns?

It was not for the first time, however, that economic value was given this form in its expression. The Chinese mathematician Chi'n Chiu-shao had in the thirteenth century already arrived at a means of reckoning up the quantity of labor in a task. In his system of mathematical computation, Ch'in set a problem of constructing towers of wood and of brick and mortar. The labor in construction was broken down in tasks, the tasks in daily rates; the rates varied according to the task and the season: spring and fall standards differed. Thus the entire product was given an abstract expression which was reckoned up in terms of units of time in days, by seasons, and kind of labor according to the division of labor, in the construction: carpenters, rope weavers, stone carvers, earth diggers, brick makers. The construction was reckoned by piece work, according to the number of beams, posts, stone plates, bricks; it is inferred that a daily rate was fixed for each task, "because salaries were reckoned per day."[9] A certain confusion should be cleared up in this connection: Demiéville has written that the work just mentioned was not measured in units of time, but by tasks.[10] But he is wrong; time was the basis of reckoning. The earnings of the laborers were measured by the amount of time, according to the season.[11] Chi'in was concerned, for complete computation, with the method of reckoning the organization of the work and the amount of piece work or tasks necessary for the completion of the construction; he was concerned with the amount of labor measured in units of time necessary for its completion. He was concerned with the relations to the natural materials, wood, stone, earth, clay, iron; with the relations between men in the social division

---

[8] Luther, Von Kaufshandlung und Wucher, 1524.

[9] Ulrich Libbrecht, *Chinese Mathematics in the Thirteenth Century*. The Shu-shu chiu-chang of Ch'in Chiu-shao. MIT Press, 1973, pp. 447ff. See Joseph Needham, *Science and Civilisation in China*. Cambridge, 1959, v. 3, passim.

[10] Paul Demiéville, Review, Che-yin Song Li Ming-tchong Ying-tsao fa che. *Bulletin de l'Ecole Francaise d'Extreme Orient*, v. 25, 1925, p. 263. Quoted in Libbrecht, op. cit.

[11] Libbrecht, op. cit., pp. 455f.

of labor; and with the amount of the labor power and labor time. The European theorists were many centuries behind the sophistication of the Chinese mathematician; his effort was isolated, however: it was not taken up in China until the eighteenth and nineteenth centuries, and in Europe. The historians of science, Needham and Libbrecht, have given Ch'in Chiu-shao his due in regard to his mathematical contributions. Here we pay attention to his place in the development of the labor theory of value.

Giovanni Botero was concerned with the source of value in the economy, but only in reference to the dichotomy, nature versus art or culture. Thus, he was bound within the frame of reference of his enemy, Machiavelli, who, we have seen, valued the work of the human hands as opposed to the bounty of nature. Botero asked, which is more important to the greatness of a state, the fertility of the soil or human industry? His answer was, the latter. Nature provides the material, but human skill gives the material its form. The products of man are more numerous and are worth more than the natural product.[12] Alone among these forerunners of the labor theory of value, Botero thought of human production as a contribution to the worth or value of the thing produced. But he did not conceive of measuring the amount of labor, still less of applying the measure to the value or worth. Luther had arrived at the second step, the measurement of the amount of labor, but he had no notion that labor was a commodity, that it had a value, and that such a value is to be measured by the amount of labor time contained therein. It is idle to tax Luther with an omission that is irrelevant to the task that he had set for himself. On the contrary, it is necessary to appreciate justly what he had achieved in the observation and consciousness of the events of his surroundings, and the expression that he gave to his observations. It is necessary at the same time to divest this appreciation of vain claims to which he neither aspired nor succeeded. Yet this is what Roscher had done, who attributed to his hero the achievement, "later taken up again by Adam Smith, of applying the common day wage labor as *measure of value.*"[13] The idea of Botero's, a half century later, is not found in Luther; the idea of Luther, of measuring, is not found in Botero. Each has a part of the thought, neither has the whole. Chinese mathematical expression had already arrived

---

[12] Giovanni Botero, *Delle Cause della grandezza delle Citte.* Rome, 1588. Bk. II, ch. 7. This was then reprinted in his *Ragion di Stato* (1589) Venice, 1598, Bk. VIII, ch. 3. See Botero, *Reason of State*, P. J. and D. P. Waley, tr., Yale 1956, p. 150.
[13] Wilhelm Roscher, *Geschichte der National-Oekonomik in Deutschland.* München 1874, p. 61: "Sehr merkwürdig ist der nachmals von Adam Smith wieder aufgenommene Gedanke, die gemeine Taglöhnerarbeit als *Wertmassstab* anzuwenden." Emphasis is Roscher's.

at the method of reckoning the labor time, but this was not taken up by the Europeans in the sixteenth century, for it was unknown to them; but Chi'n had not set himself the task of giving quantitative expression to economic value, value theory was outside his frame of reference. Botero found the term for that theory; he did not have the method for its computation. Botero followed a different line of thought from Ch'in and Luther. His problem was the relation of labor to nature, concrete labor; the problem of Luther was the relation of labor in society, or labor in its abstract side.

The relation of exchange and use value was not understood as a composite of the relations of man in society and to nature by the early writers. The Florentine banker B. Davanzati understood the problem of the relation of exchange and use value within the system of the economy, and indeed it was relevant to the problem of the sixteenth century writers, of how to secure the constancy of real value, or of real price; the two sides, value and price, were not separated by them.[14] Montanari and Belloni sought to solve the practical problems of the value of money and the balance of trade with the same system as that of Davanzati.[15] This tendency was summed up abstractly by Galiani, who had no practical problems in view as his forerunners and contemporaries. His problem was the theory of money, which has both an abstract and a concrete function: on the one side, as measure of value, on the other as the means to satisfy wants. Money is treated as a commodity by Galiani.[16]

Thomas Hobbes took up the problem of social labor, holding that it is a form of bondage, of which there are two kinds: physical bondage and bondage by contract. This is an aphoristic way of accounting for the formation of civil society. According to Hobbes, men lived at first in a state of nature; this is nonsense, and Hobbes knew better, for he contradicted himself, holding that even while in the state of nature men devised and held to covenants, being in turn held to them by virtuous sentiments. Once men had emerged from the state of primitive or simple life they lived in civil society, the polis, according to Aristotle, the city, according to Machiavelli, the commonwealth, according to Hobbes. Labor is free in the Hobbesian primitive state, it is bound in the Hobbesian commonwealth. At first the bondage is physical, e.g., slavery or serfdom, whereby civil society is

[14] Bernardo Davanzati, *Lezione delle monete*. (1582). Firenze, 1588.

[15] Geminiano Montanari, *Breve trattato del valore della moneta in tutti gli stati*. Modena, 1680. Girolamo Belloni, *Dissertazioni sopra il commercio*, Roma, 1750.

[16] Ferdinando Galiani, *Della Moneta*. Napoli, 1750. Gian (Giovanni) Rinaldo Carli, *Del valore e della proporzione dei metalli monetati con i genere in Italia*. Delle monete e dell' istituzione delle zecche d'Italia. 4 vol. Venezia, 1754-1760.

formed, and men are subjected to masters, for the first time. They are later freed from physical bondage, but are bound by contract, which is a further development of civil society, in the period of capitalism, and is the characteristic of that period. At this time, and in this condition of political economy, labor is freed, but is at the same time under contractual obligation to perform its exchange for wages.[17] The economic philosophy of individualism, radical materialism, and utilitarianism, the principle of the war of all against all, whereby, in order to constrain this belligerency political societies are formed by voluntary covenants, were introduced by Hobbes. The sovereignty of these societies, or commonwealths, is acknowledged by each of the hitherto freely contracting parties.

The economic principles of Hobbes are, in outline, the following:[18]

1. The supply of wants of a commonwealth consists in the provision of commodities. The provision is the plenty of the materials conducive to life in society, their preparation and distribution.

2. Plenty depends on the labor and industry of men.

3. Wants are supplied by commodities. These are either free or for labor purchased by mankind. [Value in use is thereby distinguished from value in exchange. The value in exchange of the commodity is the labor for which it is sold.][19]

4. "For a man's labor also is a commodity exchangeable for benefit, as well as any other thing."[20] [Hence his labor capacity is subject to contract, as any other commodity. The foundation of the commonwealth, or of political society, has the same basis in contract as the contract for labor, according to Hobbes.]

5. The trading in commodities is another form of labor. [This is not the converse of the foregoing.]

6. The produce of the territory under the dominion of a commonwealth is, with few exceptions, incapable of sustaining it. Most of these lands produce a surplus of one commodity or another. The production of a surplus and its exchange against other surpluses are interconnected.

---

[17] Thomas Hobbes, *The Elements of Law* (1640). F. Tönnies, ed. 2nd ed. M. Goldsmith. London, 1969. Pt. 2, ch. 3. Hobbes, *De Cive*. Paris, 1642, ch. II, 9 and ch. VIII, 3.

[18] Thomas Hobbes, *Leviathan*, or the Matter, Form and Power of a Commonwealth. London 1651. Pt. II, ch. 24.

[19] Marx, *Theorien über den Mehrwert* I. (*Werke*, op. cit., Bd. 26.1, p. 341):
Hobbes also has labor as the sole source of all wealth, aside from the gifts of nature, such as are found in a consumable condition. God (nature) "usually either freely giveth, or for labor selleth to mankind." (Hobbes, loc. cit.).

[20] Hobbes, loc. cit. Cf. Marx, op. cit., p. 329. Marx commented in reference to the term *labor* in this statement: "hence the use of his laboring power."

7. Commodities have an abstract expression in money. Labor, as a commodity, has such an abstract expression. Money is the abstract measure of value. [The concept of production of a surplus and its exchange was brought out by Hobbes. Wants are supplied by commodities; the surplus produced is exchanged against foreign importations; the surplus produced is surplus to the producer which is therefore the entire nation.]

8. On the division of labor in society: Everyone has either a property in land or some other commodity. Land is a commodity as any other. Likewise Hobbes wrote of "a natural property in some useful art." [But this can only mean that labor too is a commodity as any other, as we have seen.] Men have these commodities in excess; that is, they have a portion that they can spare. These are the properties in land, goods and useful arts, which are all commodities. Each owner and producer then distributes his surplus, transferring it mutually to one another, by exchange and contract.

9. "Arts of public use, as fortification, making use of engines and other instruments of war, because they confer to the defence, and to victory, are power; and though the true mother of them be science, namely mathematics, yet because they are brought into the light by the hand of the artificer they be esteemed (the midwife passing with the vulgar for the mother) as his issue."[21]

10. "The value or worth of a man is as of all other things, his price; that is to say, so much as would be given for the use of his power."[22]

Hobbes conceived of the production of a surplus both in regard to the entire commonwealth and in relation to the individual laborer or artisan; the surplus product is related to necessary production and to the distribution of the surplus. Hobbes, further, expressed the relation of mastery and bondage. He conceived of the production of commodities by labor, of the exchange of labor for commodities, and of labor as a commodity. His distinction regarding goods that are freely obtained without labor is fundamental to the conception of commodity, exchange, and exchange value of labor. He gave to commodities the abstract measure of value in money. He related labor to labor power; and he conceived both of the relation of labor to nature and the relation of labor in society. He did not arrive at

---

[21] Hobbes, op. cit., ch. 10. Marx, loc. cit., commented on this passage, which he had excerpted: "According to Hobbes, science, and not effectual labor, is the mother of the arts." And again Marx: "The product of mental labor – science – always stands far below its value. Because the labor time which is needed to reproduce it stands in no relation at all to the labor time required for its original production. For instance, a schoolboy can learn the binomial theorem in an hour."

[22] Hobbes, loc. cit. Marx held that Hobbes had arrived at the concept of labor power (loc. cit.).

the measure of value as labor time, and he did not bring together the two sides of the relation of labor, to nature and in society.

William Petty, James Massie, David Hume, Adam Smith, David Ricardo are directly in the line of development of the labor theory of value; concretely, in the line of the measure of value by labor time, Petty wrote: "Let a hundred men work 10 years upon corn, and the same number of men the same time, upon silver; I say, that the net proceed of the silver is the price of the whole net proceed of the corn, and like parts of the one, the price of like parts of the other."[23] Petty's method is to analyze the relation of labor in society; the net proceed of the product is its value, determined by the quantity of labor effectual in its production. Petty wrote down *price* instead of *value*. Ch'in Chiu-Shao, Machiavelli, Luther, Davanzati, Botero and Hobbes are part of the prehistory of the theory of value: Petty, Locke, Massie, Hume and Smith are a part of its history. All are in the line of its development, in which Ch'in and Hobbes took part on both sides, the relation to nature and the relation in society; Luther in one side, the relation in society; Petty, Massie and Hume, too, were on this side. Botero and Locke were on the side of Machiavelli: their problem was that of the relation of man and nature; Adam Smith, as we shall see, who comes most directly to the modern formulation of the theory of value begins likewise with the relation of man and nature. We have seen in the passage cited from Petty above what this means in practice. The topics dealt with by Massie differ from those of Petty but little; this is not explained by the fact that Massie wrote against Petty: Massie also wrote against Locke.[24] Hume kept strictly within the same frame of reference. His law, "Everything in the world is purchased by labor,"[25] is a modification of the formulation of the same matter by Hobbes. (See above.) The modification eliminates the phrasing relating labor to nature, and concentrates on one side, the relation in society.

The problems of economics taken up by Locke have, in general, their starting point in the relation of man and nature. In his essay, Of Property, the question of the relation to nature of human labor is twofold: 1. – How the alienation from nature, from the common right to the private right, takes place; and 2. – the affirmative of the

---

[23] Sir William Petty, *A Treatise of Taxes and Contributions* (1662). London 1679, p. 24. Marx, op. cit., p. 415.

[24] Joseph Massie, *An Essay on the Governing Causes of the Natural Rate of Interest:* Wherein the Sentiments of Sir William Petty and Mr. Locke, on that head, are considered. London 1750.

[25] David Hume, Of Commerce. (*Political Discourses*, Edinburgh 1752). Repr., Hume, *Writings on Economics*. E. Rotwein ed. Madison 1970, p. 11. See also the essay, Of Interest, op. cit.

proposition that this alienation and appropriation serves as the origin of the civilized part of mankind. The practices in England are thereby distinguished from those of the American Indians. Both the civilized Englishman and the uncivilized Indian share this in common: property in a thing is a right which is determined by labor. The labor of killing a deer marks it off from the common right of all; the sole right to it rests with him who killed it. The difference between the uncivilized and the civilized lies in the right of property in land. The measure of property, argued Locke, is set by the extent of man's labor and the convenience of life; it is labor that puts the difference in value on everything, and the greatest part of value on land.[26] Locke was but marginally interested in the relation of labor in society: money, commodities, exchange, market, are mentioned only in passing. Locke did not further analyze the categories of labor and property, nor see that they had the abstract expression of measure in common. Ch'in and Luther had already gone further in this line; Hobbes, without achieving these limits, had yet surpassed Locke in this regard. Locke wrote, "It is labor that puts the difference in value on everything." He did not show how the initial value, nor the difference, is to be computed.

Petty, who most immediately preceded Locke, actually computed the amount of labor time in the production of corn and silver. Locke was behindhand in this quantitative development as well. We shall shortly see where his contribution lay.

Adam Smith summed up the discussion of the expression of value in terms of labor:[27]

> The value of any commodity, therefore, to the person who possesses it, and who means not to use it or consume it himself, but to exchange it for other commodities, is equal to the quantity of labor which it enables him to purchase or command. Labor, therefore, is the real measure of the exchangeable value of all commodities.

> The real price of every thing, what every thing costs to the man who wants to acquire it, is the toil and trouble of acquiring it. What every thing is really worth to the man who has acquired it, and who wants to dispose of it or exchange it for something else, is the toil and trouble which it can save to himself, and which it can impose upon other people. What is bought with money

[26] John Locke, *Two Treatises of Civil Government*, 1690. Bk. II, ch. 5: On "the civilized part of mankind" (§ 30). Property in land (§ 32). On labor value (§§ 36, 40, 43).

[27] Adam Smith, *An inquiry into the Nature and Causes of the Wealth of Nations*, (1776). New York 1937. E. Cannan ed. Bk. I, ch. 5, pp. 3of. He refers to Hume, *Political Discourses*, op. cit.: "Everything in the world is purchased by labor." – See above.

or with goods is purchased by labor, as much as what we acquire by the toil of our own body.

Labor was the first price, the original purchase money that was paid for all things. It was not by gold or by silver, but by labor, that all the wealth of the world was originally purchased; and its value, to those who possess it, and who want to exchange it for some new productions, is precisely equal to the quantity of labor which it can enable them to purchase or command.

The initial value of a thing, aside from subsequent differences in value of things was ascertained by Smith; this is what Locke had overlooked. Value is worth, the real price or cost of a thing; labor is the real measure of value, says Smith, because by labor we alienate a thing from nature and appropriate it. The amount of its value is determined by the amount of the labor applied in its alienation and appropriation. Adam Smith distinguished between value in use and exchange; the latter had the abstract value of labor that is summed up in its constitution as its determination. This general formulation brings together that which was developed from Machiavelli, Botero, Hobbes and Locke, on the one side, and Ch'in, Luther, Petty, Massie, and Hume on the other. In general, those who had taken up the category of labor in relation to nature did not give a quantitative formulation to its value expression; it is the contribution of those who took up the relation of labor in society to have done so. The quantitative formulation of the expression of value as achieved by Smith leaves something to be desired, as Smith himself admitted:

But though labor be the real measure of the exchangeable value of all commodities, it is not that by which their value is commonly estimated. It is often difficult to ascertain the proportion between two different quantities of labor. The time spent in two different sorts of work will not always alone determine this proportion. The different degrees of hardship endured, and of ingenuity exercised, must likewise be taken into account. There may be more labor in an hour's hard work than in two hours easy business; or in an hour's application to a trade which it costs ten years labor to learn, than in a month's industry at an ordinary and obvious employment. But it is not easy to find any accurate measure of hardship or ingenuity.[28]

Adam Smith recognized a difficulty in the expression of value; his theory of value in society could not be expressed in quantitative terms. Ricardo[29] pointed out that Adam Smith erred in holding

---

[28] Smith, op. cit., p. 31. See also pp. 55f. and 99.
[29] David Ricardo, *The Principles of Political Economy and Taxation* (1821). London 1957, p. 9.

"that as labor may sometimes *purchase* a greater and sometimes a smaller quantity of goods, it is their value which varies, not that of the labor which purchases them; "... – but it is correct to say, as Adam Smith had previously said, "that the proportion between the quantities of labor necessary for acquiring different objects seems to be the only circumstance which can afford any rule for exchanging them for one another"; or in other words that it is the comparative quantity of commodities which labor will produce that determines their present and past relative value, and not the comparative quantities of commodities which are given to the laborer in exchange for his labor. This corresponds to one of Adam Smith's formulations; Smith contradicted this by the alternative which Ricardo held to be erroneous. But even the more plausible, Ricardian, theory of relative value of labor fails of the quantitative expression. Smith held that value is real price; but value is not any sort of price; its quantitative value is not fixed by factors external to itself. It is the factor determining the value of other commodities. This is one of the matters that Smith brought out, and after him Ricardo, who distinguished thereby between relative and absolute, real, value.

Labor is variable, says Smith, not accordingly as it is extrinsically difficult, but accordingly as it is difficult to master. The external conditions under which the labor is performed may be hard: this, however, does not increase its value. Labor in the mines, in danger and the dark, is a notorious case; labor power of miners is notoriously undervalued: black workers in the United States are given work that is "hard, hot or heavy"; I have heard this in Newark, New Jersey, and in Chicago.[30] This does not increase the value of the labor capacity or power.

---

[30] The converse was practiced in ancient Rome. Human labor was then as a rule performed by slaves, whose overseer received less to meet his wants than they because his work was lighter. Who is slave, who free? See Theodor Mommsen, *Römische Geschichte*, 6th ed. Bd. I, Berlin 1874, pp. 829f. His sources are the accounts by Cato (d. 149 B.C.) and Varro (d. 27 B.C.), both entitled De Re Rustica, of agriculture at the end of the Republic. We are dealing here with the determination of value by social labor throughout the history of civil society and economy; it makes no difference whether the social labor in question was slave or free, whether the determination of value is made by labor or by labor power in society. (On the difference between labor and labor power see Marx, *Kapital* I, op. cit., ch. 4, pt. 3. See also his pamphlet, *Wages, Price and Profit*. London 1898, pt. VII: – originally an address delivered June 1865.) In the mode of production of capital, labor power is expressed in discrete units of labor time. It is so expressed because it is a commodity. Labor as such is neither of necessity a commodity nor the expression of discrete temporal units. By virtue of its commodity relation, social labor achieves its freedom pro forma in history: thereby the labor relation of the feudal mode of production was overcome and the transition to the capitalist mode of production effected.

The factor of ingenuity, length of training, and skill of labor does, on the contrary, raise the value of the labor power, as Adam Smith correctly pointed out. Ricardo was likewise clear on the distinction between the value of labor and price or wage of labor.[31] With Ricardo, however, the labor theory of value was restricted to the relation of labor in society, and the relation to nature was excluded from his theory. He was not clear about the relation of labor to its power or time.

The service of Marx was to pull the different strands of labor theory together. The historians who were anti-labor or anti-socialist have sought to deprive Marx of the right to the authorship of the labor theory of value. This quest is vain. Marx wrote many studies of the sources of this theory, in which he combined the expression of abstract and concrete labor, the theory of labor in relation to nature and in society, of necessary and surplus labor, labor of head and hand, labor productive and unproductive.

Locke had introduced the distinction between labor and work which has been the subject of much attention and some misunderstanding. Locke wrote:

> Though the earth and all inferior creatures be common to all men, yet every man has a "property" in his own "person." This nobody has a right to but himself. The "labor" of his body and the "work" of his hands are both his.[32]

Adam Smith wrote of the division of labor and the quantity of work produced, whereby the two concepts were juxtaposed by him. Labor is the analytic category, work is the heaped up or amassed. Smith wrote of the 'productive power of labor', labor as process; work as the result that is stored, reckoned up, as the end product, or stock; labor, in his usage, is employed, and not work; labor and industry are the same in regard to productive power, as opposed to work, which is produced thereby.[33] The French *Encyclopédie* has reference

---

This mode of production is at present undergoing a further transformation, being in the process of its establishment as the mode of production of capital in general. At present as in the history of capitalism, the freedom pro forma of labor is determined by a twofold relation in society: 1. by the self-valorization of capital; 2. by the commodity relation of social labor. Labor power is distinct from labor by virtue of the commodity relation of labor, which is an exchange relation, not by relation of labor in production.

[31] Adam Smith, op. cit., Bk. I, ch. 10. See Ricardo, op. cit., pp. 12 and 28. Smith thought thereby that he could account for the higher wages of this segment of labor. This is an error; the wages of labor and value of labor are not the same.

[32] Locke, op. cit., Bk. II, 27. Thereafter in this Treatise, Locke treats of labor, more rarely of work, but never juxtaposes the two in this way.

[33] Smith, op. cit., Bk. I, ch. 1, passim. Cf. ibid., p. 86: "...to increase [labor's] productive powers, and to make a smaller quantity of labor produce a greater quantity of work." On the same theme, cf. also pp. 260 and 641.

to "la célérité du travail et la perfection de l'ouvrage;"[34] Mandeville, as Adam Smith's editor has pointed out, was the source of the phrase, division of labor; Smith's usage is in general consonance with Mandeville's; these usages have one aspect in common, they view the relation of labor and work from without; in particular, the problem of Adam Smith in the relation of the labor process and its product, the work produced; Hume says the same.[35] It is the viewpoint of the observer or theorist that is studied by Mandeville, Hume and Adam Smith. Locke's viewpoint is in this regard opposed to theirs, taking up the problem of labor from within, from the viewpoint of the toilers. Locke ascertains the right that the toiler has before he introduces man into society. (The problem is artificial, but that is a later judgment, from the standpoint of the nineteenth and twentieth centuries; but it was a valid problem in the seventeenth century.) At the time that the earth, the plants and animals on it are common to all men, yet every man has a property in his own being, his bodily organs, to which he alone has a right. The right is affirmed at this stage by the body's labor and hand's work, or handiwork, and cannot be shared with the inferior creatures; it is an exclusively human property. The labor of the body is shared with the animal kingdom. The toiler, being both human and animal, has by his animal and human effort the right to his labor and work. Hume criticized Locke's usage, but did not grasp that their problems were different, as their viewpoints were opposed. The distinction made by Locke is a means to affirmation of a right. Hume takes up only the result of the labor, or the right that is acquired thereby: "We cannot," he writes, "be said to join our labor in any thing but in a figurative sense. Properly speaking, we only make an alteration on it by our labor."[36] Locke proposes however, that there are two relations: the work of the hands, which alters or shapes a thing, and the labor of the body, which joins itself to it; the body occupies its bit of earth's surface and ultimately joins itself to the soil, returning to it.[37]

[34] Ed., d'Alembert and Diderot, vol. I, Paris 1751, s.v. Art. Cf. Adam Smith, op. cit., p. 7.
[35] On the part played by Bernard Mandeville in the idea of the division of labor, see the note by E. Cannan to his ed. of Adam Smith, *Wealth of Nations*, op. cit., p. 3. Mandeville takes his place in the history of the labor theory of value, in view of the relation of labor to nature. In his Essay on Charity and Charity Schools, included in his work, *The Fable of the Bees*, London 1723 ed., he formulated the Latin phrase, Dii laboribus omnia vendunt, the gods sell everything for Labor. David Hume, *A Treatise of Human Nature* (1739), wrote that individual labors are insufficient for the execution of any considerable work (L. Selby-Bigge ed., Oxford 1968, p. 485). See Edward Gibbon, *Decline and Fall of the Roman Empire*, 1776, ch. 44.
[36] Hume, op. cit., pp. 505f.
[37] Hannah Arendt, *The Human Condition*, New York 1959, reports on analogous distinctions in ancient and modern tongues on pp. 314, 322, also p. 72. It is also conceivable that Locke in

The insight afforded by Locke is left without development. Hume's problem, we have seen, was that of the relation of labor in society. Locke dealt primarily with the relation of labor to nature to the end of establishing a right of property. Ricardo had the same limitation as Hume, taking up the relation of labor solely in society, and the same individualist premise to his philosophy as Hume. Therefore he posited as his starting point the individual hunter and fisher, in the state of nature, isolated from society. This man of fable, however, is no more real than Robinson Crusoe on his tropical isle; it is no more than the fabled natural man of Hobbes and Rousseau. Who does not grasp the two sides of the relation of labor is condemned to a fabulation of the relation of labor. The lopping off of the relation of labor to nature has brought about the fiction of the natural man. The lopping off of the relation of labor in society has inspired the fiction of the law of the jungle in the city streets, the spiritual animal kingdom, the free market and the free businessman in the free state, the struggle for existence, and the war of all against all. Defoe, Rousseau and Ricardo on the one side, Parson Malthus and Charles Darwin on the other, St. Thomas Hobbes the father of them all.

Value of Labor and Labor Power

The difference between slave labor and wage labor is a formal one; the difference between the corresponding economic formations of

---

making his distinction regarded the opposition between rural labor and handicraft work of artisan work. It is the view of the process of production from within, as we have seen, the end of which, according to Locke, is property. Locke proceeds to this end from the consideration of the property that every man has in his own person, to the acquisition of property by its alienation from the natural state. (Peter Laslett, in his ed. of Locke's *Two Treatises*, 2nd ed., Cambridge 1970, p. 305, points to the problem of government, not of labor.) Marx, *Kapital* I, op. cit., ch. 5 incipit, recounts his own bee fable, wherein the worst human craftsman is distinguished from the best of the bees because the former has constructed his product in his head before he shapes it. This opposition, between head and hand labor is, like Locke's opposition between body and hand, the view of the laboring process from within. Marx elsewhere in his work introduces the opposition between private and social labors; here he shares Locke's interest in private labors alone. Locke moreover has the direct producer in mind, as does Marx, as the original source of value. This product therefore belongs to that producer, according to Locke. The interpretation of Locke's work in terms of the thesis of possessive individualism is valid, but too narrowly based, as it is advanced by C. B. MacPherson, *The Political Theory of Possessive Individualism*. Oxford 1970, pp. 197 et seq. Here Locke's theory is put forward as a defence of property and property right. But the right to property is established by labor and work, according to Locke; hence it is not the right of property in general that is in question, but the right of the direct producer. This was so understood by G.P. Gooch, *English Democratic Ideas in the Seventeenth Century*. Cambridge 1898, pp. 358f. Here Locke is related to the tradition of (utopian) socialism.

society is likewise a matter of form. We are therefore dealing with *one* economic system, the system of political economy, and *one* social system, the system of civil society, whether in the Asiatic, the antique, the feudal or the capitalist periods of history, throughout which the exchange and production of commodities predominate. The value of a commodity, in quantitative terms, is determined by the amount of labor expended in its production; to this idea Luther, Petty, Adam Smith and Ricardo all made their contribution. The difference between the slave and the wage system is not touched by this law of value; the difference in the form in which the surplus product and the surplus value is extracted underlies the societies both of slave and wage labor. They are both societies of political economy. A second difference between the two systems is no less formal: the wage labor is sold by its proprietors directly, the slave labor is sold indirectly. The former has the illusion, the formality, of freedom and equality, the latter none. Something is sold as a commodity in either case, whether directly or indirectly. What is sold is the labor commodity. The difference between slave and wage labor is a quantitative one: the wage laborer sells his labor time up to a certain amount; to raise that limit to the point where it includes the entire life of the workman would be to make him the slave of his wagemaster. If we therefore say *labor* instead of *labor power* in expressing the labor theory of value, it is for shortness only; it is labor power that is in question. It is not labor but labor power that is the commodity sold by wage labor; labor itself is the substance which in one form is expressed as a commodity, having a measurable value.[38] But labor is also labor in the household, the original economy; it is labor outside the political economy, in a primordial, or in a pure-communal setting. Where labor is bought and sold in the course of the production process, it is not the substance of labor but its power or capacity that is in question;

---

[38] Karl Marx, *Das Kapital* II. Hamburg 1910, p. 6. Cf. *Kapital* I, op. cit., pp. 499 and 504, and reference to his *Wages, Price and Profit*, above. The slave sells nothing, his labor and product being taken from him. The relation in the political economy and social economy, of civil society maintained by slave labor is nevertheless a commodity relation, whereby the congelation of this labor, its product, is exchanged against other commodities by the unit production in which slave and master participate. Such units in the time of the Caesars were the latifundia which, said Pliny, brought about the ruin of Italy. The direct producer as slave is a commodity under this condition. The ancient Roman mercenarius contracted for the sale of his labor power for wages; the labor power under this condition was and is a commodity. The slave then was made into a commodity over the duration of his socially productive (life-) time. No contract was involved in this relation. Certain classes of client in the ancient Roman client-patron relations were in the form of contract slaves, i.e., they contracted for the sale of their total labor, and not their labor power.

in political economy this is the case. There the unit of the measurement of labor is labor time.

The formulation of the law of value as the quantity of labor time in the production of a commodity brings together the relation of labor to nature and the relation in society. The labor process is on the one hand the material interchange with nature, the appropriation of the natural sphere for the satisfaction of human wants, purposeful activity to the end of devising values in use. However, the dialectic of labor would be onesided and defective if this were all there was to the labor relation. This is the moment of the material content, which is converted by the relation of labor in society to a formal moment. The material moment is the transformation of the natural domain in the human organism, which is labor power. This transformation is the material conversion that the labor process takes, the formal moment being the circulation process in society. It would be false to conceive that these formal and material moments proceeded pari passu; they are two moments of the same relation. You can no more separate them, in taking up the relation of labor in civil society, than you can hope to have a coin by taking its reverse alone, or a sheet of paper by taking its verso alone. The material interchange in society is the formal side of the process, of which the material process is the relation to nature. In order that the conversion of the material of nature take place, a second conversion must take place at the same time, – the conversion of labor power into its substance, labor; each conversion is the necessary condition of the other. The formal conversion is the material interchange in society, or the formation of exchangeable values. The value substance, labor, is abstracted from the direct relation to nature, its measure is not the production of useful things; now the abstract quantity of labor is measured by labor time, itself an abstraction. It is wholly in the sphere of society, abstracted from nature, that this measure takes its place. The formation of exchangeable values is a social process, the alienation of the expression of the production process from nature, and at once the abstraction of labor from the production process. The dialectic of social labor has within it the moments of abstract and concrete labor. Abstract labor is the creation of exchangeable values, it is the formal moment of social labor, the mediate relation of labor to nature. Concrete labor is the creation of usable values; it is the direct relation to nature in the production process.[39] This direct relation is converted into its opposite.

[39] Marx, *Theorien über den Mehrwert* I. op. cit., p. 329. *Kapital* I, op. cit., pp. 119, 146, 177. *Kapital* II, op. cit., p. 120. *Kritik*, 1859. (*Werke*, op. cit., Bd. 13, p. 37. *Grundrisse*, op. cit.,

The relation of labor to nature is the agency whereby nature is dominated, subjected, its materials appropriated to human use, and its laws mastered. The culture is the field in which human labor is operative. From another point of view, the culture is at once agency and field of operation of human labor, or the material-immaterial, sensory-suprasensory interchange with nature. Labor is the instrument of human society. We are referring here to the totality of the concrete human relations to nature, hence to the totality of the abstract field of culture; culture is in this sense abstract because it is the sum of all the works of the human societies, having existence nowhere save as this abstract sum. Labor is in this sense concrete because it is the labor which stands in direct relation to nature. Nature is not taken here in its totality, but only as the area, sphere or aspect to which humanity by its sum of labors relates, or the cultural field is identical with this segment or mode of the whole of nature. Labor comprises in this sense the labor of the hand and labor of the head, or mental labor, science.

On the relation of abstract and concrete labor, Engels completed the dialectic begun by Locke, writing:

> The English language has the advantage of possessing different words for the two aspects of labor here considered. The labor which creates Use-value, and counts qualitatively, is *Work*, as distinguished from labor; that which creates Value and counts quantitatively, is *Labor* as distinguished from Work.[40]

Locke, we have seen, had taken up the relation of labor and work to nature in a twofold way, from within the labor-process itself: the labor of the body is the material interchange with nature, in which the body returns to nature the entirety of what it has taken; the work of the hands is the material interchange with nature in the production of useful things. The labor of the body is the non-mediate relation; the work of the hands is mediate, the means being the instruments of work, which are specifically and characteristically human. Yet the labor of the body returns its natural burden to nature in a changed form: the human being in a later stage of the process of evolution is other than the human being at an earlier stage. The work of the hands is a part of the same process of evolution. In this sense, labor and work

p. 559. Cf. Rubin, *Očerki*, op. cit. *Studien zur Marxschen Werttheorie*, A. Neusüss-Fögen, tr. Frankfurt/Main 1973. Alfred Schmidt, *Der Begriff der Natur in der Lehre von Karl Marx*, Frankfurt/Main 1971. Rubin's focus is on the relation of labor in society, Schmidt's on the relation of labor to nature.

40 Friedrich Engels, in: Karl Marx, *Capital*, F. Engels ed. S. Moore and E. Aveling, tr. New York 1936, p. 54n. This is extended by Engels, ibid., p. 207n., where he writes, "in the Simple Labor-process, it (labor) is *Work*."

are in an interaction with each other; each is a condition of the change of the other, each is a condition of the evolution of the other. Engels took up the relation of labor from the standpoint of production, and of what is produced thereby: work as the production of use-values, labor as the production of exchange-values. From the standpoint of that which is produced, the concrete product is the useable value, the abstract, the exchangeable; from the standpoint of the process of production, the latter is the process of creating value, the former is the labor process itself.

Use and Exchange Value

Not all theories of labor express an operational relation to nature: there are many writers on the subject who have incorrectly understood the relation between productive and unproductive labor; there are likewise many writers on the theory of society who have not at all grasped the operational relation implied by the category of culture in the relation to nature, who have, on the contrary understood culture as absolutely separate from nature. The work of the hands as the shaping of useful things is an operational theory of labor in its relation to nature.

The work of the hands is not only the means of the difference between humanity and nature, it is at once the measure of the difference between the animal and the human conditions. In the history of anthropological theory, the concept of culture has been brought out in reference to these same relations, and indeed as the mark, measure and means of transition from the animal to the human condition. The theory of work and labor, however, is both theoretical and practical, at once abstract and concrete, whereas the theory of culture, as it has been advanced hitherto, is abstract only; as a concept it is theoretical, without a practical side. Moreover, the theory of labor, and of the labor theory of value, has been brought out by Marx both in relation to nature and in its social relation. The relation of culture to nature has been brought out at the expense of the relation of culture to society.

The relation of abstract to concrete labor in society bears on all of human society *in posse*. In actuality, it bears on civil society alone,[41] as we shall now see.

Marx wrote, "[Human beings] themselves begin to be differentiated from the animals as soon as they begin *to produce* their means of

[41] For discussion in relation to Aristotle's Politics, see *The Ethnological Notebooks of Karl Marx*. Assen, 2nd ed. 1974. Lawrence Krader, Introduction, pp. 19-21.

subsistence, a step which is conditioned by their bodily organization. Insofar as human beings produce their means of subsistence they produce indirectly their material life itself."[42] The implied process of the body's labor is further developed here as a condition of labor in society; *it is not the labor itself.* The production of the means of subsistence is the direct relation to nature, the production of the material life the indirect relation. The material life is life in society, in the case of humanity; in that we produce our material life only in and through society, the production is indirect. The physical organization of the human being conditions both the direct and the indirect relations to nature. These relations, both the mediate and the immediate, are two moments of the same movement, the material interchange with nature. As such, therefore, they are the material side of the process which formally is the process of circulation. The relation in society in turn has two moments, 1, the formal moment of circulation, which is itself but a determinate moment of exchange[43]; 2, the material moment of the relation in society of the human being is the necessity of life in society: the human being who is without society is either a beast or a god, either less than or greater than man.[44]

The relations of man to nature and in society are given economic expression in the processes of production and circulation. The process of production in society is a mediative relation to nature. The physiocrats naively held that the natural bounties and goods had intrinsic value; but the opposite is the case. David Ricardo was only one of many who began the discussion of value from the standpoint of labor; he is the economist of the production process.[45] But the political economy as a whole cannot be broken up into separate segments. The different parts are analyzed hypothetically, for convenience. Production and distribution, whether private or social, take place in an unbroken relation. Circulation is itself but a determinate moment of exchange; it is exchange considered in its totality; the totality is itself a moment of the dialectical movement. Exchange, again, is a mediative moment in the relations of production and distribution.[46]

Value is itself a whole, that whole is a moment of the determination of value taken as an abstraction. The exchange value is abstracted from both the relations in society and to nature. The abstraction is negated in concrete production, concrete exchange, concrete con-

---

[42] Karl Marx and Friedrich Engels, *Die Deutsche Ideologie. Werke*, op. cit., Bd. 3, p. 21.
[43] It is exchange seen in its totality. See Marx, *Grundrisse*, op. cit., Einleitung, p. 19.
[44] Aristotle, Politics, 1253a.
[45] Ricardo, *Principles*, op. cit., ch. 1, sect. III.
[46] Marx, *Grundrisse*, op. cit. Einleitung, pp. 19f.

sumption. *Value in use* is the mediated relation of civil society to nature. The mediate relation is twofold: 1. The mediation by the implements of labor. 2. The mediation by the stored up skills and traditional occupations of the society. These mediations are the cultural components, the passive moment of the relation to nature of the given social unity. The active moment is always the concrete activity of the society's members as expressers of the stored up skills and traditions.

In the political economy, the concrete value in use is completed by the value in exchange of the product. The abstract and the concrete relations of social labor thus complete each other. There is another economy in which there is little or no relation of exchange; in this economy, the unit of production and the unit of consumption coincide; this is a smallscale economy of the household, the sib, band of hunters, joint family, village community and like units. The coincidence of production and consumption takes place: (1) where there is no circulation of goods produced beyond the limits of the unit of production and consumption. In this case the household, band, etc., is self-sufficient, self-sustaining, self-dependent. If its internal means of production or consumption fail, it will disappear, eliminate itself. (2) Where the unit of production is the same as the unit of consumption. There is in this case circulation with other bands, communities, sibs, households, etc. But what is produced is produced in common, what is consumed is consumed in common. The circulation of goods produced is yet small in degree. It would be an exaggeration to speak of exchange value in this case. In the political economy it is otherwise. The unit of production and of consumption coincide only in the exceptional case, or at the beginnings of the development of the political economy: the family farm described by Hesiod, or the village community in the Asiatic mode of production, the unit of the familia, paterfamilias, servus (famul) in ancient Rome, the village community in the Asiatic mode of production.

The relations of value in exchange and use complete each other as abstract and concrete expressions of the whole. The whole is the unity of the relations of political economy, as production, exchange, consumption in society. In the political economy, the unities in which these relations and processes take place are larger than they are in the economy which is non-political. The abstract and concrete relations of value coincide with the abstract and concrete relations of labor in political society, that is, in the society of the political economy. The abstract relations of value, just as the abstract relations of labor, diminish in importance in the society which is non-political.

The relation of value in exchange and in use was not brought together, nor was it conceived as the abstract and concrete sides of the same relation, until the nineteenth century. Neither Adam Smith nor Ricardo, still less Galiani, Turgot or Say, had more than an adumbration of this relation. The two sides of the value expression, i.e., of the problem of value, are brought out separately from the six-teenth to the eighteenth centuries. We have seen that Luther was concerned with the relation of labor in society: Machiavelli, on the other hand, was concerned with the relation of labor to nature. Adam Smith took up the problem of value rather from Machiavelli's starting point than from Luther's. This means that he had not conceived the problem of value in relation to labor as that of the transition from nature to society. The problem of Hegel, and of Marx, however, was that of the internalization of the relation to nature by the relation in society. The chief movement of the transition from the one to the other is the social internalization. But this internalization is at once externalization; the boundary of the culture is extended by the re-lation to nature. The relations in society and to nature are two moments of the same movement; the external and the internal are bound in-separably together. The appropriation of the natural bounty is a con-crete relation; the relation to nature is given abstract expression in the relation in society.[47]

The means of the internalization of the natural goods is human labor and work. That work is a mediate relation to nature was brought out by Hegel. Marx brought out that labor is a mediate relation both in society and to nature; the composite relation is the deter-minant of abstract and concrete value, value in exchange and use. Thereby the strands whose beginnings are found in Aristotle, Ch'in Chiu Shao, Machiavelli and Luther are pulled together. The relation of humanity in nature is mediated by abstract labor and concrete

[47] There is a tendency to take the relation to nature alone as the starting point in the theory of value. We here propose to start from the twofold relation of labor, to nature and in society. At the same time, we begin the discussion of value in view of the twofold relation of labor abstract and concrete. Joseph Schumpeter, *History of Economic Analysis*, London 1972, p. 300, wrote of "a theory of exchange value based on value in use", and attributed this to Adam Smith and Ricardo. Any theory of value, in the light of its manifold developments, as they are traced in the present essay, cannot be restricted to this one side of the relation. Value in use is the basis for exchange value only in that value in exchange is the basis for use value. The two sides of value are mutual determinants, one of the other. In a primitive condition, on the contrary, there is no value. Lacking the abstract expression of value there are only useful things produced; lacking the exchange value expression, there is no exchange, to any significant degree, in the current sense. Lacking the relation of exchange, as here delimited, there is no abstract, exchange expression of value. Instead, there is distribution, reciprocal sharing out, and the like. Exchange and the commodity relation are mutual determinants of each other just as use and exchange value are.

labor or work. The relation of human individuals in society, on the contrary, is both mediate and immediate. Humanity does not stand in a direct relation to nature; we have distanced ourselves from nature without having taken leave of the natural order. Our material and spiritual composition are equally of the kingdom of nature. The distancing from nature, however, is the primary human condition, or the primary alienation. The mediation in the relation to nature is both an active and passive relation of mankind; the human being is both agent and recipient of the impulsions of nature. We are the initiative and the passive vessels of the natural moments. The mediation is effected by the instruments of work and the adjustments, learning, storage of learning by the hands, muscles, nerves, organs of sense, the body as a whole. These are all both passive and active relations or undertakings, whereby use-values are created and exchange-values set under way, or prepared for.

The relations in society are no less complex. Although none of our relations to nature are direct, all being mediated by our implements and stored up adjustments, adaptations and learnings, our relations in society are both mediate and direct. The transition from use-value to exchange value is effected in society and only in society, in and through the social relations. The production of useful things is not the production of use-value. Value is integral, a unity; use-value implies exchange-value and value. Abstract labor cannot be separated from concrete labor, nor labor from work in society. Each is the actualization of the potentiality of the other. Now in the political economy, these potentialities are realized. They are not yet fully realized, but are so in major part. In order to make this clear we must go back in the history of anthropology. E. B. Tylor wrote that plain cylinders of imperfect rock crystal, four to eight inches long, and one inch in diameter, are made and perforated by very low tribes on the Rio Negro. "They are not," he continued, "as Humboldt seems to have supposed, the result of high mechanical skill, but merely of the most simple and savage processes carried on with that utter disregard of time that lets the Indian spend a month in making an arrow."[48] Tylor provides us with a *terminus ante rem*,

---

[48] E. B. Tylor, *Researches into the Early History of Mankind.* 3rd ed. London 1878, ch. VII. Tylor well understood the principle of storage, holding that the world, "...when it has once got a firm grasp of new knowledge or a new art, is very loth to lose it..." – especially, he says, when it relates to the satisfaction of his daily wants. Such knowledge and new art are "acquired by man as a member of society," said Tylor in his well-known definition of culture (*Primitive Culture*, London 1871, ch. 1, incipit.) Tylor, as Marx before him, put an end to Robinsonades. Cf. Krader, *Asiatic Mode of Production*, op. cit., pp. 118, 192, 323.

the starting point of economy. It is not political economy that carries on production processes with utter disregard of time. Marx took up this thought: Capitalist society is distinguished from the primitive not through expenditure of labor in a definite time by the latter which brings him no revenue or fruits of his labor which can be resolved (transposed) into means of consumption; the difference between primitive and capitalist society is this:

1. Capitalist society applies more of its disposable year's labor in production of means of production (ergo of constant capital), which can be resolved in revenue neither in the form of labor wage nor of surplus value, but can only function as capital.

2. When the savage makes bows, arrows, hammers, axes, baskets, etc., he knows very well that he has not turned the time so applied to the shaping of means of consumption, that he has thus covered his need for means of production and no further. In addition, the savage commits a very grave economic sin by his utter equanimity regarding the use of time, and sometimes takes e.g., as Tylor says, a whole month in making an arrow.[49] The capitalist society and capitalist mode of production are the completion of the relations of political economy; in the matters of value of labor time, these relations stand opposed to the mode of production of savage society.

(The relation to nature is mediated by bows and arrows, axes and baskets. The relations in society are mediated likewise; they are also immediate. The relations between parties to a contract are mediate, as are those between buyer and seller of a commodity. The relations in both cases are at once abstract and concrete. Relations of imitation and the labor of the body are both mediate and immediate, either direct or indirect. Relations to nature and those in society are not symmetrical with each other.)

There is no value in savage society. Value in use and exchange begin in civil society, achieving their many-sided potentialities in capitalism, where, as Luther wrote, labor time is reckoned up. It was not reckoned up for the first time in history. On the contrary, it had been reckoned up long ere that time, indeed it was begun in the transition from simple or primitive to complex, class-divided society. It is the mark of the transition, as Tylor and Marx agreed, that labor time is not regarded with indifference. Luther gave an early expression of the consciousness of this effectuation, and, in China, Ch'in Chiu-Shao before him. Value in use and in exchange go hand in hand; the per-

---

[49] Marx, *Kapital* II, op. cit., p. 414; cf. also *Kapital* I, op. cit., p. 560.

spective of Machiavelli in regard to the prior condition, before the founding of Rome and Venice, bears upon the savage and barbarous conditions, not the political and civilized. By distancing himself from nature by means of his labor and work, the human being achieves his condition proper to himself.

The relations in society were adumbrated as the root of the labor theory of value by those who measured the amounts of labor time in terms of work. We have taken up the formulation by John Locke of the labor of the body and the work of the hands. The distinction is important, indeed fundamental, from the standpoint of the internal relation of production, production seen from within; it is seen thus from the standpoint of the working individual. It must be combined with the perspective from without. From this second standpoint production is the relation of labor to nature and in society. It is the reproduction of the worker and of the entire social group in all economic systems. It is the creation of value in political economy, and there alone. But value is both useful and exchangeable, value in use and exchange. For the latter it is necessary to distinguish between production and distribution. Exchange, hence value in exchange, is a mediating moment between production and consumption, together with distribution which is determined by production. The labor of the body stands in relation to the satisfaction of wants. It is useful labor, concrete labor. The work of the hands stands in relation to concrete and abstract labor, it is labor in relation to the production of value in use and exchange. The system of Locke is found only in political economy, just as the system of Hobbes. Both had already gone beyond the doctrine of the physiocrats, a century after, who derived value directly from the bounty of nature.

It is only by our labor that we stand in an instrumental relation to nature; our labor, work and toil is the instrument of that relation, which is thereby rendered mediate. It is by labor in society that we are alienated from nature in the first place, from society of any sort and condition. It is by labor in civil society that value is created, labor in relation to nature, or use-value, and labor in society, or use-values and exchange-values. This labor is at once concrete and abstract, in either aspect it is social labor, the instrument of humanization of society, at present its dehumanization. It is the instrument of socialization of the human kind and the humanization of nature.

The operations upon the natural surroundings are the medium whereby humanity produces its means of subsistence. These operations are the work of the hands; hence we say that humanity stands in a mediate relation to the natural surroundings. The labor of the body, however, is both a direct and indirect relation to nature. The human body is in a continuum with nature, it is a part of nature. The handiwork of the body, or the work of the body which is consciously aimed and directed is the means of extending the human dominion over nature, in this sense the relation is indirect. The lesser teleology of the handiwork is human; the grand purpose of the body is a myth, just as the grand purpose of nature. At the same time, the work of the hands is the mark of the difference between the human and the animal being, including, as Locke implied, the animal being of man. Therefore, the labor of the body is animal labor, the work of the hands is human. The labor of the body is continuous with nature, the work of the hands at once continuous and discontinuous. In relation to nature, the labor of the body is a continuum, flow. It has no more telos than does nature as a whole. The only telos to be observed is in relation to particular, concrete works by the human organs of production, hand, brain and their instruments. In relation to nature, the labor of the body is concrete, the work of the hands is both abstract, the planning of both labor and work in the head, and concrete, or the production of useful things. In relation to society, these matters are turned around. Abstract labor is now the continuous flow[50]; as the abstract form of labor it is in an indirect relation to nature, being alienated from it and bound to it by the total process of production. In its relation in society, work is the concrete relation, as it is to nature, being the production of useful things, in the form in which they are consumed. In its relation in society, abstract labor is the means of production of exchange value, wherein the units of the abstract labor are themselves so many units of exchangeable value, or exchange values. The units of abstract labor as exchange values are measured in units of labor time. Concrete work as it is measured in the production of use values is bound to the temporal unities of value in general, exchange value in particular. Concrete work, as it is the production of useful things, is production in direct relation to distribution and consumption; it is without necessary relation to exchange and exchange value. Production abstracted from distribution and consumption leads to production for itself, that is to the production of surplus value.

Social labor stands in a dual relation, on the one hand as labor in relation to nature, on the other as labor in its social relation, labor in society. It stands at the same time in a second dual relation, being in its relation in production on the one side mediate, and on the other

---

[50] The continuous flow of social production is abstract in reference to the relation of exchange value. That same flow is concrete, however, in reference to the material interchange with nature (der Stoffwechsel mit der Natur).

immediate or direct. The immediate producer stands in a direct relation in production, at the beginning of the process of production, whether for himself or in society. No one works for him, save in the sense that he works for himself and for others in a reciprocal relation. By the breaching of this reciprocal relation of social labor, while maintaining the remaining relations of labor abstract and concrete, mediate and immediate, natural and social, surplus value is produced. As the immediate producers are the point of origination of all production, for their own reproduction, for exchange, and surplus production, distribution and consumption, they are the original source of all labor, work and toil, of value abstract and concrete, and of surplus value. In relation to nature, human labor in general, social labor in particular, is mediate[51]; it is mediated at once by the instruments of labor and by labor of hand and head.

On the one hand the relations of social labor are manifold, on the other they are unitary. In the mode of production of capital in the modern time, the relation of social labor is formally different from that of slave labor in virtue of the sale of his labor time by the immediate producer in his social capacity as wage laborer. That this transaction is voluntary and free is a fable of our time, for it is only so pro forma. The immediate producer is necessarily constrained to sell his labor in the form of labor power under the given historical condition of production; the illusion of freedom is limned by the choice of selling it to this employer or that. Social labor, whether slave or free, whether bound by the straitness of customary or of civil law, is imprisoned by the human wants which can be supplied only by the process of production, distribution, exchange and consumption in society. The process is a whole, social labor is a whole. The difference in social labor, slave or free, is not introduced at the point where the labor enters it; for in all these cases labor enters it at the same point, as the direct producer. The difference is introduced at the point where the relation of social production is given various juridical expression. The commodity relation, which arches over all production of the political and social economy, whether unfree by custom or civil process, or free by either, is generalized to comprise the transaction between social labor and capital, whether the latter be personified by private capitalist or by the state.

---

[51] Cf. G. W. F. Hegel, *Werke*. Bd. 12. Suhrkamp 1970, p. 295: Der Mensch verhält sich mit seinen Bedürfnissen zur äusserlichen Natur auf praktische Weise und geht dabei, indem er sich durch dieselbe befriedigt und sie aufreibt, vermittelnd zu Werke. Die Naturgegenstände nämlich sind mächtig... Um sie zu bezwingen, schiebt der Mensch andere Naturdinge ein, und erfindet *Werkzeuge*. (Hegel is here supposed to have introduced only an active construction in the relation to nature. The relation of intermediation is at once active and passive.)

ON VALUE

FOUR

ON VALUE

I. ON USE VALUE AND EXCHANGE VALUE[1]

The relation between use value and exchange value, in particular, the differentiation and combination between the two, has a bearing on that economy in which commodities are bought and sold; it remains to be seen, in what follows, whether the relation in question has a bearing on any other. The exchange value of a thing produced is the amount of its exchangeability, hence the quantum of its value, relative to other goods against which it can be exchanged at a given time and place, and according to an acceptable transaction between the parties in the exchange. This is the expression of the exchange value; its determination is not accounted for thereby. The amount of value that is involved in the exchange is not determined in the exchange itself; it is determined in the relations of production in the society. As opposed to the determination of the exchange value, the commodity is not determined in the process of production in society; it is determined in the process of exchange in the society, which is the relation that one thing socially produced bears to another.

Exchange is not a universal, it is a historical condition, which is developed under given social relations. Production, on the contrary is a universal human relation. Commodity exchange takes place in the social and political economy, and takes place there alone; this mode of exchange is one of the constituents of that economy, together with the relations of production in the society. (Social production and commodity exchange are differentia specifica of the present state of that economy; other economic relations, distribution or consumption, being generally found not only in the social and political economy, but elsewhere as well.) The society in

---

[1] Adam Smith, *The Wealth of Nations*, 1776, wrote of value in use and value in exchange; also of exchangeable value. David Ricardo, *The Principles of Political Economy*, 1817, wrote of the same. Karl Marx, *Das Kapital*, 1867, wrote of Gebrauchswert and Tauschwert, Wert; this was rendered under the editorship of Friedrich Engels as use value and exchange value, value, in English. Value and exchange value are here differentiated; in the past they have not been. Why this is so will be made clear in the following pages. The beginnings of the system are to be found in the writings of Thomas Hobbes. See above, ch. 3.

question is civil society, or the society of the political economy. In order to grasp the relations between exchange, exchange value, commodity exchange, social and political economy, and social production, let us examine the unit of production, whether that unit be the village community, the plantation, workshop or factory. Production, distribution and consumption take place within such units; exchange, however, generally does not. Exchange and exchange value are not the same; exchange of commodities and the exchange value of the commodities are not the same. Exchange of commodities, together with its determinate moment, circulation, takes place where the given unit of production ceases to be, in relation to other such producing units in the society. Exchange has no place within the given unit of social production because commodities have no place there; conversely, commodities are not found where exchange does not take place. The exchange relation and the commodity relation in the social and political economy are mutual determinants, one of the other; each is the necessary condition of the other. On the contrary, exchange value is not determined in the commodity and exchange relations, it is determined in the relation of social production, by the quantity of social labor applied in its production. There are those who have sought to reveal the secret of exchange value by exploring the exchange relation in the system of price and market. Their quest is vain. Exchange value is the determinate of social labor, that is, of the relation of social production, and not of the relation of exchange, or of its particular moments, market, price, or the circulation of commodities.

The commodity, we have seen, is the mutual determinant and determinate of the exchange relation; by that relation a thing produced is transformed into a commodity. The exchange process and the commodity stand in a reciprocal relation; it is not so with the commodity relation and the relation of social production. The thing produced is transformed into a commodity by being exchanged; thereupon the category to which it belongs comprises things which are produced in society; the social production of commodities follows from their having been exchanged.

The positing of exchange value is a development of these same relations, but in the opposed sense; being the product of social labor, the exchange value is thereupon subject to exchange, its value following from its having been socially produced, and its value quantum is determined by the social production in the given amount. The exchange of values follows from their having been produced in society. Commodity and exchange value are not the same; the commodity is the exchange and use value of a thing. The exchange relation of the commodity is the reciprocal determinant of the exchange value; the exchange value does not stand in a reciprocal relation to the process of social production. Exchange and production in society are mutually determinants, one of the other. The commodity does not stand in a reciprocal relation to the process of social production, but is the determinate of that process, as may be seen from the following table of the relations of social and political economy:

Exchange → Social Production
Social Production → Exchange
Social Labor → Exchange Value
(Social Production → Exchange Value)
Amount of Social Labor → Amount of Exchange Value
(Amount of Social Production → Amount of Exchange Value)
Exchange → Commodity
Commodity → Exchange
Commodity Exchange → Commodity Production
Social Production → Commodity Exchange and Production
Commodity → Use and Exchange Value
Use and Exchange Value → Commodity
(The arrow indicates the direction of the determination. The order of the sequence is important.)

The unit of production in the commodity relation, or in the social and political economy generally, is of necessity other than the unit of consumption, the producing and consuming units being related to each other by the process of exchange. Thereby the economy is constituted as the social economy. The economic relations of exchange between the producing and consuming units are social relations, wherein commodities, having been exchanged, are thereupon produced, and exchange value having been produced is thereupon exchanged. It is not the relation of distribution that binds the units of production together in the social economy, it is the relation of exchange. Distribution is an important factor in the social economy, but it is not necessarily a social relation, whereas exchange and commodity relations are of necessity social relations. Distribution takes place within the unit of consumption and within the unit of production, not necessarily between them. (Parents distribute food to their children, they do not exchange with them, inside the family. Distribution takes place within the village community, plantation, farm, workshop or factory; exchange does not necessarily take place within these units of production or consumption, nor does the relation of buying or selling commodities. The primitive band or tribe practices distribution; exchange does not have the same function there as it does in the social economy.) Exchange is specific to the social economy; distribution is not.

Production and consumption are opposed to each other in the social economy; production and reproduction are opposed to one another in the same processes. The production of surplus value is determined by the differentiation and opposition between production and reproduction in society; the social relations of the economy are thereby transformed into the relations of the political economy: The economy, which is constituted as the social economy by the production of exchange value and the exchange of commodities, is constituted as the political economy by the production of surplus value.

In the relations of production in the social and political economy, labor time, as the determinant of value, is reckoned up. Labor time is generally not so reckoned up in the primitive condition of economy and society. The relations of production in the primitive condition are the opposite of those of the social and political economy, and of civil society. In the primitive condition the unit of production and the unit of consumption generally coincide. The hunting bands of the Yahgan, Ona, Alacaluf, Inuit, Aranda, Dieri, Paiute, generally produce what they consume; they consume what they produce. Being human, they produce their livelihoods and means of subsistence; they are active both as a part of nature and apart from nature, being at once in a relation of continuity and discontinuity with the natural surroundings and the nature contained in the human frame. The unit of production and consumption in the primitive condition of economy and society may go beyond its outer limit in order to acquire pipe clay or cowrie shells. Nevertheless, exchange plays but an insignificant part in the primitive condition; production, distribution and consumption have the sole significant functions in the social life of the primitive band. Here useful things are produced; hunting, gathering of wild plants and insects, fishing, are means of production for the group, whereby it reproduces its existence. It has been said that a surplus is therewith also produced. But it is not a social surplus. The surplus produced in the primitive condition, is produced in a way such that the reproduction of the group and its production relations in no way differ.[2] The nondifference of production and reproduction of the group, and the unity of production and consumption, are mutually determinant conditions, one of the other, in the primitive condition; because production and reproduction coincide there, production and consumption coincide; and conversely, because production and consumption coincide, therefore production and repro-

[2] See above, Dialectic of Civil Society, section II.

duction coincide. The surplus produced under this condition is a relation of production within the consuming and reproducing unit.
It is not a relation between discrete and opposed producing units,
reproducing units, consuming units; hence it is not a relation in society.
(The unity of the human kind is a noble thought that will lead to
our common weal, but it will not be proven by attributing the production of a social surplus to conditions in which it does not apply,
or by failing to distinguish between the social surplus and the surplus
within the family or the surplus tout court.)

The units of production enter into social relations with one another
as they enter into exchange relations with one another; thereby they
cease to be identical with the units of consumption. The primitive
hunting band is thus transformed into a unit interactive within a
social whole; its relations of production, division of labor and technology are therewith transformed. The society is constituted by these
interactive processes. By the relation of exchange useful things are
transformed into commodities, being now produced in society; the
economy is transformed into a social economy. The units of consumption become increasingly dependent on one another, as do the
units of social production, becoming at once increasingly specialized,
whereby the division of labor is transformed into the social division
of labor. The division of labor had up to this point taken place within
the family or other producing unit, in connection with differences of
age, sex, strength between individuals. The division of labor in the
social and political economy, on the contrary, is the social division
of labor, being based not on the differences between individuals,
largely of a biological nature, but on the differences between specialized
units of production related by the exchange process, whereby the
social economy and social unity are constituted.

The exchanges take place between the units of social production.
Values having been exchanged are produced in society; having been
produced they are exchanged. Labor is transformed into social labor,
production into social production. Exchange value is constituted
because value is produced by social labor. Value in exchange is produced because value in use has been socially produced, and conversely,
use value is produced because exchange value has been produced.
These two constituents of value are mutually determinants, one of the
other. Without use value no exchange value, without exchange value
no use value. Without the combination of exchange and use value,
no value. In the primitive condition of economy and society there is
neither exchange value nor use value, nor is value in general produced.
Useful things are produced in the primitive condition, but not

as a general rule values of use and exchange. A surplus may be produced in the primitive condition, but not surplus value. Use value and exchange value are produced in the relations of social economy; surplus value is produced in the relations of political economy. The relations of social economy and of political economy form a whole, being distinct only in the relations of value.

The system of exchange value as here set forth relates to the social and political economy, and to the successive epochs of the economic formations of society alone. That system is not found in the primitive condition. Use and exchange values, or concrete and abstract value, issue from the activity of social labor. In the social and political economy, concrete value, or use value, the necessary element of consumption, is the social product of abstract and concrete labor. These relations of labor are differentiated and combined, being the process to begin with in the relations to nature and in society of the process of social production. Use value is the form in which human wants in the civil condition of society are met. Human wants in general are met by the production of useful things. Use value does not exist apart from the physical body of the commodity, or its tangible social form in general.

Use value is not a physical property of a commodity; it is the usable value the commodity provides. Water quenches thirst everywhere in the human condition, being generally a means of satisfying a particular want. On occasion, an exchange will take place to meet that want. The useful value that water provides is not inherent in the water itself but in the society wherein the exchange relations have been constituted and take place. The value in use is not in itself but outside itself, in the society of the social and political economy.

In another sense, however, the use value lies within the thing itself. In the frame of reference of society, in opposition to the exchange value of the thing socially produced, the usefulness of the thing is the precondition of its exchangeability. The use value of the thing is that which it itself provides by having been socially produced, and which it bears unto the social transaction of exchange.

It is the quantifiable aspect of the thing to be exchanged that goes to market; it is its value that is exchanged. The exchange value has arisen on earth in the process of social labor in relation to nature in the form of a natural good. The further history of the value is transferred from the relation to nature to the relation in society, through its exchange. The value has been determined to begin with in the natural relation where it exists as a potentiality which is realized, made actual, in and by its exchangeability, through its social relation.

It alters nothing to transfer the frame of the discussion from the relations of exchange to those of social production, for within the frame of reference of commodity production the relations of exchange and social production are not separable.

The quantification of value is a twofold process, in relation to use value on the one hand and to exchange value on the other. The two processes cannot be summed up or combined. The exchange values are quantified in the various progressions, arithmetical, logarithmic, whereby social labor is increased in amount or reduced, totally, in their sum, or severally, as social labors. Use values are quantifiable as well, but in a yes-no, or as a zero-sum relation. Use values singly meet wants, which they either satisfy or they do not. The concrete value of the useful thing, its use value does not add up, neither over time nor in commerce. It is additive only in fantasy. The use value of a thing is realized by its meeting what is wanted of it, whereupon it is rubbed out. However well one has eaten today, tomorrow will be a hungry day unless one eats again. Moreover, the use value of a thing is not in itself greater or less than the use value of another thing, nor of an anterior or posterior state of the same thing, unless it or they all meet the same want. If the use value does not meet what is wanted of it then it is changed, discarded, replaced.

In respect of use, value almost helps not at all. Either there is enough water in the mill pond or there is not; moreover, it must be water and not ice or steam. By their chemical composition all these goods are forms of hydrogen and oxygen in combination according to the formula, H_2O; as use values they are different in quality, the mill race being run through in the given case by water alone.

Use values may be quantified with the piece of work in view, or the want to be met. The want once satisfied, the use value is rubbed out. Subjectively, one has no need of the water drunk once the thirst has been quenched. Objectively one can envisage a future contingency in which the same object can be applied to meet the same want again. The use value does not to market go; exchange value does.[3]

In the theory of value, the distinction has been made between the relations of the social and political economy. The relations of social economy have been considered to have a bearing on the value in use

---

[3] Cf. Arghiri Emmanuel, *L'Echange inégal*. 2nd ed. Paris 1972, pp. 342sq. R. L. Meek, *Studies in the Labour Theory of Value*. 2nd ed. London 1973. If use-value is considered to be quantifiable then it is in a different sense from the quantification of exchange-value. Meek and Emmanuel have given good accounts of exhange value, but their discussion of the quantification of use value and its relation to exchange value wants further clarification. The chapter on the early history of value explores areas outside Meek's study of the history of value, and is added to it.

and exchange of a thing; the relations of political economy have been considered to have a bearing on the production of surplus value and the relations of social classes to that surplus. The social and political economy, however, is a totality which is divided for the purposes of analysis of its composition and relations. The whole is to be reaffirmed once the purposes have been achieved.

The Question of Value versus Price

The question of value versus price as operational economic categories has been raised by some theoreticians, to the detriment of the concept of value. Price is applied by them as the measure to judge whether value is an effective category; they hold that price and market alone are valid, while value is either inferential and reflected, or else politically determined. But price and market, having had a gestation period of five millennia, are in their modernity five centuries old. Moreover, a free market and price system, in the sense that F.Hayek has set forth, have had but a short span, which has been sharply cut back since the middle of the twentieth century. The price of petroleum among other commodities has had little free movement during and since that time. The questions of parity and disparity, and of equatability between value and price are reflected in their respective histories; commodities, marketing and price are not formed by social labor in the same way that value is. The history of social labor, in respect of value, may or may not have preceded that of price; in in either case, the historical course and geographic distribution are not the same. The theory of economic relations in society independent of commodity, price, and market is available to all; in these economic relations, social labor, hence value, is expressed and developed. Commodity, price, and market, for all that their ambitus is measured in centuries, are historically ephemeral, and likewise theoretically restricted, relative to social labor, and value, its determinate form.

II. ABSTRACT AND CONCRETE VALUE; ABSTRACT AND CONCRETE LABOR

Value is abstract and concrete. Abstract value is the exchange value of a thing produced in society, concrete value the use value of the thing so produced. The thing in question is a value, or commodity, in the form of a social good, active or inert. Social labor, whether as labor or labor power, reckoned up as labor time congealed in the product distributed, exchanged, consumed, is such a commodity. Social labor, labor in general, is a unitary relation, activity, or agency, being divided into abstract and concrete labor for the sake of convenience. Value, the product of social labor, is not a unitary relation, substance or entity; it is the expression of the various forms of value, abstract and concrete, exchange value, use value, surplus value. It begins its career in society as living labor. The frame of reference of the system of social labor, abstract and concrete, labor power, labor time, surplus labor, socially reproductive labor, is not the economy generally, but the social and political economy in particular.

The relation between value and social labor is complex, being asymmetrical. Value in general is the passive form in this relation; social labor is the agent. Value is the object determined, it is not the subject. On the contrary, labor in general, social labor in particular, being the determining subject in history, are at once subject and object. Labor, in all conditions, whether in the family, the group or in the society, whether social or private, is the work of the hands in the workshop or factory; it is bodily labor in the fields.[4] It is the labor and work of hand and head. Labor is a continuous process, work proceeds to the product consumed.

The relation between concrete social labor and concrete value is a one-way determination. Concrete labor is work. It is not produced by concrete value; on the contrary, concrete labor is the producer and determinant of concrete value; concrete social labor is the producer of abstract value and abstract labor. Concrete labor belongs to the same category of useful activity performed in the primitive as in the civil condition of economy and society, being the relation between the human kind and the natural environment. In the social and political economy, concrete labor is completed by abstract labor. Each is then a determinant of the other, together forming a whole; the useful activity of the primitive condition then becomes separated and combined in the civil condition as socially concrete and abstract labor. (The order is important.)

What has happened is that a new historical factor has been introduced into the relations of labor. Labor in the primitive condition is direct labor, work or toil upon the world of nature mediated by the instruments of the group. It is neither abstract nor concrete. Labor of hand and head are not separate in this condition. In the social and political economy the relations of labor in society are developed in combination with the relations of labor to nature; labor is transformed into social labor. Labor of hand and head are increasingly separated

---

[4] This was the situation in John Locke's day. The vast increase in the capitalization of agriculture, horticulture, animal husbandry, including fishing, has changed all that. Locke's *mot* expired in the face of the rural industry of the twentieth century. On Locke see above, ch. 3.

and opposed as social labor is developed. Labor as abstraction is continuous process, as concretion discontinuous.

Concrete labor takes the form of congealed labor time, which is concrete value; in this form the social product of labor is consumed. Concrete labor and concrete value are mutual determinants of each other, as form and content of a whole, the thing produced that is consumed by the social fire, whereby the ophelimity of the process is consummated. The concrete value, being the socially useful form of the commodity, is at once the content thereof in the converse of the relation of congealed labor time in social production: the concrete value is the content, the form of which is its value in the exchange relation.

The relation between abstract labor and abstract value is other than that between concrete labor and concrete value. Abstract labor and abstract value differ from each other as the method of account in each case differs. The social and political economy is a whole, we have seen, in which people work, eat, reproduce. Consumption in this is a part of production, production as well comprises consumption; as we reproduce, we consume and produce. The method of accounting in exchange is the summing up of the abstract social values of the commodity. The method of accounting in social production is the summing up of the abstract labor; but this exceeds the sum of the exchange values of the commodities: abstract labor and abstract value are not identical. The value of the things socially produced is the abstract value, or the sum of the abstract labors that produced it. That value is a relation of exchange in the society; it is exchange value. The abstract labor is the relation of social production in the same economy, divorced from the concrete labor for the purpose of reckoning up the relations in social production. It is the flow of living labor, or social labor in abstraction from the production of useful things. As useful, concrete, work is the content of the process of social production, abstract labor is its form.

Concrete labor as content of social production stands in another relation to abstract labor as form than does concrete labor as content to concrete value as form of the same. The form that the concrete use value gives to the concrete labor is its momentary congealment in the process of production in society; the form that abstract labor gives to the concrete social labor is its momentary congealment in the process of exchange. In the latter case it is the exchange value into which useful work is transformed in the relations of the social economy; in the former case it is the abstraction itself into which the work in society is transformed in the relations of the social and political economy.

The relations of social labor and work are objective and subjective. The concrete labor meets wants as a whole, the subjective element of which comes from within the human individual. That individual is both a biological organism with hunger pangs, etc.; the human being is at the same time in a set of social relations. (The human being, apart from the biological composition of the physical organism, *is* the set of the social relations, just as human society is the expression of those relations. The relations that compose the social being of the human individual generate wants, at the same time giving particular form to the wants that are generated by the biological organism; conversely, the biological wants give particular form to the socially generated wants. The biological and social wants of the human being are each the negation of the other; each eliminates itself and the other by the satisfaction of the want in the given form.) Concrete labor is at the same time the objective element in the relations of production in society; it is the basis to which abstract value, surplus value and reproduction of the relations of social production, or reproductive value as opposed to surplus value, are related. It is the starting point of all relations in society, for here the wants of social-biological life themselves are met. The subjective element is at once subjective and objective in this case, relating to the individual as subject, and relating to that human being as subject and at once as object.

The abstract relation of social labor is wholly objective, being abstracted from the subjectivity of the human relations to self. The abstraction of social labor is at the same time its abstraction from the process of social reproduction: thus it is the alienation of the thing produced from its direct producers. The mode of its alienation is its introduction into the exchange process. The socially useful thing becomes a commodity by virtue of its having been abstracted from the process of reproduction. The relation of the commodity is then twofold: (1) By its alienation it is abstracted as a whole from the unity that produced it, the abstraction by means of exchange. (2) By its abstraction it is alienated in part from its social producers. The social product is divided into a self-reproductive part and surplus value; the part which is the social surplus is the part alienated from the direct producers. The relation of production is transformed into social production by the twofold alienation. Use value and exchange value are thus opposed and jointly produced, reproductive and surplus value likewise, in the society. The abstraction of the whole and the alienation of the part are mutually determinative relations in the political economy.

Concrete labor in the form of socially useful things produces the means of its continuation in the work process; it is reproduction of self. By the separation of use value from exchange value, reproduction is separated from social production; the first form of separation or alienation is the determinant of the second. The relations of individuals in the political economy and civil society are determined in and by the opposed relations between the units of production and consumption on the one hand, and between reproductive and surplus labor on the other. The quantity of value that is produced does not return in its totality to the reproduction of its direct producers, a part being set aside in the process of intermediation in the commodity exchange (caravanserai infrastructure and its maintenance, for example). Another part of the value total adverts to those who control and regulate the relations between the social unities of production and consumption itself. Both these parts are expressed as surplus value. The agencies of the state may assume the "charges" of intermediation, or they may fall to private hands. If the latter is the case, an interest of the public authority will diverge from and oppose the set of private interests. The public interest is identified, without further ground, with the interest of the social whole, whereby it regulates both the interests of the social class of direct producers and of the private intermediaries. The interests of the private appropriators of the social surplus are not the same as the public interest, even though the state is the organ established in the interest of these same individuals as a social class. The conflict arising from this opposition to the state interests is controlled and regulated by the state. The social surplus which its various appropriators have diverted is at the same time a totality, given abstract expression as surplus value. It is divided concretely as state, public, private ownership of the means of production, and is given abstract expression in the various juridical forms of ownership, or property. The personalities, or personifications of the process of appropriation of the social surplus, are likewise given juridical form; these fictive personalities are determined in and through the process of appropriation of the surplus value and interact with it. The alienated social product is that part which does not re-enter the process of reproduction; nor is it accumulated in any significant degree in the early periods of the history of political economy.[5] Throughout its history, whether it is surplus labor, or

[5] The original accumulation has its own historical development, connected with the functions of the intermediaries in the Asiatic mode of production. In the villages of the Mogul empire these functions covered not only collection of tax and tribute, rent and tolls, but also usury and the formation, on however modest a scale, of village capital and its personification, the village capitalist. This village capital is at once the same as capital coevally developed in western Europe and different from the latter. The personifications of capital resemble one another in

the social surplus in brute form, whether it is self-expansive, or accumulative, its value is surplus value, that which does not return to the self-reproduction of the social class of direct producers.

Abstract labor is labor in its social relation alone; concrete labor is at once labor in relation to nature and labor in its social relation. Abstract value is value in its social relation alone; concrete value is value in its social and natural relation.

The relation to nature of the social labor is mediated by the work process. On the contrary, abstract labor itself produces nothing of utility, being neither a producer in society nor out of it, neither in nature, but perhaps out of it. Abstract labor is alienated labor per se; abstract value is alienated value per se. In consequence, concrete labor and concrete value are alienated. Concrete labor and concrete value, work and use value, are alienated in part; in part they are not.

By the abstraction of social labor in the social relations of exchange and surplus production, concrete labor and value as a matter of form undergo a second abstraction: The concrete value is abstracted (alienated) from its producer in society by the relations of exchange, and at once by the relations of production in society. By its alienation through the exchange relation, exchange value is generated in the society; by its abstraction from the social producer, that is, by the opposition between social production and reproduction, surplus value is produced in the society. Joan Robinson holds that this set of relations is a political process (sc. relations of the state and law), mistaking the antecedent for the consequent in the relations of social labor thereby.

The relations of social labor to nature in political economy are two-fold, being at once mediate and direct. Human beings, in their labor, work and toil, stand in relations to nature that are mediated by acquired skills and technics, as they are by the instruments of labor applied, by the acquired skills and technics. Man goes mediately to work, in the condition of all human labor, whether in the primitive or civil condition. (There is no reason to hold that a future communal labor, or socialist labor, would bear any different relation to nature than the foregoing. This is the human condition, alienated from nature by virtue of being at once continuous and discontinuous with nature. In a utopia we sublate the alienated being of humanity, and the

---

the Asiatic and capitalist modes of production; the scale of the self-expansion of the social surplus, or its self valorization, differs vastly in order of magnitude. The formation of capital in the Asiatic mode of production and the formation of the corresponding personifications of M. le Capital and Mme. la Terre can be considered to be the same in posse that are realized and made actual in the capitalist mode of production. Capital is formed, accumulated, *valorized* in a novel and characteristic way in the capitalist mode of production. Cf. Lawrence Krader, *The Asiatic Mode of Production*. Assen-Amsterdam 1975, ch. 7.

discontinuity with nature, returning to the state of oneness with the earth, whence we arose.)

All human labor is a mediate relation to nature, being the instrumentarium of the human kind, in the process of its reproduction in society. Labor is mediate in a second sense, as medium. We do not work directly upon nature, whether inner or outer nature, but indirectly upon it. Labor as the universal human relation to nature is in this sense not differentiated; whether it is individual, communal, social, private, public, whether labor of hand or head, whether labor in the primitive or civil condition, is all one in this regard. By labor we appropriate, dominate and internalize nature, by labor we mediate our relations to nature, and alienate ourselves from it. We become human through our labor. Labor is the alienation in nature, the primary alienation, whereby we are distanced from nature, opposed to it, discontinuous with it.

By our labor we make a bit of nature our own, beginning with the mastery of the techniques of our own bodies, the sensory, muscular, skeletal, glandular systems, the nervous system and the brain. This mastery is mediated in part by the learning process. We extend the mastery to the expanding world of our knowledge. The internalized natural world is transformed into the cultural world of the human group. It is the natural world that we work, our laboratorium. This laboratorium is the passive field, the medium no longer natural on which we work. It is at once the matter through which we work, the means of work. It is the screen through which we contact, appropriate and internalize our natural surroundings. The thickness of this screen or world of culture is the measure of the degree of mastery of nature; it is the sum of means whereby mastery is acquired and expanded, intensively and extensively. The expansion is solely an outward process. We cannot claim a greater emotional control than our forebears, nor a greater dexterity of tongue or paintbrush. The screen is not a total but a selective process into which subjective and objective factors enter. The process of selection is at once an activity or means and it is the screen itself or medium.

The mediating relation of social labor in relation to society and nature is the process of reproduction. Concrete labor is the work of those engaged in direct social production. In the social relations of the economy, one labors for others. In all economic relations but those of the political economy, this is a reciprocal relation. In the relations of political economy, some labor for others, but this relation is reciprocated neither in kind nor in abstract value. Those who are the direct producers in the society of political economy reproduce the social whole, meeting the wants of others and of themselves. But they are not themselves the social whole, neither they nor themselves together with their families.

The human reproduction is opposed to the natural reproduction of the species, the former being mediate, the latter direct. The human reproduction in the primitive condition of society and economy is not differentiated from production; this differentiation and opposition, we have seen, is the relation of political economy. Reproduction in the primitive condition is production in relation to distribution and consumption alone; reproduction in the political economy is production in relation to distribution, consumption, and exchange. It is now social reproduction. Production thereby is transformed into social production. Social production, because it is the production of exchange value, is the production of surplus value; it is the production of exchange value because it is the production of surplus value. By virtue of these oppositions, the social classes of those engaged in direct production and those who are not so engaged are opposed to each other. The political relations of civil society are determined in the relations of production, exchange, distribution and consumption of the political economy, and not the converse.[6]

III. SOCIAL LABOR, SCIENCE AND SKILL

Social labor is at once the alienation of labor in society; this secondary alienation, is joined to the primary, but does not replace it. The secondary alienation is effected by appropriation of the social product, which had been in the hands of its direct producers, by the development of the conjoint relations of exchange and of production of a social surplus. This second appropriation is that whereby the common social product is divided, one part being applied in the reproduction of the social whole. The remaining part, although socially produced is not so applied. This second part is surplus value. The surplus value adverts to the social class that has not been engaged in its direct production. At the same time, individuals in that social class may participate, although not as class individuals, in the relations of social production and reproduction.

[6] Cf. Alfredo Medio, Values, Prices and Profits in Commodity Society. In: E. K. Hunt and J. G. Schwartz, *Critique of Economic Theory*. Penguin 1972. Medio has written that his description is not 'politically neutral.' His argument is forceful, but he has not got the order right. The entry of politics (in his terms) comes after the introduction of the relations of the political economy, not in medias res. He seeks (p. 344) to controvert Joan Robinson on the issue of politics in the social and political economy, but neither his position nor the one he would overthrow is well-founded. Cf. Joan Robinson, *An Essay on Marxian Economics*, 2nd ed. London 1966.

The production in society is a totality, composed of the skills of those engaged in social production, the instruments of their social labor, and the social product. The skills vary from one generation or cohort to the next in a given society. The society shares the skills, even though they be kept as industrial, technical, trade, guild, corporation, or military secrets by a close few. They are social so long as they are corporate, spread and perpetuated over the course of time; so long, that is, as they are not nonce skills.

Society as a whole is the bearer of these skills, being the unit of record in regard to their cumulation and transmission; if the skill is present anywhere in the society, it is a property of the social whole. Its presence raises the average skill of the social labor by that amount. The introduction of a scientific discovery in a society raises the average in like manner. The contradiction between the appropriation of a skill or scientific discovery by a few, in the face of its attribution to the whole, is plain to all. Compartmentalization of skills, technics, scientific knowledge is present throughout the history and geography of civil society.

"Social property" has a double meaning. It is, first, an attribute of the society; it is, second, that which belongs to the society. By separating the two meanings it is possible that some take to themselves that which is the property of the whole. The property of the few deprives the whole of its property; the separation is a privative relation, the basis of private property.

The appropriation of a scientific discovery by a few is no different from the appropriation of a skill and its social product by the same. The scientific activity is the relation to nature; the skill no different. Whether the one be new, the other old or traditional, is not a matter of moment in this connection. The skill is the relation of concrete and abstract labor to nature and in society; the scientific activity is the same. Industrial skill and scientific activity are alike in the combination of labor of hand and head of which they are constituted, the component labor of the hand being higher in the industrial skill than the same in the scientific activity, in proportion to the whole. The amount of value produced by social labor cannot be apportioned between labor of head and hand, or between industrial skill and scientific activity. The discussion of the relative value of industrial skill and science is made up of the hypostasis of both.

IV. SOCIAL LABOR, BOUND AND FREE

The history of civil society is the history of the bondage and freedom of social labor. The transition from the primitive to the civil condition of economy and society is effected by the separation and opposition between the units of production and consumption, whereby social reproduction comes to be opposed to production. The exchange between the producing unities, which results from the separation of the units of production and consumption, transforms them into the interrelated parts of a social whole. The division of labor is transformed into the social division of labor. Production is thereby transformed into social production.

It has been proposed by L. H. Morgan and Friedrich Engels that the transition from the primitive (savage, barbaric) to the civilized status is the result of the dissolution of the archaic gentes. This may be true in some cases, but it is far from generally the case. In the societies of the so-called Asiatic mode of production (so-called because the societies are found in India, Persia, China, Indonesia, other parts of Asia; but also in Europe, Middle and South America, Africa south of the Sahara, and in the ancient Near East) the transition from the primitive to the civil status was effected together with the continuity in being of the ancient communal unities, gentes, clans, tribes, village communities, etc., long after the transition was made. The Asiatic mode of production is the development of societies in which the formation and opposition of social classes arose early in history, whereby the dissolution of the primitive condition of society and the transition to the social and politial economy, and the civil society were brought about. These are the same conditions which determined the separation and opposition of the producing and consuming unities in the society.

In the Asiatic mode of production, communal relations and archaic institutions of village communities, clans, gentes, etc., were maintained in the social class of the direct producers. This class produced the necessaries for its own reproduction as a class, and a social surplus that was appropriated by the opposed social class. The latter was composed of individuals torn loose from the archaic communal institutions. The process of the dissolution of the primitive relations was asymmetrical, according to social class, the direct producers being bound to the villages and clans by custom, habit, feeling. Subsequent modes of production in the history of civil society transformed the traditional bonds of social labor into the bonds of slavery or serfdom. Whatever the form, the fact of bondage was not eliminated until the onset of the capitalist mode of production and the transformation of civil society into the modern bourgeois society.

At this point, in the history of northern Italy, England and the Low Countries, bound social labor was freed. Social labor it has remained; it is the producer of the alienated social product; the form of social labor is separated from the labor power or capacity, which is subject to contract for its purchase and sale; the seller being the owners of the labor power, living laborers.

The contract for sale of labor power against wages is a contract as any other. Unless the contracting parties are free and equal, the contract is invalid. This is a general rule throughout the history of civil society, throughout, that is, the history of contract. Social labor, as wage labor in the capitalist mode of production and in the mode of production of capital generally, including the modern socialist as well as capitalist, is free as a matter of civil right, and of legal form. The bondage of social labor by tradition is a practice of unwritten customary law. The bondage of social labor by enslavement is an explicit form of contract between two individuals, which is a breach of civil right, hence a defective contract.

ON THE DIALECTIC OF ANTHROCOLOGY

FIVE

I. SOCIETY, INDIVIDUAL AND PERSON

I. DIALECTIC OF THE RELATIONS OF THE HUMAN RACE TO NATURE AND WITHIN SOCIETY

The science of anthropology has traditionally studied the relations of the human kind to nature and the relations within society, the original condition of the human being, the preservation and overcoming thereof, the establishment of human culture, and its material, mental or artistic expression. Anthropology is founded on the presupposition of the variety of human societies and cultures, the differences between them, and the varieties in the developments and relations of each. It is an academic discipline above all, and has no internal commitment to practical undertakings. At best it has nurtured liberal spirits who embraced the "party of humanity", and who have defended the concept of the whole against any expression of innate superiority of one group over another. It is an abstract social science which has only now separated itself from a spurious natural-science view of humanity, and this latter has given birth to a monster, the biology of racism, the reduction of cultural differences to natural or innate differences, and the assignment of these to a scale of higher or lower races. This academic anthropology did not strangle its offspring until long after it had done its harm.

Karl Marx in his anthropology took up the same subject matter, the relations of the human kind to nature and in society, the relations to the animal forebears, the historical differences of the social groups.[1] But the academic nature of the discipline, its separation of theory from practice, hence its abstract character, sporadic dialectic, has removed itself from any anthropology that can call itself Marxist. The notion of a Marxist anthropology is a *contradictio in adjecto*. The work of Marx and the science of anthropology can overlap but they may not coincide, except as a potentiality of either. Their overlap consists in their common problems and what is common in their scientific method; but that method is not at all points the same in

---

[1] See *The Ethnological Notebooks of Karl Marx*, transcr. and ed., with an introd. by Lawrence Krader (Assen, 1972). Marx was one of the first to denounce the racist cant.

Marx's terms and in the science of anthropology generally, as we shall show in the following pages. The main differences lie in the necessary retreat of the academic discipline, the holding back from concrete programs of practical activity, and the lack of system in the dialectic. Anthropology as an academic profession is far from having developed a materialist basis; if it did it would simply be Marxism, or Marxism anthropology, repeating in the adjective what is expressed in the noun, as *anthropological* Marxism redundant, as *Marxist* anthropology unnecessary.[2]

We will focus on the dialectic of the relations within society and culture, and will then take up the relations to nature; at the same time the two problems are inseparable. Marx wrote:

> "*Industry* is the *actual* historical relation of nature and hence of natural science to the human being; if industry is therefore taken as the *exoteric* revelation of the human *essential powers* then the *human* essence of nature or the *natural* essence of the human being will also be understood, hence natural science will lose its abstract material or rather idealist direction and will become the basis of *human* science, just as it has become already – although in alienated shape – the basis of actually human life; and *one* basis for life, another for *science*, is a lie from the outset. Nature which becomes human history – the act of genesis of human society – is the actual nature of man, therefore nature, as it comes to be through industry, even though in an *alienated* shape, is true *anthropological* nature. [...] History itself is an *actual* part of *natural* history, of nature become human. Natural science will eventually subsume the science of man, just as the science of man will subsume natural science in itself: there will be *one* science."[3]

---

[2] The issue of a Marxist anthropology is further complicated by the controversy over the young Marx on the one hand and the mature Marx on the other. The relation of the youthful works of Marx to his mature works is a matter of continuity and discontinuity in his undertakings. By the young Marx is usually meant the author of articles in the *Rheinische Zeitung* and in *Vorwärts*, of the Kritik der Hegelschen Rechtsphilosophie, of the Ökonomisch-Philosophische Manuskripte, all from the period 1842-44. The controversy has been carried to an extreme by L. Althusser, who opposes the non-dialectical to the dialectical Marx; Althusser claims that the brand of the dialectic was stamped on those early writings and was only eradicated by him in later life. E. Fromm has put forth the opposition between Marx the humanist and Marx the revolutionist. The transition made by Marx from a philosophical anthropology to an empirical ethnology has been traced elsewhere. See my Introduction to The Ethnological Notebooks of Karl Marx; "Karl Marx as Ethnologist", in: *Transactions of the New York Academy of Sciences*, Second Series, XXXV (1973), pp. 304-13; "The Works of Marx and Engels in Ethnology Compared", in: *International Review of Social History*, XVIII (1973), pp. 223-75; *Ethnologie und Anthropologie bei Marx* (Munich, 1973), ch. 1 and 2.

[3] Ökonomisch-Philosophische Manuskripte, in: Marx-Engels, *Historisch-Kritische Gesamtausgabe* (MEGA), I, Vol. 3, pp. 122-23.

1. The relation of humanity and nature is one of continuity and discontinuity. The continuity is the original condition and the earliest relation of the human kind and the natural world; each was and is a part of the other.

2. The formation of the human species is the primary alienation of mankind from nature; all other human alienations in social and economic relations are developments out of this initial alienation, or discontinuity.

3. The separation of humanity and nature is the actual relation, the separation of human history from natural history, of human science from natural science, is the superstructure raised upon this initial separation and alienation.

4. The relation of nature and humanity is repeated in the relation of the natural and human sciences; the first relation is the determinant of the second, and not the converse. This is not a dialectical relation between the processes of the natural world and of thought; it is an opposition to the abstract material view, or the view of idealism. The unity between nature and humanity, just as the unity between natural and human science, is a potential one, a becoming; the means to the end of unity is industry, or the operation of the human kind upon nature. The reversal of the nature which becomes human, hence ceases to be itself, is a process that is limited in time, temporary, our contemporary time; the nature which has taken an alienated *Gestalt*, its human nature, will itself be reversed in turn, and the unity of nature and humanity will be developed. This is a dialectic of the double negation, first of nature, then of humanity, first by the process of alienation of humanity from nature, which process is human industry, and by its sublation.

The first part of the above passage was developed by Marx in a dialectical way, the second was dropped away: human life is given in society, social life is conceived not in the abstract but in particular historical conditions, and these are variable. Hence the definition of the human being in the different historical epochs is variable. Thus, while Aristotle in ancient Greece defined the human being as a social animal or rather as a town-dweller, Benjamin Franklin defined the human being as a tool-making animal. The relation of the ancient Greek *polis* within itself and to nature, and the relation of eighteenth-century Yankeedom, in each case posited a different conception of the human being.[4] Both of these conceptions of the human nature are

---

[4] Karl Marx, *Das Kapital*, Vol. I, in Marx-Engels, Werke (MEW), Vol. 23, p. 346. Marx took each of these conceptions of humanity in its particularity and did not advance a universal definition of his own here.

remarkable, but in neither of these societies was the limitation of the condition of humanity particular to the period overcome, and in neither case was the conception of humanity thus delimited overcome. Further, the history of invention was discussed by Marx in the context of social invention as opposed to the inventions by single individuals. He concluded that human and natural history proceeded along parallel paths.[5]

1. The material basis of the formation of the instruments of production is the natural technology of a given plant or animal species and the cultural technology of a particular human society. The natural organs of plants and animals are the instruments of the production of life of the given plant or animal form, and these organs have their natural history, just as the instruments of production of human societies have their human history. Darwin[6] called attention to the natural history of technology, Marx to the cultural history of human technology. The unit taken for his observations by Darwin was the biological species, but this unit is broken up into the technologies of particular societies in the case of the human species. The natural and cultural technologies each have their history.

2. Technology reveals the active component and relation of human beings to nature. This should be understood as the relation of particular societies, it is not general to all mankind, and must be separately mastered. The mastery of their arid habitat in the Kalahari desert by Bushmen, the adaptation of means of detection, conduit and storage of water by these people, far exceeds the ability of the later European intruders, who upset the balance between the social group and the natural surroundings. The human beings do not learn and adapt to nature as a species, but only through the traditions of particular groups; the unit of human history is different from that of the natural species.

3. The problem of production by appropriate technology contains within itself the problem of reproduction, which latter is to be understood in the natural sense of biological reproduction in the cases of the human and of plant and animal species; but in the case of humanity, in all circumstances, both of literate and non-literate cultures,

---

[5] Marx, op. cit., p. 392, note. That which was regarded in 1844 as the potentiality of the reunion of humanity and nature thus fell away, to be replaced in the later writing by the mentioned parallelism.

[6] Charles Darwin, *The Origin of Species* (1859) (Modern Library, New York, n.d.), see p. 112 on specialized and generalized functions of organs; pp. 149f. on the sting of the bee as a boring instrument; p. 370 on modifications of rudimentary structures, etc.; id., *The Descent of Man* (1871), op. cit., on specialization of organs of communication, in nature, p. 465, etc.

the reproduction process is the matter of the continued existence and furtherance of mankind not as a form of animal life. It is instead the matter of the continued existence and furtherance of particular economic relations, not merely as the abstraction – the technological basis of life and adaptational history gives way to the economic bases of human life and the history of these.

The adaptation and technics of production and reproduction of life are the same abstract categories in the case of human history as in the case of natural history: concretely they differ; the rate of development in the case of mankind is rapid and multifarious, while the biological rate of development is as a rule geologically slow. The varieties of technical adaptation of human groups are several thousand times greater than that of animal and plant species. The abstract problems of production and reproduction of the species are the same, but concretely they are realized in different ways; the differences between animals and humanity, in this regard, are great, the differences within the human species relatively small. The dialectical opposition of potential unity and actual difference is the same as that of alienation and reunification of humanity and nature. It is joined to the dialectic of the unity of humanity when considered in the abstract and the multiplicity of human social histories in the concrete cases.[7]

II. FOUNDATIONS AND NATURE OF SOCIETY

Turning to the relations of society, we take up first the nature of society itself. Society is an object that can be perceived with the senses, but it is at the same time a suprasensory object, a set of relations and the symbolic representation both of the sensory and the suprasensory object. In his treatment of commodity fetishism, Marx begins with the opposition between mysticism and sensory investigation, what is mystified and what is clear to the senses.[8] Commodities

---

[7] The theses advanced by Marx in 1844 were set forth by him again in *Capital*; the thesis of continuity-discontinuity of the relations of the human kind and nature; and the thesis of the parallel development of human and natural science. The thesis of the convergence of these sciences is a separate problem.

[8] Marx, *Kapital*, Vol. 1. In the first ed. (Hamburg, 1867), Marx wrote, p. 774: "Eben desshalb erscheinen die Arbeitsprodukte als Waren, sinnlich übersinnlich oder gesellschaftliche Dinge." *Nota bene*, the commodities are things which are sensory and at once suprasensory; being both, they are social. The social in the commodities is at once of the senses and beyond them (but there are other things in nature which are also at once of and beyond the senses). The social is of the natural order, which includes other relations beside the commodity relations, and all these are at once sensory-suprasensory. Marx took up this formulation regarding commodities in the later editions of *Kapital*: "Es ist sinnenklar, dass der Mensch [...] die Formen der Naturstoffe [...] verändert." He then considered that the table while it is still wood, unchanged, not

are both sensory and suprasensory. (It would be naive to suppose that sense-preception has no mystery attached to it, but such mystification as it has engendered leads in another direction, and is another problem than our present one.) The mystification of commodities arises from their social character, their character as the products not of social production but of the social relations between human beings, who now stand to each other not as producers in society but as buyers and sellers of the products. It is the mystification of the commodity relation; the initial mystification of the social relation, or the failure to grasp it for what it is, the relation between human beings, is the kernel of mystification carried forward into the commodity fetishism,

yet in the form of a commodity, is "an ordinary, sensory thing". "Aber sobald er [der Tisch] als Ware auftritt, verwandelt er sich in ein sinnlich-übersinnliches Ding." The mystery attached to the commodity relation, says Marx, arises out of the mystery attached to the social relation. Because we are unclear about the one, willfully mystifying and obscuring that unclarity, we mystify and obscure the other. On the dialectic of the sensory-suprasensory and the mystical, Marx proceeded to reject the mystical root of the commodity, whether in its use value or in its value determination. Yet both these economic relations have their physiological base and derivations from the head, nerves, muscles, sense organs. The social form of labor begins when men begin to work for one another. The mystery of the commodity arises out of the form of the commodity itself, which, we have seen, is a sensory suprasensory thing. By exchange, labor products become commodities: "Durch dies Quidproquo werden die Arbeitsprodukte Waren, sinnlich-übersinnlich oder gesellschaftliche Dinge." *Kapital*, Vol. 1, op. cit., pp. 85f., cf. Theorien über den Mehrwert, III, in MEW, Vol. 26.3, p. 474. We call attention first to the poetics of Marx, beginning with that which is clear to the senses, *sinnenklar*, then proceeding to the consideration of wood, an ordinary, sensory thing, then to the commodity, the form of wood as table, a sensory-suprasensory thing. That commodity as sensory-suprasensory is social; it is not social as sensory-suprasensory. Cf. *Le Capital*, J. Roy tr. (Paris, 1873-75), pp. 28f.: "sinnlich", "qui tombe sous les sens"; "sinnlich-übersinnlich", "à la fois saisissable et insaisissable"; English translation, Friedrich Engels ed., S. Moore and E. Aveling tr. (New York, 1937), p. 81: "It is as clear as noon-day", "sinnenklar"; p. 83: "commodities, social things whose qualities are at the same time perceptible and imperceptible by the senses", "Waren, sinnlich-übersinnlich oder gesellschaftliche Dinge".

    The relation of the social world to the sensory-suprasensory is a problem of the ontology of social being. See my "Critique dialectique de la nature de la nature humaine", in: L'Homme et la Société, No 10 (1968), pp. 21-39; and in: *Critique of Anthropology*, 1976, vol. 6, no. 2, pp. 4-22. Georg Lukács, Zur Ontologie des gesellschaftlichen Seins. Die Arbeit (Neuwied, 1973). The mystification of the commodity relation is a problem of the fetishism of commodities, and at the same time of the social relation. The problem of fetishism is in turn connected with the relation of religion in society and in thought; it is at once an ontological and epistemological problem. The mystery of the commodity does not arise out of the content or substance of the commodity, nor out of its social relation, but out of its form, as social sensory-suprasensory. L. v. Stein had attached much mystery to the concept of society; the certainty of the senses, wrote Stein, is not a sufficient ground for truth, since all phenomena have a basis which cannot be grasped with the senses; the concept of society is more difficult to grasp than that of the state or the economy. L. v. Stein, *Der Sozialismus und Kommunismus des heutigen Frankreichs* (1848), Pt I, ch. 2. On Stein, see Karl Marx, Die Heilige Familie, in MEGA, I, Vol. 3, p. 311.

just as its earthly core is the social relation itself, the concrete relation of human beings in a particular society, who come together in a market place and relate to each other as buyers and sellers. It is the social relation that is carried over into the commodity relation, the mystification of the social relation is the germ that has infected the commodity relation with the same disease. This carries the discussion from structure to superstructure, and will be returned to below. First we must consider the element in the Marxist social theory concerning the social relation itself.

Marx acknowledged his debt to the philosopher Ludwig Feuerbach, who criticized the Hegelian system not for its dialectic but for its idealism; but Marx had to break free from Feuerbach, which he did in the eleven theses against the latter and in the chapter on Feuerbach in the *German Ideology*. Feuerbach had written of the human essence, or the essential nature of man.[9] Marx replied: "But the human essence is no in-dwelling abstraction in the single individual. In his reality the individual is the ensemble of social relations."[10] The human individual has no essence, and exists only as a means of social relations; the essential core of humanity is nothing other than the set of human relations in society. The society in turn is not a passive category into which the human relations are poured, the society is the nexus of individual relations, just as the individual is the nexus of social relations. The collective body of individuals forms an agency whereby social conditions are formed and changed, the educators educated. The reciprocal relations of the human individual and society form an interaction, the dialectic of agent and patient, or activity-passivity.

The relations of human beings in society are various, they are not generally the same throughout the species, throughout its natural history. There is, that is to say, no species-specific behavior for mankind as there is for animal species. This is the error of modern ethologists such as N. Tinbergen and K. Lorenz. The relations of human beings vary from one society to the next, and from one era in the same society to the next. Once mankind had been distanced and distanced itself from nature, these relations became highly variable, the variability being both mark and measure of the distance from nature. The society is as much the agency of these variations as the individuals; the technological inventions should be made the subject of a critical history, and we would then see how little these inventions belong to single individuals. The scorn that Marx heaped on the fiction of

[9] Ludwig Feuerbach, *Das Wesen des Christentums*, 2nd ed. (1843). See also his *Grundsätze der Philosophie der Zukunft* (1843).
[10] Marx, Sixth Thesis on Feuerbach (1845), MEW, Vol. 3, pp. 6, 534.

Robinson Crusoe as the model of the science of society is directly related to this thesis.

The political economists of the eighteenth and nineteenth centuries fastened upon the story by Daniel Defoe of Alexander Selkirk. It is a convenient fiction, which Marx understood rightly to have concealed within it the myth of the capitalist individual. The ideological over-burden of this fiction, or its mythical core, is the self-made man, the rugged individual, who does not need society; not does he desire interference from without, in particular he wants no interference from the state in running his business affairs. The individual is the starting point of the science of society, just as, in the conception of the ideologists of individualism, the individual is the starting point of society. Society presupposes, according to this doctrine, human individuals; these individuals, on the contrary, do not presuppose society.[11] The point that Marx had made is that production, the division of labor, distribution, wants and their satisfaction are social relations and undertakings, to which social categories correspond.[12] David Ricardo had held that the primitive hunters exchanging fish and game were possessors of commodities.[13] The Robinsonade reaches over and beyond the classical economists and Marx: at the end of the nineteenth century, Marx's economic system was criticized by Eugen Böhm-Bawerk on the grounds that the individual and not the society is the starting point of economics. The Marxist standpoint was defended by Rudolf Hilferding, who accused Böhm-Bawerk of holding an unhistoric and unsocial outlook: Hilferding began, in the tradition of Marx, with the social relations of individuals with one another.[14] Böhm-Bawerk's theory of value is based on the satisfaction of individual wants; it is a subjective determination by the individual. The theory of value in Marx is objective and social, founded on labor time, a theory which is traced back to Smith and Ricardo.

[11] Marx, Zur Kritik der politischen Ökonomie (1859), in MEW, Vol. 13, p. 46. See also *Kapital*, Vol. 1, op. cit., pp. 90f.

[12] Marx, *Kapital*, Vol. 1, ch. 12, esp. § 4: "Die Teilung der Arbeit innerhalb der Manufaktur und Teilung der Arbeit innerhalb der Gesellschaft". This distinction holds for production in primitive as well as civilized societies. The division of labor in the family and in the factory does not presuppose the exchange of commodities; the division of labor in manufacture pre-supposes society, that of the family does not.

[13] David Ricardo, *The Principles of Political Economy and Taxation*, 3rd ed. (1821). In ch. 1, section 1, Ricardo wrote of exchangeable value of commodities in the early stages of society in this way. He quoted Adam Smith, *An Inquiry into the Nature and Causes of the Wealth of Nations* (1776), Book I, ch. V, to the same effect. Neither divorced the individual from society; both presupposed society in the economic undertakings of the individual.

[14] Eugen Böhm-Bawerk, *Karl Marx and the Close of his System*; Rudolf Hilferding, Böhm-Bawerk's Criticism of Marx, P. M. Sweezy ed. (New York, 1966). See p. 133 and Sweezy, Introduction, p. xx.

The viewpoint of the Austrian school of economics, of which Böhm-Bawerk is representative, is not factually wrong; the wants of the individual are undeniable. The error that they make is the same as that which Marx accused the Robinsonaders of making, that is, they divorced the individual from society, assuming that there is such a state of existence in which the individual does not need society, is independent of it, and pre-exists the society, which he joins because of a penchant toward social life. Grotius, Hobbes, Spinoza and Locke in the seventeenth century, Montesquieu and Rousseau in the eighteenth all assumed a free, unfettered life of the individual, which mankind surrendered because of the attractions of life in society, where greater riches, intercourse, gaiety would be found. The social contract whereby the civil society was founded is a consequence of the inclinations of the human beings who were already in existence. Marx, as we have seen, proposed that the individual and society are mutual determinants and determinations, one of the other. The wrongness of the Austrian school and its modern representatives, L. von Mises and F. Hayek, is not one of fact, but of the failure to bring the two sides, individual and society, into their dialectical relation.

From the starting point of Marx, the individual and society are mutually interactive and determinant. The objective side of the dialectic does not lie in the society alone, however. The individual, being formed of social relations, bears within himself both the subjective and the objective components of society; society, however, as the product of individual relations, subsists in their objective side alone. There is no subjective factor in society and history save that of the human individual; but the human individual is in turn neither subject nor object alone, he is both. During the past three generations since the death of Marx, the doctrine has spread that Marxism is the objective science of society, and this scientific side is taken up in unanimity by Karl Kautsky, Otto Bauer, G. V. Plekhanov, V. I. Lenin, although it were erroneous to say that this overt agreement on a starting point had any consequence in the practice of revolution, evolution, reform of society, or revision of Marxism.[15] All agreed, however, that the laws with which Marx and Marxists operate are objective laws of history and society. Plekhanov made the most explicit statement, and went furthest of all, in equating the individual with the subjective

---

[15] Karl Kautsky, *Ethik und materialistische Geschichtsauffassung* (Stuttgart, 1906); Otto Bauer, "Marxismus und Ethik", in: *Die Neue Zeit*, XXIV, 2 (1906), pp. 485-99; G. V. Plekhanov, *The Role of the Individual in History* (New York, 1940). See the collections by H. J. Sandkühler and R. de la Vega, *Marxismus und Ethik*, and *Austromarxismus* (Frankfurt, 1970); V. I. Lenin, *State and Revolution* (1917).

factor in history, the social with the objective, but even the Neo-Kantian or revisionist socialists, Conrad Schmidt, E. Bernstein, M. Adler accepted this view as axiomatic. The debate concerning Marxist humanism, introduced by the existentialist Marxists, carried on primarily in the light of the *Economic-Philosophical Manuscripts* of Marx, a debate which has even penetrated the parties and countries of Lenin's tradition, has not shaken the equation of Marxism with objectivity.

The objective factor in history predominates, however, because the subjective factor is suppressed, distorted and transformed by the social relations of political society. Thereby the thesis of the objective laws is given operating room; they are at work because of the conditions of civilized life that reach their peak in capitalist society. These conditions are, in the first place, the division of society into classes and, upon this basis, the alienation and reification of the human being under these conditions, hence, the objectification of the laws governing the society. The result is that the subjective side gives way, the objective side of humanity expands its role; in place of the whole individual, a simulacrum of humanity appears. The individual is divided as society is divided. How this works will be the subject of the following sections.

That is the first step in the dialectic of society; the second is the relations between the economic factor and the superstructure raised upon it in history: the state, law, philosophy, science, religion, ethics.[16] Just as there is an interrelation between the substructure and superstructure in the social whole, so there is a relation between the individual and society, each of these interrelations implying and calling forth the other.

III. THE FORMATION OF CIVIL SOCIETY

The state is an institution of civil society, it is not an institution

---

[16] Friedrich Engels repeatedly brought out the interrelations between the economic and the other factors. See his correspondence with Conrad Schmidt, Josef Bloch, Franz Mehring and W. Borgius (Heinz Starkenburg), MEW, Vol. 37, pp. 435ff., 462ff., 488ff.; Vol. 39, pp. 96.ff, 205ff. See Karl Korsch, *Karl Marx* (1938), pp. 220-29. Marx made the economic factor in history the most important one. H. S. Maine had put the moral factor first, to which Marx replied: "This 'moral' shows how little Maine understands the matter; the influences are economic before everything else, the '*moral*' modus of existence is ever a derived, secondary modus, never the primary one." *Ethnological Notebooks*, p. 329. The words "before everything else" can only mean that there is something else which the economic comes before. That which the economic precedes is given in the *Ethnological Notebooks* on p. 112: the political, religious, juristic and philosophical systems of the society.

of society in general. On the one hand, it is not a universal feature of human society, for it is not found in societies that are commonly called primitive. On the other hand, the state is not the ultimate end of society, nor is it the perfection of society; Aristotle held, to the contrary, that the Greek city-state is the ultimate nature of man, or the final end of human society. Opposed to Aristotle is the tenet that the state is a passing phase of social evolution. It will be abolished when the conditions that gave rise to it in the first place themselves disappear.

The common root of human society is life in the community, in which the opposition of the private and the public is not to be found, or is found only in a modest degree. The transition to civil society, however, the emergence of the class of new men, whose ends are at once individual and class-individual, introduces the opposition between the private and the public sector on the one hand and the continuation of the common institutions on the other. These common institutions are not overcome, they are transformed. The latter are literally the continuation of the common people, and, to an ever changing degree, the continuation of the collective institutions and the holding of the land in common. The surplus product is collected by the new class of private men, who are the public officers, who use the public offices in their private interest. Their relation to society in regard to the private interest is now twofold. Through their public control they express and undergird the private interest; through the pursuit of the private interest they achieve public control, control over the public interest and over the public, the people. All this is founded on the separation and opposition of the public from the common and the public from the private.

A lesson in etymology may make this clear. The Roman State was the republic before it became the empire. The republic is *res publica*, the public thing or matter. Civil society having been formed, the state is now called into existence, the public concern and interest is separated from the private concern, and both from the common, which is the root and stem of both. The appellation Commonwealth, the translation of *res publica*, therefore is a flat lie: commonwealth is supposed to be the civil society, but wealth is now held in severalty, and no longer in common. The wealth or social product is collected in the public interest (in the treasury of the state), but is at the same time accumulated by private individuals. It is in their interest to maintain the collective institutions; the unit for collection of the surplus in the form of rent, tax, rent-tax is by means of these collective institutions, the village, the community, the kin-village community, whereby the opposition of the public interest and the common interest is maintained and prolonged. The formation of civil society is thus a dual dialectical movement, which takes place simultaneously: 1) out of the original common concern, collective interest and life, the opposition of the public and the private interests arises; 2) the public and private interests are both opposed to the common interests of the society as a whole. That common interest was originally the predominant one in society, but in political society it is subordinate to the emergence and opposition of the public and private interests. The agencies of the state have as one of their functions the regulation of the opposition of the public and private interests, a delicate balance, in which the private is not suppressed but kept within the bounds defined by the concourse of all the parties. The extraction of surplus value from the common people, the direct cultivators of the soil, etc., is the function of the state in the early history of civil society. The private interest arises as a subjective matter, but takes a reified form in civil society, as we shall see in the following sections.

To the public sector is associated power over others, by armed men, record keepers, judges, priests; the private wealth and the public power are combined in their hands; opposed to them are the immediate producers in society. The power of the state is the expression of this wealth, armed support, learning; but it is mere appearance, externality; its supremacy has no inward root, but is the fruit of the previous external processes of increase in the social product, the means of its accumulation, storage and appropriation of a part of it in the hands of a few who, by its control, thereby gain control over the society as a whole; or rather they now control certain aspects of the life of the society, in particular, those aspects that are accessible to regulation by the state instruments: armed might for control of the interior of the society and for external conquest; the formality of the law for the control of the public, outer, formal side of the human being; religious mystification in order to obscure the origins of knowledge and of control over nature and society.

Let us turn to the human beings themselves who have been part of this joint process of division of the social product and control thereby of society; we will examine by taking this course the internal and subjective factors in history, in their relation to the aforementioned external and objective ones. Human beings had lived hitherto in an undifferentiated mass, without distinctions of wealth and power. Out of the disruption of this community of interest, the oppositions of the public and the private sphere emerge. A few individuals come forth who establish control over the public sphere in their private interest, by appropriating an increasingly larger share of the social product.

The community binds its members to itself, the members bind each other by their common life and interests, the bonds are comfortable, comforting, the opposite of despotic; the umbilicus to the community is severed, a few individuals are torn forth, the majority remain bound by custom to the whole. In the early appearance of the state, the community continues to exist for the many, while the few are gathered around the courts of the sovereignty. These few are a new social type, who put their own interests foremost, and they pursue this interest at the expense of the society as a whole, at the expense of the poor class of people, and at the expense of their wealthy congeners, or the cohort of the powerful. The working out of the individuality in society is thus onesided, it works on behalf of the wealthy and mighty few, and they work out this individuality in their own interests. This latter interest is a class interest, the individuality is that of a class of individuals. This class interest, however, has internally contradictory tendencies, for it contains within itself means both for the furtherance of the interest of the ruling class at the expense of the social whole and of the remaining class or classes, and at the same time contains means for the disruption and opposition within the ruling class itself. The state is still defined therefore as the organ of the ruling class; its functions are the domination of the entire society, of the poor class of people, of the direct workers on the land, in mines, and workshops, together with their families; but it is also the means of control over the self-interest and self-seeking of the new men, the class of the wealthy which will put the private interest of the individual even before the interest of the class to which it belongs, on which it is dependent for support, and which gave rise to that individual interest in the first place. In a first expression of this view Marx wrote:

"The apparent supreme independent existence of the state is itself merely show, and in all its forms it is an excrescence of society. As its appearance itself comes forth at a certain stage of social development, so it disappears again as soon as the society has reached a stage not yet reached. First tearing forth the individuality from the originally *not despotic chains* (as blockhead Maine understands it), *rather the satisfying and comforting bonds of the group*, of the primitive community, – therewith the onesided elaboration of the individuality. As to the true nature of the latter, it is shown only when we analyze the content, the *interests* of these 'latter'. We then find that these interests themselves again are interests common to particular social groups, interests that characterize them, *class interests*, etc., hence this individuality is itself a class individuality, and these in the final instance all have economic conditions at bottom. On this basis the state is built and presupposes them."[17]

1. H. S. Maine, *Lectures on the Early History of Institutions* (1875), had criticized the view, held by J. Austin, that the state is the result of abstraction purely within the law. Maine thought the state to be the result of moral influences, Marx criticizes Maine's view for being superficial and ignoring the economic conditions.
2. The theory of the evolution of the state is expressed by Marx in consonance with the stage theory of cultural evolution expressed by Morgan.[18]
3. The reference to the non-despotic chains by Marx is simultaneously an attack against J. J. Rousseau, *Du Contrat Social*, and against Maine.
4. The interests of the class are both subjective and objective. The definition of the state as the organ of the ruling class must be reworked in terms of the functions enumerated and in the light of the interplay of the subjective and the objective factors. First, the function of the state to control all elements of society, both the oppressors and the oppressed, must be brought out. Second, the control of the poor, exploited and oppressed by the state in the interest of the wealthy, who rule over the former through the organs of the state, is an objective factor. Third, the control of the individuals of the ruling class who act in their own interest, as opposed to class interest, is both a public and a private matter. The objective factor is the public one; the subjective aspect has been separated and subordinated to the others, thereby it has been reified, dehumanized, turned into a factor which serves the interest of others, but not of the one in whom it is a proper part.
5. Humanity lived prior to the formation of the state in collectivities whose common interests predominated over individual interests. Individuals are torn loose to form the ruling class, whereas the ruled and oppressed retain their community form and interests long after, indeed down to the beginning of the contemporary era of history. These individuals are of that self-seeking kind who put the interest

---

[17] *Ethnological Notebooks*, p. 329.
[18] L. H. Morgan, *Ancient Society* (1877). See *Ethnological Notebooks*, pp. 97-241. See also Marx, drafts of letter to Vera Zasulich, MEW, Vol. 19, pp. 384-406. Engels, Anti-Dühring, Pt II, ch. 1 (MEW, Vol. 20, pp. 137f.), had written that primitive communities had already developed the state ("der Staat, zu dem sich die naturwüchsigen Gruppen gleichstämmiger Gemeinden [...] fortentwickelt hatten"). See "The Works of Marx and Engels in Ethnology Compared", loc. cit.

of the part over the interest of the whole, and the interest of their own individuality even over the interest of the part. The state organs guard against these excesses, potentially damaging to the whole, as they guard against rebellions by the poor and against invasion from without. In the interest of the self-serving individual of the ruling class in the society, arms are sold for private profit to rebels against the state and to the invaders, at the cost of endangering the very same ruling class in the first instance and the social whole in the other. The interest of the self-serving and self-seeking individuals will go so far as to evade tax-collection or customs and excise payments, even though the pay of the state organs, army, police, treasury, which protect the ruling class, depends on these collections.

6. The tearing forth is the act of formation of the individual interests that enter into the formation of the state. The community is not destroyed thereby, but its primitive character is transformed as its members enter into relations through the age-old community with the organs of the state, which now extracts the surplus from the community in the form of rent in labor, tax in labor, rent-tax.

7. The transition from the primitive to civil society is effected by the formation of this new class of individuals, whose class interests are the individual interests, whose individual interests are the class interests and their oppositions, which therefore must be regulated and controlled by the organs of the state. The transformation of primitive institutions, among which is the community in the first place, the emergence of the new class of individuals, and the emergence of the organs of the state, together constitute the passage from primitive to civil society.

8. The class interests of the new individuals form the content of their social lives; the subjective content of the relations in society is thrown off, to be replaced by an external, objective set of social relations, and it is these which now replace the former content of the social lives of the new individuals. The onesided elaboration of the outer form of the social life is a form of reification of the whole individual; its etiology and consequence is a form of social alienation.[19]

9. The act of tearing forth of the new individuals is the primary act of alienation of civil society; the philosophy of egoism, the poetry

---

[19] On the opposition between individual and common interest see Marx, Die Heilige Familie op. cit., pp. 306-10. In his critique of Helvetius, Marx equates the individual with the private interest on the one side, the human with the common interest on the other. Thereby, the particular interest in the given society is overcome, but the critique of this interest is still to be made: the common interest is potentially the interests of all of humanity, but it is not actually so; this lies in some future time. The individual and the private interest are equated precisely in civil society, class-divided society, capitalist society.

of individualism, or freedom of the individualist from social constraints, is its ideological expression: it is a false subjectivity, the ideology of the unfettered subject that is substituted for the reality which must relate the subjective to the objective freedom. It is the second alienation of humanity as well as the first in the new form of society. The reification with which it is connected is further developed in the social relations of capital.

Marx wrote in *Capital*: "Cooperation in the labor process as we find it predominating in the beginnings of human culture, among hunting peoples or perhaps in the community of India, rests on the one hand on the communal ownership of the conditions of production; on the other hand it rests on the fact that the individual is not torn forth from the umbilicus of the tribe or community any more than the bee from the beehive."[20]

a. The sequence in the evolution of mankind from communal to individual ownership is posited. First of all, an evolution of society by stages of development is presupposed.

b. The cultivator of the soil is a member of the community of cultivators, he is not torn forth, *losgerissen*, from that community, even after the community has made the transition to membership in political society and is subordinated to the state.

c. This is the negative of the thesis proposed[21] in the notes on Maine, where the *Losreissung*, tearing forth, of the ruling individuals from the community in the process of the formation of civil society and the state is expressed.

d. The analogy between the primitive community and the beehive is a biologism, a reduction of the human kind to animal life. This is to be criticized, for the relations in the community and in the swarm are only a manner of speaking, a rhetorical trope which is contradicted by Marx himself by his reference to the beginnings of culture (*Kulturanfänge*). This reference is one of the earliest to the modern use of the word "culture", and is different in conception from the analogy drawn to the hive: culture is thereby opposed to nature.

In civil society the undifferentiated forms of human labor, characteristic of primitive society, give way to the differentiated forms. This differentiation is to begin with the opposition of private to social labor. In social labor, abstract and concrete labors are mutually opposed, each converted into the other.[22] Production in civil

---

[20] Marx, *Kapital*, Vol. 1, pp. 353f.
[21] The passage in *Kapital*, Vol. 1, dates from 1867, that on Maine from 1880-81. See *Ethnological Notebooks*, pp. 86-89.
[22] Marx, *Kapital*, Vol. 1, p. 73.

society no longer takes the form of direct and concrete, private labors for the immediate satisfaction of the wants of the individual, family, or community; production in civil society is mediate. By increasing division of labor in society the unit of production is ever more separated from the unit of consumption; the labor is now mediate labor, labor for and by others, hence social labor. It is no longer the production of useful things directly consumed by the immediate producers; on the contrary, wants in civil society are met by the labors of others, i.e., by commodity exchange and production. The products of the social labors are given an abstract expression in order to effect the exchange. Social labor is in its abstract form a commodity, but not one like any other; it is the abstract content of all exchanges, the expression of which is value. The mutual dependence of the different units of production and consumption increases as the division of labor increases, hence, as the abstract form of labor increases. The society becomes ever more abstract in its expression, or in its quality as civil society; the relations of the individuals who labor for one another become ever more abstract as the form of labor becomes increasingly abstract; in this sense they become ever more abstract individuals. The first moment, then, in civil society, is the expression of social labor as mediate labor; the medium is the relation of exchange.

The second moment in civil society is the conversion of social labor into what it is not. Here, social labor is not labor for all but for some. Civil society is society divided into classes, whereby the one does labor, work or toil for the other, but the other does not return the like amount of labor or its equivalent measure of value. The difference is the surplus produced by social labor, which is a contradiction. One class works for the profit[23] of the other. Here social labor contains a portion of non-reciprocated or surplus labor, abstractly expressed as surplus value. The contradiction is not overcome by the conversion of the surplus into private as opposed to social property; on the contrary, it is promulgated thereby. The economy of the civil society is not social economy, but, founded on the production of surplus value and on the private and privative relation of property, it is political economy. The relations of political economy are partly implicit, partly unfolded in the earlier forms of civil society, in the ancient Asiatic, classical and feudal modes of production; the relations of political economy achieve their fullest development hitherto gained in the capitalist mode of production.

Having considered the relations of civil society in themselves, to primitive society, and to society in general, we now turn to the

[23] See Marx, *Theorien über den Mehrwert*, III, op. cit., pp. 485f.

relation of the individual in society and the relation of the person to the human being, or the alienation and reification of the latter as the juridical person in civil society.

IV. THE HUMAN BEING AS SUBJECT AND OBJECT AND AS JURIDICAL PERSON

Any anthropology, whether Marxist or not, must take into account the subjective as well as the objective factors in history; human society is subjective and objective, insofar as the human being is subject and object. The objective side of the human individual has the formal social relation as its characteristic; the juridical person is the formal and external aspect of the individual, it is the individual person in its relation to law and the state. It is like a human being, having certain human qualities. At the same time the juridical person is like the legal institutions and the state, for it is wholly a social product, all of these being the inventions or figments of civil society. The juridical person is the fiction of the human being, the state is the fiction of society; the juridical person is the reification of the human being in the law, the state is the reification of society. The link between the law and the state on the one side and the human being on the other has produced a character that can convey the rules, commands, decrees of the state to its human members. Such is the formal character of the individual, or the juridical personality, which is designed to be the mechanism that conveys these rules, etc., from the formal and external sphere of social life to the internal and private one. For this reason, if for no other, the formal aspect of the human being had to be socially shaped, the subject and private formed and separated out; the reification of humanity is the figment of this formality and externality.

The agencies of the state, the courts of law, the factory, schools, the military each have a characteristic means whereby they relate to the individual, shaping the social individual to their socially derived, respective ends; the individual has a corresponding means of relating to the social institution. The way of entry into the factory is by the contract for work, which takes up the formal relation of the individual in society just as do the courts of law, which reinforce the contract. The individual is thereby alienated from his inner life; just as the worker is separated from the product, he is prevented from taking any pride in its outcome and from having love of its result. The cultivator is bound to the soil in feudalism, but the bondage is also a closeness to it, reflected in the poetry of the time. The resentment is there directed not against the means of production, the work object, for the soil is honored; it is directed against the nobility. Under capitalism, the resentment in the poetry of the working class is directed against the materials worked upon, the instruments of labor, and against the bosses.

We have seen that the social group, in making the transition to civil society, underwent a twofold opposition, the first between the social classes, the second between the public, formal, official, external and objective sphere of social life on the one side, and the private, internal, subjective sphere on the other. No such alienation and opposition is to be found in the primitive communities. The alienation of the external and public aspect of the human individual from the private and internal followed along with the social process of separation. This alienation has its history. The joint processes of social and individual division and opposition were not regarded as evil in classical antiquity. The Stoic philosophers Epictetus and Marcus Aurelius had already separated the human individual into mask and man, having regarded it as neither troublesome nor evil, but as normal that human beings sculpt their own mask, forge their own characters, make their outward features as they undergo the fortunes and vicissitudes of life.[24] But Shakespeare held that the separation of the outer from the inner face of man is evil. Hegel thus understood the problems of the person as the separation of the human individual into parts: "The individual who has risked his life can be recognized as a person, but has not the truth of this state of being recognized as an independent consciousness."[25] This recognition is a public acknowledgement, it is opposed to the inner consciousness, which is separate from the external recognition and opposed to it. The inner truth of this recognition is a further stage to be attained by the consciousness. The consciousness, which has become independent, is such by the public recognition of the person. The thesis of the person that Hegel took up is that of juridical form, the juridical person separate from the inner life, the private individuality. The question concerns an inner essence, or the mystical being, of the person. Here the separation between the inner and the outer spheres of the human individual corresponds to the separation of the private and public spheres of the society, which is likewise without an inner essence; the separation of the juridical person from the entire human individual corresponds in Hegel to the separation of the family and civil society, and both of these from the state. Hegel explored this subdivision of the individual into parts, without integra-

---

[24] Marcus Aurelius was citing Epictetus. See Marcel Mauss, "A Category of the Human Spirit", in: *The Psychoanalytic Review*, LV (1968), p. 475.
[25] G. W. F. Hegel, *Die Phänomenologie des Geistes* (1807), ch. IV, A: "Herrschaft und Knechtschaft".

tion, which he found to be the result of the division of labor in society, and Marx so understood him, taking up the same critical viewpoint.[26] The person, save when we are speaking loosely, is made by a legal fiction, and becomes our second nature when there is nothing left to the individual but his formal character mask, when the exterior is so successfully internalized that there is nothing left but the shell, which becomes the content of the person.

In the capitalist society, the human individual sells his labor capacity and labor power to the buyer, the worker to the capitalist. Both buyer and seller stand to each other as persons.[27] Formally speaking, their relation is that of equal and equally free individuals who engage in exchanges on the capitalist marketplace generally. The formality of the transaction calls forth the formal aspect of either side; the individuals who engage in it relate to each other in their formal aspect; that formal aspect has already been invented in society, it is socially useful and necessary to the particular transaction. The existence of the juridical persons in this relation is a fiction; the formal equality and formal freedom have no content, yet the form has a function, being necessary for the sale and purchase of the labor power. The equality is no less a fiction, the freedom is a deception. The juridical persons who appear in the given relation are the outward masks of human beings, but that outer form is mere appearance. The formal relations are the juridical reality, a reality which, however, is but external, apparent; in reality it is mere appearance, but in the law there is no other reality.

Marx further developed this, and in the same language. Labor power can appear as a commodity on the market only so far and because it is offered and sold by its own possessor whose labor power it is. "In order that the possessor sell it as a commodity he must be able to dispose of it, thus be the free owner of his labor capacity, of his person. He and the possessor meet on the market, and enter into a relation to each other, as possessors of commodities who are of equal birth, different only in that one is buyer, the other seller, hence both are juridically equal persons."[28]

---

[26] Id., *Grundlinien der Philosophie des Rechts* (1821), § 187, Zusatz; Marx, *Kapital*, Vol. 1, p. 385; see also D. Urquhart, *Familiar Words* (London, 1855). In Hegel's philosophy of education this parsing of the individual in social life is deplored; Marx, loc. cit., quotes Hegel with approval.

[27] "Beide Seiten stehen sich als Personen gegenüber. Formell ist ihr Verhältnis das gleiche und freie von Austauschenden überhaupt. Dass diese Form Schein ist und täuschender Schein, erscheint, soweit das juristische Verhältnis betrachtet wird, als ausserhalb desselben fallend." Marx, *Grundrisse der Kritik der politischen Ökonomie* (1857-1858) (Berlin, 1953), p. 368.

[28] Marx, *Kapital*, Vol. 1, p. 182.

We have seen that the anthropology and the psychology of the person are the dialectic of the formal, external, juridical, and that of the inner, subjective aspects. They meet in the human being in the same way that the exchangers meet on the market, or the body's members meet and oppose the belly in the tale of Menenius Agrippa.[29] The juridical person is not the human individual, but a part of that individual; again, it is a part played by the individual, the character mask. The outward character is internalized thereby; the result is nothing but that mask, the hollow husk; the external feature is the content. The materialization of the relation between human beings is taken as the relation itself, the fiction for the reality. The materialization is then transformed into the humanization of the relation between things. At the same time, the humanization of the relations between things is transformed into the materialization between juridical persons, which is what they really are. The labor capacity of the individual human being is made into a commodity, the material relation between persons. It is fetishized by being made over into a social relation between things: "As the producers enter socially into contact only by exchange of their products, it is only in the limits of this exchange that the social character of their private labors is affirmed in the first place. Or the private labors are manifested in reality as divisions of social labor only by the exchange established between the products of labor and indirectly between the producers. It results from this that for the latter the relations of their private labors appear what they are, that is, not the direct social relations of persons, in their labors themselves, but rather the material relations of persons and the social relations of things."[30]

These relations are to begin with indirect, mediate; they are *both* the material relations of persons and the social relations of things; each of these relations, from the material side and from the social side, is in a dialectic with the other, each complements and supplants the other, together forming the mediate relation of the purchasers and sellers of the private labors and making up the ensemble of the exchange relations of social labor. What they are not is direct social relations; but to take them as such leads to the fetishism of commodities. However, the dialectic of the mediate relation is not all that there is to the matter, it is but the first step. The material relations of persons alone is not the fetishism, nor is the social relations of things: these are what the commodity relations are. Their mystification rests on our having taken their indirect relation as a direct relation. On the

[29] Marx, *Kapital*, Vol. 1, p. 381.
[30] Marx, *Kapital*, Vol. 3, in MEW, Vol. 25, p. 838.

other hand, the human beings in the world of commodities and their relations stand to each other indirectly in two senses: first, in material relations as persons bearing character masks, and second, in the social relations of things. The indirect relation alone is not the fetishization of the human being, it is the elimination of the direct individual relations and their substitution by the formal, material relations that contributes to such a fetishization.[31]

The person is the juridical person engaged at once in the commodity relation and its fetishism. But that fetishism has its internal development from a simple to the complex relation. In its simple form, it is merely a mystification in the minds of the classical economists, who considered the social relations of production of men, and the determinations which the things subsumed under these relations undergo, to be the natural properties of things. This is a crude materialism, and is just as much a crude idealism, indeed a fetishism, which ascribes social relations to things which are supposed to have their determinations immanent in them, and, by conceiving them in this way, mystifies them. The fetishism is an intellectual act, not a social relation; it is a notion in the minds of the economists, which through elimination of the relations between things substituted the immanent social relations.[32] The second stage in the fetishism is also a mystification, but its setting is now transferred from the writing desk of the economist to the market place. The order in which Marx developed the thought of fetishism is the opposite of the order of its historical appearance, which is first as the relation in society, then in the minds of the theoreticians. Between these two extremes lies the simple fetishism, according to which human beings endow the product of their own creation with a life of its own.[33]

The juridical person is the same as the fictional person, or the

---

[31] In the French translation of Capital, Marx eliminated the phrase "material relations between persons" and wrote only "social relations between things" (*Le Capital*, op. cit., p. 29). In his ultimate formulation on the subject, Marx shows the fetishism of commodities to be the opposite of mediate or material relations between human beings. The fetishism is the substitution of the social by the material relation, or the direct by the indirect relation. It is the determination of the human by the material relation.

[32] Marx, *Grundrisse*, op. cit., p. 579.

[33] Marx, *Kapital*, Vol. 1, ch. 1, § 4. The fetishism of the commodity relation rests first on the transformation of the commodity into a fetish by the persons engaged in its exchange; but the persons themselves undergo a fantastic transformation at the same time, standing to each other as things exchanged. This is a second dialectic movement, a form of reification of human beings by their dehumanization, and the personification of things, which is a fantastic process. But more than this, commodity fetishism in this second dialectical movement is in turn twofold: the human being is first dehumanized and reified, second personified, made into an artificial person. See the next section, in which this movement is further developed.

persona ficta, made by conscious relations between human beings. This person is a pure figment of the law, in which relations between human beings are reduced and recreated in the formal side, as external relations invented for the purposes of commercial law, penal law, public law. It is the relation between things that is taken as the relation between human individuals. By this fiction, human beings appear as juridically equal, but their equality, even though it has a useful function, has only a formal, apparent validity. The corporate person, the joint-stock company of limited liability, has no private identity, it is anonymous, it has no private relations or life.[34] It is an automaton which is possessed by an individual whose creature it is, and who has created the creature which possesses him in turn, which he has endowed with a consciousness and will of its own. That creature is the capitalist, the creation is the business corporation. For the capitalist and the corporation have no different standing in the law; juridically, the individual entrepreneur and the private corporation are one and the same. Nor is the wage worker any different in his contract for work from the capitalist, or the representative of the corporation that engages in the contract, or the corporation. They are all juridical persons. Thereby, the subjectivity is eliminated from the social relations. By the capitalist development, human beings stand to each other as objects. But this relation is only an appearance which cloaks and seeks to destroy reality, the human being as subject-object. It is the effect of relations in civil society or, what is the same thing, civilized society, that the two sides are divided and opposed, subject opposed to object. The civil society, and capitalist society as the highest development of this, excerpts the objective side of the human being from its human context, and takes this side up alone, as the formal, juridical person, the person as business corporation.

V. THE MYTHOLOGY OF CAPITALIST PRODUCTION. PERSONIFICATION

The person is further manipulated in capitalist society; it is the personification of the non-human being and the reduction of the human being to a non-human entity, which is then personified. What is this rhetorical figure, a trope of the Homeric epic, doing as prop and mainstay of the capitalist mode of production? The rhetoricians of antiquity referred thus to the device whereby the dawn is given a human shape, Eo/Aurora becomes a name like that of any human being. The per-

---

[34] In ancient Rome, mercantile ventures were undertaken by a *societas* composed of *socii*, associates or partners. Modern social science is the child of commercial practice.

sonification of the dawn is a subjective act requiring the assent of the auditors to the words of the bard, whereby it is transformed into an objective datum; yet in ancient Greece it was not torn forth from its subjective origin thereby. In the folk epic the tropes are at once subjective and objective. In capitalism, the formal category of the person or the formal side of the human being is conceived objectively, loosened from the whole human being, made into a thing, the formal side being a personification, and the loosening from the human complex of subject-object, a reification. The personification is an invention, the figment is made into an abstract, fantastic thing. Whereas the personifications that are found in Homer were the innocent figments of natural forces in their human representations, the personification in capitalism is the reification of the human being, the objective part ripped loose from the subject, as the representation of the social relations between things. It is the social relation in alienated form.

The personification, as the composition of a mythical person, in reference to the dawn or the wind is the attribution of some human motive or a physical trait to a thing, which is by definition a non-human object. So far, it is not a reification, for a human being is not turned into a thing. Yet the attribution remains an external relation. Who can get inside the dawn? Nevertheless, Homer gave Aurora a set of human attributes. Mythology in one of its aspects is the representation of the mastery over nature in the human fantasy, and as such has given way before immodestly proclaimed recent victories over these forces. Yet our mythopoets today, though lesser talents, are no further in the mastery of society and social laws, that is, over human nature, than the mythopoets of ancient Greece, and they can refer to an entire nation as "fatherland", attributing to it bellicose or peaceable intentions, think of the whole, not of the mutually antagonistic parts that compose it, and conceive of its motives as human.[35] The objective world of the state and nations is as by magic transformed into a subjective world of human beings, which can be flattered or cajoled. But these have neither friends nor enemies, they have interests; Lord Acton well understood that the subjective feelings must give way to objective relations in history.

The personification under capitalist conditions is that of the business corporation, the attribution to capital of a will and consciousness, human qualities attributed to an inhuman thing. But the behavior of the capitalist in no way differs from that of the capitalist corporation. The capitalist is the personification of capital, in turn. The personification is, as we have seen, the making of a person in the literal sense.

[35] On the mythology of nature see Marx, *Grundrisse* pp. 30f.

Thus when we speak of a biological person, we are attributing to nature the processes of culture, for the juridical person is not made by the insemination of the ovum. The fantasy, however, has social reality, the fine paid by the corporate person or business corporation is no less real than that paid by the indvidual person. The transformation that is implied thereby attracted the attention of the ancient and medieval lawyers and theologians, from Tertullian to Sinibaldus Fliscus (Innocent IV). In the early period of capitalism the fiction of the corporate body as person was invented in order to account for this transsubstantiation of the earthly flesh. It aroused the wonder of Otto Gierke, who believed in a superorganic being that was constructed out of the human mold, but transcended it in the social whole. The wonder was given a new formulation by Auguste Comte and Herbert Spencer; Emile Durkheim sought to demystify it, but did not do so aptly. It was remystified again by A. L. Kroeber by his notion of the superorganism of human culture. The person and the group person, the corporate person and the corporation sole are social fantasies, but these thinkers have all been seized of their prodigy as Pygmalion of his Galatea.

The difficulty is that in capitalism the movement in personification is not a simple dialectic as it was in Homer. It is the transformation of thing into human by attribution of human qualities to the former; it is also the opposite, the attribution of the quality of a thing to a human being, of capital to the capitalist, and thereby in turn, the attribution of the quality of the reified human being, of the reified will and consciousness, to the thing, capital. The human subject is instated into history, by becoming dehumanized. The will and consciousness are originally the subjective relations of the human being. Marx did not eliminate the human subject from history, but considered that it is transformed, embodied in capital in the form of the capitalist, who is capital personified. Capitalists are juridical persons, the formal side of the human being; in the same way, they are the reified side of the capitalist mode of production. This personification is quite other than personfication as a mere rhetorical device, in which we speak of the marriage of *M. le Capital* and *Mme. la Terre*. The invented person enters into history and really does reduce the natural limits of human capacity to the point of least resistance for the purpose of increased profit.[36]

The person thus manufactured is a class-person, a human being as-though. The capitalist as an individual is robbed of his humanity.

[36] Marx, *Kapital*, Vol. 1, p. 425. See also *Grundrisse*, p. 356; *Kapital*, Vol. 1, pp. 99f.; Vol. 3, op. cit., pp. 832f.

In what way is he different from a corporation? The corporation does not know human sentiments of mercy or charity. If it makes a charitable contribution it is in order to gain tax relief, or because it will sit well with the public, it is good publicity. The corporation is not impersonal, it is a person, but an inhuman person. All capitalists, human or not, cause their behavior and their relations to conform to that of the corporation, which is the ideal type of capitalist; it is that person toward which the capitalist tends. Thereby the subjectivity is taken away from the human individual, who is liable to human weaknesses of mercy, charity and pity; it is deposited in the corporation, where it is endowed with will and consciousness. The subjective is thereby transformed into its opposite, the multitudinous; the plural, the multi-individual capitalist precedes the multi-national corporation both logically and in time. It is not only that the corporation has the advantageous attribute of perpetuity, as H. S. Maine thought. An individual father can perpetuate his enterprise by bequest to his son or partner. It is not only that the corporation can raise large amounts of credit. An individual can do the same, and could do so in Elizabethan times as well. It is that the corporation is inhuman and eliminates the individual, selecting certain elements of the objectivity-subjectivity, by the application of objective standards, thus introducing them into history. The form absorbs the content and makes of it something else. The formal side of the individual is all that is left. If the capitalist shows that he has human qualities, these are called weaknesses, and he will go under. It is best to leave business affairs to inhuman corporate persons.

The several institutions of society are related to human individuals, each by a characteristic means; the individual develops a feature of his character relative and conformable to the given institution, such as the juridical person relative to the law and the state. If this conformity does not take place then either the individual will go under, or, if enough individuals do not conform to the exigencies of institutional adaptation, that institution will go under. The example of the formal character of the person, which is extruded by the human being in order to comport in relation to the formal side of political society, or the law of the state, was then cited. In capitalist society the immensely plastic human individual has extruded a feature as capitalist in order to comport in relation to capital. The human characteristics of will and consciousness are applied in order to appropriate unto capital the productive power of social labor, and the productive power of society in its general form, or science. Personification is the magic wand whereby accumulated stock, which is found in all the modes of production of civilized society, whether Asiatic, ancient or feudal, is transformed into capital in the capitalist mode of production. In capitalist society the most appropriate form of the human personality for the particular end of mastery of capital has been thereby developed.[37]

The accumulation of stock takes place in fact wherever commodity exchange and production take place, wherever indeed hoarding and usury by private persons and the surplus product of society is stored in the state treasury, in the public sector of the economic whole. The characteristic of the capitalist mode of production is the transformation of the stock accumulated into capital; the means whereby the transformation takes place is the personification of capital in the capitalist. Richard Jones had written that wealth is produced by successive functions and had called attention to the gradual manner in which these successive functions are introduced by capital or capitalists indifferently. The *or* is important; it is not capital that operates, but capitalists. Things, capital, are acted upon, they are not agents in history; human beings are the agents, although they do not act as individuals, only as class-individuals. The as-if of the class-individual is a social fiction taken as real. The agency of the human beings in the transformation of stock into capital is the assumption of the role, of the character mask as capitalist; in this case the individual becomes transformed into a juridical person, and it is a matter of indifference whether it is a corporation or an individual that we have in view. Jones held that stock is capital, Marx opposed this notion, holding that the accumulated stock by becoming a person then "takes up the function of advancing wages" to men (Jones).[38] The social relations have intervened in the economic functions of stock accumulation, advancement of a wage, and formation of capital; concretely, the formation of the person is not the direct result of the relations in the economy, but of the relations in society in its juridical aspect. It is indirectly that the economic relations enter into the formation of the juridical person.

The subjective factor in history is introduced by Marx through its eradication, by absorbing it into the class-individuals, the capitalists as a class, and by providing this class with a subjective content, the embodiment of consciousness and will. This subjective content is in turn eradicated by its attribution to a juridical person, a class-person in which is deposited a host of safeguards against the arbitrary exercise of the will and consciousness of these subjective endowments. In a

---

[37] The capitalist himself is only the master of capital as its personification. See Marx, *Theorien über den Mehrwert*, I, in MEW, Vol. 26.1, p. 365; III, p. 419. See Richard Jones, *Textbook of Lectures on the Political Economy of Nations* (Hartford, 1852).

[38] Marx, *Theorien über den Mehrwert*, III, p. 420; Jones, op. cit., Lecture III.

direct way the law of property, its protection, sale, bequest, etc., is established to safeguard one of the forms of capital, private property. Crimes against property such as false stipulation and breach of contract are capitalist crimes, that is, crimes of capital endowed with a will and consciousness; corporate persons as well as individual persons are punishable by law for such crimes, which fall within the law of contract; likewise, all juridical persons are subject to punishment for breach of tax law, non-payment, evasion and the like. These crimes are different from those other crimes against property of persons such as robbery, theft and burglary, which do not presuppose a corporate person, but an individual bearing socially and legally recognized rights and obligations. The class-interest calls forth another sort of control over the subjective factor in society: the quest for profit is not free and untrammelled. The agencies of the state intervene to prevent the sale of capital, military weapons, patent-rights and services to outer enemies, such as foreign countries, or rebels in capitalist countries against the state. The motive-factor of the capitalist, the hunger after profit, is not subjective, it is reified subjectivity. It is constrained by rules that control trade both within the country and internationally. The sale of truck parts and replacements of factory machinery to Cuba during the 1960s was prevented by law in the United States, even though such sale would have produced a profit for private businessmen; the sale of similar equipment and even of commercial airplanes to Chile during the Allende government was prevented, and for the same reason: the subjective factor was constrained by law and submitted to the overriding interest of the ruling class and the state; whereby the initiative of private persons was vetoed.

Freedom is a subjective factor in history, insofar as it is contained by laws of persons, by means of which the subject is transformed into its opposite. The end-result is the formal expression of the human individual, in which the subjectivity is reduced, controlled and regulated by the social class, and by the institutions of the whole society. The formal expression is likewise the reduction of the objective side of human life to a cut-and-dried formula, life according to rule, without any degrees of freedom. The first step in the reduction of the subjectivity and objectivity of the individual is the formation of the juridical person both in time and in a logical sequence; the time covered is both social-archaeological time and the time in the life of the individual.

The psychologist Erik Erikson has written of the identity crisis of the individual in late adolescence, which is the time that he becomes a person before the law. At this time the young people take on the character masks which identify them to themselves and to others; the character masks are the personifications of social relations between persons; it is the public side of the human being that is the bearer of these relations.[39] The private side continues in its relations to family and friends, or would do so unless otherwise acted upon. The identity crisis does not come from within the private sphere, it comes from without: the official end of schooling, and the entry into the job market. The family then becomes the bearer of these forceful changes, which are borne in upon the young individual. The families do not regard higher education, unless it is normally connected with a step in a career, as a class-undertaking. For the working-class family, higher education means the way out of the working class, loss of the son or daughter; for the middle-class family it means the prolongation of idleness, failure to earn money, that is, do useful work. The students, who are in financial difficulties, have to take extraordinary steps in order to gain support, public or private, through the official acts of the public authorities directly, and indirectly through the family, which acts as the mediator and expression of the official view. The individuals do not stand to each other directly in their social relations, but only through thier character masks. The family stands to the sons and daughters indirectly, formally; it does not seek to understand the intentions of the latter, nor to support those intentions materially, but only to cause the young to adopt a doctrine for which the elders are the mouthpiece, which these elders personify. It is an economic character mask in the first place: who does not work shall not eat.

The fetishism whereby the products of labor in society appear to acquire an independent power and stand to each other as though they were relations between people is a form of the fictitious life of capital. This fetishism is a mystification of human relations, to which a further fictitious relation is appended, the figure of the person of capital, its personification; the personification assumes the garb of a human being, it is a thing that speaks with a human voice. But human beings had to put this consciousness, will, voice and figure into the thing, capital, in the first place, for in the entire realm of nature on earth there is only one subject, and that is the human subject, whose attributes are consciousness, a will, a voice, a figure, etc. We have then a twofold dialectical moment, each the reverse of the other: people endowing things with human attributes, the things then comporting, with the accord of their craftsmen, as human. The subjective factor in history has been taken away from its proper home, humanity; it becomes

[39] Marx, *Kapital*, Vol. 1, p. 100; the economic character masks of persons are but the personifications of the economic relations, who stand to each other as the bearers of these relations.

objectified. The personification, which is this subject objectified, is a necessary relation among the economic, legal and formal factors, and these are the objective ones; thereby the human being is reified, made into thing.

There was mentioned earlier a second voice in the chorus of capital relations, the equality of the contracting parties, the worker and the capitalist. Marx asked how it was that Aristotle, who had discovered the relation of equivalence in the expression of value of commodities, did not take the second step, of the composition of the substance of value through labor time, a step taken by classical economists, Adam Smith and David Ricardo at their head. The secret of the expression of value lies in the equivalence of all human labors, labor in the abstract; but this secret could only be deciphered when the concept of human equality had achieved the fixity of a popular prejudice. This, added Marx, is possible only when the commodity form becomes the general form of the labor product, and the relation of men to each other as commodity possessors the dominant social relation.[40] This process is not simple; it is just as complex as that of the subjectivity-objectivity of fetishism and of personification. The subject engages in a contract with another; this is the grammatical subject, the parties mentioned. In fact both persons show only the objective, formal and external sides of their humanity; they are dehumanized to that extent. Both parties are equal before the law, but their equality is formal, without content, without a subjectivity. The commodity relations of exchange, production and possession are the presupposition to this relation of formal equality; it is also presupposed that these commodity relations are now generalized throughout the society: we are no longer talking of society in general, but a particular one, the capitalist society, for this society has fulfilled two of the basic conditions of capitalist production, the generalization of the commodity relation to the point of dominance, and the formal equality of the parties to the work contract, of labor and capital. The objective factors in history have created a new subjectivity: equality has become a matter of popular belief, it acquires the fixity of a popular prejudice. The wage worker believes he is equal to any other person; he is a juridical person as any other, and is accepted as such by the capitalist, the law, the state, etc.

This subjectivity was not accessible to Aristotle, the commodity relation had not become general, still less predominant in ancient Greece. The lack of freedom of the slave and the formal inequality of the slave and master were the materials of Aristotle's relations in society. In ancient Greece, the Sophists Antiphon, Hippias, among

[40] Marx, *Kapital*, Vol. i, p. 74.

others, and in ancient Rome, the authors of the doctrine of natural right, held that men are equal by nature. The doctrine of equality is not supported by the social practice of the Greek *polis* and the Roman Republic and Empire; it is a subjective judgment, the objective judgment being found in Aristotle. But because of that, Aristotle could not take the second step, and it was left to a new set of relations to nature and relations in society to establish the objective conditions under which Smith, Ricardo and Marx could establish the theory of the expression of value, the substance of value and its measure. The objective conditions were made into a popular prejudice. The fictions of equality, of freedom, have no content, no social reality, they are but formal freedom, formal equality, hence they have no objective existence. With the establishment of capitalist society, the conditions of formal inequality, bondage in the form of slavery, clientage, serfdom, are all done away with. The objective condition of freedom is established, but it exists only as a potentiality. The content of freedom and equality are not achieved, therefore freedom and equality are not actual but potential. There is a popular fiction that humanity is free and equal under capitalism, but that is a judgment which mistakes form for content.

The advantage that William Petty, Adam Smith, David Ricardo and Karl Marx had over Aristotle in the establishment of the expression of value is this: objectively, the laborer had been freed from the bondage to the soil in the capitalist mode of production and is formally the equal of the capitalist; these relations are, however, but the appearance of freedom and equality, which is mistaken for their real existence in society. The latter is an illusion in which we subjectively concur. There is no doubt that the objective transformation of the social relation to production has taken place; its beginning and end points were given historical expression by the classical economists, and the historical course was given its conscious expression by Marx. The theory of value in classical economics and in the doctrine of Marx rests on both these objective and subjective conditions and considerations. History is not composed of iron laws, mistakenly propounded as objective laws by Ferdinand Lassalle and Robert Michels. The concerns of capital are with its production, reproduction, expansion and surplus production; these are assured, as they are opposed, by objective laws. In these objective historical factors and laws a subjective element is at work, and this subjective element peeps through in a distorted, reified form, as the hot hunger after profit and the impersonation of capital by the capitalist. The opposition is distorted by another subjective element, the play upon love of fatherland; that opposition is reified as economism, or the quest by agencies of the working class after material goods.

The capitalist, we have seen, is taken historically not as an individual but as the personification of a category, capital; in this form the category subsists in the consciousness of its bearers, the capitalists. The category in turn is given formal expression as the juridical personality of capital, while in a wholly parallel manner the landlord appears to represent the land as juridical personality, and the wage laborer as juridical personality sells his labor power. Capital, land and labor are determinate social forms, the trinity of political economy, they have a particular social character. Personified, they become social characters or masks and are at once things; the charade of *M. le Capital* and *Mme. la Terre* is of the same fetishized matter. Capital, however, is to begin with a relation between social beings engaged in production; it is a relation of production, moreover, of a particular social formation, in which the means of production are transformed into capital. It is a twofold relation, at once the material relation between persons and the social relation of things. In its form as fetish, capital is endowed with an independent life, will and consciousness, separate from its producers, it becomes the personification of the product and the reification of the relation of production.[41] From having been relation it becomes ever more thing, which bears the social relation, incorporates it. The means whereby this thingification is effected is the transformation of capital into a fetish; capital becomes the fetishized form of the relation, not real but fictive, a thing which relates to itself as a fantasmagorical product of the human brain, a social relation in a disguised form. As such it is not directly the social being, sensory-suprasensory, but its fantastical representation or product, which is wholly and solely imaginary, suprasensory. Capital in its forms as commodity, profit, etc., is thereby given its fetish form, the juridical personality of capital; the *persona ficta* is its practical shape.

The subjective life of the individual, wherein resides the consciousness and will, is driven out, exorcized by the ghostly essence, the stately form of the juridical person, which assumes a life of its own in the law and on the streets, and in this form, disguised as a living individual, is seen in all its finery, as the world saw Eugene Onegin, not the man, in the end, but the mask. But external form and subject are not the same, and likewise form and object are not the same; the formal side of the human being is not the objective side. Thus, the objective

---

[41] Marx, *Kapital*, Vol. 1, p. 177; Vol. 3, p. 838 and ch. 48 passim; *Theorien über den Mehrwert*, III, p. 475.

side is exhaled and banished together with the subjective, by the process of formation of the juridical personality. For the human being has both subjective and objective constituents as necessary components, each dependent on the other. In the absence of either, the human being is but a form, evoked by the relation of capital, just as the juridical person is called forth by the quintessence of formalism, the agency of the state. It is not the sensory-suprasensory being-in-society but its formalization as commodity, or alienable form of capital, and as profit, alienated form of capital, which replaces the consciousness and will of the individual as capitalist. The formalization of the individual is the fictive representation of the individual, or the fetish in one of its social characters. This fiction is the form of its reality, or the real form of its existence. It is the form in which it lives in the consciousness of its bearers, the capitalists, mirrored in their conceptions.[42] The mirroring, however, is not only the act of the consciousness, it is the consciousness in reified form. The consciousness is not only an agent, it also suffers the relation.

The last element in the trinity which makes up the capitalist mode of production is the land. The land is not the raw, disordered mass of which Ovid sang; it is neither more nor less ordered than the culture which has encompassed it. The land, moreover, is not inert, as Sartre has most recently led us to believe. In a civilization of cultivators, it is in a reciprocal relation to those who labor on it, being both agent and patient. In this matter, Lucretius is more reliable than the others.[43] The landowner who does not work the land himself has a formal relation to it, empty of content. Land has risen in value as a means of exploitation by capital, and this includes its use as housing sites.[44] The land as the field of cultivation, or location of factory, house, roadway, is the patient. As means of sustenance it is instrumental, agent. Without the tiller, no tilth; without the tilth, no tiller; no produce without tiller and tilth. It is not the fertility of the soil alone which is the determinant of value; it is not only that rent is diminished by improved methods of cultivation,[45] above all, the relation of the cultivator to the soil in this Ricardian capitalist condition is the realization of the potential relation already posited in the condition of Melanesian (Malekulan) production, and carried forward in the ancient Asiatic, Roman, etc. The landlord relation described by Smith,

---

[42] *Theorien über den Mehrwert*, III, p. 474. This is not the criticism by Marx of the mirror theory of consciousness, but it is its initial positing.
[43] Ovid, Metamorphoses, Book I; Jean-Paul Sartre, *Critique de la raison dialectique* (Paris, 1960), pp. 504f.; Lucretius, De Rerum Natura, Book V.
[44] Adam Smith, op. cit., p. 796.
[45] David Ricardo, op. cit., pp. 42ff. and 275.

Ricardo, Marx, is the abstraction and formalization of this relation to the soil. The owner of record who does not labor on the soil is the reified expression of this abstraction.

The relation of wage labor and arable, just as the relation of capital, becomes ever more thing; reification undergoes its evolution, just as abstraction, alienation, and fetishization. It does not rest quiescent, but has a potentiality which is realized in political society by labor and expansion of capital, whereby it has attained, in the capitalist mode of production, its highest development to date. Capital, labor and land have alike undergone stages of depersonalization, and in alienated form their representatives become conscious each of his reified state.

VI. SCIENCE, MATERIALISM AND RELIGION

Vico had distinguished between human history and natural history, the history that we have made and the history that we have not made, between *factum* and *verum*. The distinction was introduced in the struggle against the rules for the direction of the mind according to Descartes, and was closely followed by Marx,[46] who built upon this basis the edifice of the criticism of science and materialism, and of religion and science. In agreement with Descartes, Marx held that there is a method of the science of the human mind, but contrary to Descartes held that it is a scientific method because it is materialist. The materialism leads in two directions: it is concrete and historical, and it is critical insofar as it is concrete both in relation to science and religion, for both lead into the direction of abstraction unless they are regulated, but these *regulae* are the opposite of the Cartesian rules, which are abstract and dualistic.

The study of religion is first of all a historical science, which is critical only if it takes up directly the activities of humanity in relation to nature, to the process of production in society of human life, to the social relations connected with it, and the spiritual conceptions that arise therefrom. The order of these activities is important; they are: 1) the technical, 2) economic, 3) social and 4) mental activities of mankind. Religion *eo ipso* is uncritical, it is the abstraction of these activities and relations; the history of religion that abstracts from the material base is no less uncritical. That material base is not the technology alone, or relation to nature, nor the economic activities, but the order in

---

[46] Giambattista Vico, Dell'antichissima sapienza italica, in *Opere*, Fausto Nicolini ed. (Bari 1953), pp. 248ff., 305f.; Karl Löwith, Vicos Grundsatz; verum et factum convertuntur (Heidelberg, 1968). On Vico; see Marx, *Kapital*, Vol. 1, p. 393, note: to Vico is attributed the distinction between human history, which we make, and natural history, which we do not.

which these are introduced. In fact, technology reveals the active comportment of mankind in relation to nature, and is the starting point; the link between the relation of human beings to nature and in society is the economic process of production.[47] The representation of these relations in religion goes in two directions: the cloudy forms of religious thought have their earthly core; this is easy to show. It is more difficult to proceed in the opposite way, that is, to develop out of the actual relations of social life their celestialized form; this is in fact the invention of religion. The critical nature of the process of going from the social relation to its religious representation is a *concretum;* it is materialist and hence scientific, it is anti-abstract, a historical process.

Science is no less materialist, historical, concrete, but its spokesmen at times venture forth from their specializations, to make abstract ideological pronouncements, their abstract natural-science materialism

---

[47] Marx, ibid.: "Die Technologie enthüllt das aktive Verhalten des Menschen zur Natur, den unmittelbaren Produktionsprozess seines Lebens, damit auch seiner gesellschaftlichen Lebensverhältnisse und der ihnen entquellenden geistigen Vorstellungen." Technology does not constitute the activity of human society in relation to nature, but is the record, as fossil evidence or current form, that discloses what that relation was or is. The direct process of the sustenance of human life is appositive to the activity of the society in its natural relations which the technology has laid bare. The activity of the society is not caused by the natural relations, nor does the activity of the society act as a causal or determining factor directly; the direct process of production of the material life and the social relations are in a reciprocal relation, standing to each other as mutual determinants. Yet the order of the introduction of the members of the sequence is first, the material relations of production, and second, the relations in society. This order is underlined in the French translation of *Capital* which Marx controlled, where in place of the construction "damit auch" he caused to be inserted "par conséquent", which is more causal, making the relation in society rather more determinate, the relation to nature rather more determinant (*Le Capital*, p. 162, col. 1, note). The intellectual ideas and conceptions flow from the social relations; here the relations are clearly expressed as determinant and determinate in contrast to the relations of the relations between human society and nature and those within the society. – The problem of Marx on technology has occasioned a great debate: N. I. Bucharin, *Theorie des historischen Materialismus* (Hamburg, 1922), had proceeded directly from technology to society without taking the intervening step of introducing the economic production process, and without reference to the relations in society. Georg Lukács, in *Archiv für die Geschichte des Sozialismus und der Arbeiterbewegung*, XI (1925) (repr. Lukács, *Schriften zur Ideologie und* Politik, P. Ludz ed. (Neuwied, 1967), pp. 188ff.), had objected to this. The same accusation against Bukharin was made by Sidney Hook, *Toward the Understanding of Karl Marx* (New York, 1933), p. 142. Bukharin had in fact given a better account of his position; see his contribution "Theory and Practice from the Standpoint of Dialectical Materialism", in: *Science at the Crossroads*. Papers presented to the International Congress of Science and Technology (1931), p. 22 (repr. with new front matter by Joseph Needham and P. G. Werskey (London, 1971)). None of those participating in this discussion had made the distinction, which is clear in Marx's conception, that technology is not the relation between human society and nature, but is the record of that relation. From this it follows that we can comprehend more of the content of the relation between the human kind and nature than that which is evidenced by its formal and external side, or the technology alone.

excludes the historical process. The result is uncritical because abstract exactly as the case of religion. Materialism is the scientific method, however, only insofar as it is historically concrete and critical; the scientific spokesmen are abstract ideologists, abstracted from the context of their social labors, specialists speaking in a field for which this specialization has not prepared them, indeed disabled them, The result of their abstraction of science is just as uncritical as the religious mysticism, but it moves in another direction. The more difficult form of the religious abstraction is to proceed from the actual relations of life to the celestialized form of the same. The spokesmen of the abstract ideology of science have already performed the more difficult task, they have excluded the historical process from their activities. Structuralism, which excludes human history, has established itself in the abstract, misty empyrean. The critique of the activities of these mysterious beings is therefore the simple one of revealing their earthly core, or their material interest. Negatively the abstract science is freed from any control by practical considerations, by relations to nature and in society; positively the abstract science is related to goals that delve out the pure form of thought, the conceptual scheme which relates matter and form, and gives them their completion as structures. The latter is the more difficult form of abstraction.

In the foregoing pages the principles and contradictions of the anthropology of Karl Marx have been set forth in reference to the society of human beings. We begin with the alienation of humanity from nature, which is secured by the socialization of the human kind. But since there is no other existence than life in society, we are doomed to this alienation in a primary sense. Although alienation was, therefore, not introduced in civil society, yet it has been developed in the latter, and has been carried to its highest point in capitalist society. If alienation is the primitive condition of humanity in general, yet the separation of subject-object in society is the work of civil society, and has reached its most extreme development under the conditions of capitalist production. It comes forth in direct relation to the separation and opposition of the social classes, with the rise of civil society and the state. The result of these historical processes is, as we have seen, the reification at once of the human individual and of human society. The materials for this analysis have been taken not from the usual subject matter of academic anthropology, which is the comparison of primitive societies, but from the anatomy of civil society, or the economic relations of human beings in capitalist society, their transformation into wage workers, capitalists, juridical persons, alienated and reified people, which is the subject matter of Marx's works. The history and critique of the terms and relations of a con-

crete society, the civil society of capitalism, has been set forth dialectically, which is the only way to develop them in a manner conformable
to that of Marx.

This is in opposition to a tendency among contemporary writers who
have transformed the Marxian dialectic into an existentialism, and
have thereby parted with the frame of reference of the dialectic. Although the will to a revolutionary transformation of society in the
cases of Jean-Paul Sartre and Herbert Marcuse among existentialists
is not to be doubted, yet they have introduced the *a priori* categories of
existence, being, ontology, substance. They have made it dependent
on selected categories, which they conceive to be ultimates. This is an
anti-scientific, anti-materialist procedure, for instead of deriving the
categories from the relations of society, they have derived the social
relations from the categories. By the separation of the abstract from
the concrete society, as by the reversal of the relation of the categories
to the particular society, they have arrested the flow of the dialectic,
not in history, but in their thought. The construction of the categorical
ultimates as a stone wall is but another form of the alienation and
reification of the human individual under the conditions of capitalism.

II. RELATIONS TO NATURE; ABSTRACT AND CONCRETE LABOR

VII. LABOR, WORK AND HUMAN CULTURE

Any anthropology that calls itself Marxist must have as its starting
point the intermediation of labor between human society and nature.
The labor is abstract labor; as concrete labor it is work. The society
in question is not society in general or the human community *in
abstracto*, but a particular, historical society, whether primitive or
civilized. The question that is posed thereby is twofold: first, it is the
problem of the place in nature of the human kind, or the problem of
location; second, it is the historical problem of the transition of
humanity from the natural to the cultural order. Nature has its
history, as does the human society, but the unit that we take for the
observation of natural history is far wider than the unit of observation
of human history. In the former case it is the biological species whose
history is taken up; in the case of human history it is the communal
life of the village, and the social life of the tribe, city or nation. The
time period of natural history is geological time, which is one or more
orders of magnitude greater than the time periods of ethnography and
historiography.[1]

---

[1] The category of culture as the *differentia specifica* of the human kind is a notable contribution

The thesis of the natural science of society is that of the positive science of the nature of human society; if it is left without further development, it is a form of positivism, which is on the one side a falsification of the place of the human species in nature and a simplification of the problem of anthropology; it is the elimination of the difference between the human and natural orders, and the elimination of the difference between the sciences of humanity and nature. The natural science of human society is a potentiality of the sciences which is to be developed, but not in its present form; it is on the contrary the thesis of the science of human nature as the science of nature and its negation. The continuity between the human kind and nature is coupled with the discontinuity; the positive science of nature is inseparably linked with its negation, the science of human nature; and the latter in its abstract form is coupled with its concretion, the particular ethnographic and historical accounts.[2] T. H. Huxley, the ally of Darwin, propounded the doctrine of the continuity between man and nature and the discontinuity; the discontinuity was conceived by him abstractly, as the absence of morality in nature.[3] Max Scheler propounded the negative of this thesis, the discontinuity alone.[4] Sartre has attempted to resolve the contradiction by introducing the distinction between the objective existence of nature and the subjective category of existence *for us* in the case of humanity, but far from having "saved" the phenomenon, his proposal has only mystified the relation between humanity and nature; Sartre has invented a new name for an old disease, he has not cured it.[5]

of empirical anthropology in the past hundred years. It is proposed as the species-wide phenomenon of the human kind that is shared by no other species. The defect in the proposal lies in its abstraction, for the human capacity for production of speech or the products of labor in the form of a specific form of speech or product is only partly accounted for in this way. The category of abstract culture, or the abstraction of the human capacity, designates a field of scientific investigation; it does not express the results of that investigation in the form of laws. The interaction between the abstraction and the concretion as the means to these laws has not been developed by the cultural anthropologists.

[2] The attempt at a positive science of human society has its history. Auguste Comte and Emile Durkheim made their contributions to it; more recently it was propounded by A. R. Radcliffe-Brown, *Natural Science of Society* (Chicago, 1957).

[3] T. H. Huxley, *Man's Place in Nature* (1863); id., "The Struggle for Existence in Human Society", in: *The Nineteenth Century*, February 1888.

[4] Max Scheler, *Die Stellung des Menschen im Kosmos* (1928). This line of subjective negativity extends from A. Schopenhauer to the twentieth-century phenomenologists, among whom Scheler was a leading figure. This movement had wrought its effect on existentialism in Sartre, see the following note.

[5] Sartre, *Critique de la raison dialectique*, p. 104: "En se réservant d'étudier, dans le secteur ontologique, cet existant privilégié (privilégié *pour nous*) qu'est l'homme, il va de soi que l'existentialisme pose lui-même la question de ses relations fondamentales avec l'ensemble des disciplines, qu'on réunit sous le nom d'*anthropologie*." The subjective index in human history

The question of the place of the human species in nature was set by Marx in reference to the intermediation by labor between the human society and nature; it was then linked by him to the Darwinian conception of the continuity-discontinuity between the human and the natural order. The intermediation by labor is the characteristic relation of the human species to nature. Considered abstractly it is the initial separation, distincing and alienation from nature of the human kind; concretely it is the production and reproduction of the means of life in a given society and a given mode of production.[6] The intermediation by social labor is the cultural relation considered as an abstraction. Let us consider the three-figured field of humanity, labor and nature in their interrelations. In both anthropologies, of Marx and of the academic world, the intervention between the human kind and nature is conceived, in the one case by labor, in the other by culture. Labor and culture are in both cases conceived as social products; and in both cases the conception in the mind is related to the intervention in the life of the human species by culture on the one side, labor on the other.

is, according to Sartre, the privileged position in nature *for us*. We have by an imperious grasp accorded the privilege of position in nature to ourselves. The question is not: *quo warranto*, by what right, do we grasp; the question is, how is this imperious grasp arrived at, not its moral justification or denunciation. Further, the imperious grasp by the human kind that is here implied is the subjective evaluation of the ecological dominant, the human species in nature. That is a mere projection back, onto the past of the imperial grasp of civil society (witness Rome) and the imperialist grasp of modern capitalist societies. If it is a privileged position *for us*, then it can only be the product of civil society; primitive society knows no privilege. The doctrine of Sartre is as bad ethnology as it is bad ecology. In the latter sense it is a pseudo-natural science of humanity, the projection of the viewpoint of the naturalist onto the human being, not his proper object; distancing of the observer from the observed, as though the two were not of the same order of nature and culture. This is positivism: it is a defective dialectic because it is onesided, it does not link the positivity with its negation, and it does not repair the omission of the objective side of its thesis.

[6] Ökonomisch-Philosophische Manuskripte, op. cit., p. 83: "Das Produkt der Arbeit ist die Arbeit, die sich in einem Gegenstand fixiert, sachlich gemacht hat, es ist die Vergegenständlichung der Arbeit. Die Verwirklichung der Arbeit ist Vergegenständlichung." This thesis was conceived by Marx concretely in reference to capitalist society and production therein. It had been the thesis of Ludwig Feuerbach that man objectifies himself in creating a world of objects; it is held by many that Marx took over this thesis from Feuerbach in the Economic-Philosophic Manuscripts. (We will return to the problem of objectification at the end of this article.) The attribution of a Feuerbachian position to Marx as of 1844 is faulty because Marx had already gone beyond Feuerbach in the chapter "Die Entfremdete Arbeit", ibid., pp. 81-94. There the concept of mankind as an abstraction is overcome, and the *Gattungswesen* of humanity is taken up concretely. The alienation of labor from its product takes place in the concrete, historical society of Marx's observation, capitalist society. (The *Gattungswesen* is the generic being of humanity; see *Kapital*, Vol. 1, op. cit., p. 67, note). Marx had even gone beyond Feuerbach in 1843 when he composed his critique of the Hegelian Philosophy of Right, for in 1859 Marx referred to his own preoccupation with the material relations of life in this connection (MEW, Vol. 13, p. 8).

In this sense both anthropologies share a common principle. But this is in turn contradicted, for the concept of culture in academic anthropology remains an abstraction, whereas labor was taken up abstractly and concretely by Marx.

The theory of social labor as it was developed by Marx was posited in terms of the relation of abstract to concrete labor, and is developed as a dialectic. It is in point, therefore, to take up this dialectic, for the positions both of academic anthropology and of existential anthropology can be submitted to a joint critique thereby.[7]

Human labor is a unitary process, the purposeful expenditure of labor power. In all forms of society save the most primitive it is a social relation,[8] and in all forms of society, whether primitive or not, it is relation to nature whereby natural materials are transformed. That unitary process in its concrete form is useful labor, and as such it is labor in society whose purpose is the production of objects for consumption. Labor in its concrete form is, in relation to nature, direct labor, which transforms the natural materials into objects useful to the particular society. That same unitary process of labor has, in all but the most primitive forms of society, an abstract form. These are the societies in which commodities, hence commodity value, are produced. This form of social labor is the expenditure of human labor power in the physiological sense; it is labor considered not in relation to the usefulness of the object but in relation to the equivalence of one amount of labor and another. The purpose of the equivalence is the determination of the commodity exchange value.

Again, in its abstract form labor in society is taken up in relation to the process of circulation rather than to that of production and of consumption. We have posited therefore two types of production in society, the first or most primitive being that in which production takes place in direct relation to consumption, the unit of production and of consumption being the same. In this mode of production there is no significant amount of exchange of products between the social unities that are the units of production, whether family or kinship band, kin village, etc.; in its predominant form, labor here takes the concrete form of production for direct consumption. The second type

---

[7] A. L. Kroeber and Clyde Kluckhohn, *Culture, A Critical Appraisal* (1952); Claude Lévi-Strauss, *La Pensée Sauvage* (Paris, 1962); id. *Mythologiques. Le Cru et le Cuit* (Ouverture) (Paris, 1964); Sartre, op. cit. See also Alfred Schmidt, *Der Begriff der Natur in der Lehre von Karl Marx* (Frankfurt, 1971); Hannah Arendt, *The Human Condition* (New York, 1959).

[8] In the most primitive forms of society there is no separation of the relations of labor in the family, in the small band of kinsmen, and in society. We will leave open the question whether social labor on the one side and the division of social labor on the other can be ascertained in those circumstances. Engels thought that they could be so ascertained (MEW, Vol. 23, p. 372).

of labor is that in which the unit of production is clearly separated from the unit of consumption, and exchange of products on a considerable scale takes place between the producing units. At this point social labor properly so called is posited, and we may now take up the distinction between social labor as abstract and concrete relations to nature and in society for the first time in history. At the same time the distinction between direct and indirect labor processes is posited, or the dual forms of labor in relation to nature and in society. The increasingly indirect relation to nature is measured by the increasing number of steps in the concrete labor process or in the number of instruments to make instruments; and this constitutes a simple index of the alienation from nature, for it is the primary measurement of that form. It is production for further production. The increasingly indirect relation of labor in society is at the same time production in society for further circulation through exchange; it is production for indirect consumption. With the introduction of the relation of concrete and abstract social labor the direct and indirect relations of production and circulation in society are promulgated. These are dialectical moments of transformation of society. They are ranged on a chronological scale: the simpler or more direct takes place earlier in time, nearer to the beginnings of culture; the more complex, with more numerous stages of mediation in production, takes place later.[9] The dialectical moments of labor in society are real, being at once actual, typical and temporal. They take place in the brain and in society, for the relations of labor to nature and in society are not merely correlative to one another but are mutually determinant in their evolution from simple to complex forms.

Engels directed attention to the distinction between labor and work, which is parallel to Marx's distinction between abstract and concrete labor; as concrete labor it is work, the production of use-values; as abstract labor it is labor in short, the production of commodity value.[10] Labor as the creator of use-values is independent of any particular social end, purpose, relation, condition of human existence; as abstract labor it is abstracted from any given society, being the general material

---

[9] Marx, *Kapital*, Vol. i, p. 61. On cultural beginnings ibid., pp. 194, 353, 535.

[10] Marx, *Capital*, Friedrich Engels ed., English tr. S. Moore, E. Aveling, E. Untermann (New York, 1936), pp. 54, 207. Hannah Arendt, op. cit., writes in this connection, p. 322: "The German *Arbeit* applied originally only to farm labor executed by serfs and not to the work of the craftsman, which was called *Werk*." This is a rural urban opposition, of labor in the field and work in the town or indoors; it is implicit in the distinction between the labor of the body and the work of the hands. Both conditions were bound in the European Middle Ages, when all were *pro forma* unfree, even kings.

interchange between the human kind and the natural environment.[11] Agriculture is an application of the science of the material interchange with nature.[12] Work is the expenditure of labor power to a concrete end, on the one side the production of a given product of consumption, and of commodities on the other.

John Locke had distinguished between the labor of one's body and the work of one's hands, implying the completion of a task for a specific purpose by work, and a general relation to nature by labor.[13] The dual process in Locke's system has a twofold consequence: labor and work jointly exclude from nature the natural stuff, and appropriate it to human use, a primary alienation. But thereby the common enjoyment is excluded, and private ownership as a right is established; and therein lies Locke's naïveté. The initial distinction between labor and work in Locke was explicitly stated in another way by Adam Smith, who wrote of labor in the sense of abstract labor, and of work in the sense of completed end products; Smith cited the French *Encyclopédie*, in which the distinction between *travail* (labor in general) and *ouvrage* (a completed piece of work) was made.[14] Hegel wrote of *Arbeit* (labor) as distinct from *Werk* (work); by the former he meant undertakings relative to meeting of wants, writing in the same sense as political economists of the time.[15] Hegel opposed labor as process directly related to nature by wants and desires to work as mediated human effort: man goes mediately to work (*vermittelnd zu Werke*); the mediation of the instruments of labor is twofold, in relation to wants and in relation to the end product.[16] In Hegel as in the earlier writers there is the mental error of abstraction. Wants and desires are not natural, nor are they invariable. They vary from one society to the next, they are culturally variable, and already from the outset in seeking for a starting point of human nature we note that it cannot be found: human nature is absorbed into culture; the process disappears in the product. The generality of the human nature is absorbed in the human being; but that human being is the product of two dialectical

---

[11] Marx, *Kapital*, Vol. I, pp. 57, 198f. See Vol. 3, op. cit. p. 828.

[12] Marx, *Grundrisse der Kritik der politischen Ökonomie*, op. cit., p. 592.

[13] John Locke, *An Essay Concerning the True Original, Extent and End of Civil Government* (1690), ch. V, § 27.

[14] Adam Smith, *The Wealth of Nations*, E. Cannan ed. (New York, 1937), pp. 7, 86.

[15] Hegel, System der Sittlichkeit, in *Sämtliche Werke*, VII (1913), pp. 422ff. (here mechanical labor as negative, practical is distinguished from living labor); id., *Enzyklopädie der philosophischen Wissenschaften*, in *Werke* (Frankfurt), X, § 524. Further to this theme see: W. R. Beyer, "Der Begriff der Praxis", in: *Deutsche Zeitschrift für Philosophie*, VI (1958); I. Dubský, Hegels Arbeitsbegriff und die idealistische Dialektik [*Rozpravy Československé Akademie Věd*, LXXI, 14] (Prague, 1961).

[16] Hegel, Philosophie der Geschichte, in *Werke*, XII, p. 295.

moments, one abstract, or culture in general, and the other concrete, or the particular culture, giving particular form and intent to desires. The abstraction and concretion are to be grasped in their interrelation, as a general potentiality and its actualization *in concreto*. Marx's category of labor was expressed in parallel with his category of culture, but only the former was fully worked out. Both are necessary in reference to the abstract problem of the place in nature of the human kind.

The material interchange with nature is the abstract form of labor, whereby the natural stuff is transformed in accordance with human design. The interchange in the form of constant return allows no surplus; death leaves no excedent over, just as the second law of thermodynamics operates upon human-organic and inorganic matter. At the same time, a formal interchange takes place along with the material interchange, but that formal interchange lies wholly within the cultural sphere. Once the materials have been extracted from nature they move about for a time in society before their eventual return. The movement of the products of concrete labor in society is the metamorphosis of form of goods into commodities, commodities into money, and back into commodities.[17] The formal and material metamorphoses are both found in civil society in the circulation process. The formal interchange in circulation was systematically elaborated by Marx, whereas the material interchange with nature was set forth in aphoristic insights; it is nevertheless the material basis of Marx's value theory. The metamorphosis, as material interchange, is the transformation of matter from the domain of nature to that of culture, of natural matter, that is, into value in use in human society in general, and into value in use and exchange in civil society, in particular. As formal change it is the expression of value in the abstract form in which it circulates in the economy of the civil society, or the political economy .

The labor of the body is the means of comportment by the human kind as a whole with regard to the resources of nature. In civil society this comportment is the exploitation of the natural resources, carried through with ever increasing intensity; this relation is always temporary, even if the time period which is embraced be measured in centuries, or hundreds of thousands of years. The labor of the body is the material condition of human existence in particular and the material condition of organic existence in general. This is the ecological judgment, however, which we must make more precise, as opposed to the economic. The science of ecology studies the relations of living

[17] Marx, *Grundrisse*, p. 559; *Kapital*, Vol. I, pp. 128, 134.

organisms and species to the natural environment. The science of human ecology has taken over the models of botanical and zoological ecology, as though the human relations to nature were no different from those of trees and bees. But the science of human ecology is to this extent a pseudo-science, and the models pseudo-models, for the relations of the particular human societies to nature are both mediate and direct, whereas those studied by botany and zoology are solely direct. The economic relations, on the contrary, including the relations to nature, whereby the natural goods and bounties are exploited, are mediate. Taking the history of the human kind as a whole, in all its variations, over the hundreds of thousands of years of its existence, all the mediate relations are cancelled out; there is only the natural order, of which the genus *homo* is a part, including all the doings, works and effects of the human kind. The economic relation is negated, and the science of political economy is cancelled out therefore; there remains only the ecological relations of the world of nature. This is the converse of the teleological explanations. There the universal teleology, or the guiding line that regulates and controls human evolution as a whole, is a purely speculative conception, whereas the particular teleologies, as particular relations of means and ends, are the specific modes of comportment and relations of the human kind among themselves and to the natural surroundings. In the same way, the economic relation in reference to the human kind, when taken as a whole, is a false judgment, for it attributes a universal *telos* to the human relation to nature. There remains only the macro-ecological relation, of which the genus *homo* is a part, without an end or entelechy.

The labor of the body, as the material interchange with nature, is at once an ecological and an economic relation, in unceasing process. The ceaseless interchange between the living human body and the natural world is effected in the production of useful things; concrete wants are thereby met in concrete ways. The labor of the body is concrete labor, the original and ultimate form of labor, shared with all living organisms. The process is circular, returning in the form of wastes of the organism, and returning in death, to the soil, air and water what it has taken in life. The work of the hands, on the contrary, is human alone, being both abstract and concrete. But whereas the labor of the body as ceaseless, continual process is concrete, the work of the hands, in the form of abstract labor, is continuous, unbroken process. As concrete labor the work of the hands is the production of useful things, it is production with an end in view. Abstract labor, in the condition of civil society, is the creation of exchange value in the process of social production. The abstract labor is converted into its concretions thereupon, which are the commodities. The concrete labor is the original concretion, and remains nothing but concrete; it is the labor of the body. The natural material is given a new form by the combination of the entire relations of labor, abstract and concrete; but that labor is transformed into the interchange of forms, that is, by the exchange of equivalent values, in society. It becomes social labor. The amount of the transformation is measured by the quantity of abstract labor applied and consumed in the process of production.

The opposition drawn by Locke between labor and work is the process viewed from the standpoint of living labor, that is, from within the labor process, within the human being, from which standpoint the distinction between the whole and the part, as between the entire human organism and the belly, heart or fingers, is a vital one. The opposition between labor and work drawn by the Encyclopedists, Smith, Hegel and Engels is the same viewed from without, according to whether it is the process or the product that is considered. Marx drew the different lines together in the system of oppositions, abstract and concrete labor, living labor and dead, congealed labor time. In its content, living labor is analyzed into abstract process; in its form it is exchangeable value that is produced. In its content, again, it is use-value. The living labor power is sublated as congealed labor time, the commodity whose expression is its exchangeable value. The potentiality is thereby converted into its actuality, the finished piece of work is the actualization of the potentiality, the Hercules in the marble laid bare by the sculptor's chisel and mallet. The completed product or finished work is converted into its opposed form, the material process of interchange with nature by its consumption, whereby the product is sublated in the process. The oppositions of abstract and concrete labor, potential and actual, of labor and work, are set up historically: in reality the two sides of the opposed pairs are one. The opposition of hand labor and head labor is however an artificial one, constructed on the division of labor in civil society. The artificial opposition is now being promulgated at an ever accelerating rate, having extruded at the same time its ideological expression. The opposition of hand and head labor is, however, but a further step in social alienation. Intellectuals who have propounded this opposition in the twentieth century attribute the term "head labor" to their alienated and at once privileged state; it is in their interest to do so. But they do not ennoble themselves by this self-serving device.

VIII. ACCUMULATION AND PRODUCTION

The relation of the empirical and positive science of anthropology to its subject matter rests in no small measure on the contributions of

Darwin, who, perhaps more than anyone else in his time, established the doctrine of continuity between the human species and the natural order generally. He argued against finality in nature, whether as final cause, form or thing; further, he argued against fixed categories, and in favor of change, the movement of a species into what it is not, or its opposite. But he came upon the notions of impermanency and struggle not by reflecting on the processes of nature; they came from his reading of Thomas Malthus, the doctrine of scarcity of food and of need to restrict the numbers of the poor; his understanding of nature came through application of an ideology convenient and comfortable to nineteenth-century capitalism.[18]

The relation of Marx to Darwin was ambivalent, the relation of the systems of the two men no less so.[19] On the one side Marx opposed the Malthusian aspects of Darwin's theory, in reference to the struggle for life and the law of population.[20] On the other Marx accepted the Darwinian system of natural history as a blow against teleology in the natural sciences. The positive content of Darwin's doctrine provides the basis not for Malthusianism, but for the class struggle in history.[21] Darwin, says Marx, transfers the concepts of division of labor, competition, opening up of markets, technological inventions from English society and recognizes it among beasts and plants, summing this up in the Malthusian struggle for existence.[22] But this notion applies to human beings alone. It is the ideology of Malthusianism transformed into a pseudo-scientific doctrine, and then applied to the natural *biota*. Hegel describes civil society as the spiritual animal kingdom; Darwin turns this upside down: the animal kingdom figures as civil society.

Darwin applied the ideology, hence the categories, of English society to the study of nature; Marx applied the method of natural history to

---

[18] The alarm over depletion of oil resources is but one phase of a worldwide depletion of the stocks of nature. See Harrison Brown, *The Challenge of Man's Future* (New York, 1954). Written from a Malthusian point of view, this book raises the problem of the extraction of the natural resources for profit. As useful product the trees of the forest are hewn, as surplus product the forest is depleted.

[19] Marx offered to dedicate the second volume of Capital to Darwin, who declined the offer because of the feelings of his family.

[20] It appears to be a widespread notion that Darwin owed the idea of the struggle for life to Herbert Spencer; this has been most recently published by Jacques Monod. *Le hasard et la nécessité* (Paris, 1970), pp. 135f. But Darwin himself attributed the idea of survival of the fittest, together with its expression, to Herbert Spencer, and brought out the idea of struggle for life in connection with Thomas Malthus's notion of the geometric increase of population. On Marx's opposition to Darwin, see letter to L. Kugelmann, 27 June 1870, in Marx and Engels, *Selected Correspondence*, 2nd ed. (Moscow, 1965), p. 239.

[21] Marx, letter to F. Lassalle, 16 January 1861, ibid., p. 123.

[22] Marx, letter to Engels, 18 June 1862, ibid., p. 128.

the critique of political economy. But Darwin, we have seen, made the philosophy of nature into the history of nature, for in destroying the notion of fixity of species he proposed laws of change by accumulation of difference through natural selection. Darwin argued in favor of determination of form through function, and against the personification of nature and natural forces, and he looked on "the struggle for existence" as a metaphor.[23] The fundamental problem for Marx was, as it is for us, how the laws of human and natural history are related. Although we may acknowledge that potentially the human species and the kingdom of nature are one, in actuality they are alienated from each other, and the means for the reunification are not within reach. Nature and mankind will both be changed in order to realize this potentiality; the way to effect the required changes is subject in part to our control. We are faced, then, with the problems of changes in the dialectical moments of form in relation to function, accumulation of differences, and production in relation to reproduction.

1. Marx quoted Darwin as having written: "So long as one and the same organ has different kinds of work to perform, a ground for its changeability may possibly be found in this, that natural selection preserves or suppresses each small variation of form less carefully than if that organ were destined for one purpose alone. Thus, knives that are adapted to cut all sorts of things may, on the whole, be of any shape; but an implement destined to be used exclusively in one way must have a different shape for every differing use."[24] Darwin wrote that naturalists had devised a scale of nature in which beings that stand low are more variable than those which are higher. He continued: "I presume that lowness here means that the several parts of the organization have been but little specialized for particular functions; and as long as the same part has to perform diversified work, we can perhaps see why it should remain variable, that is, why natural selection should not have preserved or rejected each little deviation of form as carefully as when the part has to serve for some special purpose. In the same way that a knife which has to cut all sorts of things may be of almost any shape; whilst a tool for some particular purpose must be of some particular shape."[25]

Nature includes both lower and higher beings. It remains to be shown that the movement is progressive, from lower to higher, or from less specialized, variable, to more specialized, and particular in shape.

[23] Darwin, *The Origin of Species*, op. cit. Against fixed species, passim; on accumulation, pp. 66, 33, 36, 52; on natural selection, pp. 14, 29, 367; against personification of nature, p. 64; on struggle for existence as metaphor, pp. 52, 66.
[24] Marx, *Capital*, English tr., op. cit., p. 375, note.
[25] Darwin, op. cit., p. 112.

Darwin developed this in the following way: although he denied consciousness and volition to the workings of the laws of nature, yet he asserted the existence of these laws, without the active power of Deity, by natural selection, which "can act solely through and for the advantage of each being".[26] Man stands high in the organic scale, arising out of lower forms, whose traces are still to be found in the human frame; the movement from lower to higher is effected by our intellectual powers and by the social qualities of mutual aid; these powers and qualities have arisen in turn by natural selection through competition, together with the inherited effects of habit.[27]

2. The question of form and content must be separately raised before we can further consider the relations of natural to social laws in the works of Marx and Darwin. The natural laws serve either as models for the formulation of social laws or they are different versions of the same laws. In the former case they differ in their respective content; in the latter case they differ in form. The natural-science paradigm for social science assumes a like content up to a certain degree, whereas the method of the natural sciences is more highly developed and can be copied by social scientists where the likeness of content has been suggested. This may be examined relative to the concept of accumulation.

Marx distinguished between accumulation in general and capitalist accumulation in particular, showing the error of Malthus and Jones, who failed to make this distinction.[28] Capitalist accumulation is characterized by capital-begetting capital (*Selbstverwertung des Kapitals*).[29] The process of capital formation comes from the labor process, which is the means to expand the value of capital; capitalist production is nothing other than this process of *valorisation*, capitalist reproduction is a means of reproducing value as capital, as self-expanding values.[30] Reproduction is an economic process both in

[26] Ibid., pp. 64, 112. On advantage and utility of variations, p. 98; on Darwin's own utilitarianism, p. 146.
[27] Ibid., pp. 444f. There is at present a controversy over "non-Darwinian" evolution, i.e., evolution by random processes rather than selection and fitness. But Darwin had already drawn attention to maintenance as opposed to change by natural selection. It would therefore be in point to speak of randomness in maintenance as well as in evolution and change.
[28] Marx, *Kapital*, Vol. 1, p. 614.
[29] Ibid., p. 386.
[30] Ibid., p. 591. "The economic character mask of the capitalist is attached to the person such that his money functions as capital." Professor Robinson appears to have sought in vain for the inner determinant of capitalist accumulation, while criticizing Rosa Luxemburg for maintaining the thesis of an external accumulation process ("economic imperialism"). See Joan Robinson, Introduction to Rosa Luxemburg, *The Accumulation of Capital* (New York, 1951). On valorization see *Le Capital*, op. cit., pp. 257, 279.

primitive and in civilized societies, and in any mode of production, whether Asiatic or capitalist. In its simpler forms, e.g., in primitive society, or in the Asiatic mode of production, it is simple accumulation, *Häufung*.[31] The simpler forms have likewise gone through their internal development. In primitive societies, the process of development is slow, the process of handicraft manufacture is conducted unmindful of time. Implements have evolved, says Tylor, by small successive changes; he also remarks that a primitive tool maker can take a whole month for the preparation of an arrow.[32] A change in relation to time applied to laboring, e.g., in the agricultural fields, is to be seen in the Asiatic mode of production; time is now subjected to a human scale. On the contrary the hunt or gathering of wild plants in primitive societies is conducted according to the cycles imposed by natural events. Considered as an economic category, reproduction has under all human conditions a time factor to which it is associated, but under civilized conditions this time factor comes under social control to an increasing degree. The time factor in reproduction is fixed at first by natural, then by social inventions.[33]

The key to reproduction is accumulation, but in order to accumulate, one must first store up; immediate consumption is to be avoided. The physical storage of primitive economies is replaced in the capitalist mode of production by accumulation in constant capital, in means of production, in machines to make machines; in both primitive and capitalist modes of production, however, the skill of the laborers is stored up and accumulated. The storage of the computer is in this sense an accumulation; it is not a change in direction of the process from the primitive labor to capitalist labor in factories; it is, however, an increasing distantiation and alienation of the workers. Hodgskin wished to defend labor against capital as productive of value, *contra*

---

[31] Marx, *Kapital*, Vol. 1, pp. 363f. Contrary to a widely held notion in certain socialist circles and elsewhere, primitive reproduction is an economic process and has nothing to do with biological-sexual reproduction.

[32] E. B. Tylor, *Anthropology* (1881), I, ch. VIII; id., *Researches into the Early History of Mankind and the Development of Civilisation* (1865). Cf. Marx, Kapital, Vol. 2, in MEW, Vol. 24, p. 437.

[33] Lewis Mumford, *Technics and Civilization* (New York, 1963), has imagined that orderly time-keeping was invented in medieval European monasteries, and that Eastern civilizations "flourished on a loose basis of time". The appreciation of time-keeping in Asia is other in Joseph Needham, *Science and Civilisation in China* (Cambridge, 1954 and on), and in his *Clerks and Craftsmen in China and the West* (Cambridge, 1970). In civil or political society, of both Europe and Asia, concrete labor time and abstract time-keeping come increasingly under human control; both are contrasted with loose or non-existent time-keeping, or its control by natural processes, as noted in Tylor and Marx (see preceding note).

Ricardo; value is stored-up labor, according to the former.[34] He failed, said Marx, to distinguish between living and dead labor; and he did not understand the real causes of the fetishization of capital.[35] Money, according to Hodgskin, will give anyone command over the labor of some men, over the labor realized in commodities, as well as over the reproduction of this labor, and to that extent over labor itself. Hodgskin's argument to prove the dependence of the laborer on the coexisting labor of other laborers as opposed to the dependence on previous labor was intended to set aside the "storage phrase". But, wrote Marx,

"What is really stored up, although not as a dead mass, rather as living, is the *skill* of the laborer, the degree of development of labor. To be sure (what Hodgskin does not bring out, for it serves on the contrary the crude conceptions of the economists, is to place the accent on the *Subject*, on the subjective in the subject so to speak, in opposition to the matter), the separate stage of development of the productive power of labor, which is the point of departure, is present not only as capacity, ability of the worker, but at the same time in the objective organs which this labor has created for itself and daily renews. This is the true *prius* which makes the starting point, and this *prius* is the result of a developmental course. *Storing up* is here *assimilation*, continuous maintenance and at once reshaping of the already transmitted, made actual [*verwirklicht*]."[36]

Up to this point we have been concerned with the relations in society and those within the socialized individual, the human being. The skill of the worker is developed in society, stored up and transmitted; the skills are maintained and renewed in the hand, eye, judgmental capacity; they have an objective and a subjective relation in the individual. The realization of labor as work is the dead labor, the fulfillment of the capacity, that is, of the potentiality; the already transmitted is that which is finished, and is then stored up, accumulated as capital. The

---

[34] Thomas Hodgskin, Labor defended against the claims of capital; or the unproductiveness of capital proved (London, 1825).

[35] Marx, *Theorien über den Mehrwert*, III, op. cit., pp. 259ff., 285ff., The storage is unrelated to abstinence, which is falsely associated with early capitalism, Puritanism, etc., Cf. *Kapital*, Vol. 1, pp. 620ff.; Marx has many sarcastic comments on asceticism, etc. On cumulation of stock (*contra* Adam Smith) see Marx, *Kapital*, Vol. 2, op. cit., p. 142 and note. On storing up (ante-Darwin) see Marx, *Grundrisse*, p. 7: No production without stored-up past labor, even if this labor is but the dexterity accumulated and concentrated in the hand of the savage with repeated practice. (This is the caricatured presentation by the "modern" economists.)

[36] *Theorien über den Mehrwert*, III, p. 289.

stored-up capacity of the worker is transmitted by another process and has a different relation to nature. The subjective element in the storage and transmission of skills is paired with the objective element in production; the latter is the development of the productive power of labor, which is found in the hand and eye of the worker and in the instruments that he uses in his labor. The productive capacity of the worker has, again, both a subjective and an objective element, comprising the ability of all mature human beings to learn and transmit the skills of labor, which is in turn both subjective and objective, and the objective element of application in the labor process of the acquired skill. These relations of subjectivity and objectivity have their parallel in nature; the accumulation of capital is set on one side, the accumulation of the working skills on the other. This is important enough] to bring out even though it might serve the purpose of the enemies of labor, the economists who sought to stress the subjective element in the process of production, in opposition to the material. It is in the accumulation of the working skills that the parallel between the human and the natural processes was developed by Marx, who continued:

> "It is in this latter way that Darwin makes storing up through inheritance in everything organic, plants and animals, into the driving principle of its formation so that the different organisms themselves form themselves through 'storage', and are but 'inventions', gradually cumulated inventions of the living subjects. But this is not the sole *prius* for production. For plants and animals it is external nature, including therefore the inorganic, as well as their relations to other plants and animals. Human beings, who produce in society, in this way come upon an already modified nature (in particular the natural is also transformed into an organ of mankind's own activity) and particular relations of producers to each other. This accumulation is in part the result of the historical process, in part the transmission of skill in the individual worker."

Marx, who has attributed these views by a convenient fiction.[37] to Hodgskin, has drawn the parallel between natural and cultural history: accumulation through inheritance among plants and animals is the same as assimilation of skills and primitive or original accumulation among human societies.

[37] Marx is putting his own formulations into Hodgskin's mouth: Hodgskin is given a fully developed Darwinian interpretation of accumulation and hereditary descent 34 years before the appearance of Darwin's work, and is also the master of the dialectic of subject and object (see Marx, ibid., p. 290, in reference to the capitalist als personified capital).

Reproduction of the working class includes on the one hand the biological reproduction of workers, families and, where the part becomes the whole, societies. On the other it "includes the transmission and storage of skills from one generation to the next".[38] It would be false to limit the process of transmission to the relation between generations, however, as though this relation, with the implied sexual reproduction, is all that there is, as though that transmission is biologically linked. On the contrary, it is a social-cultural matter which is stored and transmitted by the learning process. The storage and transmission, again, has a biological parallel, and it would be false to separate the cultural from the natural continuum, as though humanity had no relation to nature. The statements pertaining to culture by many anthropologists, whereby culture, symbolization or reasoning are attributed to humanity in absolute exclusivity, are a defective dialectic. The storage and transmission of learned skills, being acquired during the lifetime of the individual, are not the same as the processes of storage and transmission of genetic traits. The storage process relative to acquired traits is simply analogical to the storage process relative to genetic traits; the transmission process of the acquired traits is mediated by the culture, whereas the storage of the acquired traits is mediately a natural, but immediately a cultural process. The problem of transmission of acquired traits, as it was viewed by Marx in the light of Darwin's theories, is other than the view of the matter in biological theory today; but in neither case is a direct equation between storage of skills and hereditary storage possible.

The human being not only modifies nature outside his organism, as well as the nature of his own organs, or his internal nature; the human being in society modifies the instruments though which he works upon the natural surroundings and modifies his own nature, i.e. skills of hand, eye, etc., relative to his instrumentarium. Further, we have been able to perceive since Marx's day that the field of human culture is itself not a direct continuum with the natural field, but is itself modified. Thus, if we observe the pasture in which domesticated animals graze, we find that it is discontinuous with the wild, untended pasture, even though the same grass grows in both. The pastoral animals differ, their movements, communities, numbers, density and feeding habits differ, the use that they make of the grass differs, the size of the grazing plot, the laws regulating its use are all discontinuous with the natural fields, ground and feed, while at the same time continuous; that continuum is at once direct and indirect. Before

[38] Marx, *Kapital*, Vol. i, p. 599.

proceeding into the contemporary discussion, however, we should examine the further development of Marx's own ideas.

Marx likened the division of labor in the factory, in which, be it noted, there is no commodity exchange, to a production *mechanism* whose *organs* are human beings.[39] Although the likeness of the factory to an organism is but an image, yet it is important to note for the development of the caste which petrifies a human skill and a guild which ossifies it in a particular trade and its product. "Castes and guilds", wrote Marx, "arise out of the same law of nature which regulates the division of plants and animals into species and subspecies, save that at a certain grade of development the inheritance of castes or the exclusiveness of guilds is decreed as a social law." Castes and guilds are regulated by social laws under any and all circumstances, at whatever grade of social development they arise. It is the explicitness with which their social practices of inheritance or exclusivity is decreed that varies historically. The parallel between the natural and cultural processes is further developed by Marx relative to the special skill of the Indian weaver, which is "accumulated from generation to generation and bequeathed from father to son"; and this, says Marx, provides the Hindu, like the spider, with his virtuosity. In a note to the same passage Marx comments that the Indian loom is upright and its warp is vertically stretched[40]; but this skill at the loom provides the Hindu weaver with another virtuosity than the spider's.

The reader will readily grasp the similarity and difference between the culturally determined weaver's skills and the natural skill of the spider. Here we are faced with a different dialectical moment than that of nature-culture, it is that of process and its congelation in the end result, or the relation of living and dead labor time, and this dialectic was developed elsewhere by Marx. Marx himself restored the dialectic of nature and culture, with reference to the problem of castes, in a later note that he composed on the matter, and, as the final moment of the dialectic of nature-culture, he pointed to the division of society into classes by means of caste formations. On the one side, castes are the petrification of the gentile principle, that is, the principle of blood relation, on which differences of rank are imposed. But they do not come of themselves, and Marx asks if it is not by the external factor of conquest that the castes are formed among the ancient *gentes*. Caste is the opposite of the feeling of equality, the *gens* cannot end up in a finished aristocracy.[41] The genetic course of the caste is opposed to

---

[39] Marx, *Kapital*, Vol. 1, p. 358; *Le Capital*, op. cit., p. 147.
[40] *Kapital*, Vol. 1, p. 360.
[41] *Ethnological Notebooks*, op. cit., p. 183; Introduction, pp. 14-16.

its functioning under historic conditions. The *Republic* of Plato depicts a system of division of labor which is but the Athenian idealization of the Egyptian caste organization.[42] In order to make the passage from the genesis of caste by blood relation and conquest to the functioning of castes as an ossified division of social labor, several further factors have to be introduced: bondage to the soil and in localities; the organization of communities that are not primarily agricultural but are bound by relations of social labor and kinship here and there through a nation of considerable size; the bondage, again, is not to a person as we find the case to be in slavery, serfdom, clientage-patronage, but a bondage of tradition, custom, habit or feeling.[43] These terms, which characterize the relation of the Indian peasant to the soil, are applicable to the Indian caste system generally. That is the first thesis. The second is that in a preponderantly agricultural society the relation throughout the society, whether rural or urban, courtly or common, will be determined by the agricultural relation. Thus, the form of bondage to the soil being non-personal in traditional India, the relation of bondage in the Indian caste system was the same.

The law of nature that governs the formation of castes and guilds is the same law that governs the speciation of plants and animals. That is not the same law that governs the exercise of caste functions. The parallel between nature and culture is in turn governed by individual variation. The restriction on caste development once formed and finished is the contradiction of individual variation; it is the social law that is in this case the contradiction of the natural law. The dialectical moment nature-culture is crossed by the moment of genesis-function or genesis-structure; a further contradiction is generated, but this does not decree its own elimination. Why not? Because the cultural or social law restricting human variation and innovation overwhelms the natural law; there is no contest, natural development gives way to the social decrees for considerable periods of time; the entire society must pass away before the particular contradiction can be abolished: *videlicet*, the thousands of years of ancient Egyptian or traditional Indian society. Marx propounded economics as a natural science, because of his grasp of the evolution of economic formations of society as a process of natural history.[44] He grasped both nature and society as history, hence as change; by the study of society, whose

---

[32] Marx, *Kapital*, Vol. 1, p. 388.
[43] *Ethnological Notebooks*, p. 255.
[44] *Kapital*, Vol. 1, p. 16. It is not that human science is like natural science because the latter is unalterable. On the contrary, natural is like human science because each has its history, just as nature and humanity are one in that each has its history: to this extent they are unlike the law of the Medes and Persians which altereth not.

nature is change, he came to the change of nature. The economists his contemporaries, on the contrary, appealed to laws of nature as eternal in order to affirm the same of the laws of economics which they engendered. The course goes the other way in Marx's thought: therefore economic categories of capitalist and landowner as personifications are raised up by Marx as subjectivities. The parallel with nature need not be sought because natural history is not the source of the categories; it is social. They *seem* to be objective and natural because the subjectivity in them assumes a petrified form. It is transformed into a thing; it is reified, the end result of a process of taking a whole man, subject and object, draining him of his subjective life, and substituting an objective relation of capital for the vacancy created. At the same time the converse movement takes place, the attribution to the objective moments of capital and of private property in land the subjective motivations of desire and will. The combined dialectical processes are in the one case the reification of the human being, in the other the personification of capital. The two processes are related, as we have seen, but they are not the same.

IX. OBJECT AND THING. OBJECTIFICATION AND REIFICATION

When Feuerbach wrote that man is nothing without an object, he had in mind the process whereby we create our own human condition. He held that the world of objects that we create is the means of creation of our subjective condition and thereby of our own objective nature: "Every planet has in its sun the mirror of its own nature." Further, he said, we can only know ourselves by contemplating the world as object and ourselves as object.[45] Out of this philosophy and in opposition to it Marx set forth the positions of alienation and objectification that at first caused him to be taken for a humanist. The irrelevance of Feuerbach to the human sciences today arises out of its generality; because it speaks to all humanity it speaks to no one in particular. For a related reason, alienation cannot be the starting point in the analysis of the troubles of capitalism, for it is too general a phenomenon, and while it has a bearing on our own times, yet the particularity and the generality within it have not been parsed out. It is of fundamental importance in considering the human condition in the abstract; it is a fundamental issue in the critique of capitalism, but its nature is changed when proceeding from the abstract to the concrete case.

The questions of objectification and reification are of the same sort as that of alienation, and if we treat of them it is because they have

---

[45] Feuerbach, *Das Wesen des Christentums.* (1843), Introd.

been handled and mishandled by a number of writers; their treatment, moreover, has a bearing both on the principles and the contradictions of a Marxist anthropology. Lukács took up the matter of reification in an attempt to explain the revolutionary consciousness of the proletariat; the end result of his treatment was an explanation of the decline of the revolutionary consciousness of the proletariat by the phenomenon of reification. The historical event of the October Revolution in Russia, the high point of class-consciousness associated with it in all parts of the world, the subsequent retreat of the revolutionary wave, are only partly accounted for by Lukács; his work is not an analysis so much as a segment of the protocol, bearing witness to the course of the events.[46] As a theory of revolution it lacks precision; as a theory of a social phenomenon, whether in a revolutionary period or outside of it, it is wanting in Marxian categories. Elsewhere we have shown that reification is divided as social classes are divided in capitalism,[47] but it is still not the underlying problem of society. It is the response in the head to the underlying problem. The problem of reification has been of late obscured because it has been applied indifferently as objectification.[48]

The objectification of the world is a twofold process, on the one side creation of the object, and, on the other, standing to it as object. Scientific objectivity is an aspect of the second sense; objectification of self, consciousness of self are derivative of that second sense. The first sense is a sensory act and the physical action of hands, or any other body organ. The action of objectification is necessary for life sustenance in an abstract sense; every human being creates the object that he acts upon. There is nothing praiseworthy or pejorative about objectification, the act is free of subjective valuation, and exists only in the objective world. The objective judgment corresponds to the act and is likewise free of subjective valuation.[49] We can go further into the question of value-freedom if we introduce the relation of subjective to objective value and the value-freedom on either side, but we question whether the game is worth the candle. We call attention to the naming: what is usually referred to as "value-free" is "free of subjective value"; objective value-freedom is a circularity.

[46] Georg Lukács, "Die Verdinglichung und das Bewusstsein des Proletariats", in *Geschichte und Klassenbewusstsein* (1923).

[47] Lawrence Krader, "Verdinglichung und Abstraktion in der Gesellschaftstheorie", in *Ethnologie und Anthropologie bei Marx*, op. cit., pp. 178ff.

[48] Hannah Arendt, op. cit., pp. 122, 148; Herbert Marcuse, "Re-examination of the Concept of Revolution", in: *Diogenes*, No. 64 (1968), p. 25.

[49] Max Weber, *Gesammelte Aufsätze zur Wissenschaftslehre*, 3rd ed. (1968), pp. 146ff., 489ff. Weber ought to have separated these thoughts, but did not do so.

Reification on the contrary is inseparably tied to a valuation, both subjective and objective. The creation of a thing implies the separation of the human from the thing. The act of objectification implies no such separation: we become human subjects by virtue of having made the objective world and ourselves into an object. Labor as such is a relation to the world; the making actual of labor is its objectification.[50] It is by means of a factor external to the labor relation, namely the appropriation of the object by another, that the worker becomes dehumanized, or *entwirklicht* (= deactualized). Objectification *per se* is neither a plus nor a minus, neither inhuman nor dehumanizing, it is neutral until it enters the market place. Reification, *Verdinglichung* or *Versachlichung*, on the contrary, is intrinsically inhuman because dehumanizing. The argument of the passage on commodity fetishism in *Capital* rests on the identification by Marx of the material relation of persons and the social relation of things.[51] The material relation of persons is a reification; the social relation of things is a hypostatization. The former is the materialization of the social, which is both sensory and suprasensory or material-supramaterial; the latter is the etherealization of the material.[52] In either case it is a defective because one-sided relation.

The defect of the dialectic in this case is at once the source of the reification and its result. That a social relation, which in itself is immaterial, while in its expression is at once material and immaterial, is realized in reified form as the result of its promulgation not through human beings but through persons, juridical fictions. Therefore the relation between them cannot be anything but onesided, the material relation between persons, or the reification of the social relation. The hypostatization of the relation between things, commodities, is their fantastic existence as though they were social. They are in fact the

[50] Marx, Ökonomisch-Philosophische Manuskripte, p. 83.

[51] Marx, *Kapital*, Vol. 1, ch. 1, section 4; Vol. 3, pp. 835f., 838f.

[52] It is easier to find the earthly core of the abstract relations, to show the material basis of the relations between persons; this is the task of criticism, of analysis, science and materialism. It is more difficult to evolve out of these earthly relations the mystifications, abstractions. Why do we perform the more difficult task instead of the easier one? The etherealization or hypostatization is the abstraction of the human being, his transformation into a juridical person, etc. The social usefulness of this has already been seen. Disclosure of the material relations between persons is a process that leads in two directions. First, it is the critical analysis itself; the human being has been made into an abstract, juridical person, the representation of a relation that has its material base. Second, the human being has been made into a material of the process of production, the source of labor power, whose labor time as living labor is converted into dead labor. This is the reification of the human being; it is the second dialectical moment of another process as well: the etherealization, hypostatization, abstraction of the human individual is the preparatory stage for the reification. See Marx, *Kapital*, Vol. 1, p. 393, note.

material side of the social relation which is taken to be the entirety, material and supramaterial, sensory and suprasensory, in commodity fetishism, just as the material relation between persons is the unilateral relation that substitutes under capitalist conditions of exchange for the relations between whole human beings. The juridical person is the fantastic representation of the material side of the human being, the onesided form, which, as we have seen, has been developed in society in order to realize the commodity-exchange relation, the sale and purchase of labor time, living and dead, labor capacity. This is then substituted for the whole human being. The human being under all circumstances objectifies himself in the labor relation, be the labor capitalist or communal, private labor or public, be it social labor or labor in the family. The objectification is turned into a dehumanized process, a dysvalue under the capitalist process of extraction of surplus value. The worker is reified in the process of production, the capitalist in the process of circulation of capital; the intellectual is reified in the process of abstraction. His social act is a hypostasis, whereby the subject is alienated from the object; thereby the consciousness of the intellectual is reified. Reification stands to objectification as its negation, whereby the subject is reified at the same time; but objectification is not the negation of the reification. In civil society it becomes a form of reification.

We have seen that the objective side of the human being is necessarily bound to the subjective: the human being is subject-object; without the subject, no object, without the object, no subject, without the combination of both, no human being. There are two objects, however, the object in nature and the human object. The natural object is not paired with the subject, it is neither subject nor object, but neutral. Its neutrality, as it is natural, is wholly objective. The human being is both subject and object, hence he bears his partisanship within himself. The human being can be spokesman and representative of his private interest, of the interest of all humanity, and of all nature; the human being is the bearer of all these interests, which are given subjective and objective expression within himself. He is not neutral, but bears both the subjective and the objective relations to and within society, to and within nature. These relations in no way negate each other, nor cancel each other out; they are opposite and complementary, *coincidentia oppositorum*. Further, the human being objectifies himself and makes himself into subject. These are the primary subject-object relations, and the primary subjectification and objectification.

Making the human being into a natural object, the secondary objectification, is false, for he is already object. The secondary objectification is actually a tertiary one, which comes about in this way.

The human being, having discovered the object in nature and the subject-object within himself, thereupon proceeds to a twofold projection. He projects the natural object onto the human domain, and the human object-and-subject onto the natural. The natural object and the human object are thereby taken for one another, confused one for the other, falsified and distorted. The natural object is treated as though it were the human object; and a natural subject, complete with will and consciousness, is invented. On the one side, the natural object is given the character of human objectivity; on the other, the neutrality of the natural object is projected onto the human object. The human subject is projected onto the world of nature; the subject reads his pathos in nature (waves at sea threaten, the sunny day smiles). The list of pathetic fallacies has long been made. The human subject, alienated from the human object, is projected, the one onto the other.

Social-scientific research has perpetrated the objective fallacy. Here the assumption is made that the human object and the natural object are one. The neutrality of the natural object, which makes neither moral judgments nor value judgments, is transposed to the human object. The human object is thereby artificially alienated from its natural pair. The result is the reified human object of social-science research, whereby the human being is turned not into natural object but into thing. The positive science of humanity, value-freedom and neutrality with respect to human beings are fallacies, whose grounds are not far to seek. The natural sciences have met with great success, constructing electric, electronic, atomic, chemical energy devices, from which the social sciences wish to profit. The temptation is too great to resist. But more than this, there are the undoubted successes of opinion polls and marketing analysis, together with the predictions that have followed from the pollings and analyses in political behavior and marketing behavior. These successes have been made possible because the artificial alienation of the human subject-object in the social sciences, economics, social psychology, political sociology, accomplishes in these fields what has already been accomplished in society in fact. The human being in political society has been actually reified in the process of politicking, trafficking, marketing, buying and selling himself, his labor capacity, his product. The alienation of self from self, of object from subject, is a daily event. The choice between parties, as between commodities, wares, is appearance of choice, not the reality, having as its result the false objectification of the human subject. Therefore, the social-science method is justified, but only insofar as it is not the human object that is taken up, but a false natural object.

Theodor Adorno had taken up reification not as a social, still less as an economic, but as a metaphysical category.[53] Lukács had seen in reification a condition of the consciousness formed by a condition of society. It is possible to go forward with the analysis of Lukács into the separate forms of reification in the different social classes; it is not possible to do so with Adorno's. In the latter case, the mode of treatment of reification metaphysically, instead of as it is, the deformation of social relations, and the consciousness thereof, by the spirit of spiritless conditions, by routinized labor, by formal freedom and pseudo-equality, merely evidences the spread of the phenomenon to social areas beyond its immediate field of activity. It is a part of the problem, not its solution.[54]

---

[53] Theodor Adorno, *Negative Dialektik* (Frankfurt, 1966). He writes, p. 365: "Dass der Kategorie der Verdinglichung, die inspiriert war vom Wunschbild ungebrochener subjektiver Unmittelbarkeit, nicht länger jener Schlüsselcharakter gebührt, den apologetisches Denken, froh materialistisches zu absorbieren, übereifrig ihr zuerkennt, wirkt zurück auf alles, was unter dem Begriff metaphysischer Erfahrung geht."

[54] The putative etiology of reification, which Adorno identified as its inspiration or the "wish-thought of unbroken subjective immediacy" (see the preceding note), is a symptom of the ailment first identified by Marx. Having taken the phenomenon out of society and deposited it within the domain of metaphysics, it is fitting to derive it as Adorno has done. What this derivation has to do with the phenomenon is clear: Adorno correctly distinguished between reification and objectification, but he made reification into a subjective metaphysical category instead of what it is, the elimination of the subject and of subjectivity, the substitution of relations that are external to the human being for the gap created, and the creation thereby of a new Adam and Eve who are only partly conscious of their loss. To the extent that we are unconscious of what we have undergone we are a simulacrum, the combination of pseudo-human, pseudo-subjective conditions. The processes of the elimination, substitution and new construction differ with each social class. The intellectuals, by their power of abstraction and hypostasis, which results from their abstract relations in society, can, like the bees, gather their pseudo-nectar from the flowers of evil of the other social classes. If Adorno meant Lukács by the reference to apologetic thinking, he should have said so; otherwise this remains a hidden attack; it is an *argumentum ad hominem* even if the target is not named. Reification is not a concept of metaphysical experience, but the effect on the human body, brain and consciousness of relations in society. The relations in primitive society, as recounted in the mythology, point to a primary reification; those of capitalist society point to class-divided modes of reification. On the former, see my article "Primary Reification in Primitive Society", in: *Diogenes*, No 56 (1966).

Reification has been taken up as a problem not of metaphysics but of history by H.-J. Krahl, Detlev Claussen, Oskar Negt et al., *Geschichte und Klassenbewusstsein Heute* (Amsterdam, 1971). Krahl speaks of the opposition reification-emancipation (p. 39); reification and abstract labor (p. 28); and reification in connection with legitimation theory (p. 40); Negt, Claussen and Krahl of reification and party organization (pp. 26, 41f.). The discussion moves in a direction 180 degrees counter to that of Adorno. The organization of political parties is a historical phenomenon of bourgeois-capitalist society; it is historically conditioned. The reification of the party organization does not come from metaphysics, nor from the historical conditions directly; several steps were omitted from the discussion. Reification in politics comes from the reified relations in economy and society, which set forth the political relations of party organization in reified form. Lukács's theory of reification was an explanation of the given state of the class

The contradictions within anthropology are twofold: those that can be resolved, and those that, within the given state of society, cannot. The latter are imposed by the genesis and historical course of anthropology. Academic in its origins, anthropology early had positive science, natural science as its principle. Its method and end to this extent had been the establishment of universals, iron laws, invariant abstractions of human nature in the name of objective science. But since such undertakings are derived from a fallacious image of natural science, they are in contradiction with the matter of anthropology, human life in historically concrete societies. This contradiction is irresoluble, falling outside the dialectic, hence outside scientific method, and is subject to the criticism of the latter. On the other hand, there are contradictions that may be resolved in anthropology. The criticism of the discipline is sometimes made that it is the offspring of imperialism, as though there had been neither anthropology before the moderr era nor anthropology developed by peoples subjugated through imperialism. These anthropologies exist, however, and stand both historically and synchronically in contradiction to each other; unlike the contradictions of the pseudo-scientific method, they can be overcome by their conversion from theory into the practical criticism, in the first place of the anthropologizing society, in the second of the anthropologized.

conflict (1920-23) in Central Europe; it was conditioned by the reification of the historical relations of economy and society at that time; it is a reified theory insofar as it posited, but did not criticize, its own historical foundation. A complete theory, or the step toward one, should carry these criticisms forward. Krahl (p. 19) mentions the reification of social relations and the subjectification of objective labor conditions. If by this juxtaposition a systematic connection is meant, then it should be amended: reification is the elimination of the human subject and the substitution of thing for object in the economic relations and the historical process of society. Thing and object are not the same, reification and objectification are not the same; thing and subject are not the same, reification and subjectification are not the same.

INDEX OF NAMES

Index of Names

278

Soc
JC
11
K72

DATE DUE